# Revelation Road

## Hope Beyond the Horizon

A Novel and Commentary by

# Bill Salus

*Revelation for the Road Ahead...*

# Revelation Road

## Hope Beyond the Horizon

*Bill Salus*

A Novel and Commentary by

# Bill Salus

*Revelation 19:10*

ICON
PUBLISHING GROUP

Icon Publishing Group
Customer Service: +1 877 887 0222
P.O. Box 2180
Noble, OK 73068
**www.iconpublishinggroup.com**

ISBN: 978-1-62022-001-6

Cover by Matthew Salhus with Brent Spurlock
Interior by Brent Spurlock, Green Forest, AR

**Printed in the United States of America**

# Acknowledgements

Behold, God is my helper; The Lord is with those who uphold my life. (Psalm 54:4, NKJV)

Heartfelt thanks to my wife, children, and grandchildren who inspired me to write this book. A further debt of gratitude is extended to all those below who in one way or another, through prayer, encouragement, support, research, or otherwise, genuinely blessed this book.

The Peterson family, Bob and Lynette Holmes, Brad Myers, Lynn and Dixie Wheeler, Ellen Traylor, Jim Tetlow, Dr. David Reagan, Gary Fisher, Sean Osborne, Nathan Jones, Jim Fletcher, LA Marzulli, Richard Shaw, Roger Welty, Steve Babkow, Jacob Prasch, Chris Schang, Richard Jury, Dr. Lawrence Prabhakar (Lawrence of India), Bob Mitchell (UK).

Pastors: Dave Hart, Mike Fulmer, Kevin Lea, Tom Hughes, Alyn Lloyd, Mike Harris, Dave Barton, Robert Waughman (UK).

*A special thanks to Bob Holmes and Tyler Hauer for posing for the book cover, Matthew Salhus and Brent Spurlock for book cover design, and Lani Salhus for map images.*

Best reading regards,
Bill Salus

# Contents—The Novel

# Contents—Companion's Commentary

# Contents—Appendices

# Character List

## The Thompson Family

| | |
|---|---|
| *George Thompson* | Tyler and Jami's grandfather, Martha's husband, retired Four-Star General |
| *Martha Thompson* | (a.k.a. Mimi), Tyler and Jami's grandmother |
| *Tyler Thompson* | (a.k.a. Ty), grandson of George and Martha, son of Thomas |
| *Thomas Thompson* | son of George and Martha, Tyler and Jami's mother |
| *Lisa Thompson* | wife of Thomas, daughter-in-law of George and Martha, and Tyler and Jami's mother |
| *Jami Thompson* | Tyler's sister, granddaughter of George and Martha |
| *Grandma Naomi* | Lisa's mother, Tyler and Jami's other grandmother |

## Friends and Associates of the Thompson Family

| | |
|---|---|
| *Robert Rassmussen* | (a.k.a. Razz), best friend of George Thompson, respected eschatologist |
| *Nathaniel Severs* | Razz' best friend, President of UGIC |
| *Jim Linton* | respected eschatologist and Bible prophecy teacher |
| *Harold Hirsch* | CEO of UGIC (Unistate Global Investments Corporation) |

## Political and Military

### United States

| | |
|---|---|
| *John Bachlin* | President |
| *Donald Yates* | Secretary of Defense |

### Israel

| | |
|---|---|
| *Moshe Kaufman* | Prime Minister |
| *Eliezer Moday* | President |
| *Jacob Barak* | chief military commander of the Israel Defense Forces |

| | |
|---|---|
| *Jonathan Vitow* | IAF Lieutenant |
| *Binyamin Lieberman* | (a.k.a. Benny) IAF Lieutenant General |
| *Ehud Cohen* | the Temple Foundation spokesman |
| *Avi Fleishman* | Minister of the Interior |

## Russia and China

| | |
|---|---|
| *Vladimir Ziroski* | (a.k.a. Mad Vlad) Russian President |
| *Sergei Primakov* | Russian Prime Minister |
| *Mikhail Trutnev* | Russian senior advisor to Prime Minister |
| *Alena Popov* | Russian Secretary of Mikhail Trutnev |
| *Anatoly Tarasov* | Russian Ambassador to the United Nations |
| *Li Chin* | China's Ambassador to the United Nations |

## Middle East (Arabs and Persians)

| | |
|---|---|
| *Muktada Zakiri* | Iranian President |
| *Zamani Nikahd* | spiritual mentor to Iranian President Zakiri |
| *Ayatollah Khomani* | spiritual leader of Iran |
| *Sadegh Mousavi* | President of Hamas |
| *Ahmad Al-Masri* | top General of Hamas |
| *Neda* | Sadegh Mousavi's Secretary |
| *Karim Nazari* | Al-Qaeda's new leader |
| *Muhammad Imad Fadlallah* | Secretary General of Hezbollah |
| *Hassan Tereiri* | Syrian President |

# Introduction
## (How to Read This Book)

You are invited to join me in an *one-of-a-kind* reading experience. *Revelation Road* is a story about an ordinary American family living in the end-time's generation. Without warning, the Thompsons are forced to face a series of powerful episodes that are guaranteed to change their lives forever. All young Tyler wanted was to enjoy his summer vacation, but a Middle East war of epic biblical proportion postponed his plans indefinitely. Now his aging grandparents must prepare him for the coming apocalypse.

As you engage with them in their daily struggle to survive, it becomes abundantly clear that their family tale could soon become yours. You may wake up one morning in the near future and find yourself walking in their shoes!

## More than a novel

Although *Revelation Road* begins as a novel, it concludes with a customized, non-fiction commentary section. The *Companion's Commentary* provides "biblical believability" to the adventurous scenarios depicted inside this novel. Additionally, it adds credence to the characters and their interactions, as well as veracity to the text. This format was chosen to share pertinent, timely information with the broadest possible audience.

This dual approach enables the readers to engage intimately with the novel. They can compose their own scripts inside the story line, as it progresses. This is possible because the characters are easy to relate to, and the prophetic scenarios depicted, could actually occur during the reading of the book.

For instance, one episode describes a barrage of rockets launched from the Syrians, Hezbollah, and Hamas into the center of Israel's Ben Gurion airport. These rockets severely damage the runway, stranding scores of international tourists. Grounded indefinitely with no route of escape, these travelers become instantly subjected to the dangers of an escalating Arab-Israeli conflict.

The above scene is more than a mere author creation. It is a realistic scenario that residents inside Israel grapple with almost daily. National defense drills are conducted frequently in order to prepare Israelis for a potential multi-front war. If a would-be traveler gets caught in this crossfire, while reading that chapter, they inescapably become part of the story, and automatically become cast among the characters.

## Note from the Author

It is my sincere hope that you read both the novel and the corresponding chapter-by-chapter commentaries. They can be read at the same time, or back to back; the book was designed so that either portion could be read and understood independently.

I chose this unique fiction / non-fiction crossover style of writing in order to impart timely information to as many readers as possible. The Bible speaks volumes about these uncertain times. Inside its pages lie the secrets to successful living in these last days.

Prophecy is invaluable predictive information given to us by a loving God, with 100% accuracy. In addition to equipping us for the days in which we live, prophecy authenticates God's sovereignty, spares human lives, and ultimately saves lost souls. The primary goal of prophecy is to *inform us*, rather than *impress us*. God is not someone with too much *time on His hands*; He is the one who holds all *time in His hands*. This enables Him to share and declare the end from the beginning.[1] His plan is to *pronounce hope*, rather than *announce harm*. However, He won't *denounce truth* when He foreknows it's about to overtake the world.

How God knows what He knows, only He knows. But, we can be thankful that He does, and that He is willing to share His knowledge with us.

*"God so loves us that he wants us to know what's headed our way. And, in turn, our natural response should be to worship him for caring."*

Best Reading Regards,
Bill Salus

# Revelation Road

## The Novel

NOVEL

# Chapter 1
## Iran Prepares for the Apocalypse!

"The time has come! Islam's messiah has readied for his return," declared the charismatic Shiite cleric Zamani Nikahd. "President Zakiri, we must alert the others without delay, and inform them that their multi-front attack upon the little Jewish Satan is now imminent!"

Nikahd, the mesmerizing spiritual mentor of the Iranian President Muktada Zakiri, claimed to have recently received another compelling night vision from his Islamic Messiah, Muhammad al-Mahdi.

"Zamani, you must be certain! We cannot afford any costly mistakes. Israel has recently completed the deployment of its Iron Dome defenses around Tel Aviv and Jerusalem. They will retaliate hard against us and our friends if they survive," cautioned the apocalyptically-minded president.

"There can be no doubt. The vision was crystal clear," Nikahd insisted.

"What did you see? Was he riding furiously upon his white horse again?" Zakiri anxiously inquired.

"In the night vision, al-Mahdi rode his white horse through the mushroom cloud over northern Israel again, but this time he had his sword in one hand, and the holy Qur'an held high in the other. A multitude of his followers appeared, all lining the streets of Jerusalem and praising him. They all bore the visible marks of prostration on their foreheads, from bowing down five times to pray," Nikahd exclaimed.[2]

"Praise be to Allah," Zakiri replied. "I will persuade the Ayatollah that, at last, the time of the blessed Mahdi's return draws near! I will give him the good news that the Islamic Republic of Iran shall soon reign over our Muslim brothers once and for all!"

"No need for persuasion," the Imam assured him. "I discussed this latest vision with the Ayatollah just prior to coming here. He confirmed the vision's interpretation, and blessed the plan to attack Israel. He instructed me to tell you to visit him secretly upon the completion of our meeting."

"As you know, I have been preparing for al-Mahdi's return ever since I received my divine calling to create the apocalypse that hastens his coming," Zakiri declared. "The Ayatollah's blessings and your night vision serve as my final confirmation to wipe Israel off the pages of time!"

"We must put the multi-front attack against the Jews in motion straight away," Nikahd urged. "Are the Syrians, Hezbollah and Hamas prepared to attack at your command?"

"We possess legitimate war-pacts with them all. They are obligated to act," confirmed Zakiri.

"Those pacts only come into play when one or all of us come under Israeli attack," Nikahd reminded him. "This is entirely different; we are ordering, not receiving the attack. Our proxies may fear Israel's retaliation and ignore their commitment to us."

"Absolutely not!" Zakiri insisted. "Syrian President Tereiri realizes he has no choice. He fears the loss of political power, if not his own life, without our support. Our protection kept him in power during the so-called "Arab Spring," but youth protests in that region have gotten out of hand. He needs us badly. Furthermore, our military cemented relations with his army commanders at that time. The Syrian forces are in our back pockets."

"Hezbollah and Hamas as well? Are they prepared to mobilize upon command?" Nikahd questioned.

"They seek to spill Israeli blood across the Holy Land and to drive the Jew monkeys into the Mediterranean Sea!" Zakiri exclaimed.

## Hamas Called to Iran

Sadegh Mousavi was enjoying an early afternoon lunch with his most trusted military leader, Ahmad Al-Masri, when his secretary Neda interrupted on the intercom. Excusing himself momentarily from their daily briefing, he pushed a button on the phone and picked up the receiver. "This had better be important!" he growled.

Apparently enthused by what he was hearing on the other end of the receiver, Mousavi nodded frequently as the secretary relayed a message. He finished the call by simply saying, "Tell Zakiri's office we will be there first thing tomorrow morning."

As he hung up, Mousavi leaned over his desk and boasted to his top General, "Looks like we fly to Tehran tomorrow to meet with Hezbollah and the Syrians. Neda is seeing to our travel arrangements. She will transmit our flight information to your office by the day's end."

Sadegh Mousavi had moved up the ladder to the highest rung of Hamas' organizational hierarchy. He had begun his bid for Hamas' highest post in the aftermath of *Operation Cast Lead,* in early 2009. He was the organization's most skillful diplomat and one of the primary architects behind the recently formed Hamas-Fatah unity government. Many Arabs believed that without Mousavi's political brinksmanship, the two Palestinian factions would still be warring against one another. But they weren't; their civil rivalries had ceased.

Mousavi had also succeeded in gaining the trust of Israel's liberal president, Eliezer Moday. Their strange bedfellows' friendship was creating a schism between Moday and Israel's conservative prime minister, Moshe Kaufman. Kaufman didn't trust that Mousavi's political agenda had Israel's best interest at heart.

Moday had convinced many of the liberal Knesset members that Israel's only chance to avert all-out Mideast war was to give back the land Israel had acquired in 1967. Kaufman believed, like his predecessor, Benjamin Netanyahu, that forfeiting this land would deprive Israel of defensible borders. Political head-butting was beginning to divide the country.

Looking hopefully at Al-Masri, Mousavi asked, "Has the latest weapons shipment been safely smuggled through the Rafah Crossing?"

"Yes sir," Al Masri said with a nod, "it was just confirmed to me this morning."

"Excellent," Mousavi enthused. "Have the weapons deployed immediately to the appropriate munitions locations. Alert your commanders that we are meeting with Zakiri, and that Hamas may soon be called into action against Israel!"

## Syrian President Receives Iranian Ultimatum!

Iranian President Muktada Zakiri stood behind his stately desk as Syrian President Hassan Tereiri entered his office. The two men's eyes locked on one another for a brief moment, but Tereiri was quick to lower his head. "Allah be praised," he humbly greeted.

Zakiri waved his hand at the stiff leather chair before his desk and declared, "Hassan, my compatriot, please sit. I have something important to tell you."

Without delay the Syrian complied. Zakiri gazed down on him in a show of power, before slowly settling into his own palatial chair, the mammoth desk between them. Tereiri squirmed.

"Mr. President," Zakiri said, condescendingly, "Do you know why I have asked you to meet with me alone, in advance of our sacred meeting with our Muslim brothers?"

Fidgeting, Tereiri replied, "I am blessed beyond words, Mr. President that you would choose to meet with me personally. To what do I owe this honor?"

Zakiri leaned back and exclaimed, "I have chosen to warn you in advance of the powerful information that will be conveyed, and of the behavior I want you to exhibit throughout! You must do exactly as I command, out of respect for all that Iran has done to keep you in power."

President Tereiri was stunned. "What is this warning, your Grace?"

Zakiri looked sternly at the Syrian. "As you clearly know, if it were not for my protection, the rebel dogs that are after your blood would have already prevailed against you. Iran's funding has provided you with weaponry and personnel to help you remove the Zionist pigs from the sacred land of Palestine. The time has come to put these weapons to task!"

Moving forward and placing both hands firmly on his desk, Zakiri exhorted, "I must address you bluntly regarding certain visions received from Allah by Nikahd. They confirmed that Allah has called all Muslims to this crowning moment. Nikahd's latest vision instructs that the time to multilaterally strike Israel has come!"

As Zakiri had anticipated, Tereiri evinced little enthusiasm at this pronouncement. Rising, Zakiri peered directly into his political puppet's eyes. "Did you hear me, Hassan? The long-awaited moment has arrived. I am counting on you to perform as instructed!"

Tereiri stammered, "Are...are you absolutely certain the time is right, Mr. President?"

Zakiri fumed, "Are you questioning me?"

With mounting courage, Tereiri declared, "Israel is prepared for this, and I fear my country, not yours, will suffer the brunt of the burden. The IDF has promised to destroy me and my entire posterity in the event of such an attack."[3]

"Where is your faith?" Zakiri decried. "Would you put your clan before the wishes of Allah? Certainly Allah's blessings and protection are bestowed upon us in this war against the Jews!" Then, taking a deep breath, he donned a more subdued demeanor. "Where is your faith, man? Don't disappoint Iran or your fellow countrymen. You will sit quietly, as ordered, at tomorrow's meeting, and you will support the offensive I propose to our united brothers, lest Iran be tempted to cut you off from our blessed protection. There are limits to my patience with you and your country. I warn you, don't test them at tomorrow's meeting!"

Trembling, Tereiri asked, "What, precisely, do you expect from me at this sacred meeting?"

Zakiri sat down with a sigh. "That's a much better response, Hassan. You will not question the moment that we choose to strike the little Satan. You will support the actions that are required of you and your army. This decree is not negotiable and your leadership in the destruction of Israel will garner praise from throughout the Islamic world. Now, I ask you a final time: can I count on you to support what Allah himself has declared to be our finest hour?"

Realizing that he had no choice, Tereiri donned a diplomatic smile and confirmed, "Mr. President, I will do as you propose and act according to Allah's will."

Zakiri offered a benediction, as Tereiri prepared to depart. "May Allah bestow the bounty of his blessings upon you, your family, and your countrymen."

Tereiri bowed respectfully. "As you wish, Mr. President."

Without further utterance, their private meeting was adjourned.

## Iran Instructs Proxies, Syria, Hezbollah, and Hamas, to Attack Israel!

It was a cozy group that gathered in Zakiri's chamber the next day. "Gentlemen, Iran greets you all in the blessed name of Allah," Zakiri greeted his Islamic brothers.

Similar salutations echoed back from his illustrious proxy leaders and the top commanders seated at their sides.

"As you all know," Zakiri began, "we have been waiting for that anticipated moment which Allah has appointed to bring about the destruction of Israel. I am pleased to announce that, according to a recent revelation of Muhammad Al-Mahdi to my trusted advisor Zamani Nikahd, that moment has arrived!"

Pausing, Zakiri observed the attendees seated around the oversized oval table. Except for the Syrian, Hassan Tereiri, they all nodded approvingly, and with invigorated interest.

Observing Tereiri's lack of enthusiasm, Zakiri stared him in the eye, causing his colleagues to also turn their attention toward him. Squirming slightly, in his palatial high back chair, Tereiri nodded, just as his peers had done.

Continuing with his rallying speech, Zakiri said, "The last time you all joined me here in Tehran, in 2009, we formed a war-pact against the Zionist regime. At that time we vowed to fight together against Allah's number one and two enemies, the Jews and their American supporters."

Again Zakiri paused to observe his comrades' audible responses.

The outspoken Secretary General of Hezbollah, Muhammad Imad Fadlallah, raised his voice above the others and declared, "Death to the Two Satans!"

Satisfied, Zakiri informed the group of the specific details of Nikahd's vision and concluded, "The vision signals that the time to wipe Israel off the map is now!"

At those words, Sadegh Mousavi of Hamas could no longer restrain his enthusiasm. Jumping up, he pounded the table, and blurted out, "Death to Israel! Victory shall be ours!"

His comments evoked a frenzied response from the other leaders. Even Hassan Tereiri expressed delight. The meeting had become pep rally against the Jewish State, as every man, to the last of them, testified their anti-Semitic sentiment.

Zakiri couldn't have been more pleased, and quickly moved into the war plans. "No weapon can be withheld from attacking Israel. All of your combined firepower must be unleashed promptly and simultaneously! Iran is prepared to follow in a second wave with our mighty arsenal."

This statement took some of the wind out of Tereiri's sails, causing him to exhibit a slightly soured facial expression, which President Zakiri caught out of the corner of his eye. To appease his Syrian cohort, Zakiri added, "Iran guarantees that our second wave will strike Israel early, before they can mount a serious response."

Hezbollah's Fadlallah boasted, "There is nothing to fear, Hezbollah handed Israel its head on a platter in our summer war with the Jews in 2006. Attacking together we can assuredly destroy the Zionist pigs and liberate Palestine for Hamas and our Palestinian brothers."

Continued war plotting and anti-Israel comments characterized the remainder of the four hour conference. Plans to ambush Israel from all sides were solidified behind closed doors.

When the meeting adjourned, there were no photo shoots or press releases, as the leaders from Syria, Hezbollah, and Hamas left undetected through a side door. The moment they emerged from the palace, they were escorted off in their limousines for the Tehran Imam Khomeini Airport, and their trips back to their respective countries.

Their generals, however, remained behind for secret consultation with the IRGC commanders. When Israeli intelligence picked up on the fact that the IRGC was conducting such a meeting, they perceived something dangerous was brewing, and promptly began alerting key military and political personnel throughout the nation.

✳ Iran had anticipated this response and quickly issued a reverse public relations press release to diffuse Israeli fears. *Iran Prepares Proxies for Israeli Preemptive Strikes*, the *Tehran Times* reported, thus shifting the onus onto Israel. The hope was that Israel and the world would think the commanders were meeting for defensive, rather than offensive military purposes.

The scheme apparently worked, as business in Israel went on as usual.

# Chapter 2
## Troublesome Times on Humanity's Horizon

Clearing out his desk that Friday, eleven year old Tyler Allen Thompson closed the books on his elementary school experience. Finally, the day had come that he was graduating to Eastside Middle School, a few blocks away. One last bell and a much anticipated summer vacation was all that separated him from joining his sister Jami and their mutual friends at Eastside in the fall.

Eastside was located directly across the street from the local Frostee Freeze, where all the neighborhood kids hung out after school. Although it would be Jami's final year at Eastside, he looked forward to walking to school with her and benefiting from her "miss teen queen" popularity on campus. At last, no longer would he be the only elementary school kid on their block.

At the sound of the bell, handsome Tyler spruced up his thick brown hair, courteously bid his teacher farewell, and darted out for a weekend of celebration, to be capped off with a Sunday fishing outing with his beloved Grandpa George.

Tyler was very proud of his entertaining and intelligent grandfather, and cherished the quality time they frequently shared. They were like two peas-in-a-pod and it was obvious where Tyler got his good looks. His sixty-eight year old grandfather still maintained a good physique, stylish head of silver hair, and sported a well-manicured, mustached goatee.

George Thompson was a much-decorated, retired four-star army general who seized every opportunity, especially fishing, as a tool to train Tyler in the lessons of life. In addition to his healthy lifestyle and hearty resume, George intently studied Bible prophecy and sincerely believed his grandson could be living in the final generation. Considering this, he felt compelled to prepare his only grandson for the future he believed was beginning to unfold.

Sunday morning arrived and, wishing to get an early start at fishing, George convinced Tyler's parents, Thomas and Lisa, to allow the boy to attend the 8:00 a.m. church service with himself and Grandma Mimi (her real name was Martha, but everyone who knew her simply called her Mimi). Tyler, who usually attended the local Jewish synagogue, had recently converted to Christianity as a result of his grandpa's tutelage. Tyler's conversion would eventually prove problematic with Lisa's side of the family, who came from a highly orthodox Hebrew pedigree. However, for now, the dust was settling on the religious family matter, so with a little brinksmanship George was able to maneuver his grandson into chapel.

It was Tyler's first time attending the adult service at George's non-denominational church. Apart from attending some special outreach youth events and a Christian rock concert, Tyler was basically a newcomer to the church experience. But, having become a recent convert and soon to be a sixth-grader, Tyler felt a sense of maturity sitting next to his grandparents in the sanctuary.

George was unusually energized this particular Sunday in anticipation of a guest speaker, the well-known author and "end times" expert, Jim Linton. George had read every one of Linton's dozen or so books and was eager to familiarize Tyler with one of his favorite teachers. Last week's church bulletin said Linton's topic would be, *The Importance of Bible Prophecy in These Last Days. This is an important message for Tyler's generation*, thought George, when he read his bulletin.

George's enthusiasm was further fueled by the fact that prolonged Arab protests and revolts continued to plague the Middle East region. These protests were causing wide scale governmental collapses and opened the door for radical regimes to emerge in their place. All of the unrest increasingly isolated Israel from the Arab League and opened the door for the Iranian mullahs to expand their radical Shiite Islamic beliefs throughout the greater Middle East region.

From Lebanon to Iraq, Iran was forming a formidable alliance of Arab proxy states which already included Lebanon, Syria, and Jordan. In the end analysis, the rapid formation of these unexpected alliances between Sunni and Shiite Muslims was forcing Israel into a precarious position. All of these troublesome events served to further George's feelings that mankind had been plunged past the point of no return into the biblical end times.

Linton, a noted Mideast expert who wasn't one to sugar-coat his messages, delivered a sobering sermon that Sunday. Right out of the gate he taught about a coming period of worldwide "tribulation." He warned that troublesome times were on humanity's horizon and listed a flurry of last days' signs supporting his claims. Middle East rumors of war, significant earthquakes, and the ongoing global economic crisis topped his list.

"Prepare yourselves," he said. "All of this protracted Arab unrest, coupled with Iran's recent announcement that it was on the verge of becoming a nuclear nation, will undoubtedly morph into a Mideast conflict that could open up a Pandora's Box in the Holy Land." Frightened by Linton's message, Tyler snuggled close to his grandmother's side, pressing her soft blond hair against her shoulder.

As Grandpa George feverishly penned his notes and the entire congregation sat on the edges of their pews, Jim Linton concluded by reminding them about the importance of putting their faith in Christ "before it's too late." He closed by quoting a passage in the New Testament, Luke 21:36:

"Watch therefore, and pray always that you may be counted worthy to escape all these things that will come to pass, and to stand before the Son of Man."

Dozens accepted his invitation to come forward and accept Christ as their Savior. The message had been so timely and overwhelming; Tyler was hard pressed to find a dry eye in the sanctuary. Even his grandfather, who seldom shed a tear, had trickles running down both cheeks. After the service, Tyler kissed Mimi goodbye, hopped into his grandpa's truck, and the two of them departed for their favorite fishing spot on the picturesque banks of the Colorado River.

Silence marked their travel that Sunday. George sensed that his grandson was finding it difficult to assimilate all the information he had just received. The message exceeded even George's expectations, and so he resigned himself to focusing on fishing and little else for the rest of the day.

Arriving at their destination, they got out the gear and proceeded as planned to catch some fish. However, it wasn't long before Tyler broke the ice and said, "Poppy, I'm confused about what the speaker said. Can you explain to me in kid language what he meant about the terrible times coming?"

Realizing Linton's message had left an indelible impression on young Tyler, the family patriarch pondered the overwhelming implications of the question. Baiting his pole and contemplating his answer, Poppy calmly responded, "Well Ty, remember the teacher talked about the tribulation period?"[4]

"Yes," Tyler's eyes were fear-filled. "My Mom doesn't believe in Jesus. Will she go through that?"

A moment of silence ensued, broken only by the sound of Poppy's line casting into the river.

*Oh Lord*, George silently prayed, *grant me the right words*. Although George would typically seize the opportunity to teach Tyler, he was overwhelmed by the magnitude of translating the question into his beloved grandson's level of comprehension. Swallowing hard, he uttered, "Wouldn't you rather talk about, fishing or sports, or something a little less complicated?"

Peering into his grandpa's eyes, Tyler answered, "Not today, Poppy. The tribulation seems much more important!"

Suddenly a fish snagged Tyler's pole causing him to shift his attention to the catch at hand. From that point forward fantastic fishing required their undivided attention, temporarily sparing George a painful discussion.

# Chapter 3
## Tribulation Generation

Having emptied the Colorado River of their daily fishing limit, Poppy and Ty loaded back into the truck and headed homeward. Grandpa figured the tribulation topic was destined to resurface during the thirty-minute drive. He had avoided answering Tyler's questions thus far due to spectacular fishing conditions, but during those fish-filled hours he had wisely considered his answer.

Rather than wait, he seized the opportunity to share his answer and began rather awkwardly, "The tribulation is a painful seven-year period for the world, Ty. Both people and God's beautiful creation will experience enormous suffering."

Fumbling to remove his headset and turn off his iPod, Tyler questioned, "What's that Gramps?"

"The *trip- trib*-ulation period; you asked about it earlier," Poppy stuttered. "It will be a terrible time for man and creation. There will be earthquakes, nuclear contamination, and a whole lot of worldwide devastation. The Bible says several oceans, streams, and rivers, maybe even the Colorado, will become polluted, causing many fish to die," he added.[5]

"Are you talking about a lot of major earthquakes all over the world, like the nine-point one in Japan that killed thousands of people?" Tyler asked.

Poppy swallowed. "Yes, like that one."

"We spent a few days studying earthquakes in class when the Japanese earthquake happened," Tyler said. "I remember the teacher said about a quarter-million people died in a huge earthquake in Haiti about a year before, because of their low construction standards."

Tyler's studious response slightly eased Poppy's tension about translating the tribulation into kid's language, and so he replied, "That sounds correct. It never ceases to amaze me how much fifth graders are learning these days. I feel like I can talk to you about almost anything."

Clearing his throat, Tyler corrected, "Excuse me. I'm a sixth grader now."

"Oh, forgive my forgetfulness. It never ceases to amaze me how advanced sixth graders are these days," Poppy humorously rephrased.

Grinning broadly, Tyler replied, "Well you know we are more advanced than you and Mimi were when you were in school. Don't forget we have the Internet now!"

"Oh, I see," Poppy said, holding back his laughter. "Did you know that Jesus predicted 2,000 years ago that big earthquakes would come someday?"

"Of course, that's what Mr. Linton said in church today," Tyler reminded.

"That's right. I was checking to see if you remembered," chuckled Poppy.

After a momentary interval Poppy continued, "He also said they have been increasing all over the world."

Reflecting, Tyler questioned, "Do you mean that not only fish, but hundreds of thousands of people are going to die, too?"

"Yes, the Bible book of Revelation warns that *millions* of people will die," Grandpa sadly noted.

"But why does that happen to the world? Can't people make it better so God doesn't have to punish them and the planet?" Tyler inquired.

"Good question," Grandpa mumbled.

Not expecting the conversation to swerve off into the philosophical realm, Poppy had to put on his thinking cap before responding to Tyler's intelligent questions. Collecting his thoughts, he answered, "The Bible says the heart of mankind is desperately wicked and we will continue to make matters worse because we inherited a genetic defect from Adam and Eve called 'sin.' This is why God sent his only Son, Jesus, as a sacrifice for everybody's sins. In other words, Ty, people won't make the planet a better place; it's against their selfish nature."

Since Tyler gave no immediate response, Poppy assumed he had answered Tyler's questions satisfactorily. To his relief, Tyler did not broach the subject of his mother's unsaved status in this round.

However, a few minutes later, the questions got tougher. "What about all the other religions," he asked, "And, how can someone really know if God is real?

Startled by Tyler's spiritual depth, Poppy deflected with, "What all are they teaching you kids in school these days?"

"Don't be silly, Gramps. They can't teach about religion in schools anymore. I learned a little bit about different religions at synagogue, preparing for my Bar Mitzvah."

Collecting his thoughts once again, Poppy answered, "Many false religions wrongly teach that people can become god. You know from synagogue that Satan lied to Adam and Eve in the garden of Eden. The Devil declared that by eating from the forbidden tree in the midst of the garden, they would become like God. After they ate of that fruit, they realized that he had lied to them. That lie has continued on in some of the false religions, like Hinduism and Buddhism."

Tyler replied, "We didn't learn much about those religions."

George continued, "As far as your second question, I believe that somewhere in the first chapter of the book of Romans it teaches that God can be known by observing creation. The passage says that men are to recognize there is a God through His creation."

"Makes sense," Tyler conceded.

Moments later, he inquired, "Poppy, why does this bad stuff have to happen while I'm growing up? I want to enjoy my summer and go to Eastside with my friends. Someday, I want to work with my dad in construction and have a family of my own. Are you sure there will be a tribulation in my lifetime?

"I know it doesn't seem fair," Grandpa said," but from the way the world looks now, with earthquakes increasing, and other big problems in the world, it looks like Jim Linton is right. It pains me to tell you that your generation could be the last one. But remember, Christians escape the tribulation. That is what the rapture is for," Poppy reminded.

Tyler reluctantly commented, "You're right, it's not fair. I sure hope you're right about the rapture. It didn't make sense what Mr. Linton said about it. It sounded crazy, like an episode from a Star Wars movie! Didn't he say Christians are going to disappear into the clouds by being poofed into thin air?"

"The rapture is one of the big events people need to understand," Poppy replied. "The Bible calls it a mystery. Jesus comes by surprise and takes millions of believers to heaven. The Bible says it occurs on a cloudy day and happens faster than you can blink your eyes. The people left behind will be shocked, and wonder where everybody disappeared to. It is described in several connecting Bible Scriptures."

George concluded, "If you like, someday Mimi and I can do a study with you, to help you understand it better."

"I think we should, because it sounds really weird," exclaimed Tyler. With this, Tyler turned on his iPod and put his headset over his ears once again.

# Chapter 4
## Israel Comes Under Multi-front Attack!

Observing that his grandson had checked out of the discussion and into his pre-teen music world, Poppy tuned into his favorite Christian radio station and continued homeward.

Shortly into the program, the radio station interrupted its broadcast, announcing: "This is Allen Smith, station manager at KWBC. We interrupt our regularly scheduled program to bring you an important breaking news alert! We have just been informed that a barrage of rockets has rocked Tel Aviv. Reportedly, scud missiles carrying chemical warheads were included in the assault. Although many missiles were intercepted by Israel's Iron Dome defense system, several apparently got through, hitting Israel's capital city. Unconfirmed reports suggest that hundreds of Israelis are believed injured or dead as a result of these fatal blasts."

"Hysteria fills the city streets, as several hundred thousand tourists and local residents scramble for gas masks and nearby bomb shelters. We have Sheila Abernathy, our correspondent on the ground in Tel Aviv, with us by phone. Sheila, what can you tell us?"

Turning up the volume, Grandpa immediately blurted out, "Turn off your iPod quick, Ty! We have to hear this."

"What is it Poppy?"

"Quiet please! This is important!" Grandpa exclaimed!

"Yes, Allen, this is Sheila. I'm on my cell phone shouting through a gas mask, racing to the nearest bomb shelter. Can you hear me?"

"Barely, Sheila. You're breaking in and out, but go ahead," said Allen.

Sheila frantically reported: "Panic indeed characterizes the scene here in Tel Aviv. Numerous powerful explosions hit the most densely populated portions of the city. Deadly chemical components are spreading rapidly throughout the area. Our crew is being evacuated to safety, so I have only a few moments to report what's happening here."

"In my thirty years of reporting I have never seen anything as dangerous and chaotic as this. Just down the street there are dozens of people without gas masks collapsing on the pavement. Some of the main roads are severely damaged and I fear the emergency first responders will be unable to get to them in time. This is an absolutely horrific site!"

"Sheila, this is extremely troubling! How soon until you and the crew reach safety?"

"We've neared the shelter and I have to sign off for now," Sheila responded.

"We thank the Lord that you and the crew have reached safety!" Allen said. "Dear listeners, Israel has come under serious attack and dangerous developments are occurring right now. Stay tuned to this station and we will give you further news updates on this accelerating situation as soon as we receive them. This is Allen Smith reporting from KWBC."

"Wow!" Grandpa exclaimed as he pounded his dashboard.

"Wow what?" Ty nervously asked.

"Psalm 83, that's what!" Poppy declared. "The final Arab–Israeli war might be happening right now!"

Putting the pedal to the metal in a mad dash to reach home, Poppy scanned through the radio dial, attempting to gain a full assessment of the accelerating events.

Numerous local stations were reporting the breaking Middle East news. One reported Ben Gurion airport had also been severely struck by missile fire, causing the immediate cancellation of all flights in and out of Israel. Another channel announced Hezbollah and Syria claimed responsibility for the attacks.

As the reports streamed across the airwaves, Poppy flattened the accelerator pedal to the floorboard and darted around cars, hastening homeward as if he were racing the final lap of the Indianapolis 500.

"Slow down Poppy! You're going to get us both killed!" anguished Tyler.

Shushing his grandson, Poppy said, "Don't worry! I know this road like the back of my hand. I could drive it with my eyes closed."

Panic stricken, Tyler made sure his seatbelt was buckled tight and braced for the white knuckle ride of his life.

It wasn't long before Poppy screeched into his driveway, prompting Tyler to nervously ask, "Aren't you taking me home first?"

"Not right now, Ty. I have to watch the news to find out more about what's going on in the Middle East. Come inside; Grandma Mimi will drive you home shortly," he promised.

Flinging the front door wide open, he scurried past his high school sweetheart's open arms to retrieve his Bible and turn on their big screen TV.

Focusing her aqua-blue eyes upon her grandson, who straggled in slump-shouldered a few minutes afterward, Mimi asked, "What's going on with your grandfather, and why didn't he take you home first?"

"Psalm 83, whatever that is," he whimpered.

Instantly, Mimi's countenance changed, as her compassionate heart dropped deep within her.

Pulling her grandson close to her side, she said, "Calm down. It's nothing you need to worry about. It's something your grandfather is interested in. It has something to do with what was taught in church earlier today and probably got your grandpa overly excited."

Wiping a trickle of tears from his eyes, Tyler asked, "Do you mean it's the tribulation?"

"Oh Lord, no! I don't think it's quite that serious," she replied.

"I'm scared! Why won't Grandpa tell us what's going on?" asked Tyler.

Mimi displayed her grandmotherly grin and jested, "I'm sure he will when he gets done wearing out the remote control," she said, guiding him toward the kitchen. "For now, have a fresh-baked chocolate chip cookie and try to calm down."

Taking in the fresh-baked aroma permeating throughout the kitchen, Tyler succumbed to her request. *Cookies and milk with Mimi is more fun than dealing with Grandpa's freak-out right now*, thought Tyler.

As the two of them sat across from each other at the kitchen table, Tyler asked, "Mimi, do you know about the Psalm war Poppy is concerned about?"

"Oh yes. I'm no expert, but your grandfather reminds me about it every time something gets weird in the Middle East," she sarcastically humored.

"Is it a really bad thing? I mean, do you think my cousins in Israel could get hurt?" Tyler inquired.

"Any war is bad, and people often get hurt, but Poppy says according to a book he studied called *Isralestine*,[6] Israel wins the Psalm 83 war, and becomes a safer place for awhile." Mimi comforted.

"Does this war have something to do with the problem between the Palestinians and the Jews?" Tyler queried.

"Yes, I guess you could say that; Poppy says something happens and the Arabs and Palestinians have a final war with the Jews. He says the Psalm lists a specific group of Middle East countries and terrorist groups that form a confederacy to wipe Israel off of the map forever." Mimi replied.

"That's terrible! Is Poppy sure that Israel wins?" he nervously asked.

"Yes, Poppy says Israel definitely wins," she replied.

"Ty, please don't get all worked up again. I don't know enough about all this stuff to answer your questions. We'll clean up in here and head into the parlor to see what's going on with Poppy. I'm sure everything will be fine. Your grandfather gets easily excited about Middle East news, so let's keep cool. It's probably nothing major," Mimi said in a comforting tone.

Meanwhile in the parlor, Grandpa had his Bible open to Psalm 83 and was couched closely in front of the TV, as if it were Super Bowl Sunday. Remote in hand, he flipped through the mainstream news channels like there was no tomorrow. As he suspected, they were all covering the Middle East conflict, just like they had during *Operation Desert Storm*. During that period many Americans were glued to their televisions sets, gleaning all the news they could gather. Georg believed this conflict would be even more powerful and newsworthy.

Observing out of the corner of his eye that Mimi and Tyler had left the kitchen and entered the parlor, George exclaimed "This has to be it! It's too big to be just another skirmish."

By now, further reports had streamed in, declaring Israel had launched a barrage of retaliatory missiles into Lebanon and Syria, near Damascus, and that a nationwide mobilization of all Israeli military personnel and armor was underway.

Removing her apron and placing it on a nearby chair, Mimi sat on the edge of the sofa next to George. In her characteristic angelic voice Mimi asked, "Are you prepared to calmly tell us what in the world is going on? You stormed in the house as if it were Armageddon and left your grandson weeping alone in the car."

"Forgive me, Ty. I should have been more considerate. I must have panicked you in my enthusiasm," Poppy apologized.

"You scared me half to death, Grandpa," declared Tyler. "First you have me listen to a speaker talk about the world ending and then you drove like a maniac on the freeway. Speaking about the end of the world, I thought my world was going to end because you were going to get us in a wreck!"

"How serious is this Middle East flare-up you're watching?" Mimi asked. "And please don't blow it out of proportion just because you think it has something to do with the Psalm 83 Bible prophecy."

Having lived with her husband most of her life, Mimi was well acquainted with his tendency to tell tall tales and turn current events into biblical exegesis.

Pulling his glasses down to the tip of his nose and peering above the rims, George retorted, "This is the real Mideast McCoy! No more bad rap for old George! This is the Psalm 83 prophecy many of us have been anticipating. I knew it was just a matter of time before the missiles would be blasting throughout Mideast skies."

"The other day the news reported the Palestinians and Jews were going to resume peace talks," Mimi stated.

"Wishful thinking!" replied George. "I keep telling you the Arabs and Jews probably won't make peace, because most Middle East Arabs hate the Jews and refuse to recognize Israel's right to exist. World leaders have been trying to fix the problem over there for over six-decades, to no avail; now the inevitable war has come!"

"Poppy, do you think my aunts and uncles and cousins living in Israel will be hurt?" Tyler worried.

"The Bible predicts Israel will win this war, but it is hard to know how many Israelis will be harmed while the war is being waged," answered Poppy. "News channels are already reporting serious damage and loss of life inside Tel Aviv. Fortunately, most of your family lives closer to Jerusalem. This could work to their favor, since the Arabs have holy sites there and they won't want to bomb them," Poppy comforted.

Mimi, who was obviously not an entire novice to prophecy, wondered, "I overheard the newscaster report Israel launched missiles at Damascus. Could it be Isaiah 17 has just happened, George?"

Cringing, Tyler asked, "Is that another bad prophecy? What's does that Isaiah thing say?"

"The destruction of Damascus," Grandpa declared. "Isaiah 17 predicts that Damascus will someday cease to be a city, and be reduced to rubble."

"Isn't Damascus an important city?" Tyler questioned.

"Indeed it is," Poppy replied. "Damascus is the oldest continuously inhabited city in recorded history, dating back four thousand years to the time of father Abraham. It's Syria's capital, with about four million people in and around the metropolitan areas of the city. It's a strategic target for

Israel, because every known terrorist organization has either an office or headquarters located there."

"Do you think Israel just destroyed Damascus, like Isaiah predicted?" Tyler marveled.

"This has not been confirmed, yet. All we know so far is that Israel fired missiles in the direction of Damascus. However, Isaiah's prophecy seems to suggest that Israel will be responsible for the destruction of Damascus. Isaiah also suggests the destruction is sudden, as if it happens overnight. So it's possible that's what we're witnessing," Poppy explained.

Together they watched further news reports filter in suggesting Damascus was severely damaged in the fighting, which promptly provoked an emergency meeting of the Arab League. Leaders from Egypt, Jordan, Lebanon, and all the other twenty-two member Arab states were en-route to Saudi Arabia, to convene.

Concurrently, the United Nations immediately issued an official statement condemning Israel's use of excessive force against its Arab neighbors. The statement called for the immediate cessation of all violence between Israel and Syria, Hezbollah, and Hamas, who had simultaneously begun attacking Israel from the southwest out of the Gaza Strip. It was obvious to all that this was a pre-planned, confederate effort to destroy Israel.

Meanwhile, as Mideast matters rapidly deteriorated, Tyler's mother, Lisa, came storming into the house, asking harshly, "What in the world is going on? Jami and I were clear across town at the factory outlets mall when Tyler called me, sobbing. He said his grandfather was acting strange and left him alone in the car, and we stopped what we were doing and raced over to find out why!"

Lisa had been a fashion model before marrying Tyler's father, Thomas, fifteen years ago. Once upon a time, her inviting smile and fit feminine figure adorned the covers of many popular fashion magazines, and her natural beauty epitomized the phrase "drop-dead-gorgeous." She had since become a career mom, but maintained a part-time relationship as an independent consultant for several magazine companies she had formerly modeled for. Possessing her master's degree in marketing, Lisa had standing, high-paying job offers with several companies, should she ever seek to enter the full-time workplace again.

However, she was content with motherhood, and when it came to household and family matters, she ruled the roost like a protective mother hen. Lisa did everything possible to insulate Jami and Tyler from adversity and negativity; so much so, that George often had heated exchanges with her that always began with, "You need to come off the cover, girl, and join the real world."

Suffice it to say, George and Lisa had their share of go-rounds, which Lisa usually won. Through the years, she had discovered all his hot buttons and knew when to push them. On the flip side, she also knew how to sweet talk him into her corner afterward.

"What were you both doing at such a large public place?" George challenged. "Don't you realize the country is nearly on lock down since the Department of Homeland Security elevated the terror threat level to its highest level since September 11th?"

"If you're so worried about terrorism, why did you take my son to a large church and then go fishing at a popular spot?" Lisa bantered back. "Besides, why did you make Tyler cry and leave him in the car? Did he do something wrong?"

"Calm down, dear," Mimi soothed. "Everything's under control. We are trying to explain to Tyler what is happening in the Middle East right now."

"The Middle East? Mimi, he's only a child!" she argued. "Besides, I watched some of it on the news before Jami and I left for the outlets. What's the big deal? The Arabs have been warring against the Jews from time immemorial. This conflict is nothing new!"

"Nothing new?" George retorted.

Just then Mimi, seeing Tyler's countenance fall, and fearing the conversation would worsen, interrupted. "Where's Jami?" she asked.

"Waiting outside in the car," Lisa replied.

Grabbing Tyler by the hand, Mimi led him toward the door. "I want to go say hello to her. I will get Tyler in the car for you," she offered.

Waiting for Mimi and Tyler to step safely beyond arguing distance, Lisa asked, "George, what were you about to say?"

"You need to come off the cover, girl, and join the real world!" George huffed. "We're talking about chemical warheads, gas masks, bomb shelters, and perhaps even nuclear weapons against Damascus. These aren't disgruntled Palestinians lobbing protest stones at the Jews; these are high-tech arsenals intended to wipe Israel off the map!"

George reiterated, "I have been warning you and Thomas for the past few years that the Middle East is about to go apocalyptic. Bible prophecies calling for the destruction of Damascus and a climactic Arab-Israeli war have been stage-setting since Israel fought against Hamas in *Operation Cast Lead* dating back to the time Barrack Obama was inaugurated president. I think what we are watching now could be the beginning of battles of epic proportion."

"Forgive me, father-in-law," Lisa admonished, "but being Jewish, I don't believe in Jesus! Nor do I believe in Bible prophecy. If you and Mimi want to be born-again Christians and believe in an apocalypse, that's your prerogative. However, I'm warning you not to frighten Tyler with such talk. He has enough problems growing up in this crazy world as it is, not to mention all the teen-age peer pressure he's going to face next year at Eastside Middle."

"Did you mean Eastside Middle, or 'Middle East'"? George taunted. "Because the way things are presently going over there, who knows what Tyler's world will look like by the time school resumes in the fall?"

"Enough already! This conversation is going nowhere," Lisa snapped back. "Is this what Christians want? Do they *want* war and suffering to continue between the Arabs and the Jews?"

Taken aback, George replied, "Of course not! You know I love the Jewish people and serve a God who loves both Arabs and Jews. Tyler and I were expressing our sincere concerns about the safety of your family in Israel before you arrived. But, Lisa, it takes two to make peace, and even the most liberal Jews in Israel are realizing the Arabs don't want peace!"

Frustrated, Lisa sighed, "I know you mean well, but it's getting late and I'm going to take the kids home now."

Driving off in her sporty BMW, Lisa attempted to calm Tyler down by shifting his focus back to his summer vacation plans. She told her son, "You concentrate on being a twelve-year-old and focus on having fun this summer with your sister and friends. Let your father and me deal with your grandparents regarding these grown-up matters."

Sitting shotgun, Jami asked, "What 'matters'? What's Tyler all worked up about?"

"It's not for you to worry about. It's a Christian thing and not open for further discussion."

"But, Mommy," Tyler said, "I'm a Christian! It's important for me to learn about all this Bible stuff."

"For Christ's sake!" Lisa ironically blurted. "You are just a child and unable to make major commitments."

"But, Grandma Naomi and you told me that next year I have my *bar mitzvah*, and that means I'm old enough to understand religion," Tyler argued.

Stunned by her brother's insightfulness, Jami stared at him in amazement.

Observing Jami's countenance, Lisa reminded her, "Don't forget that he's not thirteen, *yet.*"

"I'm almost twelve," Tyler rebutted.

Desperately wanting an end to the conversation, Lisa shouted, "I don't care what my mother and I said. You can't make this decision on your own right now!"

Once again, tears began to streak Tyler's cheeks.

"Now look what you've done!" Jami howled. "Why can't you and Grandma Naomi accept Tyler's decision to become a Christian? What's the big deal about Christianity? Why is everyone on your side of the family bothered by it?"

Realizing her comments had struck a sensitive family nerve, Lisa apologetically said, "I'm sorry, Son. I don't mean to lose my temper about this. I know how important being Christian is to you. It's just that my family longs for us all to move to Israel to be near them, and for you to be *bar mitzvahed* there. When I told them you recently converted, they felt betrayed."

"But, what about Dad?" Tyler reminded her. "He's been a Christian since he was my age. Your family has learned to accept him."

Lisa rolled her eyes. "Yes, but your father hasn't been practicing his religion for years! He doesn't really know what faith he is!"

Taking a deep breath, and locking in on Tyler's eyes through the rear view mirror, Lisa calmly requested, "Look, I'll try to be sensitive to your feelings about religion. For now, let's get home and have a good dinner, and try to have a better day tomorrow."

# Chapter 5
## Panic in Damascus

Beginning her expedient evacuation from Damascus, Adara Tereiri cried out to her father, Syrian president Hassan Tereiri, "What have you initiated? Our country is in utter turmoil! Syria has come under serious attack from Israel!"

With tears streaming down her frightened face, Adara continued, "Brother Kamal has warned that we all must flee immediately because Israel is coming to destroy Damascus and our dynasty. He has already prepared a place of refuge for us in Jordan."

The Syrian president replied to his daughter, "I know this situation is escalating and looks like it's spiraling out of control, but don't panic. President Zakiri of Iran has promised his country's full support to our final war with the Jews."

Adara continued to agonize, "What does Kamal mean that the Jews won't stop fighting in Syria until they have destroyed Damascus and eliminated our entire family? What have you done? Why are the Israelis specifically targeting our clan and our capitol city?" To which Hassan caustically replied, "Nonsense, your brother is speaking nonsense! He has chosen to be a coward at this critical time in our history. He is worried about Israeli Prime Minister Kaufman's empty threats to destroy Damascus, and our whole family in the event of war. These are baseless intimidations from Kaufman."

Dragging her father firmly by the arm toward the rear door of the capitol building, Adara beseeched him, "Come with me now; we can't trust Iran, we must all flee to Jordan immediately. The protestors are beginning to revolt against us again. Tens-of-thousands are communicating over Facebook and the Internet calling for fellow Syrians to kill us, and to plead for Israel's Defense Forces to back down. Brother says that protesters are already assembling to overtake the capitol. He said that if the revolutionaries don't succeed in killing us, the Bible says that Israel surely will!"

Adara fell to the floor as her father shook loose from her iron choking grip. She began pleading, "Father please, don't be foolish; come with us before it's too late, and even your grandchildren are killed. The protestors are panicking in the streets. If we don't go now, we will never survive!"

Her father's anger flared, "How dare you quote from the enemy's Bible; and you and your brother are not going anywhere. Zakiri has vowed to employ the use of his nuclear weapons to wipe Israel off of the map. This war will be over before it begins. And, you and your brother are not leaving this country. I will have no show of weakness from my family, or any of my countrymen. The protestors and the Jews will bathe in their own blood for their aggressive actions."

Instructing security close by to seize his daughter, Hassan commanded that his cowardly son Kamal also be captured. "Confine them until I decide what to do with the two of them," Tereiri ordered.

Adding complexity to Hassan Tereiri's circumstances, his son Kamal had betrayed his family's Muslim heritage by recently converting to Christianity. While touring through Bangladesh, Indonesia, and the Sudan, filming his documentary called *Can Muslims be Moderate*, he interviewed Christian missionaries who had convinced him over time that, according to several Surah's inside the Koran, there was no such thing as a moderate Muslim.

Moreover, they also succeeded in persuading him that Jesus Christ was the world's Messiah. Gaining his confidence, they eventually convinced him that Syria was clearly identified in biblical prophecy, in Isaiah 17 and elsewhere.

"Dad, the Bible declares Damascus will someday cease to be a city, it will become a ruinous heap, and I'm concerned that unless you strike peace with Israel, that day will arrive soon" Kamal had pleaded to his father Hassan, upon his return from filming overseas.

Incensed by his son's treasonous comments about Israel, Syria's capitol city, and his conversion to Christianity, Hassan Tereiri had ostracized his infidel son, and extradited him to Amman, Jordan, promptly upon his return.

Hassan Tereiri had hoped that his friend King Hussein of Jordan would be able to deprogram his son's Christian thinking. King Hussein was considered to be the most moderate Middle East Muslim leader, and the most familiar with westernized thinking. Hassan thought, *if anyone could convince his son Kamal that Muslims can be moderate, it would be his close friend Hussein.*

But, Kamal was relentless in his pursuit to warn his royal family of their pending peril.

Adara, out of love and compassion for her brother, lent his Christian preaching a sympathetic ear, and this troubled the Syrian president all the more. Although Adara was reluctant to hastily abandon her Islamic roots, she did begin wondering if Kamal was correct, and if the Bible could foretell Syria's future. With the war presently being waged against Israel, she feared Damascus could be destroyed!

Thus, now at the height of Hassan Tereiri's war distress, the thought of his children betraying his destiny with Islamic infamy was intolerable. *Incarcerate them both. How dare they disrupt this momentous moment in time*, he thought to himself.

Nevertheless, somewhere beneath his troubled Islamic-inculcated soul, he wondered if his firstborn son Kamal could be correct. What if Damascus could soon see its doom? Certainly the news he had received from the Saudi king earlier that morning *weighed heavily upon his heart...*

Departing into his office, he called President Zakiri immediately and promptly pleaded, "Where is your army, and when do you plan to launch your supposed nuclear weapons into Israel? We are under severe attack by the IDF, just as I had feared. My family is betraying me and trying to flee to Jordan, the revolutionaries are charging against my capitol as we speak, and worst of all, my chief commanders are warning that Israel is preparing to fire nuclear weapons against us. We need Iran to get involved now, without delay!"

In arrogant disbelief the Iranian president Zakiri declared, "That's preposterous! Israel would face international condemnation for such an attack. This is not a possible scenario, and your commanders' assessments should be seriously questioned."

Furiously, Tereiri confirmed, "Israel made it no secret this morning when they informed Saudi King Abdullah of their intentions to deploy their Dolphin Class submarines in the Mediterranean Sea for a nuclear mission against Damascus. King Abdullah called me immediately afterward, and said Israel wanted him to make sure Syria understood IDF's nuclear intentions. Our intelligence reports confirm that Israeli warships are on the move in the Mediterranean. Waiting to see if this is merely a rumor of war is no longer a luxury afforded to Hamas, Hezbollah, Iran, or Syria. Iran must enter, and exercise control over the Middle East war theater immediately as you promised!"

Zakiri lashed back, "How dare you issue orders to me, Hassan! I'm in command here, and I have just ordered the Secretary General of Hezbollah, Muhammad Imad Fadlallah and Sadegh Mousavi of Hamas to initiate the second stage of the war against Israel. I command you, too: follow suit, and keep in stride with our attack schedule. Iran will enter into the fight after you all have inflicted the next round of damage upon Israel, and not before."

Tired of being chastised, and realizing the imminent danger of an IDF nuclear threat, Tereiri replied, "With all due respect Zakiri, you underestimate the battlefield! Israel is already retaliating with excessive force, and they will use their nuclear arsenal. The Israelis are in a fight for their survival, and they won't leave their best weapons on the shelf. First Damascus, and then Tehran will be their targets. The Jews know that you have commanded this attack, and they will seek revenge against Iran, as well. By your own admission, you miscalculated Israel's response. You think the IDF will authorize only a measured response, but I tell you they will nuke both our countries!"

Irately, the Iranian president commanded, "You shall do as I say, or you won't have to worry about the protesters or the Jews; Iran shall have your head! I have instructed the deployment of IRCG troops to our western borders, and intend to shut down the Strait of Hormuz tomorrow, according to our joint military plans. The world will condemn Israel when Iran chokes off its major artery of oil distribution. Israel will not use nuclear weapons against you for fear that doing so will provoke the wrath of the world upon itself!"

Before Tereiri could reply, the dial tone rang in his ear. Zakiri had hung up, leaving the Syrian president no alternative but to stay true to their apocalyptic course. However, now he realized that all the warring parties were in a no-stops final fight for survival, and that Syria was on its own!

# Chapter 6
## There's Trouble in Tehran and Destruction in Damascus

Throughout the next few days, George Thompson and his faithful companion of forty-four years, Mimi, remained generally fastened to the sofa and focused upon the TV, watching Mideast matters significantly worsen. Additionally, George entertained a steady stream of phone calls from fellow prophecy buffs interested in comparing notes as to the biblical ramifications of the escalating Mideast mayhem.

Apart from the occasional visit to the latrine, as retired General George often referred to their bathroom, and their daily workout in their garage conversion gym, they hunkered down in the parlor for what they anticipated could be a very long haul. They were quite content remaining indoors because they were fixated upon the mainstream news; but, more importantly, the Department of Homeland Security (DHS) had raised the American terror alert level to its severest condition, as a result of the current Arab-Israeli war.

The alert level began its upward ascent a year earlier, during the widespread protests in the Arab Spring of 2011. But, the escalating multi-front Middle East conflict sent the United States terror level soaring to new heights.

Intensifying matters, Iran was mobilizing its IRGC troops to move westward toward Israel and moving several warships into the Red Sea. Moreover, Iran closed off the Strait of Hormuz, causing oil prices to skyrocket, stock markets to plummet, and great concern within the international community.

If all the above wasn't troubling enough, Iranian president Zakiri vowed to unleash thousands of terror cells deeply imbedded in the United States, in a massive nuclear Jihad against Americans.

Iran's hostile actions and troubling threats prompted many Americans to storm the gas stations to top off their tanks, for fear of further gas shortages and price spikes. Additionally, panicked consumers stampeded grocery and big box stores, emptying shelves of emergency goods like food, water, basic weapons, and first aid kits.

However, George, being an end-time's survivalist, already had his stockpile of gold, guns, and goods in order, and wasn't caught up in the frenzy.

Many Americans were refraining from going to public centers of interest, like sporting events, malls, and movie theaters, for fear of chemical, suicide, and other types of terror attacks. These fears were further nurtured by the fact that the New York City and Los Angeles police departments were utilizing newly developed radiation detector devices on a daily basis, to search for dirty bombs potentially concealed somewhere within their city limits.

Although initially George wasn't overly concerned about all these above developments, his disposition was rapidly changing, now that Israel had come under fire from Iran's proxies. He realized Iranian terror threats against America were equally as credible. He commented to Mimi, "It may not be wise for Lisa and Jami to make their mother-daughter mall visits, anymore."

"How do you propose to stop them, after your recent spat with Lisa?" Mimi asked. "And, if that's the case, then it's not advisable for you and Tyler to go fishing again, until all this Mideast dust settles."

Her fishing comment, reminiscent of Lisa's barb to the same effect, hit below the belt, provoking George to respond, "That's overkill! Terrorists are not going to blow up fishing holes. For Pete's sake, they don't even know where the good ones are located!"

\* \* \* \* \* \*

It was near dusk on the Sunday after the war broke out, when their solitude was interrupted by the sound of the doorbell, announcing a surprise visit from George's old army buddy and best friend, Robert Rasmussen. Robert, always clean shaven and lightly splashed with Old Spice cologne, had shared in several overseas tours of duty with George. But now, like George, he was enjoying the rewards of retirement.

"The Man with the Midas Touch," as George often referred to him, was a man of means. He possessed a portfolio worth millions of dollars, which was partially from inheritance, but mostly from sound investing. Robert had been away on an extended business trip when the war broke out, and was grateful to be back in his home town.

Robert's house was a stone's throw from George's, and having lost his wife, Ruth, to cancer a few months earlier, he spent much time at the Thompson residence. On this occasion, George was especially pleased to see Robert, because he wanted to get his prophetic slant on Mideast events.

Rasmussen was no novice when it came to understanding Bible prophecy. Author of hundreds of widely published prophecy articles and an invited guest of numerous radio and TV shows, he was considered by many to be an end-times expert. The slightly balding Robert, at six-foot-four, maintained a strong physique and keen mind. Sixty-two and retired, he also maintained a well-trafficked prophecy blog/website, which normally received several thousand unique visitors daily.

Razz, short for Razzmatazz (George's nickname for Robert), strongly believed the next Middle East war would fulfill prophecies contained in Ezekiel 38-39. These two chapters, he believed, described a Russian-Iranian led coalition against Israel in the end times.

The moment the Middle East war broke out, George had a hunch Razz would identify it with Ezekiel's war, rather than the Arab-Israeli war predicted in Psalm 83. Finally, with Razz back in town, he could find out if his suspicions were correct!

Upon greeting Razz at the door, George led him toward the parlor, where Razz asked, "George, have you and Mimi been watching the Middle East go apocalyptic this past week?"

"Absolutely! Mimi and I have become dysfunctional couch potatoes since the war broke out. We're afraid to turn off the news for fear we'll miss some late breaking event. And, we hesitate to leave the house for fear of meeting up with an Islamic suicide bomber," George replied.

Razz chuckled at George's half-serious comment. "The latest news warns that Iran is coming into the Mideast fray militarily. Everyone in the military circles we travel, recognizes that Iran has instigated its proxies of Syria, Hezbollah, and Hamas to wage this multi-front war against the Israelis. That is going to force Israel to attack the rogue state, and attempt to destroy their nuclear weapons program. I can see all this leading to the fulfillment of Ezekiel 38 and 39."

"Oh brother, here we go again!" George sighed. He then called out to Mimi, "Dear, will you fire up a pot of coffee, please; and I'll attempt to set Razzmatazz straight about where these Psalm 83 events are headed?"

As if to ignore George's passing Psalm 83 comment, Razz quickly interjected, "The Israel-US covert cyber war, initiated in the summer of 2010, seemed to slow down Iran's nuclear program dramatically, but my sources all confirm Iran is about to become a *bona fide* nuclear nation, and may already be armed and dangerous with several undetected nukes hidden somewhere in their underground nuclear facilities. If so, this is concerning to not only Israel, but America as well." Former UN ambassador John Bolton has been warning us that the world will probably have to accept a nuclear Iran, which will reshape the balance of power in the Mideast.[7]

"That may all be true Razz, but what is going on in the Middle East presently is primarily an Arabs verses Jews conflict, not a Russian, Turkish, and Persian verses Israel event!" George replied. "Besides, some of us are fully expecting Israel to strike Iran's nuclear sites, especially in Bushehr, in fulfillment of Jeremiah 49:34-39."

With a deer in the headlights stare at George, Razz replied, "What in the world are you talking about? Are you referring to the prophecies regarding ancient Elam? I am under the impression Jeremiah's Elamite prophecies were historically fulfilled during the conquest of the Persian Empire."

As Mimi handed him his fresh cup of java, Razz said, "George, refresh my memory about Elam."

George replied, "As you well know, Ezekiel was not the only Old Testament prophet predicting Iran's end-time fate. His contemporary, Jeremiah, prophesied against Elam. Ezekiel 38 identified today's Iran as Persia, which was Iran's former name until it changed in 1935. However, Jeremiah labeled at least part of modern-day Iran as Elam. At that time, about 2,600 years ago, Persia encompassed the majority of modern-day Iran, but Elam, with its capital city of Susa, covered most of what is now west-central Iran, including the area of Iran's main nuclear site at Bushehr."

Realizing his extensive recent research had piqued Razz' curiosity, George continued, "Elam dates back approximately 4,000 years, to when Chedorlaomer was the Elamite king. Abraham conquered him in his quest to free his nephew Lot from captivity.[8] Recently, several end-time scholars, like Dr. Arnold Fruchtenbaum, John McTernan, and Sean Osborne have been teaching that Jeremiah's Elamite prophecies will find fulfillment in the last days.[9] Considering you are one of the experts on Iran in end-time's prophecy, I'm surprised you haven't been apprised of their important studies," George concluded.

NOVEL

While sipping upon Mimi's fresh brew and momentarily reflecting upon George's Elam comments, Razz suddenly sprayed out a mouthful of coffee. "What's that, George? Is that a satellite feed of Damascus?"

Huddling together in front of the TV, the three of them listened intently as the newscaster announced,  "We have just received confirmed reports that the city of Damascus and its surrounding metropolitan areas have been destroyed. Repeat, Damascus has been destroyed." The broadcaster went on to say, "The satellite images you are watching right now vividly illustrate the entirety of Damascus reduced to rubble!"

Jumping up, George shouted, "That's it! There you have it! The fulfillment of Isaiah 17:1 has just occurred!"

While his wife sank into a state of shock, he began pacing the parlor.

"Unbelievable!" he cried. "We knew this was coming!"

"But watching it unfold before our very eyes breaks my heart!" sobbed Mimi.

Razz, his voice quaking, groaned, "This is the point where our hearts overtake our heads. We can hypothesize till doomsday, but to realize that hundreds of thousands of people have just been incinerated..."

His words trailed off as George bent over to grip his friend's shoulder. Mimi placed a hand there, as well, and the three wept.

# Chapter 7
## Israel Attacks Iranian Nuclear Sites

"What went wrong?" Iranian president Muktada Zakiri inquired of his spiritual advisor Zamani Nikahd. "How could Israel use nuclear weapons against our closest allies? Were we not all, including the Syrians, under the divine protection of Allah, and called to hasten the return of messiah Muhammad Al-Mahdi?"

Nikahd replied, "Fear not, my vision of his return was crystal clear. Mahdi is coming! We are only to know when, not necessarily how, Muktada, and his time is near."

Unimpressed with his advisor's vague and cliché-like comment, Zakiri asked, "Then what am I to do, sit around and wait for Hezbollah, and Hamas to be destroyed alongside, before Iran attacks Israel? There is no word from Syrian president Hassan Tereiri, or his chief commanders, so I fear they all died during the blast, and lie buried deep beneath the Damascus rubble."

Nikahd looked upward, as if entering into a trance, and said with a patronizing voice, "You must be patient, Muktada; I'm awaiting another vision to direct us."

"Be patient!" shouted Zakiri, "There is no more time to be patient. Nikahd, if you have ill-advised me, I will have your head on a platter."

Cowering backward a few steps while slightly prostrating, Nikahd muttered, "Allow me to depart from here, my esteemed president, to my holy chambers to pray to Allah for our answer. I'm certain Allah will guide me in this matter."

Zakiri frowned at him and commanded, "You have twenty-four hours and not a minute more to bring me back Allah's message. And, if you fail to return with Allah's guidance I will consider you to be a false prophet and have you killed. Meanwhile, I will put our capitol and nuclear sites on high alert in preparation for an Israeli strike. I fear President Tereiri was right, and the multi-front attack against Israel was premature. Tereiri warned me that if Damascus came under nuclear attack from the Israelis, that Tehran would be targeted, as well."

## The Night of the Israeli Air-strike

It was past dusk in the Middle East, and the sun had settled in the western skies, when Israel Prime Minister Kaufman gave the green light to attack Iran's chief nuclear sites, including their main one located in Bushehr.

"We have succeeded in destroying the capitol of our nearest neighbor to the northeast, and now it's time to neutralize our foremost existential threat, the rogue state of Iran. We must send their nuclear program back to the stone age, like we did to Iraq in 1981, and Syria in 2007," Kaufman announced to IDF military chief of staff General Jacob Barak.

Barak replied, "Very well, we will put *Operation Samson's Storm* into overdrive against the Iranians. This command comes not a moment too late, prime minister, because our window of opportunity to strike Iran's nuclear sites was rapidly closing. IDF intelligence suggests the Iranians are merely weeks away from incorporating the Russian S-300 missile defense system into their IRGC arsenal. This state-of-the-art Russian missile defense system would jeopardize all future IAF stealth attack capabilities."

"Those Russian traitors," replied Kaufman in frustration. "They can never be trusted!"

General Barak cautioned, "It will be an extremely dangerous air campaign with unpredictable consequences, because our intelligence suggests Iran may already be expecting our attack. Also, we suspect that President Zakiri of Iran has already acquired, or possibly developed several nuclear weapons devices. If anything goes wrong, Israel should be prepared for a retaliatory nuclear attack within moments afterward. We must prepare all our emergency services beforehand, and you must be isolated to safety."

Kaufman replied, "My administration will take all necessary precautions to protect our citizens and ourselves from potential harm this nightfall."

Barak consoled, "The good news is that we have crippled Syria by destroying Damascus, so Iran will be worried about the similar thing happening to Tehran. This should cause them to think twice before retaliating against us."

"This night will go down in infamy as the night we ensured Israel's national survival. May the blessings of HaShem be upon you and our valiant fighters this night General Barak," Kaufman responded, with praise in his voice.

Early the following morning the presses, airwaves, and Internet social networks like Facebook, YouTube, and Twitter were streaming with unconfirmed reports that Israel had attacked Iran.

"*Israel Strikes Iranian Nuclear Sites,*" read the headline of the *US and World Daily Chronicle.* The article stated that Iran had anticipated an Israeli airstrike, but was unable to prevent it, and in the end suffered great loss at the hands of the Israelis. It appeared as though Israeli sorties struck their nuclear targets with precision, and won an incredible dogfight in the air against the Islamic Republic of Iran Air Force (IRIAF), in the process.

YouTube and television news footage showed a barrage of Iranian anti-aircraft fire streaming through the blackened skies, but not one Israeli Air Force (IAF) plane was reportedly struck down. Additionally, numerous Iranian fighter jets were caught on camera exploding in the skies. For many Americans watching on their TV sets at home, it was reminiscent of the night skies over Baghdad in 1990-1991 during *Operation Desert Storm*, but much more riveting.

Furthermore, the night canvas was splattered with unexplainable events. IAF pilots recounted stories of how a mysterious iridescent cloud cover formed around their fighter jets, providing a protective shield that hid them from view, absorbed the sound of their jets, and seemingly deflected Iranian anti-aircraft fire from harming their crafts.

"The experience was entirely surreal, like being animated in the air. If we weren't involved in a serious aerial conflict with the Iranians, we would have thought we were simply floating silently in the clouds, and suspended in time. We heard and saw the Iranian fighter Jets surround us, but before they could see us we tagged them, and took them down. It was nothing short of a miracle," remarked IAF Lieutenant Jonathan Vitow, shortly after returning back from the battle.

Moreover, some pilots stated the stealthy illumination only seemed to be visible when flying inside the clouds. They sincerely believed the cloud canopy obscured their planes from the vision of the oncoming Iranian fighter jets, which seemed to be expecting the IAF attack.

"No doubt about it; they were expecting us. The element of surprise was non-existent, we became the ambushed, but our forces survived unscathed. This can't be said of the Iranians," confirmed IAF Lieutenant General Binyamin (Benny) Lieberman, assessing the mission.

Oddly, although the night skies over Iran seemed like a Walt Disney World fireworks display on the fourth-of-July, multiplied times ten, no illuminated clouds were caught on camera. However, reports coming out of Iran declaring that their advanced radar systems were unexplainably jammed throughout the night, seemingly added credence to the IAF pilots' eyewitness accounts. Iran's nuclear facilities had been strategically struck, and the damage on the ground was being assessed, but for the time being it appeared as though Israel had dodged the Iranian nuclear bullet for a little while longer.

As news reports streamed in across the TV, George and Razz were astonished at how the IAF had escaped the tactical air-strike unscathed. Razz posed the question: "How does one record such a miraculous war effort in the military journals? Does the author write, 'While narrowing in on their nuclear targets, the IAF was ambushed by protective cloud-cover that enabled them to see, but blinded their enemy?'"

Humoring his friend, George answered, "Sounds good to me Razz. It's just another typical Israeli war story, like when Gideon destroyed the Midianites in Judges 7:16-22."

Razz concluded, "This attack against Iran is going to send Russia through the roof. Russia is heavily invested in Iran's nuclear program and is currently exporting their S-300 missile defense system to the Iranian president Zakiri. This could disrupt the flow of Iranian money desperately needed by the Russian economy. At the very least, we can expect this to cement Russian-Iranian national relations all the more tightly."

George responded, "Let me guess, you think this IAF attack against Iranian nuclear sites will cause Russia to form its Muslim coalition with Iran, Turkey, Libya, and the other in fulfillment of Ezekiel 38 and 39."

"Absolutely, it seems logical to me," answered Razz.

Contemplatively, George responded, "I disagree, and think Psalm 83 will result. But, with all that is happening in the Mideast it appears we will soon see who is correct."

## Iranians Flee from Nuclear Fallout

Later that day, news reports were coming in that nuclear fallout from the IAF air-strikes was creating a Chernobyl-type condition in west-central Iran. The Bushehr nuclear reactor was emitting high levels of radiation, necessitating a mass evacuation from the area. Affected populations were fleeing hand-in-hand with their children and any personal belongings they could carry in their cars or on their backs.

Tens of thousands were scattering in differing directions. Reportedly, some were heading up into northern Iran, and some downward toward the south. Iraq and Kuwait were opening their adjoining borders temporarily to those Iranians seeking to flee the country. A humanitarian crisis of epic proportion was developing, amidst the backdrop of all the other Mideast chaos.

George, Mimi, and Razz couldn't believe what they were witnessing.

Teary-eyed, Mimi lamented, "Things just went from bad to horrible in the Middle East."

Embracing his wife, who was visibly shaken by what she was watching, George tried to console her, "Mimi, all we can do is pray for the Iranian people. Most of those precious souls are victims of the Ayatollah's radical regime. They tried to protest their government's actions repeatedly over the past decade, but were either beaten, imprisoned, or executed by President Zakiri's henchmen. The smart Iranians will exit into the neighboring countries until the fallout settles, and the Zakiri regime topples."

Razz sympathized and said, "At least many of the protestors from the Arab Spring had the ability to assemble, but the Iranian protestors were always denied that privilege."

Composing herself slightly, Mimi suggested, "Maybe if there is any silver lining to this tragedy, it will cause many people to consider how crazy and out of control the world has become; and how important it is to trust in God."

# Chapter 8
## Arabs Unite to Fight:
## Is it Psalm 83, Ezekiel 38 or Armageddon?

The world seemed to spin off its axis that apocalyptic summer. It was as if Damascus had become the apex of the universe and its total destruction somehow shifted the earth out of planetary alignment. Oil rich Arab states turned into hardened lava flows overnight, as more OPEC nations retaliated against Israel. Saudi Arabia, Iraq, Kuwait, Bahrain, Qatar, and the United Arab Emirates, coupled with the North African OPEC nations of Libya and Algeria, all played the oil card alongside Iran, attempting to provoke international condemnation against Israel's aggression.

The League of Arab States had scarcely concluded its weeklong meeting before Syrian casualties numbered in the hundreds of thousands, and equally as many refugees from both Syria and Iran flooded the desert sands of Iraq. Syrians crossed over Iraqi borders from the northwest and Iranians from the southeast.

Without delay, Arab armies began to mobilize against Israel. All twenty-two members of the Arab League declared war against the Jews, including Egypt and Jordan, who discarded previous peace accords, and renounced Israel's right to exist. Overnight, Arab skies were filled with the smoke of burning Israeli flags and chants of "Al Mawt Li Israel!" (Death to Israel!)

So much was happening so fast, that Razz all but moved into the Thompson residence. Reflecting on their Desert Storm days, Razz and George encamped in front of the TV 24/7, monitoring war events. With their laptops on and Bibles open, they acted as if they were deployed on a fact finding mission for the US intelligence community.

It was almost comical, how they compared notes and shared night watch duty to ensure they didn't miss any breaking news. At one point, their military madness crossed the demarcation line of insanity, causing Mimi to chastise them both for arguing about whose turn it was to visit the latrine. "Boys if you don't start behaving, I'm going to turn off the TV and kick you both out of the house! I know you are trying to correlate the war events with Bible prophecy, but frankly, I'm appalled at how insensitive you have both become! Human lives are at stake around the world!"

Humbled by her comments, the two of them retreated, hangdog, to the garage gym. They admittedly had become numb from watching so much devastation. Countless disheartening pictures of charred and contaminated victims bombarded the news channels. In addition, an endless stream of Syrian and Iranian widows and orphans were filmed wandering aimlessly in the barren Mideast deserts.

Concurrently, a large exodus of Syrian Kurds began to migrate toward the north, concerning the Turkish government. The Turks were still recovering from the Kurdish refugee crisis resulting from the Syrian revolts of 2011. At that time, thousands of Kurds crossed the adjoining Turkish-Syrian borders, attempting to flee persecution from the Syrian Alawite regime.

All of these pictures and powerful events were too much for even the most calloused to process. Still, they knew the worst was yet to come, that the destruction of Damascus was only the start of much more disaster to follow.

As they reclaimed their humanity that afternoon, Razz came up with a brilliant idea. "George," he said, "we should start blogging daily about what's going on and field questions that must certainly be developing. You can handle the Psalm 83 questions and I'll tackle the Ezekiel 38 ones. All the while, we should seize this opportunity to further the gospel to the concerned."

Although they were still split as to what prophecy was finding fulfillment, undoubtedly an epic holocaust had begun. Perhaps it was too premature to know whether Psalm 83 or Ezekiel 38 would unfold in the wake of Damascus's destruction, but what mattered was getting the good news about Jesus Christ out to as many people as possible. They both agreed that time was of the essence, because, in their estimation, the rapture could occur at any moment.

They began blogging, and Razz' website hits quadrupled immediately. They began receiving a constant barrage of blogs, emails, and phone calls. It was as if the Lord opened the floodgates to the harvest field.

As they anticipated, people had lots of questions. Many were about Psalm 83 and Ezekiel 38, but mostly folks sought instructions on what to do in the midst of the Mideast peril.

Collectively, the two of them responded to hundreds of questions daily. One blogger was so impressed, he called them the *End-times tag-team extraordinaire.*

They treaded the blog-waters as long as they could, until finally, Razz called in reinforcements. He began forwarding many of the emails and phone calls to his inner circle of trusted eschatologists, who included George's favorite teacher, Jim Linton. These were peers with whom Razz had volleyed emails back and forth through the years. Whenever Razz discovered a new prophetic insight, he sought their professional opinions before going public.

Razz and George needed their support now, more than ever. They were receiving hits and inquiries from scores of believers and unbelievers who had Google-searched fodder phrases like "the rapture," "apocalyptic Middle East," "Magog invasion," "Psalm 83," and "Damascus destroyed," which, in turn, led many to Razz' site, email, and cell phone.

This increased activity reminded Razz of his trip to ground zero, in the immediate aftermath of September 11, 2001. Those terrorist attacks had spawned a harvest field of hungry souls seeking answers to what had occurred on that infamous day. At that impressionable time, he fielded questions like, "Is it Armageddon?" and "Does the Bible have anything to say about terrorism?"

Like then, the bloggers and callers were asking apocalyptic questions in the aftermath of Damascus's destruction and Iran's radiation fallout crisis.

"No it's not Armageddon; it could be Ezekiel 38," Razz echoed to numerous callers. Similarly, George was directing callers to Psalm 83.

However, more importantly, they and their colleagues seized the opportunity to present the gospel to hundreds, if not thousands, during the latest round of the Middle East conflict.

# Chapter 9
## Psalm 83:
## The Final Arab–Israeli War

As the war progressed, it became apparent to both George and Razz that Mideast developments resembled the prophetic descriptions detailed in Psalm 83, rather than Ezekiel 38 and 39. Hezbollah to the north, Egyptians and Saudis to the south, Hamas to the southwest, Palestinians and Jordanians to the east, and even Iraqi forces, had assembled alongside the seriously beleaguered Syrian troops, to surround the Israelis.

As specified in the Psalm, the time had arrived wherein the Arabs stood united against Israel. The "Mother of all Mideast Wars" was inevitable. Although the United Nations Assembly was furious with Israel for reducing Damascus to rubble, their hands were tied, and they were becoming increasingly pre-occupied with the burgeoning Iranian refugee crisis. All previous land for peace proposals calling for the Palestinians and Israelis to live securely side by side were discarded. Diplomacy had failed, staining the legacies of several US presidents and leaving all-out war as the only option.

It was bottom-line time; Damascus was destroyed, the Iranian nuclear threat was minimized, and now the Arabs and Jews were going to have to "duke-it-out" on their own terms in the Holy Land. The international forum had proven to be a fruitless dead-end street. Moreover, the weaponry of the imminent clash was certain to make all previous Arab-Israeli wars seem like minor skirmishes.

This time, only one kingdom would be left standing when the final bell rang. George and Razz confidently concluded that according to the Lord's promises to Abraham, Isaac, and Jacob, inscribed inside the Bible, that Israel would be the victor.

The Arab confederacy invoked their god Allah with a mandate to destroy Israel. They boldly announced, almost word-for-word, what had been prophesied in Hebrew 3,000 years before: "Halak Kachad Goy Shem Yisrael Zakar Lo Od" (Come let us *(Arabs)* wipe them *(Jews)* out as a nation that the name of Israel be remembered no more.) The "seer"[10] Asaph saw this world-changing event coming,[11] and warned that the Arabs would confederate to destroy Israel, in order to possess the Promised Land.[12]

Watching satellite shots of the massive mobilization of multinational Arab armies near Israel's borders, George asserted, "They never wanted peace with the Jews; they wanted peace without the Jews!"

"You are absolutely correct! They weren't seeking a two-state solution; they had a one-state solution in mind all along," Razz responded. "They wanted one more Arab state called Palestine."

"Those poor Arab souls," said George.

"What do you mean?" asked Razz.

"The Arabs are about to go toe-to-toe with the 'exceedingly great army' of Ezekiel 37:10, that has already demonstrated its regional superiority against Damascus and Iran," George answered.

Nodding in concession, Razz said, "I know I'm supposed to be an end-times expert, George, but I've been so preoccupied with Ezekiel 38, I apologize for not giving Psalm 83 more attention. I'm familiar with the *whos, whats, whens, wheres,* and *whys* of Psalm 83, but please describe for me *how* you believe this war will play out."

Striving not to gloat over his scholarship, George humbly replied, "Unlike the Ezekiel 38 invasion, wherein the Lord personally destroys the invaders, the Israeli Defense Forces are instrumental in defeating the Arab confederacy of Psalm 83. Several Old Testament passages in Ezekiel 25 and 35, Obadiah, Jeremiah 49, Zechariah 12, Zephaniah 2, and Isaiah 11 describe an empowered IDF destroying Israel's surrounding Arab enemies. It seems the Lord raises up this mighty army primarily for this purpose, since it plays no vital role in either the Ezekiel invasion or during the events of Armageddon that follow both," George expounded.

"Good point," acknowledged Razz. "Have you discovered any Scriptural clues as to the length of the Psalm 83 battle?"

"Not really; but, we both know Israel doesn't have the luxury of waging a war of attrition. They have to act expeditiously and decisively to counteract formidable Arab arsenals. The recent destruction of Damascus is a good example," reminded George.

General George was continuing to pour out his prophetic insights when Mimi cleared her throat loudly, her notorious way of signaling, "It's a wrap; pack it up; that will be enough for today." She had been twiddling her thumbs, while listening to their laborious conversation. In her you're-boring-me-to-death voice, with which George and Razz were very familiar, she beckoned, "Would you officers mind adjourning to another area of the compound, so I can have some time alone?"

"Mimi, aren't you interested in all this?" George objected.

Sarcastically, she answered, "Dear, for the past fifteen minutes I have been listening to you both flap your gums and entertain your egos. Whenever you get on a roll, talking about this stuff, I know it could be hours before you come up for air."

"We're not entertaining our egos," George rebuffed. "These are important facts!"

Giving him the if-looks-could-kill stare, she replied, "Yes, I'm sure they're important facts to retired Generals and prophecy buffs, but they're boring me to death! In fact, I fully intend to boot you boys out of the room and turn the channel to Home and Garden Television Network (HGTV), if we don't resume some normalcy in this house for the afternoon!"

Before the Mideast war broke out, Mimi would watch HGTV most every night after dinner, to unwind from her day. Her comments to switch the channel to her favorite TV network made it obvious to both George and Razz that Mimi was on information and emotion overload. Suffering from a loss of hope that life would ever be the same again, she wasn't quite ready for the world to fall apart, or for Jesus to whisk her away into the rapture clouds just yet.

She desired to see her grandkids go to college and get married. She wanted to travel and enjoy retirement with her husband. Earthquakes and holy wars were intruding on life, liberty, and the pursuit of her happiness!

Fortunately, after forty-four years of marriage, George knew when it was time to back down and afford Mimi her space. She had been a trooper up 'til now, allowing Razz and he the run of the house. But he clearly recognized she was about to have a meltdown.

"Can I get you anything, or do anything for you, dear?" George gently asked.

Mimi blinked back tears. "When was the last time you got on the phone with your son, or called your sister, or did anything besides go round and round with Razz about Middle East Bible prophecies?" she whimpered.

Realizing rhetorical questions like this weren't intended to be answered, George made eye contact with Razz and gestured for a smooth, but swift departure. "What say we adjourn upstairs for awhile, ol' buddy," he suggested, and delicately handed Mimi the remote control.

The two of them decided to empathize with Mimi's frustration for the remainder of the day. They watched some baseball and shot some pool in the bonus room. Instead of fielding prophecy questions, they called some friends and family to bid them well.

Razz even headed home relatively early, to give George and Mimi space to regroup as a couple.

At least for that night, they both took a leave of duty.

# Chapter 10
## The Russian – Iranian Nuclear Connection

Stuffing the classified dossier hastily into his brown leather attaché case, Mikhail Trutnev whisked suspiciously toward the back exit door of his office, startling his secretary. The silver-haired receptionist that seldom donned a smile, Alena Popov, had set nearly every one of his appointments over the past ten years, and was unprepared for his dubious departure.

"Wait a minute. You have a full schedule of appointments today! Where are you going, and when will you return?" She bellowed.

"Clear my calendar for the rest of the day, I have something pressing to go over with Prime Minister Primakov, and don't know when I'll be returning," he called over his shoulder.

Trutnev was the Russian prime minister's closest confidant. Sergei Primakov relied exclusively on him for all of his intelligence on internal and nuclear affairs. Mikhail became a highly decorated General for his leadership roles in the Soviet-Afghan War, waged between 1979-1989, first and second wars with Chechnya, between 1994-1996 and 1999-2000 respectively, and successes in the Russian invasion of the Democratic Republic of Georgia in August, 2008.

Mikhail maintained extremely close ties to several veteran agents in Spetsnaz GRU (the Special Forces of the Foreign Military Intelligence Directorate), which is staffed by the most experienced and elite of Russia's special operators since its creation in 1949, at the onset of the Cold War against the West. The prime minister depended to a fault upon Mikhail and was about to be confronted nervously by him at his desk.

Prime Minister Primakov instructed his personal secretary to let General Trutnev into his office. Closing the door securely behind his visitor, Prime

Minister Primakov calmly said, "Good Morning, General. Have some hot tea; it's my favorite blended brew, just given to me by Chinese Ambassador Li Chin."

Fixated on the pressing matter at hand, Trutnev ignored the invitation and hustled the critical documents out of his briefcase and placed them on Primakov's desk, almost tearing them in his haste.

Puzzled, Sergei gestured to a chair in front of his desk, "Mikhail, what is this about?" Then, looking about the room suspiciously, Primakov jested, "Have you come to warn me of an assassination plot?"

Trutnev swallowed nervously, "I wouldn't say that, at least, not yet," he replied.

Taken aback, Primakov gazed piercingly into his confidant's eyes, and proceeded to pour Mikhail some tea into a rare porcelain cup from the Romanov era.

"Tell me then," Sergei said, "what is so urgent?"

"Sir, you must be briefed immediately about distressing information I recently received. This information is extremely troubling in light of Iran's current nuclear radiation crisis. I have been delivered highly classified information about the missing tactical nuclear devices that I reported to you several months ago."

Prime Minister Primakov's heart sank. Speaking with a hint of annoyance in his voice, he replied, "That report was incomplete and not verifiable, if I remember correctly, Mikhail."

"The investigation was as complete as possible at the time Mr. Prime Minister," Mikhail replied.

"Are you insinuating that I let the matter fall through the cracks?" Primakov challenged.

Taken aback, Mikhail clarified, "No, no, no, Mr. Prime Minister! I just wanted to brief you about the sealed report my secretary delivered to me when I entered my office this morning. Normally, she greets me with my hot coffee when I arrive, but instead she handed me this distressing report. It reveals that several tactical nuclear devices are unaccounted for, at three of our more loosely monitored military installations. I know we lacked information on that, since my last report, and given the dangerous implications of these details, I feel your attention to this matter is of utmost importance."

Realizing he had procured Primakov's undivided attention, Mikhail scooted the report toward the prime minister, who was now seated across from him at his oversized, rectangular oak desk. Shifting to the edge of his high-back leather chair, Primakov promptly picked up the report and began reading silently.

Mikhail stirred restlessly across from him, twiddling his fingers and glancing nervously about the room. The prime minister's eyebrows rose higher with each page. His countenance had changed dramatically since he had poured Mikhail's tea.

Mikhail was increasingly fidgety, and standing, began pacing about the office. The prime minister, deeply engrossed in the documents, failed to notice Mikhail's mounting anxiety.

The communiqué clearly spelled out that several "suitcase" nuclear devices had entered Iranian Revolutionary Guard Corps hands. The report also outlined IRGC plans to use these devices for "strategic" purposes if Israel or the West struck Iranian nuclear facilities, or other specific targets.

As the prime minister completed the report, he looked up sternly into Mikhail's eyes, stopping him in his tracks. "Has President Ziroski been briefed on this?" Primakov snapped. Moving within whisper distance of the prime minister, Mikhail reluctantly answered, "Perhaps, I'm uncertain."

"What do you mean, 'uncertain'?" The prime minister said with a grimace.

Mikhail muttered, "My secretary said the envelope showed up mysteriously on her desk this morning, with no memo or trace of origin. She said she had spotted an aide to President Ziroski in the hallway moments before she stepped out of her office to visit the lounge."

"Hmm," the prime minister grunted. "Please continue."

Mikhail proceeded on. "When she returned, the sealed dossier was sitting in plain view, in the center of her desk. She said that whoever left the folder purposely brushed aside several other papers to make room for it. Her guess was that the confidant strategically positioned the document on her desk, expecting it would be passed to me expeditiously."

Ignoring Mikhail's obvious attempt to speak softly, Primakov blurted out, "This means that the president knows everything!"

The prime minister's harsh tone caused the General to step backward. Visibly shaken, Trutnev, asked meagerly, "What are we to do?"

Primakov let out a deep sigh as he leaned back into his overstuffed chair and reached inside the lapel of his suit coat to extract his handkerchief. Blotting beads of sweat from his brow, he sat eerily still for a few minutes.

Looking for some sort of cue from his superior, Mikhail stood speechless.

NOVEL

Having gathered his thoughts, Primakov at last stood up from behind his desk. Smoothing his suit, and firming up the knot of his tie, he calmly gazed at his closest comrade. By now, Mikhail resembled a deer frozen in the headlights of an oncoming car. Both, he and his untouched cup of tea, had grown cold inside.

With as much professionalism as he could muster, Primakov said, "Mikhail, I thank you for bringing this report to my attention.  Apparently President Ziroski is sending me a message.  I will have to meet with him personally to let him know that his message was received.  I will let you know if you can be of any further help in this matter." The prime minister gestured toward the door and Mikhail gladly seized the opportunity to exit the office.

Once Mikhail had departed, Primakov calmly reached for his desk phone and pushed the intercom button.

"Yes, Mr. Prime Minister," his secretary answered.

"Please set up an appointment for me to meet with the president, as soon as possible, he ordered."

"Of course, Mr. Prime Minister, what shall I say it's regarding?" she asked.

Ignoring her question, the prime minister slouched back down to his chair and braced for the wrath he expected to soon receive, from Russia's cruelest Czar.

## President Mad Vlad

Meanwhile, Russia's president was meeting with his UN Ambassador, Anatoly Tarazov, addressing other important classified matters inside of his expansive office.

"Is it true Anatoly, that the cabinet members of the politburo have begun sinisterly calling me the Mad Vlad behind closed doors?" The ruthless Russian inquired.

Accustomed to closely guarding his responses, Tarasov nervously replied, "Such rumors are circulating Mr. President."

Stepping beside his life-size picture of Joseph Stalin, Ziroski asked, "And you, dear comrade, have you ever made such remarks?"

"No," Tarasov insisted, "Absolutely not; perish the thought!"

Ziroski jeered, "Your response pierces me comrade! I am surrounded by spineless fools who feel threatened by me, and I find few to trust anymore. Mother Russia requires the strictest allegiance from her servants in these turbulent times. In the past you have caused me to question your loyalty; am I to believe things have changed with you now?"

Buckling under scrutiny, the Ambassador whined, "All that you have ever asked of me, I have performed, since that unfortunate episode. I will never let you down again."

Ambassador Tarasov referred to the time he had fumbled a few critical words during an important speech regarding Russia's intentions for Iran's nuclear development program. Russian fuel rods that had been recently loaded into Iran's primary nuclear facility had become a hot button of controversy in the halls of the General Assembly.

Anatoly Tarasov was under strict orders to diffuse the debate. Ziroski had scripted the exact wording to be spoken, and was beyond furious when Anatoly Tarasov deviated from the teleprompter speech. Mad Vlad had said Anatoly's disobedience bordered on treason.

Mad Vlad spoke directly to his point, "The United States continues to antagonize the Iranian President Muktada Zakiri, even after Israel has violated Iranian airspace and caused the Bushehr nuclear reactor crisis. We must persuade them to lift their ongoing sanctions upon Iran swiftly. Zakiri is becoming increasingly desperate and out of control!"

Anatoly agreed, "Anything, Mr. President; what would you have me do?"

Ziroski replied, "China is prepared to criticize America and several European nations severely for still harboring what they are now calling "inhumane sanctions" against Iran. These countries are still suspecting Iran has nuclear devices undetected somewhere that Israel didn't destroy, and as such refuse to lift the sanctions. I have inside information that their assessments are accurate, and Iran does possess nuclear devices."

Anatoly gasped and echoed his earlier comment, "Perish the thought!"

Ziroski then instructed his chief diplomat, "You must lock arms with Chinese Ambassador Chin, and lobby in the assembly against America's charge to maintain and strengthen sanctions. These sanctions are crippling Iran and will provoke Zakiri to lash out!"

Tarasov consented, "I am very close with Ambassador Chin, and we know how to turn the political tables on the American delegation. We have made it extremely difficult through the UN in the past, for America to get broad support for deeper sanctions against the Iranians, and with Iran's radiation fallout crisis, we can humiliate America for certain."

"Ratchet up the pressure to a point of embarrassment," Vlad commanded. "I want the United States isolated in their campaign against Iran. Get the

European nations to distance themselves from America on this matter, or else I guarantee Zakiri will take matters into his own apocalyptic hands. He informed me yesterday that his crazy Imam Zamani Nikahd has received another ridiculous vision that their Mahdi won't come unless the Great Satan America is attacked!"

Confused, Tarasov replied, "I thought you, too, were fed up with the Americans?"

"I am," Ziroski answered, "but, I want Iran to focus its aggression toward Israel, rather than attempt to terrorize the United States. Attacking America will awaken a sleeping giant and complicate world matters. The Jewish State is threatening our energy plans for the region. Jewish exploits need to be stopped, before they discover oil, in addition to all their recent natural gas discoveries."

Just then the president's intercom sounded and his secretary announced that the prime minister had arrived for their meeting.

Brushing the Ambassador out the door, as if he were an annoying fly, Mad Vlad barked, "Off with you now, and go take care of our business in the General Assembly."

## Mad Vlad's Sinister Plan

President Ziroski had received and reviewed the classified report well in advance of forwarding it strategically to Prime Minister Primakov. Suspecting the missing nukes would soon be utilized against Israel or the West, he needed a high level scapegoat. Hence, the prime minister had become the fall guy for Mad Vlad's diabolical plan.[13]

Primakov entered the room punctually at 3:00 p.m. As Ziroski's secretary closed the door behind him, Primakov pulled the classified dossier from his satchel and commented, "I thank you Mr. President, for agreeing to meet with me, I have a very pressing matter to discuss with you."

Playing possum, Ziroski questioned, "What pressing matter, Comrade; I'm very busy today?"

Primakov pulled a nearby chair close to Mad Vlad's desk, proceeded to sit down, and held out the document asking, "Sir, are you familiar with this document regarding our missing "baby nukes"?

"What missing nukes?" Ziroski growled, glaring intensely at Primakov.

Primakov placed the report squarely in the center of Ziroski's desk and stammered, "Mr. President, forgive me if I'm mistaken, but I assumed that you had seen this."

Ziroski stood up and leaned over his desk, fists planted on either side of his desk pad and declared, "You assumed right! Do you, for one moment, think that I am not aware of everything that is going on in my administration, long before you read your damaging reports?"

Primakov squirmed, realizing his problems were mushrooming.

Ziroski angrily continued, "You previously assured me that there would be no further fallout from that matter, that you and comrade Trutnev's department had matters well in hand. And now, as Iran undergoes a radiation crisis, I find out this troubling information. If Iran uses our nukes against Israel or American targets, there will be severe consequences!"

Slamming down his fist on the dossier, Mad Vlad thundered, "What can you add to this report?"

Primakov sputtered, "Mr. President, my staff is investigating the accuracy of these findings, as we speak."

Leaning across his desk, as if to bite Primakov's head off, Ziroski bellowed, "What kind of a fool do you take me for? I know for a fact that you just found this information and have had no time to investigate it further. You knew nothing of this major problem until I had my confidant deliver the dossier to your office. I knew about it long before you even got wind of it. I've already conducted my own internal investigation and confirmed these details to be true."

Tongue-tied, the prime minister timidly muttered, "Mr. President, I only meant..."

"You only meant what?" Ziroski interrupted. "You told me Trutnev had matters under control and that this issue was put to rest. Now we learn that some of our "baby nukes" are in rogue Iranian hands! You fool! Zakiri informed me this morning that Israel did not destroy these nuclear devices, and I fear he intends to use them against the United States."

"I will offer Zakiri double their value to repurchase them back," suggested Primakov

But, Ziroski countered, "I have already made Zakiri a more than generous offer, and he is not interested. He said the IRGC paid top dollar for these nuclear devices and refused to divulge how and when they were procured."

Primakov tried one more time to placate his superior, "Certainly, the IRGC can be pleaded with. Let Trutnev and me attempt to reason with their commanders."

"No way!" Ziroski shouted. "Zakiri is extremely upset as a result of your failure to deliver the S-300 missile defense system to the IRGC on schedule.

NOVEL

He feels that Iran could have averted the recent Israeli air-strike, if the system had been operational. He has become like a ticking time-bomb since Israel attacked his nuclear program and any interference from you or Trutnev will certainly set him off."

Primakov moved to stand up, stating apologetically, "Mr. President, according to Trutnev, these suitcase nuclear weapons were all accounted for."

"Your lies never cease," Ziroski retorted. "You and Trutnev are setting up Mother Russia for a hard fall. But, as always, I'm way ahead of you Sergei. You will be the one who takes the fall if Iran utilizes these nuclear weapons. As prime minister, you will shoulder sole responsibility for the disappearance of these nukes."

Becoming increasingly unnerved, Primakov replied, "Zakiri would be a fool to launch these weapons against Israel or America. It would be a death wish."

"Let me assure you," Ziroski avowed, "Iman Nikahd has convinced Zakiri that he has been called by Allah to this end. When Zakiri uses these weapons, and I expect he will, the two of you, along with Mikhail Trutnev, and Zamani Nikahd will all be tried and hung by the International Court! Then the Ayatollah and I can rebuild Iran's nuclear program and seize control over all the vast resources of the Fertile Crescent."

# Chapter 11
## Terrorists Attack America Again!

Following Mimi's momentary meltdown earlier that week, George thought it would be therapeutic to host a weekend barbeque with some friends and family. So, that following Saturday, he invited Lisa, Jami, Tyler, Razz and a few close friends over for his specialty: seared rib-eye steaks, marinated in a richly seasoned soy-Italian sauce.

Unfortunately, his son Thomas was still out of state working on a commercial construction project and couldn't attend. In light of volatile world events, his prolonged absence from home was causing Lisa many restless nights. Her sleeplessness was beginning to show in her tired eyes and the dulling of her usually vibrant complexion.

Knowing how conscientious Lisa was about her beauty and parenting skills, Mimi commented, "You're holding up quite well in light of playing the role of two parents lately. George and I couldn't be more pleased with you as a daughter-in-law."

Setting down her kitchen utensil and turning toward Mimi, Lisa affectionately replied, "Well, that's very nice of you to say, Mimi. I haven't been sleeping well, while Thomas has been away. Normally, I do okay in his absence, but I'm worried about him, the kids, my job, and my family in Israel. It's almost impossible to get any beauty rest anymore."

"Well, beauty isn't everything, and besides, God made you absolutely adorable," replied Mimi.

Lisa shrugged. "You're being kind," she said, "but I don't feel very adorable these days. My eyes are puffy, my neck aches, and I plucked out my first gray hair this morning!"

"Mimi resembled that remark," George heckled, intruding into their conversation.

"Yeah, about thirty years ago. Thank goodness for make-up and hair-color," Mimi jested.

"Poppy, how long 'til we eat?" asked Tyler, entering the kitchen.

Grandpa knew that Tyler's question was code for, "Can I steal a bite before dinner?" George had spoiled his grandson with taste-testing throughout his childhood. As a result, Tyler had developed an incurable habit of loitering around the grill, expecting his grandpa to sneak him tasty morsels before dinner was served.

Winking, George slyly replied, "Why don't you come out and help me turn the steaks in about ten minutes."

"You got it, Gramps," Tyler laughed, running back to the patio.

While the Thompsons attempted to resume normalcy on the home front, the developing Middle East humanitarian crisis had the international community reeling in shock. The UN pleaded for, and achieved, a brief ceasefire so relief workers could tend to the hordes of dead and wounded in the Middle East. This allowed for a momentary calm before the pending storm of Holy War in the Promised Land.

Unfortunately, this was not the case throughout Muslim communities in Europe and elsewhere around the world. Muslim protestors crowded numerous city streets from Paris to London to Jakarta to Khartoum. Molotov cocktails, tear gas, rubber bullets, and "Death to Israel" signs made much of Europe look like the streets of downtown Cairo, in the days leading up to the resignation of Egyptian president Hosni Mubarak. Worldwide Muslim protests were beginning to make the Arab Mideast protests and revolts of 2011 pale in comparison.

Between the destruction of Damascus, the Iranian radiation crisis, and worldwide Muslim protests, there weren't enough newscasters or news cameras to cover all the breaking news. The major news channels had to pick and choose from a plethora of newsworthy events, the ones they felt deserved special coverage.

The picnic tables were set up, the potatoes were baking, and the barbeque was fired up, when suddenly Razz stormed into the backyard. "Come, quick! America has just been terrorized!" The chatty gathering was stunned to silence. "Yankee stadium is ablaze!" gasped Razz. In an instant, the patio cleared as the party moved into the parlor to catch the breaking news.

It looked like September 11, 2001, all over again: panic-filled streets, blaring sirens, and smoke in the air. "A powerful bomb has just exploded during the middle of the Yankee versus Red Sox game!" one newscaster announced. "Details are sketchy, but traces of radioactive fallout have been detected. As you can see on the screen, HAZMAT teams are already mobilizing on the scene, suited up in full protective gear, as first responders quarantine the area."

News footage of the blast was shocking and evidenced that the explosive was no amateur device. Immediate indicators pointed to the possibility that a tactical nuclear weapon had been detonated. Aerial images of Yankee Stadium made it look like the recent destruction of Damascus had spilled over into New York. Intensifying matters, a decent sized crowd was in attendance to watch both teams battle for first place. Fans that would otherwise refrain from attending, for fear of terrorism, made an exception for this particular game. Initial news assessments all confirmed that the prospects for survivors appeared very grim.

As George feverishly flipped through the news channels, reports streamed in that hundreds of wildfires were blazing throughout various parts of the country. These fires reeked of arson, causing commentators to deduce that a multi-pronged terror attack had been launched against America.

Observing the shock in his guest's faces, George assumed the role of General. He encouraged everyone to remain calm and stay for dinner. "Razz will keep an eye on developing events for us," he volunteered. "Besides, we can't let the terrorists win by ruining a perfectly good barbeque!" Although eating was far from their thinking, they wanly smiled, and agreed to support one another by sharing the meal together, while watching the events unfold.

Unfortunately, the remaining events that unfolded that Saturday evening made the terror of September 11, 2001, pale in comparison. They could only pick at their meals, because the catastrophic events of the day stole their appetites.

Thousands lay dead in and around Yankee Stadium. Meanwhile, first responders throughout the country were mobilizing to put out scores of wildfires. As these developments continued to unfold, more devastating blasts occurred at Wrigley Field in Chicago, and, simultaneously, at Chavez Ravine Stadium in Los Angeles. Although far fewer fans filled these arenas than at Yankee Stadium, those in attendance were all feared dead.

While the country was grappling with the scope of developing events, reports came in that a similar blast had apparently been averted at Tiger

Stadium in Detroit. Stadium security officials had been investigating suspicious activity in the docking area, accosted a delivery vehicle, and ended up shooting and killing its driver as he attempted to flee. A detonation device was located inside the vehicle and carefully disarmed. While the stadium was being evacuated, the bomb squad was cautiously searching for the whereabouts of the bomb.

Additionally, several Jewish synagogues across the country were blown up, as suicide bombers, shouting "Allahu Akbar" rushed in during Saturday Shabbat services. Hundreds of Jewish worshippers across America were believed killed or injured.

Viewing these reports, Lisa shuddered. "That could happen in *our* neighborhood," she gasped. "That could be Tyler in one of those buildings!"

George hugged her tightly and said, "Tyler's alright; he's safe right here. We will never let anything bad happen to him." Within their embrace, the centuries old Jewish-Christian divide was temporarily bridged. In that instant, a Jew and a Christian had found common ground by facing the shared enemy of Islamic fundamentalism.

Now both Israel and America were under siege; but in America's case, the specific enemy was difficult to identify.

Initial reports implicated Al-Qaeda. WikiLeaks documents had reported the Pentagon believed that Al-Qaeda possessed one or more nuclear devices. However, intelligence findings were being confounded by the fact Karim Nazari, Al-Qaeda's new leader, had recently relocated from the caves of Afghanistan to protective obscurity inside Iran. His unconfirmed whereabouts complicated matters, causing the Pentagon concern that a concerted terror campaign involving Al-Qaeda and the rogue state of Iran was unfolding.

Was Iran making good on Zakiri's promises to create an apocalyptic condition inside Israel and America, to hasten the coming of the Twelfth Imam? And, was Al-Qaeda running interference for Iran, by igniting widespread wildfires and blowing up Jewish synagogues nationwide?

The Twelfth Imam, also referred to as the Mahdi, is the Shiite Islamic messiah. In recent months Iranian Shiite Mullahs had boasted that combined attacks on Israel, the "Little Satan," and America, the "Great Satan," would invoke the Mahdi's end-time return. Iranian president Zakiri was echoing similar apocalyptic sentiment through Al-Jazeera television and the Tehran Times newspaper.

Additional concerns were directed toward Hezbollah, headquartered in Lebanon. It was common knowledge that cell groups from this Iranian-backed military organization had entered America by crossing the border of Mexico. Several known members of the terror group, which had recently been detained in Texas, admitted this. Furthermore, they informed authorities that Hezbollah had maintained an operative presence in the countries of Mexico and Venezuela for years.

Despite all the above, no smoking guns were jumping out at investigators and due to Mideast volatility, America had to proceed with the discovery process cautiously. What was certain was that the responsible party would receive the harshest of punishment. Meanwhile, Americans were told to go on lockdown and watch their TVs for further developments and instructions.

From the moment the stateside terror began, Lisa had been attempting to contact Thomas on his cell phone. Nationwide connectivity was hindered, due to the enormous call volume. Finally, after dozens of attempts, she got through to him and was relieved to hear he was in his car, headed home.

"Hallelujah!" she shouted. "Thomas will be here tomorrow night. They postponed construction temporarily so he and his crewmembers could head home."

Mimi asked anxiously, "How is he, and what did he say?"

"He's in shock" Lisa responded. "The minute they heard about Yankee Stadium, they shut down the construction, and he grabbed his crew and headed home. He was thankful to hear from me because none of them have been able to get through to their loved ones by phone. He wants me to get home and contact all the workers' family members, right now."

"I will follow you home," George offered. "We should take the service streets as a precaution."

"I'm riding with Poppy," Tyler cried.

"Lisa, I think you should grab the address book with worker's phone numbers and an overnight bag for you and the kids. Stay at our house until Thomas gets home," Mimi urged. "We can call everyone from here."

"Thanks, Mimi, but I'll feel more comfortable at home," Lisa replied. "We'll be fine. Hopefully, the worst is about over."

Realizing Lisa was firm in her decision, George asserted, "Let's get you all home, then."

Exchanging farewell embraces with Mimi, Lisa and Jami jumped into the BMW and headed out; George and Tyler shadowed them in the pick-up. Observing his grandfather place a shotgun in the backseat of the truck before departing, Tyler asked, "What is going to happen to America? Are we going to be okay?"

George blinked back some tears and gave a reply he only half believed: "I'm sure Americans will rally together quickly, like we did after September 11th. In no time the country will get back to normal. Until then, everyone will have to make adjustments, like your dad leaving his job and us following the girls home tonight. America is a strong country and we will get even with the terrorists. Afterward, our streets will be safe and you will be hanging out at Frostee Freeze, again."

# Chapter 12
## The Arabs Surrender

By the time Thomas and his crew arrived home, American terrorism experts were alternately pointing fingers of blame at Iran, Al-Qaeda, and Hezbollah. Although none of them had claimed responsibility; all were prime suspects. And even though the enemy remained unidentified, the Joint Chiefs of Staff advised US Secretary of Defense Donald Yates and newly elected President John Bachlin to prepare for a multi-front Mideast war.

Pre-scheduled plans for full troop pullout in Afghanistan were promptly postponed, as that war torn country is strategically located on Iran's eastern border. Ground, air, and naval forces were put on ready alert, and massive amounts of heavy military equipment was being readied for rapid redeployment. Although US President John Bachlin had campaigned against further US military involvement in the Middle East things had changed drastically.

Meanwhile, the Middle East predicament was heating up again. Like a kettle boiling over on the stove, the newly formed Islamic Unified Arab Forces (IUAF) were preparing to face off with the IDF. Some US military analysts suggested the terrorist attacks in America were staged as a diversionary tactic, enabling the IUAF to garner more time to assemble and strategize. These pundits believed the Arabs relied on the terrorists to eliminate America from the Mideast equation, by terrorizing the country from within.

Others disagreed, claiming the concerted terror campaign had to have been months in the making. No matter which side was right, it looked like David and Goliath had been resurrected for a final battle in the Middle East.

Finally, after several failed attempts to reach his father over the crowded land telephone lines, Thomas got through on his cell phone. "Dad, I missed you and mom immensely. How are you both doing?"

Attempting to console his only son, George replied, "Under the circumstances we are doing fine son. We are so relieved that you got back home safely to be with Lisa and the kids."

In a seemingly helpless tone, Thomas said, "I just hate having to leave Lisa and the kids alone, but I have no choice, it's so hard to find good work anymore.

Observing his son felt a sense of guilt about the matter, George praised his son for doing what it takes to be a good family provider. "Son we are so proud of you and know that you have to do what it takes to survive these tough times. And you know your mother and I will always be here for all of you."

Unable to contain his emotions, Thomas said tearfully "What in the world is going on? I am so very concerned for everyone's safety. Do you think things are going to get worse?"

"That's no easy question son?" replied George. "The world's falling apart at home and abroad."

"Is this it? Do you and uncle Razz believe the Bible predicted America would come under siege?" Thomas inquired.

"I don't know about that, but we do believe Middle East events are driving all the chaos, and are about to accelerate into the biblical wars of Psalm 83 followed by Ezekiel 38," George answered.

Composing himself somewhat, Thomas confided, "I'm glad you taught me the fundamentals of survival as a child. I have my gold, guns, and goods in place."

"That's all important under the circumstances, but what's most critical is your faith in God," reminded George.

"I agree," confirmed Thomas. "I'm back on board with the Lord, and when war broke out in the Middle East, I started following uncle Razz' daily blog."

Unfortunately, the call was abruptly disconnected because of over-crowded phone lines, but George was delighted to hear his son was trusting God again. He attempted to reconnect over the phone with Thomas throughout the day, even utilizing his landline as an alternative to his mobile phone. But, the heavily trafficked lines rendered a perpetual busy signal, prohibiting further contact.

That day, the sound of Mideast war drums were quickly drowned out by the sound of Scud missile blasts and advanced rocket explosions. Unfortunately for the Arabs, the advanced rockets were primarily launched from Israel's side. Before America could render a final verdict on whether or not to get involved, the Arab–Israeli war had kicked into highest gear.

The Arabs were taking a shellacking.

Over the next two weeks, as America tarried over what terrorists to fight, her citizens gradually went back to work, and Razz, George, and Mimi watched the capitals of the Psalm 83 nations surrender to Israel one-by-one. Before the radioactive dust from Damascus and Bushehr settled, the kings, princes, prime ministers, and presidents of Amman, Beirut, Cairo, Gaza City, Riyadh, and Ramallah were waving white flags and bowing in defeat toward Jerusalem.

It was obvious the IDF had previously formulated a fool-proof, prison-rules plan for dealing with this multi-front Arab attack. It was as if someone had tipped off the Israeli Defense Minister to Psalm 83 ahead of time.

With extreme precision, Israel's army attacked the jugular vein of the Arab States. Airstrips, munitions sites, military headquarters, capital cities, and more, were hit with sortie upon sortie, loaded with tactical weapons. The Mediterranean Sea could not be quieted, as nuclear-tipped warheads were launched from Israel's Dolphin class submarines upon strategic targets in Egypt, Saudi Arabia, and portions of Northeast Syria near the borders of Iraq. Not even the holy cities and shrines of Islam were off IDF limits.

The Al Aqsa Mosque and the Dome of the Rock in Old Jerusalem had been captured by IDF ground troops. Air strikes had severely damaged Islam's two holiest sites, at Mecca and Medina. Muslims were temporarily stranded without a place to pilgrimage.

But probably most shocking was the way Arab "friendly fire" slaughtered many within IUAF ranks. It was as if a drunken stupor had overtaken their armies, like when Gideon fought against the Midianites, recorded in the biblical book of Judges. Many military analysts believed Israel utilized advanced strategic EMP technologies against IUAF centers of command and military installations, causing Arab attacks to backfire.

In the aftermath, some Middle East Muslims began questioning Allah's "Akbar" (greatness), while others continued to rally worldwide against the Jewish State with intensified violent protests. Before the "fat lady" could sing her closing chorus, Israel was taking prisoners of war and hoisting Israeli flags over many Arab capitals.

Among them was Egypt, Israel's ancient nemesis. Home to about 80 million Egyptians, their homeland was turned into desolation as a result of Israel's retribution. Egypt's cruel leader from the Muslim Brotherhood,

NOVEL

Muhammad Al-Barwahi, who had seized military power during the vacuum created by the Egyptian protests, had played the lead role in forming the IUAF. He had armed Hamas to the hilt, and then pointed all of Egypt's firepower at Israel, forcing the Jews to almost wipe Egypt off of the map.

Hundreds of thousands of Egyptians were either dead, injured, or in need of quick deportation. Egypt's desolation made portions west of the Nile almost uninhabitable, due to radiation fallout. Nuclear experts feared it could be forty years before some of the remote parts of Egypt could be repopulated. Miraculously, shifting wind patterns kept the fallout from approaching Israel, enabling the IDF to advance its front lines into areas east of the Nile.

One day, toward the war's end, Razz pointed to the TV and commented, "Look at all these Arab prisoners being escorted to prison camps. It reminds me of the Gulf War images, when thousands of Iraqi prisoners waved white flags and begged for mercy. I can't imagine where they plan to detain them all." George joined in with the speculation, "You just watch, Razz! POW camps will start popping up in southern Lebanon, and remote parts of the Negev and Sinai deserts. The IDF will choose these locations to keep their enemies isolated."

Razz was reminded of a related prophecy in the book of Obadiah. Opening his "New King Jimmy" Bible to the specific passage, he read: "'... and the *captives of this host* of the children *of Israel* shall possess the land of the Canaanites as far as Zarephath.' Zarephath was a Phoenician town inside ancient Sidon, today's Southern Lebanon," Razz explained.[14] George took his turn, adding, "Obadiah also predicted Israel would possess the Gaza, West Bank, southern Jordan, and most of the desert area of the Negev and Sinai in addition to southern Lebanon. And, Jeremiah 49:1-6 tells us that after Jordan's capital, Amman, is destroyed, along with many surrounding cities and villages in northern Jordan, Israel will take over Jordan. Jeremiah seems to have foretold the surrender of Jordan."

Razz agreed. "After the destruction we just witnessed, the Israeli Air Force (IAF) hammering upon Cairo, Suez, and Luxor, it appears Isaiah 19:18 will soon find fulfillment, as well."

"What does that say?" asked George.

Flipping his Bible to the pertinent passage, Razz read, "In that day five cities in the land of Egypt will speak the language of Canaan and swear by the LORD of hosts; one will be called the City of Destruction."

"What's the language of Canaan?" George questioned.

"Today it's Hebrew, of course," Razz responded.

Normally, Mimi would have interrupted their bantering back and forth, but on this occasion she startled them by speculating, "Conditions in the aftermath of Psalm 83 will probably bring more Jews into Israel."

"How do you figure, Mimi?" Razz responded.

George jumped in. "She's right! Israel could become the land of opportunity for Jews around the world. It'll be a safer place, and Arab oil and other commercial industries could be exploited; not to mention the large natural gas and oil deposits recently discovered there."

Clearing her throat, Mimi said, "Excuse me, there is one too many Mimis in this conversation. As I was attempting to say, Muslims are in a mob mentality throughout the world, making it unsafe for Jews living outside of Israel. This is why I think they will now flee to Israel, to escape mounting persecution."

Applauding her insight, Razz responded, "If what you both predict comes to pass, then the stage could rapidly be set up for the fulfillment of Ezekiel 38 and 39. It won't take long for Israel to 'dwell securely' and become the prosperous nation Ezekiel describes. Their new opportunities will require increased manpower. You two might be on to something."

Pleased that Mimi was involved in the conversation, Razz asked her, "Didn't Lisa's siblings recently move to Israel to join their parents and other relatives?"

Delighted by Razz' family-related question, she answered, "That's correct. And some of them live near the war zone. The crowded phone lines have prevented her from communicating with them."

"What about emails?" asked Razz.

"Lisa said they're not getting through, either," Mimi reported.

"Regarding Lisa and Jami, George and I are very concerned about their rejection of Christ. Thomas hasn't exactly bannered his Christianity on his sleeve and Tyler is a newborn babe in Christ; so thus far, neither of them has convinced Lisa or Jami to accept Jesus into their hearts as their personal Lord and Savior. If you and George are correct that Isaiah 17 and Psalm 83 are fulfilled now, I'm frantically concerned the rapture could occur at any moment and they'll be left behind."

Razz asked her, "How soon are you expecting the rapture to occur?"

Carefully choosing her words, Mimi responded, "George and I share in your belief the rapture could occur at any moment. The fact it didn't happen before this major war means it's nearer now than ever before, don't you think?"

Razz agreed and added, "I also believe it is an imminent event and think it might occur before Russia, Iran, Turkey, and the other Ezekiel 38 invaders confederate against Israel."

Razz' Ezekiel 38 comments piqued George's interest, prompting him to ask, "What makes you say that?"

Razz answered, "Several things; one being that Ezekiel identifies the Jewish people as 'My people Israel' three times during the episode. To me, this means the event is very Jewish centered and raises questions as to the whereabouts of the church by that time."

"Ezekiel 38 and 39 clearly identifies Israel in the last days. I have often used these chapters to refute Replacement theology, which is the belief God is done with the Jews and the church has taken their place. It is impossible to put the church in place of Israel in this prophetic episode."

"Furthermore..." he said, when Mimi interrupted, asking, "Why is there a furthermore? How did we go from family talk about Lisa's and Jami's salvation to discussing Ezekiel 38? Can we agree the rapture is near and we need to pray and plead for their salvation before we vanish? I'm looking for constructive ideas to help them, not details about an event you don't think we will even experience."

Razz apologetically agreed and suggested that they pray for Lisa and Jami. Mimi began, "Beloved Lord, we lift up Lisa and Jami before your throne. Have mercy on their souls. Save them, Lord! By your design they were created. They are your children. Their salvation is your heart's desire. We agree with you that they are precious. Lord, make their salvation assured through the blood of Yeshua, Jesus Christ. Seal them in your hand for eternity. In the name of Jesus, we pray."

Together, the three of them said, "Amen."

# Chapter 13
## Israel, the Next Emerging Market

Cleaning up the carnage from *Operation Israeli Freedom*, which became the secular title for Psalm 83, proved to be an enormous task. Undoubtedly, the IDF had earned itself the reputation of becoming an "exceedingly great army,"[15] but there was collateral damage on both sides of the Arab – Israeli fence. Unlike *Desert Storm*, which primarily experienced Arab casualties, *Op Israeli Freedom* was a far cry from being a sanitary war.

Even though the Arabs suffered a sweeping defeat, scores of Israelis were killed or injured during the conflict. Mopping up the mess and restoring Middle East infrastructures could take months, perhaps years, and require more Jews to migrate into Israel to accomplish the herculean task.

In an attempt to replenish its wounded and lost population, Israel's Ministry of the Interior launched a global campaign called *Tzion Levav*, meaning "Zion's Heart" in Hebrew. This campaign promised a "Greater and Safer Israel." It entreated Jews living abroad to migrate back to their ancient homeland and become the heart and soul of a new, expanding Israel. The slogan read, "Escape Anti-Semitism, Experience Religious Freedom, and Enjoy Economic Opportunity; Come Home to the Holy Land!"

The campaign was extremely successful, and without delay Jews worldwide heeded the invitation. One by one, family upon family, community upon community, multitudes of Jews began flocking into the victorious Jewish State. As a result of the IDF victory, Israel was becoming a safer place. The threat of war and Arab terror was subsiding and the Jewish State wholeheartedly welcomed the immigrant manpower.

Meanwhile, the broader Gentile world was thrust into a state of flux, wondering whether to condemn Israel or cooperate with the victorious

Jewish State. As George and Razz suspected, humanity had questions, and a harvest field was forming.

America was pleased that, in short order, the IDF had done much of its war business for it. Those responsible for terrorizing America would exact the harshest punishment imaginable, but for now *Op Israeli Freedom* had dealt a lethal blow to Hezbollah and Al-Qaeda. Both terror groups were severely punished by the IDF for their antagonistic participation in the war. Surviving members of both groups were among the first to be processed in the POW camps. According to US assessment, both groups had been involved with Iran in the terror attacks inside America.

For Iran's involvement, the US began deployment of 80,000 additional troops into the region. The troop surge was primarily directed toward Afghanistan, due to its strategic location on Iran's eastern border. Iran feared harsh American retaliation, and quickly called upon Russia to increase its military presence in the region. Reportedly, Russian president Ziroski promised the Ayatollah of Iran his countries full support, and deployed of an equal number of Russian troops into Turkey and Iran. This complicated American military plans and was certain to revive the Cold War.

Meanwhile, back at the Thompsons', George and Razz quickly discovered that many so-called Christian leaders were clueless about the prophetic relevance of *Op Israeli Freedom*. Statements out of the Vatican and the World Council of Churches condemned Israel's action, demanded the return of Arab POWs to their homelands, and called for the formation of a Palestinian State. Thus, the preponderance of the Christian church failed to appropriately associate the Arab – Israeli war with its Psalm 83 counterpart.

While Israel was mopping up in the aftermath of the IDF victory over the Psalm 83 Arab nations, Razz received an urgent phone call from his close friend Nathaniel Severs. Severs was the president of Unistate Global Investments Corporation, one of the largest investment firms in America. UGIC managed more high profile accounts than any other brokerage house in the country. Severs ranked among the nation's top economists and sported a resume more extensive than the presiding Federal Reserve Chairman, Benjamin Bernard.

Razz and Nathan were high school friends, who had played on the varsity football team together. Although their careers subsequently sent them in different directions, they kept in frequent contact, and like a fine wine, their friendship had sweetened with age. Nate, as Razz referred to him, had never married. His successful career had taken him to almost every country on the globe, earning him the respect of many world leaders and a good share of romantic relationships with female celebrities along the way.

Speaking several languages and epitomizing the "tall, dark, and handsome" cliché, Nate didn't limit his options to famous American women only. His lavish lifestyle often prompted Razz to ask, "When are you going to slow down and let one of these starlets catch you, before you go to your grave lonely?" Nate, who possessed an endless repertoire of one-liners, would always volley back with something like, "Marriage is like religion: there are so many to choose from and until you're certain you've identified the right one, it's best to keep on looking."

In return, Razz would warn, "How many failed relationships and brushes with bad religions will it take before you realize Jesus is the way, the truth, and the life, and the only way through to the Heavenly Father?"[16] It pained Razz to realize that Nate was still undecided about Christ, even though he had shared the gospel with him countless times.

"Hello, Nate, and to what do I owe the honor of this call?" answered Razz.

"I was hesitant to make this call," Severs said, "and sincerely wish it was merely a friendly one, Razz. However, world economies are unraveling by the minute, as you can imagine. I personally wanted to encourage you to make immediate major protective moves with your UGIC accounts."

"What do you advise, Nate? I'm already overloaded with futures, commodities, gold, cash, and rare coins," declared Razz.

"It's hard to say; things are so unpredictable at present. We just need to stop the bleeding. My staff informed me your investment accounts, like most everyone else's countrywide, have dropped approximately forty-five to fifty percent since all the chaos began," replied Severs.

Visibly disturbed, Razz asked, "What about investing in Middle East oil? Some news channels are saying Israel hopes to quickly contract with several American petroleum companies to get some of the conquered OPEC oil circulating into global economies again."

"Israel is definitely interested in bringing order to the Mideast chaos by flooding world markets with oil," Severs replied. "However, investing in oil futures right now is extremely risky. Before everything blew up, crude oil was closing at $152 per barrel. However, since OPEC shut down production a few weeks ago the price per barrel shot up to $398 a barrel."

"Yes," groaned Razz. "I'm already feeling it at the pump. Yesterday I paid $11.38 a gallon. It cost me almost $200 to feel up my SUV!"

Overhearing their conversation, George chicken-scratched a quick note and placed it in front of Razz: *Remember Israel – Ez. 38—lotsa $$$ B4 Russia invades.*

Razz nodded, then proceeded to tell Nate, "I sincerely think Israel is the place to invest at this point."

"Really? Explain," Nate urged.

"According to Bible prophecy, Israel is going to become very prosperous someday. It appears that day draws near," replied Razz.

"How can you know that with certainty?" asked Nate.

"If you recall a couple of lunches ago, before all the mayhem, I warned you that Russia was going to hook up with Iran and several other nations to invade a safe and extremely wealthy Israel," Razz reminded.

"Yes, I recall, but why do you feel Israel stands at that point, presently?" Nate questioned.

"Well, Israel decisively defeated its Arab enemies and can now dwell securely and exploit Arab oil, commercial, and agricultural resources," asserted Razz.

Nate warned, "It could take months before Israel gets OPEC drills pumping, and the Suez Canal and Strait of Hormuz open again. Moreover, Iran will certainly attempt to prevent Israel from using the Persian Gulf to export its oil and commerce. Not only that, but it's almost impossible to get phone or internet service in most of the Middle East; no incoming or outgoing mail is being processed throughout most of the area; tourism and commercial travel is at a standstill; and a majority of the oil refineries and Arab infrastructures are severely damaged."

Razz responded, "Then months it is. Besides, it's better to bless Israel and be patient with my investments than to continue losing money in volatile world markets."

"Well, the latter is certainly the case!" Nate agreed. "As you command, we will invest in the wealthy Israel you are anticipating. The UGIC staff will promptly prepare a pro-Israel *pro forma* for your preview."

As soon as Razz hung up, George asked, "Well, what's the economic expert experiencing?"

"World markets are collapsing and all investments are erratic! He's reluctantly going to research investment potentials developing inside Israel," answered Razz.

"Do you think investing is relevant in light of the imminent coming rapture?" George asked. "What?" Razz laughed. "You were the one shoving a post-it about greater Israel under my nose when I was on the phone!"

"*Touché,*" George chuckled. "We can't be utter escapists. We have to occupy the earth and be good stewards of our finances in case the Lord tarries a little while longer."

"Ezekiel 38 teaches that Israel will garner 'great spoil' just before Russia invades," Razz reminded. "It must be referring to spoils of war from the Arab conflict."

"Razz, do you still believe America shows up as merchants wanting to conduct commerce with Israel in the Ezekiel 38 prophecy?" George inquired.

"Certainly, why wouldn't I?" Razz reiterated.

"In light of America's horrible economy and major recent terrorist attacks, America's not the same stable superpower it once was. This has caused me to rethink America's role, if any, in end-time's prophecy. Frankly, I'm not sure anymore that the US is in Bible prophecy," George explained.

Razz reflected, "America needs Israel right now. The roles are reversed; instead of Israel depending on us for their survival, we now depend on them to survive our struggling economy. Israel has already rescued us from Al-Qaeda and Hezbollah, and now America absolutely has to come alongside Israel and help the expanding Jewish State emerge into its full potential."

"I hope you're right Razz. Our country is in dire straits right now," George said with a sigh.

"Stop being such a downer, George. The US is about to bless Israel and be blessed in return,' Razz opined.

# Chapter 14
## Greater Israel Makes Plans for a Third Temple

The following afternoon George was able to get Thomas back on the phone. It was an abbreviated call and upon hanging up, George informed Mimi, "Thomas and Tyler are on their way here." "Oh, that's wonderful!" she replied. "Do you realize we haven't seen our son in over a month?"

"Cherish the remaining moments we have with him," George responded.

"What's that supposed to mean?" Mimi wondered.

"Supposedly, Thomas and Tyler have something extremely important to discuss with us," George added.

"Did he say what it was?" Mimi asked anxiously.

"Something about Lisa wanting them all to move to Israel immediately," George announced.

Mimi's hand flew to her mouth. "My worst nightmare come true," she cried. "I just knew when Lisa's family moved over there they would pressure her to follow!"

Seeing her reaction, George reconsidered. "Let's not jump to any conclusions," he said, "Let's hear what he has to say."

Overhearing, Razz offered, "It's temporarily safe, though in the long haul maybe not smart."

"Why do you say that?" asked Mimi.

"Because the Russians are coming," Razz reminded.[17]

Anxiety began to set in. "Stop beating around the bush," Mimi pleaded. "What's that supposed to mean?"

"The Russian - Iranian led invasion of Israel predicted in Ezekiel 38 and 39 will overshadow this recent Arab – Israeli war," Razz clarified.

"He's right, dear," George echoed. "But, the coming invasion will make this last one look like small potatoes."

Mimi concernedly responded, "I thought you military experts believed we won't be here for the Magog invasion."

Razz reiterated, "We can't be certain, Mimi. The rapture is an imminent event and we are not told anywhere in Scripture about its exact timing. All we are reasonably certain about is that we are not appointed to wrath, as the Bible puts it."[18]

"There are good reasons to believe the church escapes the entire battle, but not all expositors are convinced about this. I don't want to panic you, but it's possible many Israeli residents could die as a result of this massive invasion. If Thomas moves his family to Israel, he could be putting them in harm's way," warned Razz.

Overwhelmed with concern for Thomas and his family, George asked, "Razz, would you please stay and share these concerns with Thomas?"

"Don't you think for one second about leaving," Mimi chimed in. "We need you to help us rid our son of this ridiculous notion to move to Israel. This is absolutely absurd. It's a war zone over there. What's he thinking?"

"Certainly, I'll stay! I'm very concerned that he thoughtfully, and prayerfully, considers this major move at such a time as this," replied Razz.

At that point, George felt compelled to share what Thomas told him over the phone the day before. "I neglected to inform you both that Thomas is reading his Bible and frequenting Razz' daily blog-site to keep up with Mideast events."

"Hallelujah! Finally some comforting news," exclaimed Mimi. "Train your child up in the way he should go, and when he is old he will not depart from it," Mimi quoted Proverbs 22:6, her favorite child-rearing Bible verse.

"If we can't convince him to stay in America, at least he takes Christ with him to Israel," commended George.

Awaiting the arrival of Thomas and young Tyler, the three of them watched further significant Mideast events unfold on the news.

It was indeed an eventful day that saw Israel make several controversial sovereign moves. In the morning, the Israel Land Administration (ILA) was delegated the responsibility of annexing sizable allotments of Arab lands, including the Sinai Peninsula and portions of Egypt, Jordan, and Lebanon. By capturing these additional lands, Israel could increase its size by over 35,000 square miles.

Upon hearing this announcement, Razz said, "Amazing! The Israelis fought for over six decades to maintain control over a meager 8,000 to 9,000 square miles, but after their decisive victory in *Operation Israeli Freedom* they can now call the shots."

Shortly after the ILA announcement was made, the Israeli Minister of Defense called for the 403 mile long "West Bank Barrier Wall" to be demolished without delay. Reminiscent of President Ronald Reagan's famous "Tear down this (Berlin) wall" challenge to Mikhail Gorbachev, the Israeli leader cried, "Tear down this fence of terror!" This wall had served its purpose by separating Palestinian terrorism from Israel proper. However, in the aftermath of Psalm 83, Israel anticipated that all Arab terrorism would subside, rendering this wall no longer necessary.

Recalling events from the previous day, Razz recounted how significant it was that the Ministry of Religious Affairs granted the Jewish Temple Foundation permission to go forward with the construction of the third Jewish temple, where the Islamic Dome of the Rock had once stood.

At the time of the announcement, Ehud Cohen, the Temple Foundation spokesman, boasted that the Temple Foundation estimated the altar could be set up, temple instruments readied, and Levitical priesthood operational in a matter of days. The temple instruments had been previously prepared, and the Levite priests already identified, making Cohen's comments a definite possibility. He further declared the actual temple could be constructed within the span of one to two years.

"Well, George and Mimi, to me, the Religious Affairs temple announcement puts the end-times' frosting on the last days' cake," said Razz.

"I totally agree, Razz. We have to make sure Thomas realizes how fast prophetic events are occurring in Israel, right now!" George exclaimed.

Razz further added, "It will be a cold day in Hades before the international community tolerates the construction of this temple. The altar may be erected, a few priests ordained, and subsequently some animals sacrificially slaughtered, but it won't be long before a public outcry is voiced by Muslims, Catholics, Orthodox Christians, and even animal rights activists, worldwide. After all, this site is holy to Christians and Muslims, as well as Jews."

As they were conversing, Thomas and Tyler arrived. Right away Mimi noticed Thomas didn't look like his vibrant self. Normally, his complexion was tanned, muscles toned, and his smile infectious, but this visit he seemed pale, worn-out, and downtrodden.

"What's wrong, Son? You don't look quite like your chipper self today," she commented.

"I'm fine, Mom, just a little stressed by what's happening in the world," he replied.

After exchanging endearing hugs and we missed yous, they adjourned upstairs to the family room for their important meeting. This secluded area of the house was where pressing family matters were traditionally discussed. As they seated themselves, Tyler fastened himself to his favorite place of refuge, at Mimi's side. Mimi realized things were weighing heavily upon her grandson's mind.

"Thomas," George began, "I invited Razz to join us because of his expertise concerning what's transpiring in the Middle East."

"Absolutely," Thomas responded. "I wouldn't have it any other way."

"So what's up with this talk about moving to Israel?" asked George.

"Lisa's brother, Joseph, who has been living in Israel the longest of all her seven siblings, is a close friend of Israel's Minister of the Interior, Avi Fleishman. Because of Lisa's extensive background in tourism advertising, Joseph has recommended her to Avi, who is seeking experienced Jewish employees for his rapidly expanding agency."

"Fleishman, who is becoming one of Israel's most respected leaders, has offered her a high ranking government position. He wants her to be an associate director of marketing for the *Tzion Levav* campaign. She will be working alongside Avi and several of his key staff administrators."

"Also, her family has offered to gift us a large down payment toward the purchase of a home in Israel, so we can all live close to each other. They are telling us that the Israeli government is developing an incentive plan to encourage home ownership. They want more Jews to move to Israel right away. Especially, Jews who would like to inhabit the former Arab territories, although the housing incentive applies anywhere in Israel."

"Supposedly, individuals who can prove at least one spouse comes from Jewish descent receive a 0% interest loan for the first ten years, while the nation expands. Her entire family over there is enthusiastic about the prospects of what they are calling a 'Greater Israel.'"

Unable to contain her dismay at this sudden turn of events, Mimi opined, "We were under the impression that Lisa was finding it difficult to communicate with her family over there, and now you're informing us you're packing up, moving abroad, and buying a house!"

"I'm amazed, myself," Thomas answered. "She *was* having trouble connecting with them. These recent plans have developed over the past forty-eight hours and now she has her mind set on accepting the job and making the move. Please don't act so surprised mother. Lisa has previously warned us she wanted to someday move to Israel. Nonetheless, Tyler and I are struggling with the sudden timing of this, and that's why we wanted to tell you what was going on."

"How soon is all this supposed to take place?" questioned Razz.

"Mom was booking her and Jami's flight on our way over here," whimpered Tyler.

Turning her attention toward her grandson, Mimi asked "How do you feel about moving to Israel, Ty?"

Snuggling even closer, he replied, "I'm upset because I was looking forward to going to Eastside Middle School with Jami. And I'm scared because of the war over there. Also, I don't want to move that far away from you and Grandpa."

Puzzled, George asked Thomas, "Son, I'm curious: why is Lisa booking a flight so suddenly, and why are Tyler and you remaining behind?"

Thomas explained, "We have a split decision in our household on this matter. I just returned from a month of seven-day work weeks in Florida and haven't had time to digest all this. Barely arriving through the front door, I was bombarded with Jami's plans to move to Israel and attend a private school with her cousins."

"Tyler and I are uncertain about shipping off to Israel so soon after the major war. I believe it was the war of Psalm 83, according to what I read on Uncle Razz' blog-site. And Tyler confirmed that's what you told him on the way home from fishing, when the war broke out."

Empathizing with Thomas's concerns, Razz chimed in, "I'm in solid agreement with you, Thomas. The dust hasn't settled over there yet. The place is still a dangerous war zone. Your parents and I have been monitoring recent announcements coming from Israel's government. They're making major land acquisitions, tearing down the partition wall, and making preparations to construct their third temple. I'm also concerned that Israel will have trouble incarcerating all the Arab POWs. The makeshift detention camps they set up are temporary facilities, at best."

George added, "Muslims across the globe are sure to unite, to prevent Israel from implementing these plans. The world will be appalled when animal sacrifices commence on a new altar in Jerusalem. Israel needs to be cautious regarding such matters, or they'll provoke worldwide Anti-Semitism. World governments and economies need time to digest what just happened over there."

"Not to mention, it looks like Russia and America are about to go to war in Iran and Afghanistan!" declared Razz.

Drawing a deep breath, Thomas announced, "I appreciate all your concerns, but in the end analysis, I fear that Tyler and I must move with them to Israel."

"But, why, Son?" George pleaded. "You just said you and Lisa were divided on this."

Shrugging, Thomas admitted, "Actually, your own words have convinced me! It seems clear that Bible prophecies are being fulfilled at an accelerated pace. First the destruction of Damascus, followed by Psalm 83, and now they are planning to construct the Jewish temple. This implies Christ could be coming for believers at any moment!"

"That's right, but..." George faltered.

Thomas looked sympathetically at his parents. "Unfortunately, Lisa is clinging to her Jewish roots and is influencing Jami to do the same," he confessed. "Their Jewish heritage is blinding them to the truth about Jesus as the Messiah. It breaks my heart that they continue to reject him as their Lord and savior. I feel a deep sense of guilt for not being a better Christian husband and dad. I'm hoping that, by making this move and sticking by them, I can finally lead them to the Lord. Recent events could create a change in their hearts."

"That's noble, Son; however, you admitted, yourself, that these events are causing them to cling to their Jewishness, instead," his father reminded.

Thomas saw only one alternative. "I'm left with no choice but to follow them to Israel and continue to love and witness to them."

Tyler suddenly stiffened. "Why do I have to go with you? Please don't make me move! I can live with Mimi and Poppy and go to school in America!"

Weeping alongside her grandson, Mimi pleaded, "Thomas, let him stay behind with us. Your father and I will raise and protect him here inside our home. Please don't subject him to the uncertainties over there. It's not safe! Your father and Razz believe that Russia will soon invade Israel. They believe all of you will be in harm's way if you move there."

Leaping to his feet, Thomas pleaded, "Don't do this to me, Mother! We can't have this conversation! My mind is made up and I'm not leaving my son behind. You can't expect me to abandon my family at this critical time. That's all there is to it!"

George raised a hand to calm him.

"No, Dad! Listen! Lisa will have a good job and I will have no problem getting work as a general contractor over there. Her brother informed me this morning that thousands of new homes are in planning stages to be built, to absorb the Jewish influx into Israel. Nobody can predict how soon any invasion will occur. It may not happen for many years, or even decades!"

Breathless, he slumped to his seat again. "The best thing you can do is pray for us!" he insisted. "If anything changes, I will let you know, but for now, this matter is closed."

Huddling together, they wept and prayed. George asked God to protect, preserve, and prosper them in the new Israel.

Thomas struggled to separate his son from Mimi's tearful embrace. "Come, Son," he said, determination ringing in his voice. "Let's get ready to go to the Promised Land."

# Chapter 15
## Russia Forms an Evil Plan to Invade Israel

The next several months proved to be extremely fruitful for Israel. Gaining regional superiority, the enlarging Jewish State commanded the attention and respect of many world leaders and global markets. The little nation of Israel, which much of the Muslim world had wanted to wipe off the map, had morphed into Islam's arch nemesis.

Meanwhile, many Muslims no longer made a distinction between Israel and America; they called them singularly the "Great Satan."

As Razz had predicted, America immediately began assisting Israel to acquire and exploit Arab assets by investing and contracting with the "greater and safer" Jewish State. Reciprocally, the struggling US economy received a much needed shot in the arm, as Israel offered Americans many economic opportunities. Israel required American ingenuity and manpower, and shelled out the shekels to hire the best the United States had to offer.

Russia, on the other hand, began coveting Israel's burgeoning prosperity and plotted a comprehensive campaign to divert Israel's newfound spoils into its own national coffers.

"My dearest friend! How are you? Thank you for coming to my country on this momentous occasion," in humblest salutation, the Russian president Vladimir Ziroski greeted Ayatollah Khomani.

The Ayatollah had just arrived at the request of president Ziroski, to solidify Iran's involvement in the multi-nation coalition Russia was forming in opposition to Israel. Russia's leader proposed that the strictest of sanctions should be imposed upon Israel for plundering the Arab states. His plan intended to enforce the sanctions by preventing Israel to export its commerce into world markets. Ultimately the plan contained war strategies, if Israel failed to comply with the coalition's wishes.

The supreme leader of Iran shook his Russian counterpart's hand and said "The honor is indeed mine, dear president. We have many common interests to discuss these days."

Ziroski conceded, "Most certainly we do, supreme leader of Islam. Iran and Russia must collaborate on a mutual plan to eliminate Israel, and elevate Islam under your exclusive leadership, if the Jews resist our coalition's mandate. The Israelis have made a grave mistake by attacking your country and unleashing its nuclear arsenal against our Arab brothers. Already the nuclear fallout from Bushehr is beginning to clear from Iranian skies, and Israel's glory will soon wane thin if our combined forces invade their soil."

The Ayatollah lamented, "Millions of my people still scatter into the nations for fear of the radio-active fallout, and Israel must not go unpunished! *There is no if, Mr. President we absolutely must invade Israel!*

Ziroski concurred, "We are on the same page of history together on this my friend. Israel will not survive our concerted effort."

"Our foolish president Zakiri and his mystic friend Zamani Nikahd have caused much hardship in my country," the Ayatollah replied, "and they are soon to be exiled and replaced with leaders who will make certain that this time the state of Israel gets wiped off the pages of time forever."

"Praise be to your all powerful god Allah," said Ziroski, in a most patronizing tone.

Khomani continued, "The three-phased plan you set forth against Israel with our Muslim brothers in Turkey, Libya, the Baltic States and African countries is fool proof. Allah gives his blessings to go forth with *god-speed*. Israel should not be allowed to bask for long in its glory for the killing of our Arab brothers. The Arab possessions and lands should be returned to them, after our coalition takes its just rewards."

Ziroski agreed, "Russia is extremely honored to call Iran our partner, along with the other Muslim countries in this matter. There will be ample spoils of war to share. Our coalition is already mobilizing to blockade all the waterways the Jews want to use to export their plunder. The commercial relationships they are attempting to form with America, Asia, Australia, Canada, and the European countries will never get off the ground. Our coalition will prevent them from making good on their promises to export their newfound booty overseas. Our consortium will see to it that no waterway to their east, north, west, or south will be open to them."

Applauding his comments, the Ayatollah commented further, "Iran is saddened to hear the Saudis have opted to refrain from joining the fight against Israel with us. They would have proven to be a strategic ally. They could prevent the Jews from transporting commerce through the Arabian Peninsula. But after the damage Israel afflicted upon them in their recent war, I guess they have proven to be true Sunni cowards."

With anger in his eyes, Mad Vlad Ziroski replied, "If the Saudis allow the Jews safe passage upon their soil we will invade their kingdom alongside the Jewish kingdom. This was declared to them when they chose not to join our coalition."

"Excellent, no longer will they be a thorn in Iran's side," the Ayatollah concluded.

After the Iranian supreme leader departed homeward, Mad Vlad finished making his international rounds with the coalition countries. One-by-one, about a dozen nations signed on to the cruel Russian leader's foul campaign against Israel. He became obsessed with the desire to stop the burgeoning Israeli economy dead in its tracks. Mad Vlad's thinking was constantly sinister. His thoughts were continuously evil toward Israel.

"When I destroy the Jews, I will thank them for harnessing all the Arab wealth into one coffer, making it easier for Russia to seize. When my hordes bury their dead bodies, I will be sure to spit on their coffins, and pillage their cities and ravish their widows," he inscribed one night in his private journal. Israel's celebration over their surrounding Arab enemies would turn out to be short lived, as Mad Vlad Ziroski had quickly put his evil plan in place.

Ziroski seized every opportunity to harness the hatred of Israel among the Muslim countries that enlisted in his confederate alliance. Skillfully, he solicited the nations that most hated Israel, bordered strategic waterways, and desperately needed economic revival. Most of them housed significant Muslim populations, such as the former Soviet Union republics of Kazakhstan, Tajikistan, Turkmenistan and Kyrgyzstan. Additional key coalition members, which were also predominately Muslim, included Tunisia, Algeria, Sudan, Ethiopia, and Somalia.

Mad Vlad's league had to be strategically located along all the important waterways surrounding Israel. The northernmost African nations of Libya, Tunisia, and Algeria were called upon to patrol the Mediterranean Sea to the south, while Turkey manned the maritime responsibilities on the northern part of Sea. The East African countries of Sudan, Ethiopia, and Somalia were to monitor all commerce commuting via the Suez Canal, down through the Red

Sea. Iran was designated exclusive accountability for guarding the Strait of Hormuz and all Israeli export efforts through the Persian Gulf.

Russia even attempted to enlist Yemen, to prevent Israeli commerce from diverting on land through the Arabian Peninsula to the Arabian Sea. But the Yemenites, like the Saudis, opted out of the coalition. These two countries were still recovering from the devastating Psalm 83 war.

It was widely speculated that if it weren't for Israel's desire to capture OPEC oil under Saudi soil, Saudi Arabia would have been destroyed alongside Damascus. Furthermore, it was reported that the Saudis wanted no further part in a campaign against the "God of Israel," whom they believed had empowered the IDF against them and their Arab cohorts.

US President John Bachlin still threatened revenge against Iran for terrorizing America; but meanwhile, Americans were counting their blessings, considering Israel's military victory and economic expansion as the medicine Wall Street needed.

However, Russia's newly forming coalition, bent on preventing Israel from conducting international commerce, caused American war drums to pound loudly. Painful reminders of the Cold War and Mutual Assured Destruction (MAD) were rekindled, as raging rhetoric emanated from Washington and Moscow.

Both countries were heavily deployed throughout the Middle East. Russian troops were stationed in Turkey, Iran, and several Baltic States; the US Navy had deployed a full armada of nuclear-equipped fleets into the Persian Gulf and Mediterranean. US Naval commanders were on strict orders to monitor all maritime activities and assure safe passage of Israeli ships destined for international ports.

A showdown between America and Russia's confederacy seemed imminent, causing President Bachlin's administration to hastily attempt to form its own coalition of allies from Europe. Although this slowed Russian plans, it also aggravated their will to attack Israel.

Russia made no bones about it: Israel faced an existential threat from the north. The Russian-led consortium contested Israel's ownership of conquered Muslim lands and Arab spoils of war. Muslim hordes, assembled by Ziroski, demanded that Israel release all Arab prisoners of war and return their lands to them. Russia promised to help its partners recapture the Arab territories, and line their pockets with plunder and booty in the process.

All of these developments occurred before map makers could redraw atlases of the reshaping region.

Just when Israelis thought the worst was behind them, they stood at the threshold of an even greater danger. It appeared another genocidal attempt was being formulated on a far more formidable front.

Although the IDF had achieved the status of an "exceedingly great army," Israel realized their defense forces were outgunned by Russia's nuclear-equipped confederacy. Israel resigned itself to reliance upon American mediation and muscle, but in this go-round the Jews questioned the trustworthiness of America's resolve and military might. America was still recovering from terror at home and exhaustive military campaigns in Afghanistan, Iraq, Libya, and elsewhere.

Additionally, Israeli leaders were very concerned that, in the process of protecting Israel, America might extract revenge against Iran and ignite further widespread war. One miscalculation could trigger a domino effect, preventing Israel's "great spoil" from reaching Asian and European markets.

Leaders of the European Union were working feverishly to create calm and stability in the Middle East. EU President Hans Vandenberg, was working tirelessly with his parliament to resolve geo-political disputes emanating in the aftermath of *Operation Israeli Freedom.*

He even solicited input from the Pope and other religious leaders, due to the religious underpinnings of the regional volatility. Only a comprehensive plan, addressing all economic, political, geographical, and religious concerns, would stand a chance of bringing peace to the Holy Land.

Meanwhile at home, it was blatantly clear to George and Mimi that their loved ones, now living in Israel, were in harm's way. Thomas and his family were already moved into their new home near Jerusalem, the grandkids were attending local schools close by, and Lisa and Thomas were gainfully employed. As suspected, the events described in Ezekiel 38 and 39 were stage-setting for rapid fulfillment.

"Thank God, you were able to give Thomas and Lisa that video before they departed!" Mimi told George.

"What video was that?" asked Razz.

"Linton's latest DVD, dealing with end-times prophecies," replied George. "It had barely hit the retail shelves before Psalm 83 occurred. It's a masterful work, sequencing prophetic events, including the rapture, on through to Christ's second coming."

"Yes, I've heard about that one," Razz recalled. "Isn't that the one where he predicts the rapture occurs between Psalm 83 and Ezekiel 38?"

"Yes, it is," George confirmed. "And he presents many of the same arguments you teach. In fact, he credits some of your work at the end of the video."

Razz nodded, humbled. "Do you have an extra copy we can watch right now?"

"Unfortunately not, I only purchased one copy from his table when he spoke at our church," George stated in regret. "I got it for Mimi, but felt compelled to give it to Thomas to show to Lisa and the kids when they settled down in Israel."

"Did Linton get into my teachings about Gog's evil plan?" Razz questioned.

"Yes, and he agreed with you whole-heartedly. In fact, Linton devotes about five minutes to Russia's attempt to blockade the waterways."

"So, he agreed with me that Russia's coalition is strategic," Razz mused.

"Yes," George assured him. "He echoed your sentiments exactly. Linton even included footage that mimics what Russia and its coalition are accomplishing at present."

"Has Thomas shared the DVD with the family, yet?" Razz wondered.

"No. He says Lisa and Jami are too up caught in the family's religious crossfire."

Mimi sadly added, "Lisa and her family refuse to consider anything related to Jesus or Bible prophecy. In fact, Thomas told me Lisa's mother recently said, 'It was Jehovah, not Jesus, who protected Israel in the recent war.'"

"Of course she would say that!" Razz replied.

George agreed, "It fits with what Paul says in Romans 11:25. The Jews are hardened to the truth about Jesus until the 'fullness of the Gentiles' is completed."

Mimi bristled. "Of course, it doesn't help that, in the name of Christ, Jews have endured centuries of bigotry and persecution! Why would Christians expect they should be open to the gospel?"

Razz' face reddened. "That's all too true, Mimi. I am sure that factors into the scenario!" Clearing his throat, he added in a conciliatory tone, "Maybe it helps to know that the next verse says after the fullness of the Gentiles is completed, 'all Israel will be saved.' Unfortunately," he said, hesitating and shaking his head, "before Israel acknowledges Christ as Messiah, they go through two more genocidal campaigns."

Mimi groaned, "What do you mean 'two more genocidal campaigns'?"

"The Ezekiel 38 invasion will happen, followed a few years later by the Antichrist's final pogrom. Zechariah 13:8 predicts he will annihilate two-thirds of the Jewish population dwelling in Israel at the time." He went on, "Since Gog is already forming a coalition, these two genocidal attempts will probably occur in Lisa's and Jami's lifespan."

As tears welled in Mimi's eyes, George remarked, "That's why time is of the essence for them to watch that DVD! Thomas informed me he has told them about the video and placed it in their home safe, where they keep their emergency funds. He believes that, should the worst happen, Lisa will rescue the cash from the safe and hopefully watch the video at the same time."

"Good plan!" Razz declared. "And, if Christians are not raptured prior to the battle, Thomas can try one more time to open his family's eyes to the good news about their Messiah!"

# Chapter 16
## The Christian Exodus into the Clouds

"Scooting to the edge of his chair, financier Nathaniel Severs suddenly shouted, 'Unbelievable!'"

Severs was celebrating the success of Razz' portfolio with him over lunch, when his attention was abruptly drawn to the restaurant big screen TV.

While quickly turning about in his chair to share in the excitement, Razz asked his host, "*What*? What are you looking at?"

To their collective astonishment, a strange luminous image was flickering brightly on the oversized television. "The Virgin Mary appears above Vatican City," the ticker tape stated, as it streamed across the bottom of the screen.

Instantly, the room went silent as patrons shifted their attention to the event coverage. Hastily, the young hostess grabbed the remote, and maximized the volume just in time to hear, "A Mary apparition is apparently occurring in the heart of Vatican City."

The newscaster, who could barely compose herself, continued, "The large luminescent image you can probably make out on your screen is said to be the Virgin Mary! Our local affiliates tell us that the radiant image is well defined from their vantage point inside Vatican square. They are giving us confirmed reports that an apparition is indeed appearing at this very moment. Please stay with us as we continue to broadcast the image, while attempting to connect with one of our reporters on location."

Squaring around to face his friend, Razz blurted out, "This is huge! I'm getting a very eerie feeling right now, Nate!"

"Me, too! Do you think this apparition has anything to do with the weird atmospheric conditions shrouding the planet," Nate queried.

What Severs was alluding to was a week-long cloud that had enveloped the earth unexplainably. Unprecedented monsoon weather patterns, normally confined to the southern hemisphere that time of the year, overtook the northern hemisphere, as well. West African, Asian, Australian, and North, Central, and South American skies were all overtaken by towering cumulonimbus clouds reaching well into the stratosphere.

Eerily, at the same time, most of Europe became obscured underneath towering ash-clouds emanating out of the Icelandic Eyjafjallajökull volcano. The volcano that briefly brought European air travel to its knees in 2010, had recently erupted again, spewing out volumes of caustic cinder high into the surrounding skies.

Making matters worse, the sun could scarcely be seen, and satellite views pictured skies blanketed in gray. Top meteorologists declared the atmosphere had never experienced such abnormal conditions, causing great concern across the globe. The planetary picture was so portentous it prompted Israeli weather forecaster, Jonathan Levinson, of *Israel Network News* (INN), to label the looming tempest the "Exodus Eclipse," reminiscent of the Hebrew escape from Egyptian bondage approximately 3,600 years before.

To the astonishment of his countrymen, Levinson compared the present weather predicament to the pall of darkness alluded to in Exodus 14. He reported Pharaoh Ramses[19] was plagued by similar bizarre weather patterns, and posed the question, "Where's Moses when you need him to part the gray skies?" Although he intended the comment in jest, it almost cost Levinson his job, in light of the severity of the unprecedented weather phenomenon.

Worldwide gloom quickly spawned feelings of widespread doom, causing conspiracy theorists to speculate that a secret global cloud-seeding experiment had metastasized out of control, threatening humanity's existence. Conversely, New Age spiritualists predicted mankind's alien creators were opening hyper-dimensional atmospheric portals through which to return to recapture the planet. World governments gave no good explanation, leaving people in a dismal emotional state.

Amidst the backdrop of the densely overcast troposphere, Catholics had converged upon Vatican City to discover who would become the newly elected Pontiff. Pope Pius XIII had recently passed away and the Cardinals were deliberating inside the Sistine Chapel with their ballots in hand.

With baited breath, throngs of the faithful waited in the square outside to hear the bells of St. Peter's Basilica sound, and to see the white smoke billow from the chapel's furnace, indicating a new Pope had been decided upon.

It had been over six days, and the multitudes were growing impatient. They had witnessed the summer skies mysteriously darken, and rumors began circulating that the heavenly firmament was transmitting a troublesome sign. Fueling the emotions of the faithful was the increased presence of the Swiss Guard. These Vatican security forces continuously poured into St. Peter's square on heightened alert for potential terrorist attacks.

As the crowds inside the square grew increasingly tense, the Marion apparition suddenly occurred. The enormous luminous figure appeared overhead, hovering close atop the high cross on St. Peter's Basilica. Her radiance was so intense; the worshippers fell to their faces.

Miraculously, beams of sunlight penetrated through the thick cloud-cover, magnifying the pierce marks upon her outstretched hands and majestically illuminating the cross below. In possibly the only place on the planet where sunshine could be seen, the rays were so concentrated that fire appeared to be burning into both her hands, yet they were not consumed.

The prostrate crowd fell silent as the apparition began communicating her message to the minds and hearts of many onlookers. These selected visionaries suddenly rose to their knees and started shouting aloud, "The Lady of All Nations has come to reconcile the world to her immaculate heart!"[20]

Moments later, a host of others cried out, "The time has finally come for the Co-redemptrix to redeem all of her children."

Apparently the apparition had anointed a random host of onsite voices. Clearly, they communicated the same messages, and repeated them several times. After the announcements had ceased, the visionaries began chanting, "Hail Mary, full of grace." Their hypnotic incantations mesmerized the rest of the faithful and morphed into a choir echoing throughout St. Peter's Square.

Despite the apparition's near-blinding glow, television crews were able to video the spectacle. Clear images were hard to capture, but, it was clear to all who witnessed the spectacle that something supernatural was occurring.

After telling Severs that there was no way of confirming that the Marian apparition had anything to do with the bizarre weather scenario, Razz turned around to watch further developments at the Vatican.

Camera crews and reporters at the site began broadcasting the chants of the visionaries. Through their voices, the supposed Marian messages resonated throughout the world, as thousands of television and radio networks covered the event. As her messages streamed across the TV ticker, Severs asked, "Do you believe that's a true Marian apparition appearing over the Vatican?"

"It's hard to make out *what* it is from these images," replied Razz. "But, the visionary communications seem credible. My guess is that it is."

"Are you suggesting that Mary, the mother of Jesus, really does appear to the faithful?" Nate marveled.

"Absolutely not!" Razz exclaimed. "I *do not* believe that's the Mary of the Bible presently surfing the skies above Vatican City! Whoever, or whatever, that is, has to be demonic!"

"Demonic?" Nate gasped.

"The biblical Mary would never make such outlandish claims to be a Co-redemptrix, on even par with Jesus Christ! The book of Luke quotes her as saying she, herself, 'rejoiced in God her Savior.'[21] She can't *be* a savior if she *needs* a Savior!" declared Razz.

Nate sat back in bewilderment. "Well you have to admit this *is* a miraculous event," he argued.

"Don't be fooled by her enchantments," cautioned Razz. "Scripture tells us even Satan can deceptively transform himself into an angel of light."

Nate shook his head and crossed his arms. "Are you suggesting that Satan has duped the Catholics all these years into thinking he's the Virgin Mary?"

"Hardly," Razz replied, trying to reason with Nate. "Let me give you some Scriptural insights about the 'queen of heaven's' apparitions, and their role inside Roman Catholicism. The book of Revelation warns about a coming false world religion identified as 'Mystery Babylon the Great, the Mother of Harlots' and...."

While his words still filled the space between them, in the blink of an eye Razz disappeared inexplicably from sight!

Nathan couldn't believe his eyes. In an instant, his best friend had vanished into thin air without a trace. Frantically, he jumped up and cried out, "Razz, Razz, where did you go?" Pulling closely to his heart Razz' clothing, which had fallen to the floor, Nathan started to weep profusely.

On several previous occasions, Razz had forewarned his worldly friend that the day would come when Christians would be caught up into the clouds in the twinkling of an eye; Nathan came to grips with the fact that this was what had just happened.

Stricken with grief, he dropped to his knees. It wasn't long before he heard the sound of others weeping and noticed more abandoned garments sprinkled about the restaurant floor. Reluctantly pulling himself up to the table, he looked about him, only to view a sea of tears cascading down the cheeks of those left behind.

It was about five minutes later that Nathan realized the television broadcast of the Mary sighting had abruptly shut off. He had no idea what was taking place at Vatican City.

Immediately, he tried to pull up the internet on his cell phone, but no service was available. He darted outside to listen to the radio in his Mercedes and was shocked to see what looked like an apocalyptic episode out of the "Twilight Zone" occurring on the bustling city streets.

Sirens blasting, car alarms blaring, and shouts of "Please help me!" echoed resoundingly throughout the chaotic business district. Cars were wrecked, fire hydrants were gushing, and people were running frantically every which way, like headless chickens.

Nathan felt as though his soul had been ripped out, as he realized that Jesus had just come for the Christians. In that powerful moment, he knew that Razz had been preaching the one true religion to him, all along. He recalled the numerous times Razz had reminded him that Jesus was the Way, the Truth, and the Life, and that he alone was the pathway to heaven.

As he wove in and out of wreckage *en route* to his home, he remembered Razz' last request, made during their luncheon: "Since I have no children of my own, please promise me that you will make sure Thomas Thompson and his family receive my full inheritance when I die or...get raptured."

Razz informed him during their luncheon that he volunteered him alongside George Thompson as co-executor of his trust, enabling this wish to be accomplished. "I know you can be trusted, and knew you wouldn't mind, so I had my attorney take care of the paperwork."

As recently as that very day, Razz had mentioned the rapture. How sorrowful Nathan felt that, throughout all of the years, Razz' preaching had fallen on his own deaf ears! *How hard could my heart be, that I wouldn't trust the advice of my high school buddy?* He thought. And now, it was too late; the rapture had passed him, and countless others, by.

Once the power came back on and Severs could get internet service again, the Mary apparitions had ended. The world was now asking serious questions about the whereabouts of the Christians, and whether the "Queen of Heaven"[22] would reappear to bring peace to Earth, as she pledged?

# Chapter 17
## After the Rapture, the World Gets Religious

The disappearance of Christians profoundly affected America and portions of Europe, whereas in Muslim-dominated countries like Turkey and Iran, life went on relatively unchanged. American forces stationed in the Middle East had become fractured by the heavenly departure of nearly a quarter of their troops and commanders. The rapture had rendered the US military extremely vulnerable against a potential face-off with Russia's coalition in the Holy Land.

Similarly, on the American home front, the country was rapidly deteriorating into a condition of chaos, prompting the US government to enact martial law nationwide. Anarchy plagued much of the country, as utility companies frantically attempted to restore services to municipalities and diminished National Guard forces mobilized in metropolitan areas.

It was the aftermath of Hurricane Katrina, multiplied by ten thousand, all over again. However, in this case, there was no US President to blame for slow response times, since President Bachlin and many members of Congress were numbered among the departed. Unbelievers were left behind to fend for themselves, and America's future remained uncertain.

Unistate Global Investments Corporation, Nathaniel Severs investment firm, was teetering on the verge of collapse, given all that had happened worldwide. It became blatantly clear to Nathan that the "god of money" had made his final exit from America when the Middle East chaos erupted. He recognized Razz had hit the nail on the head about investing in the new Israel, and decided to direct his company's focus on the emerging Jewish State.

Furthermore, Nathan began to grasp the significance of what was occurring worldwide, and spent several days in prayer and fasting, reviewing

Razz' website articles and attempting to understand what the post-rapture future held in store. Fortunately, his dear friend had compartmentalized his site, making it easy to find future event time charts, as well as learning how to become a "born again" believer.

Those were the two foremost topics on Nathan's mind: "What's next?" and "How can I be saved?" Razz even posted articles about how Mary apparitions could increase after the rapture and mislead the masses into the worldwide worship of Mary.

"Father please forgive me, for I have sinned," Nathan prayed, upon kneeling at the foot of his bed one fateful evening. "Please receive me into your kingdom family through the blood of Jesus Christ. I believe you sent him, your only begotten son, to die for my sins, and I am so grateful for that!"

Nathan pleaded for pardon from the Lord. He patterned his salvation prayer on Razz' website roadmap and began reciting the Lord's Prayer[23] often throughout the ensuing days. He became blessed by an unexplainable peace that comforted and guided him.

Assured that he had his spiritual house in order, Nathan proceeded to explain the rapture event to his unbelieving UGIC staff. Due to the magnitude of world circumstances and their utter admiration for their boss, most were receptive and some accepted Christ as their Savior.

Nathan informed his personnel that he intended to expand UGIC's reach into Israel. He put his right hand man, Harold Hirsch, in charge of American and Global operations and proceeded to secure his belongings for a permanent move to the emerging Jewish marketplace.

With Razz' burgeoning Israel-centered investment portfolio in hand, Nathaniel Severs boarded up his estate and flew to Israel to locate Thomas Thompson. He had previously attempted to contact George and Mimi Thompson, but after leaving about a dozen unanswered phone messages, he surmised they had both been caught up in the clouds alongside Razz and the rest of the born-again believers.

Leaving instructions for his staff to locate the possible whereabouts of the Thomas Thompson family in Israel, Nathaniel Severs began his pilgrimage to the Holy Land. Uncertain whether Thomas had been raptured, he still intended to uphold his promise to Razz, and hand over his portfolio to him or his family. He suspected Lisa and Jami Thompson were left behind, because Razz informed him during their final luncheon that the girls were Jewish unbelievers.

In addition, he realized from Razz' website that the Jews would eventually need a crop of Oskar Schindler[24] prototypes to comfort and protect them in the last days. According to Razz' article series entitled the "Jew in the Last Days," Nathan understood that the Antichrist would soon attempt a final Jewish genocidal campaign that would make the Hitler holocaust seem like a walk in the park.

"Righteous Gentiles," Razz had called them. He wrote that Jesus would pull them close by his right side, like a shepherd gathers his sheep into their sheepfold, and would say to them, "Come, you blessed of my Father, inherit the kingdom prepared for you from the foundation of the world."[25]

Severs promised the Lord that he would become a righteous Gentile like Schindler, even if it cost him his life in the process. He planned to start with Thomas Thompson's Jewish relatives and subsequently work incognito to set up an underground network through his extensive global connections, that would be ready when called upon to facilitate the exodus of Jews to safehouses throughout the world.

* * * * * *

About one-month passed between the rapture and the rap upon the front door of Thomas' residence in Beit Shemesh, Israel. Not knowing what to expect, Nathaniel Severs stood outside the Thompson family door, briefcase in hand. He had met Thomas and his family on several holiday occasions, but wondered if they would recognize him, since those visits occurred when Tyler was but a small child.

He had refrained from previously contacting the Thompsons to alert them of his visit, because he was preoccupied with battening down his own hatches in America, and getting settled into his new location in Israel. He wanted to have his boots on the ground prior to conveying Razz' good intentions and sizable portfolio to the Thompsons. And, most importantly, he felt it insensitive to break the news about Razz' departure over the phone.

Sizing up the tall, suited, gray-haired businessman standing at her doorstep, Lisa said in surprise, "Is that you, Mr. Severs?"

"It is," replied Nathan.

Escorting him inside to the living room, Lisa inquired, "What a pleasant surprise. What brings you across the pond to our humble abode?"

"You're uncle Razz named Thomas and all of you as the beneficiaries of his sizable trust, so I promised to personally present it to your family," he announced.

Immediately Lisa's eyes started to well up with tears, prompting Nate to ask, "What's wrong, dear?"

"Didn't Razz inform you that Thomas and our son Tyler were Christians?" she asked.

"Yes, Lisa, I figured as much from our last conversation," Nathan acknowledged. "When I was unable to reach Thomas' parents to get your family's whereabouts, I knew they, too, were gone."

"Tyler, Thomas, George and Mimi were all taken away!" Lisa sobbed, clutching at her heart. "Things were finally going well for us. The Arab war had ended. We were moved into our new home and the kids were attending local schools. I came home from work one evening and Thomas and Tyler were gone!"

Nathan recounted to Lisa, "I was eating lunch with your uncle Razz, watching the Marian apparition on the restaurant TV, when, poof! He disappeared without a trace!"

Startling Severs, Lisa retorted, "I'm going to be furious with Jesus if he's got anything to do with the disappearances of Thomas and Tyler!"

"What do you mean, 'furious with Jesus'?" Nate asked.

"I've heard speculations that Jesus came like a 'thief in the night' and took the Christians to heaven! When we realized they were missing, Jami and I scoured the countryside for days looking for the two of them. Every waking moment, we wait for them to show up at our doorstep. If it's true that he's to blame, how could a so-called loving Christian Messiah ruin so many families across the world?"

"So you understand what happened then?" Nathan asked cautiously.

"No, I don't want to understand! I want my family back!" Lisa said in anguish.

"Lisa, they were taken to heaven to be with the Lord and are in a better place," Nathan offered.

Breaking down, Lisa clutched Nathan and wept on his shoulder. "I'm a wreck. I'm angry, lonely, and my husband and son have been taken from me. Israel's on the brink of a major war again, and Jami and I feel so lost and alone!"

During that sensitive exchange, Jami made a surprise entrance into the room. "What's going on mother?" she asked in a disapproving tone. "Who is this man?"

Releasing herself from their innocent embrace, and trying to compose herself, Lisa introduced Nathan Severs as a long time friend and business consultant of Uncle Razz. "Uncle Razz asked Mr. Severs to assist us through these difficult times," explained Lisa.

"How is uncle Razz? Jami wondered. "I miss him."

Severs was silent, but Jami realized from his facial expression that there was no more Uncle Razz.

"Don't tell me that he's been stolen away, too!" Jami cried.

"That's why I moved to Israel, to help you and your mother cope with what's happened and about to happen," Nathan conveyed.

Bewildered, Jami sighed, "I don't understand."

Lisa wiped her teary face with her sleeve. "I'm a poor hostess," she sniffled. Taking Nate by the arm, she suggested, "Why don't we all take a seat in the family room. You can explain why you've come, and what you think is going to happen."

Seated comfortably together on the oversized sofa, Nate began, "For starters, I have Razz' Irrevocable Trust and Summary of Assets inside my briefcase. He left you both a sizable fortune worth, approximately 150 million shekels, to survive upon. He requested that I guarantee your family is well provided for, in the event of his death or…disappearance."

Lisa was amazed. "Are you suggesting he anticipated his own disappearance?"

"I am. In fact he predicted the possibility just before it occurred at our luncheon that fateful day," Nathan replied. "He said in the event I die or get raptured, I want you to…"

Interrupting his sentence in midstream, Lisa blurted out, "'Raptured'…did he really say that?"

"Those were his exact words," Nate confirmed.

Lisa shivered, rubbing her hands up and down her arms.

Nate leaned close. "What's so troubling?" he inquired.

"Raptured is the word circulating in Jerusalem, for what happened to the Christians. An upstart movement of Jews is creating a ruckus in the city, claiming the raptured Christians are evidence that Christ is the Messiah!"

"Are you referring to the 'Royal Jews from the Twelve Tribes of Israel'?" Jami asked.

"Yes, I believe so," Lisa answered. "How did you hear about them?"

"Recently, a lot of teachers at school have been warning their students to beware of false teachings that are spreading across the country," Jami reported. "Supposedly, they number 12,000 from each of the ancient twelve tribes, totaling 144,000, spread out in Israel and other parts of the world. They are teaching Jesus is the Messiah and that he is coming to judge humanity and set up a new kingdom, like the ancient garden of Eden. One of my teachers said their message is extremely dangerous, and is purposely intended to drive people away from Judaism."

"Their movement is already gaining steam in America and parts of Europe," Nathan said. "In fact, your Uncle Razz posted several articles about their end-time's ministry on his website."

"Uncle Razz predicted his own mysterious departure and the arrival of these 144,000 Yeshua-believing witnesses?" marveled Lisa. "How could he have known?"

"He gleaned it from years of Bible study," said Nathan. "I would show you where he writes about these subjects on his website, except his and many other Christian sites have been removed from the Internet over the last two weeks."

"Why's that?" Jami inquired.

"Obviously because the world leaders don't want people to connect the disappearance of millions of Christians with the rapture," Nathan deduced.

"Are you suggesting that some group of global elitists is pulling the strings now?" Lisa gasped.

"Yes, but it's far beyond that; according to Razz' writings it's outright demonic!" warned Nathan.

With a puzzled expression, Jami questioned, "'Demonic!' Doesn't that mean inspired by the devil?"

"That's how I would interpret it," Nate agreed. "Razz often used the word when he described prophecies or powerful events intended to deceive people. For instance, he told me just moments before he disappeared, that he believed the Marian apparition occurring right then was demonic."

"That Marian spectacle was amazing!" Lisa recalled. "It was big news here in Israel, at the time. All the newscasters reported on it, but since the Christian disappearances, or should I say 'rapture,' it has been hard to find any more information about the strange events at the Vatican that day."

"Mr. Severs," Jami said fearfully, "I have been worried about where my father and brother vanished to. Every day, I surf the web and watch the news for clues. I wonder if the Mary appearance had anything to do with the Christians leaving." She swallowed hard. "What do you think?" she asked.

Nate studied her pensive face. "It is very coincidental," he agreed. "But, others are saying the disappearances relate to some bizarre alien scenario. Purportedly, humanity is being prepared to meet its alien creators, who are going to help us evolve to a higher consciousness." His tone betrayed his lack of respect for such notions, and Jami didn't know whether to laugh or cry.

"This doesn't surprise me," she admitted.

"What do you mean?" Lisa wondered.

"People are obsessed with this extra-terrestrial stuff!" he replied. "UFOs, abductions…It's on TV and the internet all the time."

Lisa threw up her hands. "Alien abductions! I thought the rapture argument was over the top. But, this theory is absolutely crazy!" she exclaimed. "Official disclosure about alien creators; I thought the Christian rapture argument sounded like pie-in-the-sky, but this theory is absolutely crazy,"

"Call it what you will, Lisa, but it's certainly no laughing matter, and groups suggesting the Christians were raptured in fulfillment of Bible prophecy are being mocked and persecuted. These 144,000 you're hearing about are encountering an enormous resistance," Nathan reported.

Lisa shook her head wearily. "Nathan, you're welcome to stay with us until you get settled, but this is too much for us girls to process right now."

"No, Mother!" Jami cried out. "Don't ignore what's going on! I want to watch the DVD Grandpa George gave Dad," she pleaded.

"What DVD is that?" asked Nathan.

"It's about the 'last days.' Dad begged and pleaded with us time and again to watch it, but we ignored him," moaned Jami. "Please, Mother, go get it out of the safe so we can watch it with Mr. Severs. Maybe he can explain it to us."

Nathan saw Lisa's countenance change dramatically at the mention of the DVD. He sensed Lisa feared the content would serve as a haunting reminder of her rebellious attitude.

Nathan gently grasped her hand in both of his and said, "Lisa, I'm no expert on the Bible. If I were, I would probably be having dinner in heaven with Razz and the others, right now. But, I believe with all my heart that your husband would want you to watch this DVD, to prepare you for what's coming. And, I would be honored if you would allow me to watch it with you and your daughter."

Turning pale, Lisa managed, "Very well. There's no sense in postponing the inevitable. I'll go get the DVD."

# Chapter 18
## Left Behind, the Heavenly Love Letter

As Nate laid out Razz' portfolio on the dining room table, Jami and her mother made their way through the narrow hallway to the safe. Jami was relieved the time had come to unlock the family vault and retrieve her dad's DVD. Finally, she could fulfill her father's wish that she watch the video and discover its crucial content!

Upon opening the safe, Lisa was surprised to see the video staring back at her atop all the important family records. Only a few months prior she had fumbled through the safe and purposely buried it beneath the cash and papers. She recalled thinking, at the time, *Out of sight, out of mind; maybe if Thomas doesn't see it, he will quit pestering me to watch it.*

Noticing its new strategic location, she realized Thomas had since placed it on top of the stack. *Why?* She couldn't help wondering at the time. *Did he believe his disappearance was near at hand?*

Removing the DVD from its case, she was amazed to see a letter gracefully float out and land face down upon the nearby credenza. Startled to see the letter waist high and scarcely an arm's length away, Jami and she stood breathlessly still for a moment. They wondered which of them would muster up the courage to pick it up.

Finally, Jami asked, "Well aren't you going to read the letter, Mother? It's probably a message from Dad to us."

"Of course," Lisa said, frozen in place.

After another pause, Jami asked, "When?"

"When what?" Lisa said brokenly.

"When are you going to read Dad's letter," Jami queried.

Brushing aside a teardrop, Lisa pressed the letter to her lips and gently Eskimo-kissed it with her nose, receiving a refreshing whiff of her favorite masculine fragrance. Her husband had anointed his love letter with the exotic cologne she given him on their last anniversary.

Sitting side-by-side on the sofa inside their makeshift home office, Lisa opened the letter and said, "You're right; it's from your dad."

She began reading aloud, "'Beloved Lisa and Jami, you and Tyler are the best things that ever happened to me in my life!'" Lisa's heart gave a momentary flutter. Collecting her composure she continued, "'Oh, how I love you with all my being, and want you, Lisa and Jami, to receive this letter with open hearts and minds.'"

Already, the girls could scarcely see through the wellsprings of tears brimming in their eyes. These were Thomas' final thoughts and most cherished words to them. The letter's significance, in light of his permanent absence, pierced beyond the fabric of their hearts into the depths of their innermost beings.

"Read more," pleaded Jami, "I have to hear Dad's last words."

"'By now, you probably realize that Jesus came for Tyler and me. Please don't worry about us. We are in heaven, united with my parents, uncle Razz, and other loved ones who shared our faith. Oh, how desperately we wish you were both with all of us here!'"

Lisa gulped and went on: "'Although we're apart, please be assured that no distance could ever separate me from the love I have for the two of you. You are both so beautiful, loving, and caring! The Lord truly blessed me with the best his creation had to offer, by allowing me to play such an intimate role in your lives.'"

"'As I pen these final thoughts, I'm swept up in a sea of emotions. The possibility that I may never see either of you again, if you remain obstinate toward Jesus, is more than my heart can handle. I'm weeping right now, as our lives together are memorialized forever in my mind.'"

Her heart swelling, she continued, "'I recall seeing Jami take her first breath on the delivery table, as if it were yesterday. Never before had I experienced such a wonderful and powerful moment. I remember her first word, step, birthday, bicycle, braces, braids, and pesky puppy.'"

"'Jami, honey, words can't explain how proud you make me. You are all that a father could have ever hoped for. I pray from the bottom of my heart that you have many wonderful remaining days upon the earth; but, above all else I beg you to accept Jesus into your heart as Savior. Please don't delay!

Do it even now as you read this letter and watch this video. I promise you, that you will be with us in heaven, forever.'"

Lisa set the letter down to hug her daughter who was now weeping uncontrollably.

"What is this, Mother? What has happened? What are we waiting for with Jesus? I want to be with my dad and brother. I can't take it any longer!" she sobbed grievously.

The power of the moment was overwhelming, prompting Lisa to say, "I know, honey. It is all going to work out. We still have each other."

"Don't you get it, Mother?" Jami complained. "It's not going to all work out, without Jesus! Don't you understand what Dad's trying to tell us?"

"Certainly, I do," Lisa replied. "I, too, long to be with your father and brother."

Sponging Jami's tears with her sleeve, Lisa picked up the letter and read further.

"'Lisa, the beloved wife of my youth and best friend in life, forgive me for leaving you alone at such a critical time. Please don't be upset at God. Even though our departure may not make sense right now, this is all part of His perfect plan.'"

Clutching the letter next to her broken heart, she looked toward the high heavens and anguished, "How? How can this be a perfect plan?"

Turning her face aside in frustration, she continued to read her husband's final words.

"'Please, as hard as it is for you to consider, remember that I told you that someday Tyler and I could disappear into thin air, with millions of other Christians. If you experience this, please realize that Jesus has come for His church!

"'I plead with you, don't shut out the significance of what has happened, because it will lead you to Jesus, and ultimately here to be with us someday, soon. I wouldn't tell you this if I didn't believe it with every ounce of my heart; and you will also need to share this good news with your family someday.'"

Lisa tossed the letter aside and grabbed her chest gasping for breath. She was turning white and seemed to be hyperventilating.

"Mother, what are you doing? Are you okay?" asked Jami.

"I... I... I can't... I can't take it anymore," stuttered Lisa. "I have to st...st... stop, before I f...f...faint!"

Jami began feverishly fanning her mother's face with a magazine.

"I have done this to us!" Lisa wailed. "My stubbornness has caused us both to be left behind! Sobbing and crying out at the top of her lungs, she pleaded, "Forgive me, Jami! Forgive me, Jami!"

Jami had never seen her mother so distraught, nor held her so tight, as she did in that gripping moment.

Lisa's cries were so loud, Nathan rushed down the hallway to look in on them. "What's happened?" he bellowed anxiously.

"I have ruined my daughter's life! It's my fault she can't be with her father!" Lisa wept.

"Lisa, she can...you both can!" comforted Nathan. "I felt the same way when Razz left me alone that day in the restaurant. I felt so guilty and ashamed for not trusting what he tried to warn me about. Razz tried to teach me about Jesus whenever he could."

"I know. So did my beloved husband," Lisa wailed.

"Mother, you're not completely responsible. Dad and Tyler kept trying to warn me also. I made up my own mind not to trust what they were saying," Jami confessed.

"Look, girls," Nathan intervened, "I recently accepted Christ as my Savior, and if you ever want to see Thomas and Tyler again you need to do the same. But, salvation is much more than a ticket to Thomas; it is the promise of eternal peace, love, and happiness. It is God's gift to us through Jesus Christ. Receiving His gift is the most important thing we can ever do. Your beloved Thomas realized that his sin soon stood between him and his Savior, so he repented and committed his life to the Lord Jesus. So please... do as Thomas instructs, and don't put it off any longer!" he implored.

Regaining some composure, Lisa said, "Thank you, Nathan. What a wonderful friend you are! Undoubtedly, the Lord has sent you to Jami and me."

After Nathan assisted Lisa to her feet, Jami picked up the letter and the DVD and said, "Let's go into the TV room and calm ourselves down, so we can watch Dad's video together."

\* \* \* \* \* \*

After a refreshing beverage and snack, Jami gazed into her mother's eyes. "Are you ready for this?" she asked, holding up the DVD.

"I am," Lisa replied.

"Are you sure you want to view Linton's video before meeting Jesus?" Jami asked.

"Yes, your father told me that it would convince me that Jesus is the Jewish Messiah," Lisa hedged.

"As you wish, Mother." Jami consented.

As Jami inserted the disc into the DVD player, Nathan asked, "Is this a recent picture of Thomas and Tyler?"

He had innocently grabbed the video case from the coffee table and turned it over to the backside to preview Jim Linton's content comments. In the process, he noticed the picture inserted between the outside plastic and the disc sleeve.

Grabbing for the video case, Lisa gasped, "What picture? What did we miss?"

There it was, in plain view, a picture of the two most important men in her life taken just days before their disappearance. Caught up in the sweeping emotions of the love letter, she and Jami had failed to notice the picture inside the DVD housing.

"There was no picture here, before!" Lisa gasped. "I remember looking at both sides of the DVD last time I was in the safe, and this picture wasn't there!"

Leaning against her mother's shoulder to glimpse the photo, Jami surmised, "This is a new picture. It must have been taken right after Dad shaved off his mustache, about a month ago."

"You're absolutely right. I distinctly remember that he shaved the morning Tyler and he took their father-son field trip to the Jordan River," Lisa recalled. "I asked why he was shaving, and with foam all over his face, he said, 'It's time for a change. I had no mustache until after we were married and I want to remind you of our first dates.' Then, he immediately bear-hugged and Eskimo-kissed me, making sure to get half of his shaving cream all over my face," she laughed. Then, soberly, "His exact words that followed our messy embrace were, 'Remember, we used to bear-hug and Eskimo-kiss, back then? That stopped around the time I grew my mustache.'"

"They must have taken the picture during their trip to the Jordan. That's the actual river in the background," Jami commented.

"Wow, you're absolutely right!" Lisa confirmed.

Tears began flowing down the girls' cheeks when Nathan said, "This certainly can't be easy for the two of you."

"No it's not that," Lisa commented. "It's just that the way they took the picture is a message to us."

"How so?" Nathan inquired.

"See how they embrace with one arm, but their free arms are extended outward, motioning toward the camera, rather than resting naturally by their sides?" Lisa pointed out.

"Yes, that does seem staged," Nathan acknowledged.

Jami explained, "They are reaching out to mother and me for our daily group hug. Every waking morning Dad would huddle us together for a group hug and prayer before he allowed us to step into the new day. He started this family ritual when we moved here to Israel."

"It became my favorite part of every day," Lisa reflected. "I even learned not to cringe every time they closed the prayer in the name of Jesus."

Lisa handed the DVD case to Jami and requested she use her long manicured fingernails to navigate the photo out of the slipcover.

"Hurry! Let's see if the boys wrote anything on the back," she instructed.

Noticing abbreviated comments on the photo's reverse, Nathan politely asked, "Would you prefer I leave the room, while you read the boys' message?"

Holding his hand, Lisa answered, "No stay here with us, Nathan. You are part of our family, now."

She read the inscription:

"'Group hugs anyone? We are only a salvation prayer away from you right now. We are waiting for you on the shores of heaven with Jesus and our open arms, longing for our family group hug. Believe and be-living with us, now, before it's too late.'"

"'PLEASE, WE BEG OF YOU, DO WHAT OUR LETTER SAYS!!!'"

"'Love, your favorite two boys...T n T'"

Lisa clutched the photo fondly to her bosom, choking back tears.

"Well, that settles it for me, Mother," Jami announced. "I'm taking my leap of faith for Jesus, right now. Tyler told me that when he received Jesus into his life, that his sins were forgiven and that he was a new creation. I saw the change in him, from that point forward. He was more kind and loving toward me as his sister. Jesus changed him. I want to become a Christian and then watch the video, with the comfort of knowing my future is secure with Jesus Christ. I want to live a changed life like Tyler, from this point forward. This is what Dad and Tyler always prayed that we would do."

"Yes, Daughter, I agree 100%," Lisa consented. "I have a peace in my heart about this. It's time for me to stop hiding from the truth, and to receive God's gift of salvation through Jesus Christ. I can almost hear Grandpa George telegraphing me from the shores of heaven: 'Come off the cover girl, and jump on board the Jesus train.'"

Turning to Nathan, she said, "Mr. Severs, we would be honored to have you pray with us to receive Jesus Christ."

Upon hearing her invitation, Nathan could hardly contain his joy. God had honored his prayer to become a righteous Gentile, starting with the Thompson family. "Lord, great is thy faithfulness," he declared. As he wrapped his strong arms around the girls, he said, "Let the group hugs and prayers continue now and forever!"

Leading them in the sinner's prayer, which he had seen on Razz' website, Nate introduced Lisa and Jami, descendants of Abraham, Isaac, and Jacob, to their Lord and Savior, Jesus Christ!

\* \* \* \* \* \*

Tears drying on their faces, the three sat down to watch the DVD together. Preparing to insert the disc in the player, Jami switched on the TV. Suddenly, they we're shocked to hear a newscaster announce, "**We repeat, Russia has invaded Israel**."

With a gasp, Lisa cried out, "*OH MY LORD!*"

*To be continued*

# End Notes—The Novel

[1] Isaiah 46:9-10

[2] A sign of the Mahdi, the Islamic messiah, "It is clear that this man is the Mahdi who will ride the white horse and judge by the Qur'an (with justice) and with whom will be men with marks of prostration on their foreheads [Marks on their foreheads from bowing in prayer with their head to the ground five times daily]." http://www.answering-islam.org/Authors/JR/Future/ch04_the_mahdi.htm

[3] A real threat was issued from an Israeli foreign minister to Syrian President Assad which can be read over the Internet as of 9/7/11 at this link: http://www.maannews.net/eng/ViewDetails.aspx?ID=259178

[4] The tribulation is a term Christians often use to describe the last seven-year period on this present earth's time line. This period is characterized by the outpouring of divine judgments upon Christ-rejection humanity.

[5] Revelation 8:5, 11:13, 16:18 (earthquakes); Revelation 9:13-19, Zechariah 14:12 (wars); Revelation 8:8-11 (seas, streams, and rivers).

[6] *Isralestine, The Ancient Blueprint of the Future Middle East,* is authored by Bill Salus and is available through Amazon or Bill Salus' personal website.

[7] John Bolton told a group, including the author, that the world may have to accept the fact that Iran will become a nuclear nation. He suggested the only alternative to this would be if some nation attacked Iran's nuclear program. He believed that only Israel would consider this, at the time that he spoke. This was on 9/10/11 at a banquet held in his honor in Beverly Hills, CA.

[8] Genesis 14:17

[9] Dr. Arnold Fruchtenbaum of Ariel Ministries identifies this in section C-6 of chapter 20 in his *The Footsteps of the Messiah*. John McTernan's article of August 23, 2010, regarding this subject is linked at http://johnmcternansinsights.blogspot.com/2010/08/elamiran-in-latter-days.html (accessed 12/2/2010). Sean Osborne's article of September 15, 2010, regarding this subject is linked at http://eschatologytoday.blogspot.com/2010/09/jeremiah-49-will-coalition-of-nations-html (accessed 12/2/2010).

[10] 2 Chronicles 29:30 informs us that Asaph was a seer at the time of King David. The Hebrew word for seer is *chozen* and identified Asaph as a beholder of vision likened to a prophet.

[11] Psalm 83:4

[12] Psalm 83:12 indicates that motive of the Arab confederacy is to possess the Promised Land.

[13] Use of these tactical nukes against the West would leave a no-alibi forensic nuclear fingerprint pointing at Russia and directly incriminate "President Siroski," given the narrative above. The late (some say, and I believe, assassinated) General Alexander Lebed assured the US Congress and the American public via the CBS News program *60 Minutes*, in September 1997, that between 84 and 100 of Russia's 250 1kT tactical nukes were missing. These tactical nuclear weapons were under the direct control of the Spetnaz GRU, according to General Lebed. (Notes to author from Sean Osborne on 6/25/11)

[14] Obadiah 20a; emphasis added

[15] Ezekiel 37:10 speaks of an exceedingly great army.

[16] John 14:6

[17] Based on the Nathaniel Benchley juvenile novel, *The Off-Islanders*, the movie which tells the Cold War story of the comedic chaos which ensues when the Soviet submarine accidentally runs aground near a small New England island town. Information accessed on 2/22/11 from the internet at http://en.wikipedia.org/wiki/The_Russians_Are_Coming,_the_Russians_Are_Coming

[18] I Thessalonians 5:9-10, 1:10 and Revelation 3:10 (the church of Philadelphia is kept prophetically from the "hour or trial"). Many scholars associate this phrase with events in the tribulation period.

[19] There is some dispute as to whether Pharoah Ramese ruled at the time of the Hebrew exodus out of Egypt. Some scholars believe he ruled subsequently and advocate that Amenhotep II was Pharoah at the time. Informaiton was accessed 5/5/2011 from the internet at: http://wiki.answers.com/Q/Was_it_really_Ramses_II_who_was_the_Pharoah_when_the_Exodus_happened

[20] Isaiah 47:5 speaks of a Queen of Kingdoms, or Lady of Kingdoms in some Bible translations.

[21] Luke 1:47

[22] "Queen of Heaven" is another title used by Mary visionaries for the Lady of All Nations. More explanations are given in the commentary section.

[23] Matthew 6:9-15. After this manner therefore pray ye: Our Father, which art in heaven, Hallowed be thy name. Thy kingdom come, Thy will be done in earth, as it is in heaven. Give us this day our daily bread. And forgive us our debts, as we forgive our debtors. And lead us not into temptation, but deliver us from evil; For thine is the kingdom, and the power, and the glory, for ever. Amen. For it ye forgive men their trespasses, your heavenly Father will also forgive you: But if ye forgive not men their trespasses, neither will your Father forgive your trespasses. (KJV)

[24] Oskar Schindler (28 April 1908 - 9 October 1974) was an ethnic German industrialist born in Moravia. He is credited with saving almost 1,200 Jews during the Holocaust by employing them in his enamelware and ammunitions factories, which were located in what is now Poland and the Czech Republic, respectively. Internet accessed 5/11/2011 at http://en.wiki.org/wiki/Oskar_Schindler

[25] Matthew 25:34

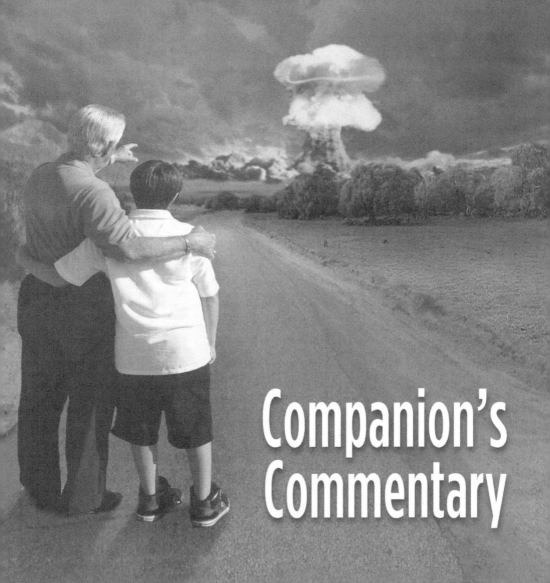

# Revelation Road

## Companion's Commentary

# Introduction
## to Companion's Commentary

Welcome to the commentary section of the book. As stated in the introduction, this segment provides "biblical believability" to the adventurous scenarios depicted in the novel. It's designed to enhance the fiction section, but has been conveniently positioned behind the novel for those who choose to read it independently. This dual format was selected to cater to both fiction and non-fiction audiences.

Maximum enjoyment and enrichment can be achieved by reading both the novel and the commentary together. This can be accomplished through either a chapter-by-chapter, or section-by-section, review of the book. Some might prefer to *breeze* through the novel before reading the supporting commentary. Others may seek to study the prophecies as they unfold one chapter at a time, by flipping back and forth between the novel and the corresponding commentary.

Throughout man's history a multitude of masterpiece manuscripts have been written. Many of them were based on true stories. Whereas those were inspired by people and events of the past, this story could easily become based upon the true accounts of someone in the future. This is entirely possible because, even though the characters are made up, their last days life struggles are realistic.

Certainly, we know from Revelation 19:10 that the testimony of Jesus Christ is the spirit of prophecy, and thus we confidently conclude that the Bible is based upon his story. However, as the powerful scenarios depicted inside *Revelation Road* unfold, they will undoubtedly serve to shape numerous additional autobiographies.

The question is, whose? Who will become the wiser for the reading? The world is about to undergo a significant period of unprecedented tribulation.

Who will discern the times and heed the signs? Who among us will rise to the occasion and shine forth in the last days like a beacon of light in a dark world?

Some of the episodes explored in this commentary section deal with predicted events that the author believes could happen in the *near* future. Based upon prophetic precedence, this means they could happen before, during, or shortly after you read this book, but probably sometime within your generation.

The author *is not* making this statement because he claims to be a prophet, but because the world stage is set for the near-fulfillment of the primary prophecies described inside *Revelation Road*. These include, but are not limited to, the dozens of prophecies spread throughout portions of Jeremiah 49; Isaiah 11, 17, 19, and 47; Psalm 83; Obadiah; Zephaniah 2; Zechariah 5 and 12; 1 Corinthians 15; 1 Thessalonians 4; Ezekiel 35-39; and Revelation 17.

That's right; the stage appears to be set up for dozens of prophecies to find near-fulfillment. If they don't occur in Grandpa George's lifetime, they will probably happen within his grandson Tyler's generation. This is a daunting possibility qualified by the fact that every weapon is fashioned, technology developed, empire-revived, and confederate-alliance-formed, enabling all end-time's prophecies to be fulfilled.

Prophecies were issued through the ancient Hebrew prophets in both *near* and *far* formats. The near prophecies had to be fulfilled during the prophet's lifetime. Upon fulfillment of a near prophecy, the person earned the right to be identified as a true prophet, verses a false prophet.[1] False prophets presented misleading information that often led to idol worship or loss of life. As such, they were punished by death.[2]

The fulfillment of a near prophecy authenticated the prophet, and accredited all of his or her[3] far prophecies. The logic was, if the prophecy occurred exactly as foretold during the person's lifetime, then all the prophet's future predictions could also be counted on to be fulfilled exactly.

Although the prophecies in the *Companion's Commentary* were *far off* prophecies when written centuries ago, they are rapidly approaching their *near future* fulfillment. Only those once *far,* but now *near,* prophecies that the author believes are soon forth-coming, are identified in this book.

*Revelation Road* is only the first book in a series. Each subsequent book picks up where the previous left off. Ultimately, the series intends to identify chronologically the prophecies scheduled to occur between now and the second coming of Jesus Christ.

*Note:* Only when a prophecy becomes history, can its exact details be known. Anticipating the coming of a prophecy by understanding its biblical description, and discerning its stage setting signs, is like looking through a glass; no matter how clear the glass, perfect vision is impossible. Describing a coming prophecy or ordering it chronologically, is an imperfect science. Therefore, the ordering of prophetic events outlined in *Revelation Road*, is the educated estimate of the author, and cannot be chronologically guaranteed!

COMMENTARY

# Chapter 1—
## Iran Prepares for the Apocalypse!

*Topics covered:* Can the Future of the Middle East be Known?; Overview of Psalm 83

The world cries "heaven forbid," but does heaven *foreknow* if a Middle East war between the Arabs and Jews is coming? Ancient texts from the Hebrew prophets seem to confirm what humanity has recently begun to realize: that over six decades of Mideast violence, pro-Palestinian UN resolutions, and failed "land-for-peace" deals have left a final Arab-Israeli war as the only remaining option.

It appears the Bible predicted that the longstanding Arab hatred of the Jews would perpetuate throughout time, and climax into a concluding "Mother of all Mideast Wars!" The fifty-million dollar questions are: *when*, and *who wins*?

*Revelation Road* attempts to answer these questions by combing through the pertinent Hebrew scripts to uncover the predicted outcome. Much of the groundwork for *Revelation Road* was accomplished through the research poured into my first book, *Isralestine, The Ancient Blueprints of the Future Middle East.*[4] *Isralestine* takes an exhaustive look at the future Mideast wars of Psalm 83, Ezekiel 38, and Armageddon that were predicted in the Bible, and as such, is an important reference resource for this book.

# Can the Future of the Middle East be Known?

Can the outcome of the Arab-Israeli conflict be known in advance? According to the prophet Isaiah, the answer is yes.

> Remember the former things of old, for I am God, and there is no other; I am God, and there is none like Me, *declaring the end from the beginning, And from ancient times things that are not yet done*, saying, 'My counsel shall stand, and I will do all My pleasure,' (Isaiah 46:9-10; emphasis added).

Isaiah declares that only the Lord can foretell the future. It was the calling of the Hebrew prophets, like Isaiah, Jeremiah, Ezekiel, and more to inform of future events, and in so doing showcase the supreme sovereignty of their God. *Revelation Road* identifies a plethora of prophecies regarded with the future of today's Arab-Israeli conflict, that when aligned together seems to present a clearer picture of its foreseen conclusion.

What the world has witnessed in the Middle East over the past six decades appears to have been anticipated thousands of years in advance. Due to the spiritual significance of the Arab-Israeli struggle, it can be expected that the prophets had plenty of prophetic information to pen for our understandings about today's complex Middle East scenario.

Several Scriptures stated that the Jews would re-gather from the nations into their historic homeland of Israel, and be greeted by unabated Arab aggression. According to the ancient seer named Asaph, an Arab confederacy will someday form to destroy Israel and possess their Promised Land.

> "They [the Arabs] have taken crafty counsel against Your [Jehovah] people [the Jews], And consulted together against Your sheltered ones. They have said, "Come, and let us cut them [the Jewish state] off from being a nation, That the name of Israel may be remembered no more. For they have consulted together with one consent; They form a confederacy against You: . . ." "Who said, "Let us take for ourselves The pastures of God for a possession." (Psalm 83:3-5, 12).

The novel, the *Companion's Commentary*, and associated appendices included in *Revelation Road* are intended to impart new insights, and invaluable information, so that the reader can better prepare for prophesied Middle East and world events.

This first chapter of the novel thrusts the reader into a high level war meeting hosted by the Iranian president, Muktada Zakiri, in his host city of Tehran. Iran and its proxies Syria, Hezbollah, and Hamas strategize to destroy Israel, for their own diverse interests. Iran is interested in creating an apocalyptic war against Israel in order to hasten the return of the Islamic Shiite Messiah, Muhammad al-Mahdi. Hamas wants Israel eradicated in order to facilitate the creation of a Palestinian State. Syria and Hezbollah have their own self-interests, as well.

Although the novel depicts a fictitious scenario, it closely resembles the geo-political threats on the ground in the Middle East today. Syria, Hezbollah, and Hamas are commonly referred to as Iran's proxies in the media. Reportedly, in 2009 the four of them formed war-pacts together.[5] Moreover, Israel conducts "Turning Point" civilian defense drills on a regular basis. These drills are primarily intended to prepare Israelis for a multi-front attack from Iran, Syria, Hezbollah, and Hamas. Due to dire concern that such a multi-front attack may be imminent, the Israeli government passed out millions of gas masks to its citizens in 2010.[6]

The Arab Spring of 2011 has increasingly destabilized an already explosive situation in the region. Many Mideast pundits are concerned the Arab protests and revolts that led to shifts in the political landscapes of several predominately Muslim countries, will encourage the spread of pro-Palestinianism, anti-Semitism, and governance by Islamic Sharia law. As such, many familiar with the Psalm 83 war are wondering if the event is about to find final fulfillment.

## Overview of Psalm 83

Psalm 83 describes a climactic concluding Arab-Israeli war that was prophesied by Asaph the seer about three thousand years ago.[7] The actual text of the Psalm has been included for your reading convenience in the commentary's chapter called *Israel Comes Under Multi-front Attack!*

It is my firm assessment that the Psalm is more than an imprecatory prayer concerned with Israel's ancient enemies; I believe it also predicts a Middle East war that is now imminent. Geo-political events involving the Arab Spring of 2011, the Palestinian quest for statehood, and several decades of failed diplomatic efforts to swap Israeli land for Arab peace, has primed the populations listed in Psalm 83:6-8 to confederate against the Jewish state in direct fulfillment of this prophecy.

Since Psalm 83 is commented upon throughout several chapters and appendices within *Revelation Road*, only a brief overview is provided in this section of commentary.

The Psalm identifies an inner-circle of Arab states that share common borders with modern-day Israel. This is in stark contrast to an outer-ring of nations listed in a separate coalition described in Ezekiel 38. Although some eschatologists attempt to merge the two prophetic episodes together, these appear to be two differing Middle East wars.

The Ezekiel 38 war, commonly referred to as the *Magog Invasion of Israel,* is exposited upon in later sections of this commentary. If the reader is not familiar with the Ezekiel invasion, an overview of the event is available in the commentary of the chapter called *The Russian – Iranian Nuclear Connection.* The populations involved in both Psalm 83, and Ezekiel 38 are displayed in the images section (appendix 26) of *Revelation Road.* Interestingly, Iran is involved in Ezekiel 38, but not Psalm 83. The possible reasons for this are discussed in this commentary in the chapter called *Israel Attacks Iranian Nuclear Sites.*

The Arab confederates of Psalm 83, which seem to include the Palestinians, Hamas, Hezbollah, Syrians, Jordanians, Egyptians, Saudis, Iraqis and more, form a collective strategic war plan to destroy Israel. Their ultimate goal is to eradicate the Jewish state and confiscate all the land it presently possesses. This would include the land captured by Israel in the Six-day war of June, 1967.

Presently, most of the international community and the Arabs are pressuring the Israelis to forfeit much of this land, in order to form an independent Palestinian state. Psalm 83 suggests the Arabs will someday abandon diplomatic efforts and opt for war instead. This will prove problematic for the Arabs because the land in question belongs to the Israeli descendants of Abraham, Isaac, and Jacob, rather than the Arabs.

> On the same day the LORD made a covenant with Abram, saying: "To your [Israeli] descendants I have given *this land*, from the river of Egypt to the great river, the River Euphrates— . . ." (Genesis 15:18; emphasis added).

Moreover;

> And God said to him, [Abraham's grandson Jacob] "Your name *is* Jacob; your name shall not be called Jacob anymore, but Israel shall be your name." So He called his name Israel. Also God said to him: "I *am* God Almighty. Be fruitful and multiply; a nation and a company of nations shall proceed from you, and kings shall come from your body. The land which I gave Abraham [in Genesis 15:18] and Isaac I give to you; and to your descendants after you I give this land." (Genesis 35:10-12).

Psalm 83 describes a blatant Arab attempt to confiscate this Promised Land. *Revelation Road* provides Scriptural support attesting to the fact that the final Arab-Israeli war will be won by the Jews. The guiding principle to this understanding is found in Jeremiah 31.

> Thus says the LORD, Who gives the sun for a light by day, The ordinances of the moon and the stars for a light by night, Who disturbs the sea, And its waves roar (The LORD of hosts is His name): "If those ordinances depart From before Me," says the LORD, "Then the seed of Israel shall also cease From being a nation before Me forever." Thus says the LORD: "If heaven above can be measured, And the foundations of the earth searched out beneath, I will also cast off all the seed of Israel For all that they have done," says the LORD. (Jeremiah 31:35-37)

Psalm 83:3-5, 12 informs that the Arabs will confederate for the explicit purposes of destroying Israel and capturing their Promised Land once and for all, something Jeremiah 31:35-37 says is utterly impossible. Unless the Arabs can alter the ordinances governing the universe, they will not succeed.

Currently, the Jewish people are repopulating this land in fulfillment of several Bible prophecies. The Jews are returning into the land after centuries of dispersion into the Gentile nations of the world. According to these prophecies this process appears to be irreversible. This appears to be the reason that the Jewish state is expanding, rather than contracting. This reality is attested to by the fact that the Arab-Israeli wars of 1948, 1967, and 1973 strengthened, rather than weakened the resolve of the Israelis. The Jews continue to make aliyah to Israel and nothing the Arabs have done to date has been able to prevent their return.

Thus, in a nutshell, Psalm 83 predicts that Israel's ancient Arab enemies, which happen to be Israel's most observable Arab foes today, will at some point in the future, *confederate, form a war strategy to destroy the Jews and their state, eradicate the name of Israel forever, and confiscate the Promised Land.*

According to connecting prophecies in Obadiah v. 18, Ezekiel 25:14, 37:10, Jeremiah 49:1-6, and elsewhere, the Israel Defense Forces (IDF) prevail in the Psalm 83 war. The war, its conclusion, and imposing aftermath affects are discussed throughout various portions of this book. As you read, understand, and apply these prophetic passages to Psalm 83, it is important to recognize that the Arabs are attempting to curse the Jews. As such, they must be cursed according to the divine foreign policy issued in Genesis 12:1-3.

COMMENTARY

"Now the LORD had said to Abram: 'Get out of your country, From your family And from your father's house, To a land that I will show you. I will make you a great nation; I will bless you And make your name great; And you shall be a blessing. I will bless those who bless you, *And I will curse him who curses you*; And in you all the families of the earth shall be blessed.'" (emphasis added)

Herein lies all Gentile foreign policy: those who bless Abraham will likewise be blessed, but those cursing him, will be cursed! It is commonly understood contextually, that these verses extrapolate from Abraham to his Hebrew descendants through the genealogies of Isaac, Jacob, and Jacob's twelve sons, who formed the twelve tribes of Israel. Hence, the Genesis 12:3 principle applies to the Jewish descendants of these twelve tribes today. Moreover, there is no valid reason to conclude that this Gentile foreign policy isn't still applicable.

At the time the Genesis 12:3 foreign policy was issued, the world was populated with people. Out from the masses, one was divinely called, and that was Abraham. In essence he became the first Hebrew, and many translate the word *Hebrew* to mean *to pass over*.[8] Hence, they regard it to mean *the man who passed over*. Abraham, which in the Hebrew language means, "father of multitudes," passed over from ungodly men, to become a man of God. The common understanding from that point forward was that humanity was comprised of Abraham and his Hebrew descendants, and everybody else called Gentiles.

The reason this is important to note is to confirm that the God of the Bible is a just God, with age-old Gentile foreign policy in place. He is not a God that renders divine judgment upon the undeserved. The Psalm 83 Arabs, by their own choice, ignore the foundational understandings contained in Jeremiah 31:35-37, and fundamental precepts in Genesis 12:3. They seek to destroy the Jews, which means they will extract lethal judgment upon themselves. Rather than pity their unenviable plight, it is better to warn them beforehand.

There are naysayers who don't believe Psalm 83 is a *bona fide* Bible prophecy. Some believe it is merely a prayer of lament. Others don't separate it out as a distinct Middle East war, apart from Ezekiel 38 or Armageddon. Many of the objections to my hypothesis that Psalm 83 is a distinct and imminent war have been encountered since the summer 2008 release of *Isralestine,* and are addressed inside portions of the commentary and appendixes of this book.

If one considers Psalm 83 to be a prayer and not a prophecy, then it is doubtful that they will raise the red flags of warning to the Arabs beforehand.

Or, if someone doesn't believe the Psalm war is imminent, they may lack a sense of urgency to inform the Arabs to form an immediate exit strategy into a safe destination. As for me, I intend to send a clear message in *Revelation Road*, that the Arabs need to watch out, because it appears the war of Psalm 83 is about to occur and they are in imminent danger.

One can't be dogmatic about such matters, especially when there are some eschatologists that argue against Psalm 83 being a prophecy. But, due to the severity of the potential Arab-Israeli war, it is better to err on the side of safety, than to risk taking the chance that many of us are mistaken about the Psalm's prophetic implications.

At the time *Revelation Road* was being composed, the Arab Spring of 2011 was commencing. Some believe the Arab protests and revolts have supernatural origins, others think they are the result of a global conspiracy, while liberal pundits suggest it's merely a youth bulge responding to the freedoms they are learning about over the Internet social networks like Facebook, YouTube, and Twitter.

Of all these alternatives, the one that appears to be most biblically supported is that of the supernatural origins. We can conclude this from a declaration made by Daniel the prophet.

> Daniel answered and said: "Blessed be the name of God forever and ever, For wisdom and might are His. And *He changes the times and the seasons; He removes kings and raises up kings*; He gives wisdom to the wise And knowledge to those who have understanding." (Daniel 2:20-21; emphasis added).

One thing for certain about the Arab Spring of 2011: the seasons of change appear to have arrived in the Middle East. Moreover, Arab leaders like Zine al-Abedine Ben Ali of Tunisia, Hosni Mubarak of Egypt, Muammar Gaddafi of Libya, and Ali Abdullah Saleh of Yemen have been removed, making way for others to be raised up. Daniel attributes these types of sovereign events to the supernatural doings of the Lord. It is my sincere prayer that *Revelation Road* will be inspired supernaturally to impart *wisdom to the wise* and *knowledge to those who have understanding*.

*Please read the next novel chapter now.*

# Chapter 2—
## Troublesome Times on Humanity's Horizon

*Topics covered:* Basic Introduction to the Tribulation and the Rapture; The Pre-Tribulation Prophecies; The Gap Hypothesis

## Basic Introduction to the Tribulation and the Rapture

This chapter in the novel draws attention to what many Christians commonly call the "tribulation-period," nicknamed the *trib-period* for future commentary purposes. Pastor Jim Linton announces "troublesome times" are coming, alluding to the trib-period. He follows with a flurry of significant indicators signaling this perilous period rapidly approaches. In large part, *Revelation Road* is a compilation of many of these pre-trib, tell-tale warning signs.

For those readers unfamiliar with the trib-period; in a nutshell, it is generally believed to last seven years, conclude this present earth's timeline, and be characterized by apocalyptic judgments that decimate most of the planet. Due to the severity of these judgments, a majority of human and other life forms are destroyed in the process.

These judgments include fiery-like hailstones that burn up one-third of the world's grass and trees in Revelation 8:7; a falling star or comet that penetrates into the earth's atmosphere and contaminates one-third of the earth's rivers in

Revelation 8:10-11; also a locust invasion that torments men for five months and destroys much of the planet's vegetation in Revelation 9:3-6. All told there are twenty-one judgments contained in the book of Revelation. These include seven seal, seven trumpet, and seven bowl judgments.

In essence, it is the period reserved for divine judgments upon a sinful, Christ-rejecting world. *Revelation Road* concerns itself with some of the world-changing prophecies leading up to the trib-period, and reserves the majority of trib-period prophecies for a later sequel in this book series.

Importantly, Linton's message concludes by introducing a way to escape the trib-period through Jesus Christ. In so doing, he alludes to another powerful prophetic event called the "rapture." The rapture is explained in greater detail in the commentary, in the chapters called *The Christian Exodus into the Clouds*, and *After the Rapture, the World Gets Religious*. However, a brief overview is provided below, because it's germane to this chapter's commentary.

The rapture is a miraculous event characterized by the departure of millions of Christians worldwide. In what amounts to the greatest disappearing act of all time, true Christian believers are whisked away to spectacular places previously prepared for them in heaven.[9] This includes true believers living at the time, as well as those believers previously deceased.[10]

At an unspecified time, Jesus Christ removes them all instantly, leaving the preponderance of those left behind without rhyme or reason as to why they vanished, or where they relocated. For those familiar with the bestselling *Left Behind* book series, authored by Tim LaHaye and Jerry Jenkins, the rapture is the central theme of their first book.

To the skeptic, the event undoubtedly ranks atop the "Most Ridiculous" lists of prophecies in the New Testament. However, for the Christian it rates among faith's greatest rewards. Because the biblical description of the event in 1 Corinthians 15:51-54, and 1 Thessalonians 4:15-18 is seemingly so bizarre, young Tyler compares it to a *Star Wars* movie when he first learns about it in chapter two.

# The Pre-Tribulation Prophecies

*Revelation Road* evidences that important Bible prophecies occur before the trib-period commences. There are four primary reasons this statement can be supported. These reasons are listed and briefly explained below;

- Seven years of trib-period are not enough time to fulfill all remaining prophecy.

COMMENTARY

- There is an unspecified time-gap existing between the rapture and trib-period.

- Pre-trib prophecies have been fulfilled, setting precedent that more will follow.

- There are non-conforming prophecies that don't fit inside the trib-period.

For years the predominant teaching among prophecy scholars was that the rapture would occur and the trib-period would promptly follow. In essence the teaching model was that the rapture was the trigger-point of the tribulation. For this reason many end-time's experts, called "eschatologists,"[11] believed all remaining Bible prophecies had to find fulfillment during the trib-period.

Consequently, this caused the relatively short trib-period, spanning only seven years, to become the catch-all closet of all remaining unfulfilled Bible prophecy. Since some pending predictions could require a considerable amount of time, rather than merely a few years to develop and come true, this teaching becomes prohibitive.

As an example, although events depicted inside the *Revelation Road* story line play out relatively quickly, in reality the prophetic episodes described could be separated by years, rather than weeks or months. As the commentary section will continue to point out, there are good reasons to believe the majority of the *Revelation Road* prophecies discussed are pre-tribulation events.

*Seven years of a trib-period are not enough time to fulfill all remaining prophecy.* Some forthcoming Bible prophecies have definite timeframes associated with them; whereas, most do not. Therefore, eschatologists are wise to allot reasonable interludes of time between events. For instance, the Bible foretells the coming of a world religion that flourishes for a time, but then is destroyed and replaced by the Antichrist's religious system. Additionally, the Bible predicts the formation of a global order that segues into ten separate kingdoms in Daniel 7:23-24.

It seems illogical to restrict the rise and fall of such major international events to the confines of a seven-year time span. And, these are just four prophetic events, leaving dozens more of equal or greater importance remaining. Certainly, many events occur simultaneously, but others require the fulfillment of a prior event from which to build upon.

Thus, seven years of tribulation seemingly provides insufficient time for some prophecies to find their final and complete fulfillment.

*There is an unspecified time-gap existing between the rapture and trib-period.* Lately, the realization has set in among many teachers and students of prophecy that the Bible teaches the trib-period begins by the confirmation of a false covenant confirmed by the Antichrist with the nation of Israel, rather than the rapture. Isaiah 28:15,18 and Daniel 9:27 are the Scriptures providing details regarding this covenant. Because of Daniel's prophecy, the trib-period is more appropriately called Daniel's Seventieth Week.[12]

According to Isaiah's and Daniel's descriptions, this cunningly devised covenant is a seven-year peace-pact intended to lure Israel into a false sense of security. Those critical seven years result in a period of unprecedented worldwide woes. Armageddon, the mark of the Beast, and Mystery Babylon are just a few of the popularized biblical terms defining this period.

Somehow the content and confirmation of the Antichrist's false covenant becomes the straw that breaks the camel's back, provoking the Lord to finally judge unrighteous mankind. For this reason the *true content* of the *false covenant* must be appropriately understood and is among the challenges this book series undertakes.

Some teach the treaty will be what brings about a temporary Mideast peace between the Arabs and / or Palestinians and the Jews. It is believed to be temporary, because the Antichrist breaks the treaty at the midpoint of the seven-year period. However, this teaching is primarily driven by geopolitical Middle East events, rather than sound biblical exegesis. Nowhere in Scripture does it appear to state that the false covenant alludes to a peace that is crafted between Arabs and / or Palestinians and the Jews.

According to Bible prophecy, Arab-Israeli peace appears to be achieved militarily, rather than diplomatically. The evidence supporting the military resolution is contained inside my book *Isralestine, The Ancient Blueprints of the Future Middle East*, and will be expounded upon further inside various segments of this book.

## The Gap Hypothesis

Since the reality has set in that the trib-period commences with the confirmation of the false covenant, rather than the rapture, some scholars wonder about this unspecified time-gap between the two major events. For instance, Tim LaHaye, the co-author of the aforementioned *Left Behind* series, and I discussed this possible gap interval in December, 2009, at the Pre-Trib Rapture Research Center conference in Dallas. In a postscript to our conversation, Tim emailed me this statement in the early part of 2011, representing his current thoughts on the matter:

COMMENTARY

> Pre-Trib. scholars are not agreed on whether the rapture starts the
> Tribulation (Nothing in scripture says it does). Daniel 9:27 says the
> Antichrist will confirm a contract with Israel for one week (or seven
> years), which leads me to believe that starts the Tribulation. There is
> a high possibility that the Rapture could take place prior, but only God
> knows how long.

This gap interval has many pondering its post-rapture, pre-trib duration.
Is it a day, month, year, decade, or possibly longer? Furthermore, which Bible
prophecies find fulfillment during the gap? For instance, will the Antichrist
emerge on the world scene during the gap period? Obviously his entrance into
the Middle East Theater must precede the tribulation period, since the treaty
he confirms with Israel is its likely start point. Simply put: until the Antichrist
surfaces, he can't confirm a treaty with Israel and therefore, the trib-period
can't commence.

Additionally, 2 Thessalonians 2:5-9 suggests this "lawless" leader will be
revealed "in his own time." However, until then, divinely appointed restraint
hinders his rise to power. Some scholars believe the removal of restraint
coincides with the rapture. If they are correct, this positions the emergence of
the Antichrist, the first horseman of the apocalypse in Revelation 6:1, inside the
post-rapture / pre-trib interval. This suggests at least one of the four horsemen
of the apocalypse is a "gapper."[13] If so, does he ride solo into this period or are
there other apocalyptic horsemen, characters, or prophetic events that partner
up with him inside the gap?

Unfortunately the Antichrist, also referred to as the seed of Satan,[14] does
not appear to go it alone in the gap. Subsequent commentaries in this book
series identify his cohorts, their battlefield schemes, and the human casualties
left behind in their wake. For reasons explained in book two of this series, I
believe all four horsemen of the apocalypse in Revelation 6:1-11 surface inside
the post-rapture / pre-trib gap period.

Moreover, during the gap period the world witnesses geopolitical
upheavals, a resurgence of paganism, deceptive signs, mystical wonders,
cosmic disturbances, increased natural disasters, a greater Israel, and a
Christian revival amongst a multitude of those left behind after the rapture.
Tragically, for many this becomes a period plagued by Christian martyrdom.

*Pre-trib prophecies have been fulfilled setting precedent that more will
follow.* As stated above, most of *Revelation Road* is concerned with prophecies
the author believes could find their fulfillment prior to the commencement of

the trib-period. Several prophecies have been fulfilled during the church age that set precedents which other pre-trib prophecies might follow. For instance:

- The destruction of the second Jewish Temple in 70 AD by the Romans fulfilled Matthew 24:1-2 and Daniel 9:26.

- The worldwide dispersion of the Jews also occurred in 70 AD, in fulfillment of Ezekiel 20:23 and elsewhere.

- World War I and World War II seem to have fulfilled Christ's prediction in Matthew 24:7 that predicted "nation will rise against nation."

- The Nazi Holocaust appears to be what Ezekiel's dry bone vision in Ezekiel 37:1-11 foretells. Some, like eschatologist David Dolan, also believe the Holocaust was predicted in Psalm 102.[15]

- The re-gathering of the Jews into the reestablished nation of Israel occurred in 1948, in fulfillment Ezekiel 36:24, Isaiah 11:11, Ezekiel 37:12 and elsewhere.

These are just a few of the apparent fulfilled pre-trib prophecies. Additionally, appendix one, called *The Final Century—Christian Survival versus Pagan Revival,* points out that the entire church age exists in fulfillment of pre-trib Bible prophecy, according to the prophetic applications within the seven letters to the seven churches of Revelation chapters two and three.

*There are non-conforming prophecies that don't fit inside the trib-period.* When one understands the chronology of events predicted to occur during the trib-period, it becomes relatively clear that certain other remaining prophecies don't seem to fit well inside the trib-period. For instance, the first half of the trib-period is characterized by a feeling of peace and security inside Israel. Thus, any prophecies depicting the Israel Defense Forces (IDF) fighting their Arab enemies, especially in Psalm 83, *don't fit* the descriptions of false Mideast peace occurring during this first half. (Three and one-half years.)

Conversely, the second three and one-half years, often referred to as the "great tribulation," find Israel fleeing from the genocidal campaign of the Antichrist. Thus, the IDF won't likely be fending off their Arab foes during this period either. Therefore, prophecies relating to the IDF fighting the Arabs like in Ezekiel 25:14 and Obadiah v. 18 seem to occur prior to the trib-period. It would be improbable that the Arabs and Jews will fight after the trib-period concludes, because the messianic kingdom is established shortly thereafter. The kingdom period is characterized by peace rather than war.

By now some of you may be wondering if Tyler successfully reeled-in his fish and grandpa ever answered his tough tribulation question. Inquisitive Tyler has only begun to scratch the surface when it comes to understanding pertinent prophetic matters. Throughout this book he asks Grandpa George many more pertinent questions about the Bible prophecies his younger generation might face. This necessitates grand-fatherly, rather than "grand–scholarly" responses. Follow this family duo along their treacherous trail as this end-time's tale unfolds. New prophetic insights and additional characters pop up along the way.

*Please read the next novel chapter now.*

COMMENTARY

# Chapter 3—
## Tribulation Generation

*Topics covered*: End-Time's Christian Survival; End-Time's Christian Denial; The Final Generation has been Pre-appointed; Faith's Final Frontier; The Two Types of Last Days Christians; Humanity's Last Day's Heart Condition

While Poppy and Tyler head homeward, let's analyze some of their important conversational points. One of Tyler's understandable questions is, "Poppy, why does this bad (tribulation) stuff have to happen while I'm growing up?"

If you followed their conversation closely up till now, you understand he is essentially asking his grandfather, "Why has my generation apparently been singled-out to be the last generation to exist on this earth?" This question presupposes that there will be a final generation that experiences the apocalyptic judgments, which bring this earth to its end.

A plethora of Bible passages predict the passing away of this earth, and with it a concluding generation. We can't be certain if it's pre-teen Tyler's generation, but the signs of the times, coupled with several key prophecies, strongly suggest it is!

2 Peter 3:10-13 tells us this earth will be replaced by a new one filled with righteousness. Matthew 24:13-14 teaches that this occurs after the gospel is preached throughout the world as a witness to all nations. Matthew 24:21 predicts that dangerous end-time events will necessitate the shortening of Earth's existence, in order to prevent human extinction. Revelation 12:12

COMPANION'S COMMENTARY

141

informs us that even Satan recognizes when this end-period nears, and the last generation exists.

Rather than attempting to identify all the prophetic passages predicting this wicked world will end, let's postulate that it will, and possibly quite soon! This daunting prospect has caused some Christians to kick into a *survival* mode. They stockpile gold, guns, gas, and goods in order to survive. However, many others choose the path of *denial*. In so doing, they tend to shun Bible prophecy, and search out seeker-friendly pulpits willing to tickle their ears with positive messages favoring an inoffensive social gospel.

These competing Christian mentalities of *survival* verses *denial* transmit mixed messages to unbelievers, many of whom actually worry the world is about to implode. Increased natural disasters, Middle East rumors of war, mortgage meltdowns, worsening world economies, and more, have many unbelievers justifiably wondering if things will worsen into an apocalypse of epic biblical proportion.

Below is a brief comparison between end-time's Christian *survival* verses Christian *denial*. For additional reading relative to end-time's Christianity, read the appendix called *The Final Century, Christian Survival verses Pagan Revival*.

In chapter two, Poppy tells Tyler that Christians are to *escape*, rather than *endure*, the trib-period. He cites the rapture as the means of their departure. The Scripturally supported arguments for a pre-trib rapture are present in the commentary chapter called *The Christian Exodus into the Clouds*, and in the appendix called *Old Testament Allusions to the Rapture*. However, the specific timing of the rapture is unknown, and it is not the only potential pre-trib event to be watching for. Other prophetic events could precede the rapture.

## End-Time's Christian Survival

Since these powerful events are forthcoming, it's prudent to prepare for them in advance. There is biblical precedent for prophetic preparedness. It's smart to fill the storehouses with food in advance of a pending famine—that's what Joseph did in the Genesis 41 historic account. Joseph possessed invaluable insights into the future, and took the necessary measures to provide for the Egyptians. *In the process, his Hebrew posterity was also preserved.* Joseph's actions were blessed, because they glorified God, and were in alignment with the Lord's plan for that time.

If a Christian exemplifies the lessons of Joseph by preparing for prophetic events, his or her actions, if rightly motivated and appropriately understood, can serve as a testimony to an unbelieving spectator. The goal is to temper the survival efforts with a clear demonstration of whole-hearted faith in Christ, and a wholesome understanding of Bible prophecy.

The believer's behavior should resemble that of Noah's.[16] While his ark was being constructed, he used the opportunity to preach to those curious about his foreknowledge of the flood. Although only his immediate family heeded his warnings, the inaction of those in denial did not deter him from taking the necessary survival measures. *In the process, his posterity was also preserved.* Noah's actions were also blessed because they glorified God, and were in alignment with the Lord's plan for that time.

Additionally, stockpiling some cash, gas, and goods, in advance of the fulfillment of a Bible prophecy can insulate the believer from the predictable panic and hysteria that could follow. Long gas lines, food shortages, and inaccessible ATM machines for instance, can be temporarily avoided. This buys time for some resemblance of normalcy to resume. *In the process, the believer's posterity can also be preserved.*

## End-Time's Christian Denial

Surprisingly, even though the end-time signs are plentiful and abundantly clear, many Christians don't believe they live in the last days. The fact that the eschatological message is not being taught from many pulpits has a lot to do with this. Ignorance about the end times keeps many from realizing they live within them. For those of you in this category, the fact you are reading this book is encouraging. Hopefully, *Revelation Road* will pique your interests into continued Bible prophecy studies.

However, these next few paragraphs are intentionally written for those Christians falling into a different category. There are those who believe, or at least think it possible, that there is such a thing as an end time, but they shudder at the possibility that those trying times have officially been ushered in. In essence, they choose the path of denial. Rather than prepare for the end, they opt to ignore it.

One of the reasons for this is that they are young, and seek to live long, healthy, and happy lives. Or, they're older and have children or grandchildren growing up that they want to send to college, or marry off. To them, the end times just doesn't fit into their lifelong plan. In fact, some in this category even hope the blessed rapture gets postponed way off into the distant future.

Even though times are worsening, they cling to the hope that world economies and geo-political events are going to get better. Unfortunately, if there is an end times, and if they are upon us, this mentality of denial is dangerous.

Certainly pursuing a noble aspiration, like sending a child through college, is a good thing, but if mankind has been plunged into a period of time whereby hunting and fishing for survival is more essential than getting a four-year business degree, then what's in the best interest of the child? Should he or she be taught to fish, or how to sell Sports Utility Vehicles (SUVs) when gas is priced at an unprecedented premium?

This example may sound facetious, but it speaks directly to the point. For instance, Christ says,

> For then there will be great tribulation, such as has not been since the beginning of the world until this time, no, nor ever shall be. And unless those days were shortened, no flesh would be saved; but for the elect's sake those days will be shortened. (Matthew 24:21)

This passage predicts a time is coming, which will be characterized by great worldwide tribulation. It implies that earning a college degree, or getting married and having a baby, is illogical. This coming "great tribulation" will *necessitate survival*, and *eradicate denial*. Everyone alive at the time will be forced to realize that the world is about to end! Christ is referring here to the final years of the trib-period, but some generation will experience this *great tribulation* first-hand!

This isn't about being anti-marriage or minimizing the importance of a good education, it's about being aware of the signs of the times. The timing of this specific prophecy is detailed further in this chapter's commentary, but is used here to warn against Christian denial. The fact many pastors avoid teaching about these last days, does not negate the fact that these last days need to be taught about. According to Acts 20:26-28, pastoral responsibilities require that the full counsel of God be taught from the pulpit. The full counsel includes Bible prophecy. Below is a quote that puts this into perspective.

> J. Barton Payne, the author of the *Encyclopedia of Biblical Prophecy*, lists 1,239 prophecies in the Old Testament, and 578 prophecies in the New Testament. That works out to a total of of 1,817, by his count. And prophecies involve 8,352 of the Bible's verses. And because there are 31,124 verses in the Bible, this works out to be about 27 percent of the total, meaning one-fourth of the Bible is prophecy.[17]

Picking and choosing what preaching is more conducive to filling the pews is not an option for an end-time pastor. Presenting about sixty-three percent of the Bible to a congregation, does not fulfill the requirements of Acts 20:26-28. 2 Timothy 3:16-17 says that all 31,124 Bible verses are divinely inspired, including the 8,352 regarding prophecy. Additionally, these two passages teach that even the prophetic Scriptures equip the man of God for service.

> All Scripture is given by inspiration of God, and is profitable for doctrine, for reproof, for correction, for instruction in righteousness, that the man of God may be complete, thoroughly equipped for every good work. (2 Timothy 3:16-17).

# The Final Generation has been Pre-appointed

The tough lesson for the final generation to learn is that they were pre-appointed to unprecedented perilous times. We are talking about *tribulation such as has not been since the beginning of the world until this time; no, nor ever shall be*, according to Christ. Pre-appointed describes this generation's unpleasant predicament, because we are informed of the following in Acts:

> He, [the Lord of heaven and Earth], gives to all life, breath, and all things. And He has made from one blood every nation of men to dwell on all the face of the earth, and has determined their *pre-appointed times* and the boundaries of their dwellings. (Acts 17:25b-26; emphasis added.)[18]

When one understands the grievous implications of living in the tribulation generation, it is understandable that denial occurs. Denial is the first of the five stages of grief.[19] However, the sooner the individual graduates through the subsequent stages of anger, bargaining, depression, and acceptance, the better off he or she will be.

These five stages of last days grief are evident in Christianity today. Many *deny* they live in the last days. The fact that eschatologists trumpet an end-time's message *angers* them. They *bargain* for a less-threatening allegorical interpretation of end-times prophecy. But, when end-times telltale signs remind of the urgency of the hour, they become *depressed*. In the end, they are left no choice but to *accept* the fact that they have no control, and must trust completely in the Lord and in the inerrancy of his prophetic word.

COMMENTARY

# Faith's Final Frontier

Every previously pre-appointed generation has showcased individuals motivated by inspirational faith. *Foxe's Book of Martyrs* is lined with accounts of Christians who gave their lives for their faith between the first and sixteenth centuries. The tribulation generation will evidence that faith has reached its maturation point. Their faith will be purified through the trials of the trib-period.

The apostle Peter informs us that faith is more precious than gold to God. However, like gold, it is tested by fire.

> In this you greatly rejoice, though now for a little while, if need be, you have been grieved by various trials, that the genuineness of your faith, *being* much more precious than gold that perishes, though it is tested by fire, may be found to praise, honor, and glory at the revelation of Jesus Christ, whom having not seen you love. Though now you do not see *Him,* yet believing, you rejoice with joy inexpressible and full of glory, receiving the end of your faith—the salvation of *your* souls. (1 Peter 1:6-9)

We know from the book of Revelation that many believers in the tribulation generation will demonstrate a true, tried, and tested faith. Revelation 6:9-11, 7:9-17, 20:4 and elsewhere teach they will pay a martyr's price for believing in the gospel. Their plight will be further detailed in book two of this series.

The testimonies of these martyrs will come during a time when the Antichrist rises to power through power, signs, lying wonders, and all unrighteous deception. His devilish program, fueled by strong delusion, will appeal to the preponderance of humanity.[20] To choose Christ at that time will be more than unpopular; it will be a certain death wish. The Revelation passages below tell us that they will possess a patient faith, one that believers today would do well to emulate.

> He who leads into captivity shall go into captivity; he who kills with the sword must be killed with the sword. Here is the *patience* and the faith *of the saints.* (Revelation 13:10; emphasis added).

> Here is *the patience of the saints*; here *are* those who keep the commandments of God and the faith of Jesus. Then I heard a voice from heaven saying to me, "Write: 'Blessed *are* the dead who die in the Lord from now on.'" "Yes," says the Spirit, "that they may rest

from their labors, and their works follow them." (Revelation 14:12-13; emphasis added).

Some of these eventually martyred individuals could be alive today. They would be unbelievers at the time of the rapture, that convert to Christianity subsequently. If they are, then they have been pre-appointed to an unprecedented period of perilous times. Believers today have the hope of the rapture to look forward to. Perhaps, severe Christian persecution could befall today's believer beforehand, but the hope of escaping the trib-period still applies. This is not so for the post-rapture believer. Their martyrdom will become both their testimony, and their blessing, according to Revelation 14:12-13.

With this in mind, it is important to conduct our lives in awareness of the times we live in. Some of our family members, friends, neighbors, co-workers and acquaintances may be numbered among the Christian martyrs of the tribulation generation. What they see in you, and hear from you, can impact their life decisions from this point forward.

# The Two Types of Last Days Christians

The historical accounts contained in Numbers 13-14 point out that there were two types of Hebrews at the time of Moses. Courageous Joshua and Caleb represented those who had faith to die for. They realized the power God possessed, and relied entirely on him to get through the giant obstacles— literally—that stood between them, and the Promised Land. They understood the days they were pre-appointed to. They must have realized the Genesis 15:12-16 prophecy given to Abraham, predicting 400 years of Egyptian servitude had ended. Thus, they recognized the time had come to enter into the Promised Land in fulfillment of part two of the prophecy.

> Now when the sun was going down, a deep sleep fell upon Abram; and behold, horror *and* great darkness fell upon him. Then He said to Abram: "Know certainly that your descendants will be strangers in a land [Egypt] *that is* not theirs, and will serve them, and they will afflict [enslave] them four hundred years. And also the nation whom they serve I will judge; afterward they shall come out [the Hebrew Exodus] with great possessions. Now as for you, you shall go to your fathers in peace; you shall be buried at a good old age. But in the fourth generation they shall return here, [the Promised Land of Canaan] for the iniquity of the Amorites *is* not yet complete." (Genesis 15:12-16)

COMMENTARY

Joshua and Caleb realized they were part of the fourth generation, the one destined to return and possess the Promised Land. Realizing they existed in fulfillment of this Bible prophecy, they exhibited the faith necessary to rely whole-heartedly on the Lord to deliver upon His prophetic promise made to the patriarch Abraham. They trusted the Lord would perform and safely deliver their generation home to the Promised Land.

Conversely, their counterparts were spineless. When they spied out the land promised to them, they were intimidated by the enemies and were unwilling to war against them. Even though they probably understood the above prophecy, and even saw the Red Sea swallow up Pharaoh's army, they still *underestimated* God's power. In so doing they undermined his glory. For their lack of faith and courage, they were severely chastised and wandered in the wilderness, where all but Caleb, Joshua, and those under the tender age of twenty, died over the next forty years.[21]

Both groups were pre-appointed to those hard times. They were all forced to live under the last, harshest days of the Egyptian bondage. Subsequent to their exodus, they were all expecting to enter into the Promised Land in fulfillment of Abraham's prophecy. But only one group possessed the faith required to stand up to the challenges. One group represented *survivors* and the other *deniers*.

What is your condition in comparison? Do you possess the unshakable faith of Caleb? Are you willing to acknowledge the end of time draws near? Can you muster up the courage of Joshua, required to face the challenges appointed to the final generation? In the book of Joshua the word courage or courageous appears seven times, illustrating the importance of possessing a fearless faith. Or, are you destined to wander aimlessly in the wilderness of denial, anger, and depression, while your unbelieving loved ones face the real threat of missing the rapture and being plunged into the tribulation period? Are you a Christian survivor or denier?

# Humanity's Last Day's Heart Condition

In chapter two young Tyler asks another innocent question linked with the prevalent humanistic thinking in the world today. The boy asks, "Can't people make it better so God doesn't have to punish people and the planet?"

Humanism believes in the dignity of man and is grounded in the belief that man's heart is inherently good, rather than evil. Humanists believe man can control his destiny, and given sufficient time right his wrongs, can control world woes and avert humanity's self-destruction.

Generally speaking, the humanist puts his faith in man, rather than God. Many view humanism as a man-centered religion. Below are a few interesting facts and quotes about humanism as religion.

- In the 1961 case of Torcaso v. Watkins, the U.S. Supreme Court held that Secular Humanism is a religion.

- Secular humanist John Dewey described Humanism as our "common faith." Julian Huxley called it "Religion without Revelation."

- The first Humanist Manifesto spoke openly of humanism as a religion."[22]

The Nuclear Non-Proliferation treaty is a prime example of humanistic thinking. It intends to limit the spread (proliferation) of nuclear weapons with the ultimate aim of total disarmament, hoping in the end all nuclear technologies will be utilized solely for peaceful purposes.[23] It is naïve to think rogue nations like Iran and North Korea, or terrorist organizations like the Taliban, Al Qaeda, or Hezbollah, under their present leaderships, wouldn't use nuclear weapons to advance their political or ideological agendas.

North Korea already possesses nuclear weapons, and Iran is developing them at the time of *Revelation Road's* composition. Once they possess nuclear weapons they could deliver them into the hands of their proxy, Hezbollah. Additionally, it is commonly understood that the Taliban and Al Qaeda are actively pursuing the confiscation of all or part of Pakistan's nuclear arsenal. Estimates are that Pakistan presently has over sixty nuclear weapons.[24]

It would only take a handful of nuclear weapons to wipe Israel off the map, and sixty strategically placed and detonated, could prove fatal for America. Recently, respected authors like Dr. Mark Hitchcock, Dr. David Reagan, and Terry James have written books about America's role in end-time's Bible prophecy.[25] In each of their respective writings they posed the possibility that a nuclear attack could come upon American soil. The topic of America in Bible prophecy will be discussed in greater detail inside the chapter commentary called *Terrorists Attack America Again*.

Poppy dispels young Tyler's humanistic thinking by saying, "People won't make the planet a better place; it's against their selfish nature." Jeremiah 17:9 validates this statement by declaring that man's heart is inherently deceitful and desperately wicked.[26] It is for this reason Christ died sacrificially for man's sins.

The Bible predicts sin will evolve into an incurable cancerous condition in the tribulation period whereby if left unchecked, would lead to the destruction of all mankind forever.

COMMENTARY

> For then there will be great tribulation, such as has not been since the beginning of the world until this time, no, nor ever shall be. And unless those days were shortened, no flesh would be saved; but for the elect's sake those days will be shortened. (Matthew 24:21)

The "great tribulation" (great-trib) referenced in this passage is commonly understood to be limited to the last three and one-half years of the trib-period. The passage alludes, in part, to the devastating world effects resulting from the "bowl" judgments of Revelation 16, that are poured out during this period. These judgments are reserved for those within humanity that epitomize Christ-rejecting sinners.

Many of those adversely affected by these great-trib judgments will by then have whole-heartedly accepted the "mark of the beast."[27] In so doing, they will have embraced the Antichrist and his world religious system, and consciously reject Jesus Christ in the process. Since this passage declares "no flesh would be saved," it appears that, in addition to the bowl judgments, this passage implies that worldwide nuclear warfare also occurs.

The Greek word Christ uses for saved is *sozo*, and can also be interpreted as, preserved, or safe. The inference is that mankind would self-destruct through the means of its own devices and divisiveness, unless the Lord restricted the "great tribulation" to its short, but disastrous, three and one-half year period.

Furthermore, the apostle Paul declares mankind's wickedness increases in the last days creating perilous times.

> But know this, that in the last days perilous times will come: For men will be lovers of themselves, lovers of money, boasters, proud, blasphemers, disobedient to parents, unthankful, unholy, unloving, unforgiving, slanderers, without self-control, brutal, despisers of good, traitors, headstrong, haughty, lovers of pleasure rather than lovers of God, having a form of godliness but denying its power. And from such people turn away! (2 Timothy 3:1-5)

Extended reading of chapter two's commentary is located in the appendix called *The Three Types of Christian Tribulation*. This section also addresses the "abomination of desolation," which triggers the period of "great tribulation."

*Please read the next chapter of the novel now.*

COMMENTARY

# Chapter 4—
## Israel Comes Under Multi-front Attack!

*Topics covered:* The Mideast Stage is Set for the Apocalyptic Wars; The Text of Psalm 83; The Potential for Psalm 83 Israeli War Casualties; The Three Trains of Thought on Psalm 83 Israeli War Casualties

## The Mideast Stage is Set for the Apocalyptic Wars

In October of 2011, Syrian President Bashar Assad threatened to attack Tel Aviv with missiles if the NATO alliance intervened on behalf of the Syrian protesters.[28] At the time his comments were made, an estimated 3,000 Syrian protesters had been killed by the Assad regime, during year-long protests. NATO intervention in Libya a few months prior to Assad's statement had led to the toppling of Libyan President Muammar Gaddafi, causing Assad grave concern that he could be ousted similarly. Graphic images of Gaddafi with a bullet hole in his head undoubtedly prompted Assad's warnings to NATO and threats against Israel.

Additionally, the Syrian president stated that he would call on Hezbollah to launch a simultaneous missile attack into Tel Aviv, and for Iran to prevent US and European warships from entering into the Persian Gulf. Israel's response to Assad's threats was to retaliate against the Syrian capital of Damascus. Prior to Assad's rumors of war, this novel chapter, which introduces a fictitious chemical missile attack upon Tel Aviv, had been authored.

Presently, Israel is concerned about such a multi-front offensive, and regularly conducts civilian defense drills called *"Turning Point,"* as a preparatory measure. Many Israelis possess personal gas masks, and know the location of nearby bomb shelters in case such an attack occurs.

Scud missiles are mentioned in the Tel Aviv attack. White House correspondent Bill Koenig, of www.watch.org, informed me at the end of 2009 that Syria was reported to have the most advanced Scud missiles in the world, including Scud B,C and D missiles. Many US lawmakers believe Scuds were transferred to Hezbollah from Syria in early 2010. *The Washington Times* reported on 4/22/2010 that the Senate Select Committee on Intelligence Chairman Dianne Feinstein, California Democrat, told *Agence France-Presse*, "I believe there is a likelihood that there are Scuds that Hezbollah has in Lebanon. A high likelihood."[29]

In addition to Scuds, many analysts believe that chemical weapons exist in Syria's and Hezbollah's arsenals. The Kuwaiti newspaper *Al-Siyasa* revealed this in March of 2009.[30] Reportedly, components capable of being converted into chemical weapons have been transferred from North Korea, through Iran and Syria, into Hezbollah's hands. Along these lines, many suspect Saddam Hussein's weapons of mass destruction were transported into Syria just before America invaded Iraq in 2003. Thus, a chemical attack like that described in this novel chapter is entirely possible.

Although the Bible doesn't specifically predict a chemical weapons attack targeted against Tel Aviv, it does prophesy about several end-time's Israeli war prophecies. Those wars, along with many other Bible prophecies, are the subject of this *Revelation Road* end-times book series. Because these predicted attacks are coming, and these dangerous weapons already adorn the arsenals of the attackers, there is a high degree of likelihood that they will be utilized during the coming conflicts.

These conflicts could be coming soon, in light of increased regional instability brought about by the Arab Spring of 2011. Almost every affected Middle Eastern or North African country is involved in either Psalm 83 or Ezekiel 38. Liberal pundits suggest the protests and revolts are nothing more than Arabs seeking life, liberty, and the pursuit of happiness. Many of them believe that the social networks of Facebook, Twitter, and YouTube have enabled the sizable Arab youth bulge to look beyond the confines of state censored medias, and seventh century Islam. They hope democracies will spring up across the region as a result.

However, apart from Israel, democracies haven't characterized the Middle East. Historically, power shifts in the region have occurred through revolutions, assassinations, rigged elections, or combinations thereof. The fact of the matter is that these are predominately Anti-Semitic Muslim populations that support the Palestinian plight. When it is all said and done, it is likely that these populations will oppose Israel and support the quest for a Palestinian state. If this turns out to be the case, the wars of Psalm 83 and Ezekiel 38 may occur soon, sequentially, and without much delay between.

This is because when these wars come, they appear to happen in rapid succession. Seemingly, each world-changing war sets the stage for the next one. For instance, this chapter suggests the multi-front attack upon Israel leads to an IDF retaliatory attack upon Damascus, which segues into the larger Psalm 83 Arab-Israeli War. Syria is only one member amongst ten populations listed in the Psalm 83:6-8 confederacy. Therefore, any attack upon Syria's capital city of Damascus could easily escalate into the larger Arab-Israeli war of Psalm 83.

Similarly, my first book about Psalm 83, called *Isralestine, the Ancient Blueprints of the Future Middle East* and considered the prequel to this book, suggests that Psalm 83 sets the stage for the larger Russian-Iranian led coalition to invade Israel, as described in Ezekiel 38-39. Ultimately, after the Ezekiel invaders are defeated, the Middle East Theater becomes primed for the Armageddon campaign.

The battle staged in the Armageddon campaign caps off all the Middle East wars predicted to occur upon this present earth. Armageddon is more than a battle, which is pointed out in the commentary of the chapter called *Arabs Unite to Fight – Is it Psalm 83, Ezekiel 38 or Armageddon?* A major battle within the Armageddon campaign is fought between Christ and all the remaining armies of the world, led by the Antichrist.[31] Revelation 19:11-21, in connection with Isaiah 63:1-6, teaches that Christ will prevail over the Antichrist and his armies. 2 Thessalonians says the lawless Antichrist will be no match for the mere brightness of Christ's coming.

> And then the lawless one will be revealed, whom the Lord will consume with the breath of His mouth and destroy with the brightness of His coming. (2 Thessalonians 2:8).

There are ten members in Psalm 83 and nine different populations in Ezekiel 38. Comparatively, there are over 195 countries in the world at present.[32] If the Psalm 83 and Ezekiel 38 armies are destroyed, that still leaves 176 countries left in the aftermath to align with the Antichrist against Israel, in Armageddon.

Psalm 83, the final Arab-Israeli war, and Isaiah 17, the destruction of Damascus, Syria are thoroughly discussed in this book. The Ezekiel 38-39 Russian-Iranian led invasion of Israel is given a modicum of coverage in this book, but is addressed more exhaustively in Book 2. The campaign of Armageddon involving the Antichrist will be covered extensively in Book 3 of this series.

However, Isaiah 17, Psalm 83, Ezekiel 38-39, and the Armageddon battle, may not be the only major Middle East showdowns yet to come. Other apocalyptic

COMMENTARY

episodes, like a preliminary confrontation between Israel and Iran, seem to occur in the Fertile Crescent, as well. Jeremiah 49:34-39 suggests that Iran, as Elam, appears in another end time Middle East military confrontation. More information about Jeremiah's Elamite prophecies are explored in the commentary of the chapter called *There's Trouble in Tehran and Destruction in Damascus*.

Since Psalm 83 is a major theme of this book, it is included verse-by-verse for your study purposes below. Interpretive information about the Psalm is spread throughout *Revelation Road*. Many of the appendices have been converted from my former articles that addressed questions or objections about the Psalm that were posed to me after the release of *Isralestine*.

In a nutshell, the passage below points out that an Arab confederacy forms to destroy the nation of Israel. The coalition forms a cunning plan to wipe Israel off the map and capture the Promised Land. According to verse four, the Arabs want the name of Israel to be "remembered no more," which modern interpretation infers that they want the name of Palestine to replace it. An apropos contemporary way of phrasing the coalition's motto is, "Death to Israel, and Viva la Palestine."[33]

Asaph is the psalmist of this particular Psalm and he petitions the Lord to deal with the Arab confederacy similarly to the ancient military examples chronicled in Judges 4-8. In those historical accounts, the Israelites defeated their enemies through the Lord's empowerment, and eliminated all future oppression from the specific enemies referenced. *Revelation Road* warns that Psalm 83 is a prophecy that appears ready to find fulfillment soon, and contains Bible Scriptures and commentary that support that conclusion.

# The Text of Psalm 83

1.  Do not keep silent, O God! Do not hold Your peace, And do not be still, O God!

2.  For behold, Your enemies make a tumult; And those who hate You have lifted up their head.

3.  They have taken crafty counsel against Your people, And consulted together against Your sheltered ones.

4.  They have said, "Come, and let us cut them off from being a nation, That the name of Israel may be remembered no more."

5.  For they have consulted together with one consent; They form a confederacy against You:

6. The tents of Edom [Palestinians refugees including West Bank Palestinians] and the Ishmaelites [Saudis]; Moab [central Jordanians] and the Hagrites [or Hagarenes— Egyptians];

7. Gebal [Lebanese], Ammon [northern Jordanians], and Amalek [Arabs of the Sinai area]; Philistia [Palestinians of the Gaza, including Hamas] with the inhabitants of Tyre [Lebanese, including Hezbollah];

8. Assyria [Syrians and northern Iraqis] also has joined with them; They have helped the children of Lot. Selah

[Refer to the images section (appendix 26) to see the connecting table identifying the modern-day equivalents of the Psalm 83 populations in verses six through eight above.]

9. Deal with them as with Midian, as with Sisera, as with Jabin at the Brook Kishon,

10. Who perished at En Dor, who became as refuse on the earth.

11. Make their nobles like Oreb and like Zeeb, Yes, all their princes like Zebah and Zalmunna,

12. Who said, "Let us take for ourselves The pastures of God [Promised Land] for a possession."

13. O my God, make them like the whirling dust, like the chaff before the wind!

14. As the fire burns the woods, and as the flame sets the mountains on fire,

15. So pursue them with Your tempest, and frighten them with Your storm.

16. Fill their faces with shame, that they may seek Your name, O LORD.

17. Let them be confounded and dismayed forever; Yes, let them be put to shame and perish,

18. That they may know that You, whose name alone is the LORD, are the Most High over all the earth. (Psalm 83)

COMMENTARY

# The Potential for Psalm 83 Israeli War Casualties

Upon hearing about the Psalm 83 Arab-Israeli war, young Tyler expresses sincere concern for the well-being of his Jewish kin residing in Israel. He asks, "Poppy, do you think my aunts and uncles and cousins living in Israel will be hurt?" When Tyler first posed a similar question to his grandmother Mimi earlier in the chapter, she responded by saying, "Any war is bad, and people often get hurt, but Poppy says Israel wins the Psalm 83 war, and becomes a safer place for awhile." His grandfather's subsequent response to the question was, "The Bible predicts Israel will win this war, but it is hard to know how many Israelis will be harmed while the war is being waged."

As the Psalm 83 scenario is presented fictitiously throughout the novel, and exposited upon in the non-fiction commentary, it becomes clear that the final Arab-Israeli war it describes will be no meager skirmish. It will be a war of epic biblical proportion and numerous Arab casualties are predicted. But what about the Israelis, will they sustain many injuries and deaths? Rather than postponing that discussion it will be covered here.

Obviously there are casualties on both sides of every major war, and this one will probably be no different. Even though Israel will essentially manhandle their opponents, according to several Scriptures identified throughout *Revelation Road*, they will probably not go entirely unscathed in the process.

Even though the Lord has been re-gathering the Jews into Israel since 1882 with wider Jewish immigration, established them as a nation in 1948, and has end-times plans for the Jewish people, historically, they have suffered human loss during the wars fought against the Arabs in 1948, 1967, and 1973. Although these wars weren't the final fulfillment of Psalm 83, they appear to have partially fulfilled the Psalm, in that they evidenced the Psalm 83 Arab enmity toward Israel, and set the stage for the final showdown. The attitude of hatred, which motivates the Arab confederates to want to wipe Israel off the map, is spelled out in Psalm 83:2-5.

In 1948, Israel won the war, but 6,373[34] Israelis were killed in the process. This represented about one percent of its Jewish population of approximately 650,000 at the time. In the Six-Day war of June, 1967, there were 777 Israeli soldiers killed, and 2,585 that were wounded.[35] In the Yom Kippur war of 1973, 2,812 Israelis were estimated to be killed.[36] Because of the slender geography of Israel, wars in that region do not tend to last long. There are no long, protracted wars between modern-day Israel and her enemies.

From a *historical war perspective,* Israeli casualties from Psalm 83 are likely, especially since the Psalm 83 war will probably make all past Arab-Israeli wars pale in comparison. Due to the magnitude of the event, they could easily exceed all casualties combined from the 1948, 1967, and 1973 wars. *But, will they?*

From the biblical perspective, there are three trains of thought on this matter. They are listed and briefly discussed below. The fact is, the Psalm doesn't directly address this topic, but other Scriptures may.

# The Three Trains of Thought on Psalm 83 Israeli War Casualties

- Divine intervention in Psalm 83 limits Israeli casualties.

- The Israel of Ezekiel 36 mitigates Israeli casualties in Psalm 83.

- Isaiah 17:1-6 potentially predicts severe Psalm 83 Israeli casualties.

*Divine intervention in Psalm 83 limits Israeli casualties.* This train of thought takes into consideration the possibility that God will put a protective hedge around Israel. In the process, a lesson is to be learned by mankind. Because of this invisible defensive hedge, Israeli casualties will be minimal or non-existent. Additionally, according to Ezekiel 25:14, the IDF is divinely empowered, enabling them to defeat their Arab foes.

The lesson humanity can glean in the aftermath of Psalm 83 is that God's foreign policy expressed in Genesis 12:3 is still intact. This passage says that all who curse Abraham (or his Israelite descendants) will be cursed. The Psalm 83 confederacy, bent on destroying Abraham's descendants and eradicating Israel forever, is a clear attempt to curse Israel.

Psalm 83:6 lists the "tents of Edom" first in the Arab confederacy. The Edomites are descended from Jacob's twin brother, Esau, according to Genesis 36:1, 9. Jacob was later called Israel in Genesis 32:28 and 35:10. Thus, the Israelites are Jacob's posterity and the Edomites are Esau's. Esau's Edomites, who have some ethnical representation in today's Palestinians, will be decimated, according to Obadiah v. 18 and Jeremiah 49:10-11, for attempting to destroy Israel in Psalm 83.

After the Edomite-led confederacy is defeated, the reasonable rhetorical question left for humanity to answer is: "If the Lord did not spare the descendants of Jacob's own twin brother Esau, from the promise of cursing contained in Genesis 12:3, how can anyone attempting to oppress Israel not likewise be cursed?"

The Arab defeat in Psalm 83 will be a "curse-for-curse-in-kind" lesson straight out of the Genesis 12:3 playbook. The Arabs will have sought to wipe out Israel militarily; but instead, the IDF will wipe out the Arabs militarily. Thus, the Arab attempt to annihilate Israel in Psalm 83 provides sufficient grounds for their total destruction, regardless of Israel suffering any casualties of war or not. This argument finds further support from the historical episodes identified in Psalm 83:9-11. Asaph, the seer,[37] petitions the Lord in these verses to deal with the Arabs of Psalm 83 like Gideon did to the Midianites, and Barak did to the Canaanites.

These historical accounts are written in Judges 4-8 and provide important information on how the Lord intends to deal with the Arab confederacy of Psalm 83. The Midianites had oppressed the Israelites for seven years. Outmanned and outgunned, Gideon took 300 warriors and destroyed 120,000 Midianites.[38] It appears as though no Israeli casualties resulted from Gideon's war against the Midianites. Furthermore, it doesn't seem that the Midianites ever oppressed the Israelites again.

The same holds true in the Israelite-Canaanite war described in Judges 4-5. The Canaanites oppressed the Israelites for twenty years. Subsequently, the Canaanites suffered a bitter defeat by Barak and the "Israel Defense Forces" of that time. No mention of Israeli casualties of war are reported as a result of that conflict either, nor are there any indications the Canaanites ever oppressed the Israelites again. In both examples, the Israelites were operating under divine empowerment and protection. Additionally, both enemies of Israel were defeated from top to bottom. Even their kings, nobles, and princes were killed alongside their soldiers. Importantly, these particular enemies ceased to ever oppress the Israelites or their Promised Land again.

Presently, the Arabs oppress the Jews and want to dispossess them of their Promised Land. Ultimately, they will confederate in a final attempt to wipe Israel off the map. They lose decisively, and like the Midianites and Canaanites, become incapable of ever oppressing Israel again.

Some scholars believe that Psalm 83 was fulfilled in 2 Chronicles 20, or in the 1948 or 1967 wars, or both. Those arguments are refuted in the attached appendix called *Has Psalm 83 Found Final Fulfillment?* The fact that the Arabs involved in Psalm 83 currently oppress Israel evidences that the prophecy remains unfulfilled.

If the IDF suffers nominal casualties against the formidable forces of Psalm 83 similar to these historical examples, it will clearly evidence the Lord's hand of protection over the Israelis and their land. I believe this protection exists now and will continue to be in place throughout Psalm 83 and Ezekiel 38-39.

However subsequently, due to the false covenant the Antichrist confirms with Israel, as described in Daniel 9:26 and Isaiah 28:15, 18, the Lord's hand of protection over Israel is temporarily removed. We know from Zechariah 13:8 that potentially millions of Israeli deaths occur at the hands of the Antichrist and his armies. These casualties will confirm the temporary removal of the divine protection.

"And it shall come to pass in all the land [of Israel]," Says the LORD, "That two-thirds [of the Jews] in it shall be cut off and die, But one-third [a faithful remnant of Jews] shall be left in it:" (Zechariah 13:8)

Although many casualties of war will occur during the Armageddon campaign, this may not be the case in Psalm 83, provided the Lord's protection covers the nation of Israel as it did during Gideon's and Barak's time.

*The Israel of Ezekiel 36 mitigates Israeli casualties in Psalm 83.* The second train of thought, subscribing to a lack of casualties in Psalm 83, is best articulated by Gary Fisher of *Lion of Judah Ministry.*[39] I had the fortunate opportunity of interviewing Gary on the *Prophecy Update Radio Show* for KWBB, when we were together at a prophecy conference in Dallas, in December of 2010. Our timely interview can be heard in 4-parts at this web link: http://isralestine-blog.blogspot.com/2011/05/ezekiel-warned-in-end-times-israel.html.

About midway through part two of the interview, Gary suggests that the Lord is going to supernaturally judge the ancient Arab hatred spoken about in Ezekiel 35, and that Israel might not even fire a shot in the Psalm 83 war. He finds clear connections between Psalm 83 and Ezekiel 35-36, and believes that the passage below describes the Arab hatred of Israel that exists today. He believes "in the time of the iniquity of the end" alluded to in this passage refers to these end times.

> Because thou hast had a perpetual enmity [ancient hatred], and hast given over the children of Israel to the power of the sword in the time of their calamity, *in the time of the iniquity of the end*; therefore, as I live, saith the Lord Jehovah, I will prepare thee unto blood, and blood shall pursue thee: since thou hast not hated blood, therefore blood shall pursue thee.(Ezekiel 35:5-6, ASV; emphasis added)

Fisher furthermore states, "I see some miraculous judgment on those (Arabs) that are intent on destroying Israel." Then he quotes Ezekiel below to encourage the possibility that Israel might survive the Psalm 83 conflict relatively unscathed.

> But ye, O mountains of Israel, ye shall shoot forth your branches, and yield your fruit to my people Israel; for they are at hand to come. For, behold, I am for you, and I will turn unto you, and ye shall be tilled and sown; and I will multiply men upon you, all the house of Israel, even all of it; and the cities shall be inhabited, and the waste places shall be built; and I will multiply upon you man and beast; and they shall

increase and be fruitful; and I will cause you to be inhabited after your former estate, and will do better *unto you* than at your beginnings: and ye shall know that I am Jehovah. (Ezekiel 36:8-11, ASV)

In summary, Fisher suggests that Ezekiel 36 pictures Israel as a blessed and bountiful nation after Psalm 83, suggesting that Israel may not be hit very hard by the Arabs during the Psalm war.

I believe Fisher is correct to connect parts of Ezekiel 35 and 36 with Psalm 83, and hope he's correct in his optimistic assessment of minimal Israeli casualties. Fortunately, during the interview, he left open the possibility that Israel may fire shots at their Arab enemies in Psalm 83, because I think it's clear from prophecy that they will. According to my extensive research on Psalm 83, it appears that the IDF is the military tool utilized by the Lord to defeat the Psalm 83 Arab confederacy. Refer to the following attached appendices to understand the probable IDF role in Psalm 83.

> ***Appendix 4:*** Is Ezekiel's Army About to Face Off with the Arabs?

> ***Appendix 5:*** Divine Vengeance—The Israel Defense Forces in Bible Prophecy

> ***Appendix 6:*** Ezekiel: Israel's Dry Bones Can Fight

An exhaustive exposition of today's IDF in Bible prophecy is written in the "Exceedingly Great Army" chapter inside my book *Isralestine*.

*Isaiah 17:1-6 potentially predicts severe Psalm 83 Israeli casualties.* Some eschatologists, myself included, connect Isaiah 17 with Psalm 83. Isaiah predicts the destruction of Damascus. In our story, Poppy aptly points out to Mimi and young Tyler,

> "Damascus is the oldest continuously inhabited city in recorded history, dating back 4,000 years, to the time of Father Abraham. It's Syria's capital, with about four million people in and around the city."

Syria appears to take part in Psalm 83 under the banner of Assyria. Therefore, the destruction of Damascus could certainly occur during, or within close proximity of, the fulfillment of Psalm 83.

At the time Psalm 83 was written about 3,000 years ago, Assyria comprised modern-day northern Syria, and northern Iraq. In 1,150 BC, Assyria began invading Syria (ancient Aram).[40] The first Assyrian king to mention Carchemish is Tiglath-pileser I (circa 1,268 BC), who states that he plundered "from the neighborhood of the land of Suhu (the Shuhites) as far as Carchemish of the land of Hattu" in one day.[41] Carchemish was an ancient capital of the Hittites, located on the west bank of the Euphrates in northern Syria.[42]

Approximately 1,000 BC, Assyria defeated the Hittites,[43] enabling them to seize portions of modern day northern Syria. At that time, Damascus was located in the southern section of ancient Aram. Aram generally comprised much of what is now modern-day southern Syria. Because Aram is not listed in Psalm 83, it is possible that the destruction of Damascus predicted in Isaiah 17:1, occurs apart from the Psalm war. I believe the destruction of Damascus is either a precursor, or a part of Psalm 83.

If Isaiah 17 occupies at least a peripheral part of the Psalm 83 scenario, then Israel could suffer severely according to what Isaiah 17:4 declares.

> In that day it shall come to pass That the glory of Jacob [Israel] will wane, And the fatness of his flesh grow lean. (Isaiah 17:4)

This verse portrays Israel in a dire condition. The expressions "the glory of Jacob will wane," and "the fatness of his flesh grow lean" are self-explanatory. Israel becomes war-torn, "in that day," alluding to the day of Damascus's destruction. Israel's lean condition seems to be the result of a serious conflict between Israel and Syria, in which Syria suffers the most damage.

According to the passages below, it appears as though Israel is responsible for the destruction of Damascus, and that the city is reduced to rubble overnight, well within a 24-hour period.

> In that day his [Damascus's] strong cities will be as a forsaken bough And an uppermost branch, Which they left because of the children of Israel; [IDF] And there will be desolation. (Isaiah 17:9)

> At evening time, behold, terror! Before morning, they [Damascus and its strong cities] are no more! This is the portion of those who despoil us, [Israel] and the lot of those who plunder us. (Isaiah 17:14, RSV)

*Please read the next novel chapter now.*

COMMENTARY

# Chapter 5—
## Panic in Damascus

*Topics covered:* Isaiah 17—The Destruction of Damascus

K amal Tereiri, the Syrian president's son, warns his father in this novel chapter that the Bible predicts the future destruction of Damascus. He says, "Damascus will someday cease to be a city, it will become a ruinous heap, and I'm concerned that unless you strike peace with Israel that day will arrive soon."

Kamal Tereiri is referring to Isaiah 17:1, which says:

> The burden against Damascus. "Behold, Damascus will cease from *being* a city, And it will be a ruinous heap."

Kamal's concern is that without a peace-pact between Syria and Israel, the destruction of Damascus could occur soon in the *Revelation Road* story line. He makes a valid point, because Isaiah 17:9 suggests Israel is responsible for the toppling of Damascus, and Isaiah 17:14 seems to teach that the Syrian capital city is reduced to rubble overnight.

Connecting prophecies about Damascus are identified in the commentary chapter called *There's Trouble in Tehran and Destruction in Damascus*, but below is a verse-by-verse study of the entirety of Isaiah chapter 17.

\* \* \* \* \* \*

# Isaiah 17—The Destruction of Damascus

(Isaiah 17:1-2)—The burden against Damascus. "Behold, Damascus will cease from *being* a city, and it will be a ruinous heap. The *cities of Aroer are forsaken*; they will be *for flocks* which lie down, and no one will make *them* afraid." (emphasis added)

These first two verses inform us that the Syrian capital city of Damascus will be destroyed, causing it to cease from being a city. Since Damascus exists today, this prophecy remains unfulfilled. Additionally other cities "of Aroer" are adversely affected, causing them to be "forsaken." The Hebrew word used for forsaken is *azab*, and means abandoned, withdrawn, left behind, released, or neglected.[44]

Since these cities eventually become agriculturally zoned "for flocks," the best understanding is probably that the destruction of Damascus necessitates the withdrawal of the surrounding city populations, which ultimately leads to their release and rezoning. Whichever government is sovereign over this area at that time, will reevaluate the highest and best use of the territory to be agricultural.

*Parson's Bible Atlas* lists three possibilities for Aroer: *Aroer Judah, Aroer Sihon,* and *Aroer Gad.*

- *Aroer Judah* was located about twelve miles southeast of Beersheeba, which places it as the furthest away from Damascus of the three options.

- *Aroer Sihon* was a city situated on the northern banks of the Arnon River, which was formerly located inside the tribal territories of Reuben. This places Aroer Sihon in ancient Moab (central Jordan), which is still fairly far south from Damascus.

- *Aroer Gad* becomes the likely option, because it was located in the area of ancient Ammon, (northern Jordan).[45]

Damascus is located in southern Syria, and Amman (Aroer Gad), the capital of Jordan, is in northern Jordan, where most Jordanians live. Only 109 miles separates the two Arab capitals, which is a shorter distance than the distance between the two most populated California cities of Los Angeles and San Diego. Approximately 120 miles, less than a two hour drive, separate these two US cities.

Aroer Gad was part of the tribal territory of Gad. Numbers 32 informs us that the tribe of Gad was generally agriculturalists and as such, Gad requested this territory because it was suitable for his sizable flocks. Thus, the destruction of Damascus apparently spills over into northern Jordan. Jeremiah 49:1-2, seems to give more detail about these northern Jordanian cities.

> Against the Ammonites [northern Jordanians today]. Thus says the LORD: "Has Israel no sons? Has he no heir? Why *then* does Milcom inherit [Aroer] Gad, And his people dwell in its cities? Therefore behold, the days are coming," says the LORD, "That I will cause to be heard an alarm of war In Rabbah of the Ammonites; It shall be a desolate mound, And her villages shall be burned with fire. Then Israel shall take possession of his inheritance," says the LORD. (Jeremiah 49:1-2)

The sequence of events should be as follows. Damascus and Rabbah are destroyed, probably in the same war effort. In the aftermath, Israel takes possession of northern Jordan including ancient Aroer, and rezones much it for agricultural purposes. Milcom was the Ammonite god when Jeremiah wrote. Since Milcom and all the other pagan Arab gods have all since been replaced by Allah, Jeremiah likely alludes to Islam in his prophecy. Jeremiah asks why do Arab Muslims dwell in the cities bequeathed to one of Jacob's twelve sons?

Ultimately, in the aftermath of a war, Israel possesses "his inheritance," represented by the cities of Aroer Gad. Ammon is a participant in the Psalm 83 Arab confederacy. Thus, the war in question is probably Psalm 83. If this is so, then the destruction of Isaiah's Damascus and Jeremiah's Rabbah are probably closely related Psalm 83 events. Assyria, which comprised part of modern day northern Syria when Psalm 83 was written, is also part of the Arab confederacy.

> (Isaiah 17:3)—"The fortress also will cease from Ephraim, The kingdom from Damascus, And the remnant of Syria; They will be as the glory of the children of Israel," Says the LORD of hosts.

Assyria conquered Aram, the location of Damascus, around 732 BC and the "fortress" of Ephraim ceased to exist, when the Assyrians conquered the northern kingdom of Israel in 722 BC. Isaiah, whose ministry spanned between 740–701 BC, appears to have authored chapter 17 prior to the Assyrian conquests.[46]

This could explain the first part of Isaiah 17:3, but fails to address the latter part, which identifies the remnant of Syria with the glory of the children of Israel. At the time of the Assyrian conquest of Damascus and Ephraim, there was no Syrian "remnant" under Israeli rule, "as the glory of the children of Israel."

Therefore a dual fulfillment of the prophecy may be coming. What Isaiah could be warning about is that strongholds in northern Israel (Ephraim) will become war-torn at the time of Damascus's destruction. The Syrian refugees (remnant) thereby, become captured by the IDF (children of Israel). Isaiah 17:9 below suggests Israel is responsible for the downing of Damascus. Isaiah concludes verse 3 by informing us, even though Damascus will cease to exist, a remnant of Syrians will survive.

> (Isaiah 17:4-6)—"In that day it shall come to pass *That* the glory of Jacob will wane, And the fatness of his flesh grow lean. It shall be as when the harvester gathers the grain, And reaps the heads with his arm; It shall be as he who gathers heads of grain In the Valley of Rephaim. Yet gleaning grapes will be left in it, Like the shaking of an olive tree, Two *or* three olives at the top of the uppermost bough, Four *or* five in its most fruitful branches," Says the LORD God of Israel.

These verses open with "In that day." Isaiah uses this expression four times throughout the chapter. The fact that he first uses this in verse four suggests that the preceding three verses all serve as the antecedent to the phrase. In other words, "In that day":

- Damascus ceases to be a city (v. 1),

- The cities of Aroer are forsaken (v. 2),

- The fortress of Ephraim, and kingdom of Damascus ceases (v. 3), and

- The Syrian remnant becomes subservient to the glory of the children of Israel (v. 3).

If so, than at the time all the above occurs, Isaiah 17:4-6 finds fulfillment. These verses picture Israel in an undesirable condition, suggesting the Jewish nation comes under attack at that time. Some believe these verses occur at the time of Armageddon, because Israel will suffer severely at that time. The problem with aligning the "in that day," with Armageddon at the end of the tribulation period is that verse nine clues us otherwise. Isaiah 17:9 informs us that the cities that become forsaken are abandoned because of the Jews. Any cities abandoned during the campaign of Armageddon will be abandoned because of the Antichrist's war related activities, not Israel's.

In conjunction with Israel's suffering, Isaiah 17:4-6 mentions terms, idioms, and locations, like heads of grain, Valley of Rephaim, gleaning grapes, olive tree,

COMMENTARY

olives, uppermost bough, and fruitful branches. These usages suggest there will be casualties in Israel. The Valley of Rephaim, is located in Israel, and is now called *el-Bukei'a*.[47] This valley was the site of two historic wars the Israelites successfully waged under King David against their arch enemy the Philistines. Coincidentally, Philistia is listed in Psalm 83. Perhaps Isaiah is telling us that, like David defeated the Philistines in the Valley of Rephaim, so will a lean and waning war-torn Israel bring about the destruction of Damascus before or during the Psalm 83 war episode.

But, Jewish genocide will be averted as Jews will survive in northern Israel (uppermost bough), and even more will survive in the more populated cities (fruitful branches).

> (Isaiah 17:7-8)—In that day a man will look to his Maker, And his eyes will have respect for the Holy One of Israel. He will not look to the altars, The work of his hands; He will not respect what his fingers have made, Nor the wooden images nor the incense altars.

COMMENTARY

These verses teach that the overwhelming events "in that day," cause humanity to question the power of its false gods of religion, technology, and materialism. The events surrounding the destruction of Damascus adversely affect all of mankind, prompting some to consider their creator, and his protection over the nation Israel.

The American Standard Version translates Isaiah 17:8 as follows:

> And they shall not look to the altars, the work of their hands; neither shall they have respect to that which their fingers have made, either the Asherim, or the sun-images.

The Hebrew word used for *Asherim* is *Asherah*. *The Holman Bible Dictionary* defines *Asherah* as,

> A fertility goddess, the mother of Baal, whose worship was concentrated in Syria and Canaan and the wooden object that represented her.

By using *Asherah*, Isaiah seems to emphasize that the false god of Syria will suffer disrespect. *Asherah,* like most other Mideast gods, gave way to Allah worship around the seventh century, when Islam was officially conceived. Allah is the would-be Syrian god today, that will suffer disrespect when Damascus is destroyed.

(Isaiah 17:9)—In that day his strong cities will be as a forsaken bough And an uppermost branch, Which they left because of the children of Israel; And there will be desolation.

In this verse Damascus is personified by the pronoun "his." In that day, that destruction of Damascus and "his" strong cities (of Aroer, v. 2) are forsaken; it will be a scene of "desolation." At the time Damascus meets its doom, it is characterized by "strong cities" about it. It is not a picture of weakness, but of a militarily strong Syria.

The "children of Israel" are responsible for this desolation and these forsaken cities. This verse implies that the IDF may have something to do with the destruction of Damascus. The devastation appears to also extend into cities north of Damascus, identified as "an uppermost branch."

(Isaiah 17:10-13)—Because you have forgotten the God of your salvation, And have not been mindful of the Rock of your stronghold, Therefore you will plant pleasant plants And set out foreign seedlings; In the day you will make your plant to grow, And in the morning you will make your seed to flourish; But the harvest will be a heap of ruins In the day of grief and desperate sorrow. Woe to the multitude of many people Who make a noise like the roar of the seas, And to the rushing of nations That make a rushing like the rushing of mighty waters! The nations will rush like the rushing of many waters; But God will rebuke them and they will flee far away, And be chased like the chaff of the mountains before the wind, Like a rolling thing before the whirlwind.

Isaiah 17:9 previously informed Damascus that *his* strong cities will be desolated apparently because of Israel. Isaiah 17:10-13 foretells why this desolation comes. Damascus, identified by the pronoun "you" in this instance, is not mindful of God.[48] But in addition to that, the Syrians are amongst a multitude of mighty waters that are rushing like roaring seas. This suggests that Syria, represented by Damascus, comes against Israel forcefully in a confederate effort with other nations.

Seas typically represent the Gentile nations, and in this instance they are noisily roaring and rushing like mighty waters.[49] This pictures a massive military invasion. We can safely assume this invasion is targeted at Israel, because verse 9 implies that Israel retaliates. The fact that they come against Israel evidences they have forgotten the "God of their salvation." The God of Israel is the God of salvation, and he promised in several Scriptures that Israel could never be destroyed.[50]

COMMENTARY

Isaiah says the war campaign results in a "heap of ruins," and characterizes the whole episode as a "day of grief and desperate sorrow." Isaiah 17:13 seems to connect with Psalm 83:13-15. In Psalm 83, Asaph petitions the Lord to do what Isaiah 17:13 says occurs to this confederacy. This implies that the destruction of Damascus and desolation of the surrounding cities could be related in some way to the Psalm 83 scenario. They both use the same six Hebrew words of *galgal, paniym, ruach, har, radaph,* and *suphah,* as comparatively highlighted below.

> O my God, make them like the whirling dust, [*galgal*] Like the chaff before [*paniym*] the wind! [*ruach*] As the fire burns the woods, And as the flame sets the mountains [*har*] on fire, So pursue [*radaph*] them with Your tempest, And frighten them with Your storm [*suphah*]. (Psalm 83:13-15)

Compared to Isaiah 17:13 below:

> The nations will rush like the rushing of many waters; But God will rebuke them and they will flee far away, And be chased [*radaph*] like the chaff of the mountains [*har*] before [*paniym*] the wind, [*ruach*] Like a rolling [*galgal*] thing before [*paniym*] the whirlwind [*suphah*].

If this is the case, then the nations that rush mightily like many waters are the Psalm 83:6-8 Arab States. If the destruction of Damascus occurs in a related Psalm 83 event, this would help explain why Syria, under the banners of either Aram or Assyria, doesn't appear listed in the Ezekiel 38:1-6 coalition of Magog invaders.

As stated above, the destruction of Damascus seems to occur at the hands of the IDF, according to Isaiah 17:9. This suggests that the "day of [Damascus's] grief and desperate sorrow" is a pre-tribulation event for the following reasons:

- The first three and one-half years are characterized by Israel dwelling in a false peace.
- The second three and one-half years are characterized by attempted Jewish genocide.

During the first half of the tribulation, Israel is dwelling in a false sense of national security. The covenant confirmed with them by the Antichrist in Daniel 9:27 creates this period of deceptive calm. The IDF appears to let its guard down, as a result.

At the mid-point of the tribulation, the Antichrist enters into the third Jewish temple and abominates it, as Christ prophesied in Matthew 24:15. This violation of the temple commences an unprecedented Jewish genocidal attempt by the Antichrist, which characterizes the last three and one-half years of "great tribulation."

Regarding the Israel Defense Forces' inability to prevent the "abomination of desolation" discussed above, Dr. Arnold Fruchtenbaum points out that the IDF can't even curtail the event. He suggests this evidences a weakness, or complacency, characterizing the IDF during the first half of the tribulation period. You can listen to Dr. Fruchtenbaum's entire radio interview with me, called *Is Psalm 83 a Great Tribulation Event?*, on *Prophecy Update Radio* at this link: http://prophecydepot.blogspot.com/2009/12/is-psalm-83-great-tribulation-event.html

Conversely, the second half of the tribulation period is not characterized by IDF complacency, but by IDF catastrophe. Israelis and their soldiers appear to be on the run from the perils plaguing that period. Zechariah 13:8 says that two-thirds of the Israelis in the land will be killed. The Antichrist and his troops are on the rampage to annihilate the Jews. Both Dr. Fruchtenbaum and I concur, that this will probably prompt the IDF to flee, rather than fight.

Interestingly, Isaiah 17:13 speaks of mighty rushing nations, but the prophet doesn't use the usual Hebrew word for nations, which is *goy*. *Goy* is the Hebrew word utilized in the classic Armageddon passages like, Joel 3:2, Zechariah 12:3, 9, Isaiah 34:1-2, and Psalm 2:1. *Goy* is found approximately 512 times in Scripture, evidencing it as the typical word to describe the "Gentile nations." Isaiah uses the term *goy* sixty-six times throughout his sixty-six prophetic chapters, but never uses it once in Isaiah 17.

Instead, to describe the mighty rushing nations, Isaiah opts for the Hebrew word *leom*. This word appears approximately thirty-one times in Scripture and Isaiah 17 repeats it twice in the same context. The word means "to gather, a *community:*—nation, people."[51] The plural use of the word is *leummim*, and it is translated as "*communities*; an Arabian, or a descendent from Dedan, which was formerly located in modern day Saudi Arabia."[52] The usages of *leom* in the passage below identifies populations that ultimately appear to participate in Psalm 83.

The first biblical usage of *leom* is found in Genesis 25, describing two peoples whose descendants end up in Psalm 83; the Israelites and the Edomites.

> And the LORD said to her: "Two nations [*goy*] are in your womb, Two peoples [*leom*] shall be separated from your body; One people [Israelites of Jacob—*leom*] shall be stronger than the other, [Edomites from Esau - *leom*] And the older shall serve the younger." (Genesis 25:23).

The first and only biblical usage of the word *leom* in the plural, as *leummim*, is also found in Genesis 25, as an Arab descendent of Dedan. Dedan formed an area in what is today Northwest Saudi Arabia. Saudi Arabia is also in Psalm 83 under the banner of the Ishmaelites.

> Jokshan begot Sheba and Dedan. And the sons of Dedan were Asshurim, Letushim, and Leummim. (Genesis 25:3)

These two above passages identify Edomites, which have ethnical representation in the Palestinians today, and descendants of Dedan, which are modern-day Saudis. Both Palestinians and Saudis are involved in Psalm 83. For the above reasons, it is reasonable to presume that the destruction of Damascus, the desolation of the surrounding strong cities, and the disrespect toward Allah, all find a correlation to the events prophesied in Psalm 83.

> (Isaiah 17:14)—Then behold, at eventide, trouble! And before the morning, he is no more. This is the portion of those who plunder us, And the lot of those who rob us.

Isaiah concludes his oracle against Damascus by describing the length of time it takes for the city to become reduced to rubble. Overnight, this historic city is destroyed. One evening Damascus flourishes, but by the next morning it's obliterated. This occurs as the penalty portion of Genesis 12:3. Syria's capital city is reduced to ruins, because Syrians attempted to plunder Israel, probably in Psalm 83. It is a curse-for-curse-in-kind disciplinary duty, outlined in the Lord's Gentile foreign policy of Genesis 12:3.

> I will bless those who bless you, [Abraham and his Hebrew descendants] And I will curse him who curses you; And in you all the families of the earth shall be blessed. (Genesis 12:3)

Jeremiah 49:23-27 appears to give more detail on how Damascus gets destroyed overnight. Jeremiah's correlating passage is detailed in this commentary's chapter called *There's Trouble in Tehran and Destruction in Damascus.*

The bottom line is that Damascus can presently be destroyed overnight by the weapons technologies Israel presently possesses. Unless Syria changes its hateful disposition toward the nation of Israel soon, humanity could wake up one nearby morning to a flood of Syrian refugees exiting out of the Damascus rubble.

For more commentary on the future of Damascus read the appendix titled: *When will Damascus be destroyed?*

*Please read the next novel chapter now.*

COMMENTARY

# Chapter 6—
## There's Trouble in Tehran and Destruction in Damascus

*Topics covered:* The Destruction of Damascus; The Attack Against Iran's Nuclear Sites; Jeremiah 49:34-39 Commentary; Historical Overview of Jeremiah's Elamite Prophecy; Iran Fiercely Angers the Lord; The Future of Iran; The Lord Establishes Authority Over Elam

Two important prophetic events are highlighted in this chapter: the destruction of Damascus and the attack upon the "foremost" of Elam's might, possibly alluding to Iran's present nuclear program. The primary passages detailing both episodes are listed and commented on below. Regarding Damascus, this section of commentary is intended to expand upon the Isaiah 17 study, contained in the previous chapter's commentary called *Panic in Damascus*.

## The Destruction of Damascus

The burden against Damascus. "Behold, Damascus will cease from *being* a city, And it will be a ruinous heap." (Isaiah 17:1)

In that day his [Damascus] strong cities will be as a forsaken bough And an uppermost branch, Which they left because of the children of Israel; And there will be desolation. (Isaiah 17:9)

Then behold, at eventide, trouble! *And* [overnight] before the morning, he *is* no more. This *is* the portion of those who plunder us, [Israel] And the lot of those who rob us. (Isaiah 17:14)

These three Isaiah 17 verses seemingly teach that Damascus will someday be reduced to a heap of rubble (verse 1) overnight, between some sunset and sunrise, because Damascus attempts to "plunder" and "rob" "the children of Israel," (verse 14) who in return retaliate (verse 9). The Hebrew word used for both plunder and rob is *bazaz*. This dual usage infers that Syria, represented by its capital city Damascus, will be guilty of plundering and pillaging Israel.

In direct alignment with the mandatory cursing aspects defined in Genesis 12:3, Syria's punishment is formatted similar to its aggression. Genesis 12:3b can be understood, "I must curse those who curse you." The pronoun "you" refers to the Israeli descendants of Abraham, Isaac, and Jacob. Simply stated, those seeking to curse the Israelis, must be cursed. Syria someday seeks to plunder Israel; therefore, Israel someday is empowered to plunder Syria in retaliation.

The Isaiah 17:9 verse informs us that Syrians from "strong cities" are displaced, inferring Syria is guilty of attacking populated or strong cities inside Israel. Isaiah 17:6 refers to these heavily populated Israeli cities as "fruitful branches," and announces there will be some survivors. The bottom line, according to Isaiah 17, is that Syria will experience widespread desolation, seemingly because they preemptively attempt to create desolation inside Israel.

Damascus will be destroyed, leaving Syria with no capital city, because Syria will apparently attempt to destroy Israeli claims to Jerusalem as its future capital city. This theme against Jerusalem seems to collaborate with the Damascus verses found in Jeremiah 49:23-27.

> Against Damascus [southern Syria]. "Hamath [northern Syria] and Arpad [northern Syria] are shamed, For they have heard bad news. They are fainthearted; There is trouble on the [Mediterranean] sea; It cannot be quiet. Damascus has grown feeble; She turns to flee [Syrian refugees], And fear has seized her. Anguish and sorrows have taken her like a woman in labor. Why is the city of praise [Jerusalem] not deserted, the city of My joy? Therefore her young men shall fall in her streets [civilian casualties], And all the men of war shall be cut off in that day [military casualties]," says the LORD of hosts. "I will kindle a fire in the wall of Damascus, And it shall consume the palaces of Ben-Hadad [Syrian capital buildings]." (Jeremiah 49:23-27).

By connecting Jeremiah's passage to Isaiah's we get a grander picture surrounding the destruction of Damascus. Although some expositors teach that Jeremiah 49:23-27 found fulfillment during Jeremiah's time through the

COMMENTARY

173

Babylonian conquest over Damascus, clues in Jeremiah's passage suggests otherwise. For instance, Jeremiah asks Damascus, "Why is the city of praise not deserted, the city of My joy?" This alludes to Jerusalem, which was destroyed and deserted during Jeremiah's lifetime. Therefore, Jeremiah's rhetorical question to Damascus about Jerusalem would prove pointless at the time.

Additionally, Jeremiah says Damascus becomes fainthearted because "there is trouble on the sea," which "cannot be quiet." The Babylonian conquest of Damascus was by land, rather than by any surrounding sea. Unless Jeremiah wants us to view the term "sea" allegorically to mean the Gentile world, like it does in Revelation 13:1 and elsewhere, or figuratively as a manner of speaking to a point, we must conclude Jeremiah's prophecy about Damascus was not fulfilled at the time of the Babylonian captivity.

Conversely, Jeremiah's passage makes complete sense when aligned with Isaiah 17. For instance Hamath and Arpad, two northern Syrian locations, are shamed because they receive troubling news. They become distressed along with Damascus, because they are all about to become battle zones.

These ancient cites, mentioned dozens of times in the Bible, historically ranked among the more important cities of Aram (modern-day Syria). Hamath is approximately 120 miles north of Damascus, and Arpad over 200 miles northeast of Damascus, about twenty-five miles north of today's Aleppo. Therefore, when Isaiah 17:9 predicts Syria's "strong cities will be as a forsaken bough And an uppermost branch," we presume from Jeremiah's descriptions the IDF's retaliation against Syria will cause the abandonment of several formidable "strong" Syrian cities in addition to Damascus.

The trouble on the disquieted sea is a literal threat today, since Israel supposedly has nuclear weapons concealed in Dolphin class submarines off the Middle East coastline of the Mediterranean Sea. Perhaps some surface to air missiles containing nuclear warheads could be launched toward Damascus by Israel from the Mediterranean. Could this be why Jeremiah says Damascus is seized by fear, grows feeble, and turns to flee as if anguished like a woman in labor? Is this why "young men shall fall in her streets, And all the men of war shall be cut off in that day?"

Notice Jeremiah predicts all the men of war, not a just a few troops, will be destroyed in this coming war. Presently the Syrian armed forces are over 646,500 strong and include many "young men" 18 and older.[53] Jeremiah's prophecy causes us to consider the depths of Syria's defeat. Furthermore, the young men he alludes to may include both civilians and military personnel. Certainly, an assault that devastates an entire city like Damascus will cause much civilian loss of life. Consider the following information contained in the *Encyclopedia of the Nations*.[54]

> The population of Syria in 2003 was estimated by the United Nations at 17,800,000, which placed it as number 55 in population among the 193 nations of the world. In that year approximately 3% of the population was over 65 years of age, with another 41% of the population under 15 years of age. There were 102 males for every 100 females in the country in 2003. According to the UN, the annual population growth rate for 2000–2005 is 2.38%, with the projected population for the year 2015 at 23,018,000. The population density in 2002 was 95 per sq km (245 per sq mi), but most of it was concentrated in a small area; 70% of Syria's people live in Damascus and the six western provinces.

Damascus is the capital of one of Israel's main enemies and is a strategic target for Israel, in the event of a multi-front war with Iran, Hezbollah, Hamas, and Syria. Syria is among the Arab countries that refuses to recognize Israel's right to exist. They have warred against Israel in 1948, 1967, and 1973. Unlike Jordan and Egypt, Syria has refused to make peace with Israel because it wants the Golan Heights returned, which Israel captured in 1967. Technically, Syria is still at war with Israel, and tensions between the two countries remain high.

On September 6, 2007, Israel attacked a suspected nuclear reactor in the Deir ez-Zor region of Syria, as part of Operation Orchard. Threats and rumors of war have characterized the standoff between the two countries. In an interview with BBC TV on June 17, 2010, Syrian president Assad accused the reigning Israeli administration of Benjamin Netanyahu of being a "pyromaniac government," and stated that there was no way to achieve peace with such a government.[55] His comments came on the heels of the Mavi Marmara incident, where nine Turkish activists died on a flotilla bound for Gaza.

A few months prior, in February of 2010, Israel's blunt-talking foreign minister, Avigdor Lieberman, warned Syria's president, Bashar al-Assad, that the Assad family would lose power in any war with Israel. In a speech at Bar-Ilan University, near Tel Aviv, Mr. Lieberman said: "I think that our message must be clear to Assad. In the next war, not only will you lose, you and your family will lose the regime. Neither you will remain in power, nor the Assad family."[56]

Syria's arsenal includes the most advanced scud missiles in the world.[57] Additionally, Damascus is one of the closest major cities to Israel's borders and could be used as a staging ground for a ground and air attack into Israel, due to its ideal location between Iran to the east and Lebanon to the northwest.

COMMENTARY

Reportedly, many Middle East terrorist organizations are headquartered in, or at least affiliated with Damascus, further heightening IDF concerns about humanity's oldest continuously inhabited city in recorded history. Damascus is thought to be between 4,000 to 5,000 years old.

Logically, if Israel comes under a multi-front attack from enemies possessing weapons of mass destruction, it will have to act aggressively, expeditiously, and decisively. Israel is the approximate size of the state of New Jersey, meaning a couple nuclear bombs could wipe the Jewish state off of the map. Israel doesn't have the luxury of waging a war of attrition. It's a matter of survival for the Jewish state and the destruction of Damascus by the IDF would indicate to its enemies that the war has become an all-or-nothing proposition.

## The Attack Against Iran's Nuclear Sites

In the novel, George surprises his best friend Razz with this comment: "Besides, some of us are fully expecting Israel to strike Iran's nuclear sites, especially in Bushehr, in fulfillment of Jeremiah 49:34-39."

The Jeremiah verses George alludes to contain an interesting prophecy that seems to remain unfulfilled, and could involve Iran's nuclear program. The subject of Jeremiah's prophetic utterances is Elam. During the prophet's time, Elam comprised what is today considered the central western portions of Iran. Persia, spoken of by Jeremiah's contemporary Ezekiel, in Ezekiel 38:5, encompassed most of today's northern Iran at their time. The following Scriptures from Jeremiah 49 and commentary below it, suggests that Iran could be involved in dual end time prophecies. This would include the prophecies of Elam by Jeremiah and those regarding Persia in Ezekiel 38-39.

Jeremiah 49:34-39

The word of the LORD that came to Jeremiah the prophet against Elam, in the beginning of the reign of Zedekiah king of Judah, saying, "Thus says the LORD of hosts: 'Behold, *I will* break the bow of Elam, The foremost of their might. Against Elam *I will* bring the four winds From the four quarters of heaven, And scatter them toward all those winds; There shall be no nations where the outcasts of Elam will not go. For *I will* cause Elam to be dismayed before their enemies And before those who seek their life. *I will* bring disaster upon them, My fierce anger,' says the LORD; 'And *I will* send the sword [*military campaign*] after them Until I have consumed them. *I will* set My throne in Elam, And [I] *will* destroy from there the king and the princes,' says

COMMENTARY

the LORD. 'But it shall come to pass in the latter days: *I will* bring back the captives of Elam,' says the LORD." (emphasis added)

# Jeremiah 49:34-39 Commentary

The most important declaration to note in this passage is that Elam has done something that has fiercely angered the Lord, "My fierce anger." As a result, the Lord has Jeremiah declare eight times, "I will" bring about a judgment against Elam. Nine related prophecies result as listed below. "I will:

1. Break the bow of Elam, the foremost of their might,

2. Bring the four winds from the four quarters of heaven,

3. Scatter them [Elamites] toward all those winds [worldwide],

4. Cause Elan to be dismayed before their enemies and before those who seek their life,

5. Bring disaster upon them, my fierce anger,

6. Send the sword after them until I have consumed them,

7. Set My throne in Elam,

8. Destroy from there the king and the princes, and

9. [in the latter days] bring back the captives of Elam."

Items #1-3 above appear to result from the expressed intentions described in #4-6. As stated above, the key to grasping the why's and wherefore's of Jeremiah's utterances against Elam is in recognizing that the Elamites have done something to anger the Lord as per #5. Because they have aroused the Lord, they will be "dismayed" in #4 as "disaster" in #5 befalls them. The nature of the disaster is by the "sword," meaning militarily related, in #6.

The disaster is severe in #6, "until I have consumed them." And, it is witnessed by Elam's "enemies" and those who "seek their life" in #4. If the event were to happen in the near future, the enemies seeking to end Iran's quest for regional power, and dispossess the rogue state of nuclear weapons would be: America, Israel, and / or some predominately Sunni Muslim countries like Saudi Arabia, Egypt, and the United Arab Emirates. Additionally, several other countries are concerned about Iran's perceived attempts to conquer the greater Middle East. (Refer to the appendix called *Iranistan* for more information about Iran's hegemonic attempts to form a Shiite Crescent within the Fertile Crescent.)

COMMENTARY

# Historical Overview of Jeremiah's Elamite Prophecy

COMMENTARY

Elam was a son of Shem, Noah's oldest son. His descendants settled in what is today central western Iran, east of the Tigris River. Their capital city was Susa. Today, Susa's city ruins are located in Southwest Iran, about 150 miles north of the Persian Gulf.[58]

The Elamites were a war-like people, according to Genesis 14:1-9.[59] Jeremiah issued this prophecy regarding Elam about 597 BC, one year prior to Nebuchadnezzer's conquest over Elam around 596 BC.[60] There is some evidence that the Babylonian king put Elamites under his subjugation, but as a whole the Elamite culture and language remained intact and the Elamites were not dispersed worldwide, as called for in the prophecy.

Subsequently, Cyrus of Persia conquered Babylon about 539 BC, beginning the Persian Empire period, which lasted until around 330 BC.[61] The Persian Empire extended throughout most of the Middle East and parts of northern Africa, and encompassed Elam. However, Ezra 4:9 reveals the Elamites still had political representation during the time. And, Ezra 2:7, 31 states that the Elamites returned to their homeland after the Babylonian captivity.

Even though power shifts occurred after the Persian period, the Elamites still survived in Elam. Acts 2:9, written several centuries afterward, around the time of Christ's first advent, informs us that the Elamites and their language still existed. Furthermore, Jeremiah 25:17-29 and Isaiah 11:11 evidence the existence of an end time's Elam.

The above historical tracking, aligned with the nine prophetic requirements of Jeremiah, suggests that the pertinent Elamite prophecies remain unfulfilled. Importantly, none of the above indicates that Elam aroused the fierce anger of the Lord, also suggesting an event in waiting.

********

We are told that the "bow" of Elam will be broken. Iran will be struck at the "foremost of their might." The Hebrew word used as foremost is *reshith*, and can also be translated at the chief, choicest, or finest point of its might. Additionally, we're informed that Iranian refugees will flee into the nations of the world. Importantly, we are informed: "it shall come to pass in the latter days." This infers the following:

## Come to pass in the latter days

Since this prophecy does not appear to have been fulfilled historically and applies to the "latter days," the foremost of Iran's power may include its nuclear facilities.

Along the lines of this being an end-time's event, Dr. Arnold Fruchtenbaum, founder of Ariel Ministries, records the following in his book *The Footsteps of the Messiah*:[62]

> "Although Persia or Iran (ancient Elam) is not an Arab state but a Persian one, its future will be examined here because it shares the same religion (Islam) with Moslem Arabs. Peace will come between Israel and Iran by means of destruction, according to Jeremiah 49:34-39. In verses 34-38 Jeremiah described the destruction of Elam, with the inhabitants being completely dispersed all over the world. But then verse 39 declares: 'But it shall come to pass in the latter days, that I will bring back the captivity of Elam, says Jehovah.'
>
> The destruction of Iran will be partial, and the dispersion will be temporary. Eventually the inhabitants will return and resettle Iran. The future of Iran is similar to that of Egypt, but the length of time they will be in dispersion is not revealed. So peace will come between Israel and Iran via destruction, dispersion, and then a conversion and a return. There will be a saved nation of Elam (Persia or Iran) in the (Millennial) Kingdom."

Dr. Fruchtenbaum points out that these Jeremiah verses represent a forthcoming event. He acknowledges, "The destruction of Iran *will be* partial, and the dispersion *will be* temporary."

## Break the bow

Isaiah 22:6 tells us that the Elamites were experts in archery. Jeremiah appears to pick up on this theme in his prophecy. The prophet utilizes the Hebrew word for an archer's bow, which is *qesheth*. Without a functional bow, an archer is unable to launch arrows at his target. This implies Iran may be unable to launch rockets or nuclear warheads as a result of being struck militarily, by the "sword," at its place of foremost might.

## Foremost of their might

This suggests Iran will be strategically targeted at the pinnacle point of its power, which today includes its developing nuclear program. This could also include its military installations, headquarters, and armories

As George declared earlier in the novel chapter, Iran's chief nuclear site is in the area of Bushehr, and is located today inside the boundaries of ancient Elam. It is possible that Jeremiah predicted an attack upon Iran's nuclear site(s) approximately 2,600 hundred years ago.

Could such an attack create a Chernobyl-effect inside part of Iran, causing many to evacuate into various nations of the world? Is that what Jeremiah 49:36 alludes to when it states "Against Elam I [the Lord] will bring the four winds from the four quarters of heaven, And scatter them toward all those winds [away from the radiation fallout]; There shall be no nations where the outcasts of Elam will not go."

Jeremiah uses the Hebrew word *kol*, which rather than being translated as a scattering *toward*, or into, the four winds, means a thorough dispersion into everywhere, or throughout. In essence, it suggests that an event happens in Elam predicating a massive evacuation in all geographic directions. Presently, at the time of authoring this section, the Bushehr nuclear plant is loaded with nuclear fuel rods, and if struck militarily, could cause radiation fallout to occur.

It is doubtful that Jeremiah's prediction of an Iranian worldwide dispersion has occurred historically, meaning it is probably, as Dr. Fruchtenbaum suggests, a pending prophetic event. Furthermore, Iran's involvement in the Ezekiel 38-39 prophecy prohibits the possibility that all Iranians experience a worldwide dispersion prior to the fulfillment of Ezekiel's prophecy. Iran appears to be one of Russia's primary allies in Ezekiel's prophecy, meaning Iran maintains an army, although it may be weakened, at the time.

Thus, if the breaking of Elam's bow and the worldwide dispersion of Elamites has not occurred historically, then Jeremiah 49:34-39 and Ezekiel 38-39 could be separate, or the same event(s). Perhaps the breaking of Elam's bow occurs before Ezekiel 38 and temporarily adversely affects Iran's military prowess, but does not permanently eliminate it. Then the worldwide dispersion occurs separately as a result of Ezekiel 38.

There is another possibility: maybe the broken "bow" (nuclear weapons or nuclear facilities like Bushehr) is broken, causing some isolated geographical contamination. This could force the affected populations to disperse out of Iran into uncontaminated neighboring nations. As stated earlier, ancient Elam represents only a portion of modern-day Iran. Thus, it is plausible the Iranian exodus is not nationwide, but limited to the affected populations. This would enable Iran to muster up an army in the gap-period, between the breaking of its bow and the joining in with the Ezekiel invasion.

## Iran Fiercely Angers the Lord

As stated in #5 above, disaster befalls Elam because they provoke the Lord to fierce anger. Since the Lord is not easily angered, what might Elam, or Iran today, be guilty of?

Perhaps the fact that Iran's apocalyptically-minded President Ahmadinejad threatens to wipe Israel off the map, and that he is developing a nuclear program to accomplish that dastardly deed, could have something to do with it. Iran publicly denounces the Jewish state's right to exist, and is guilty of antagonizing Israel through its proxies, Hezbollah, Syria, and Hamas. Additionally, Iran has fomented terrorism and violence since the Iranian Revolution in 1979.

According to Zechariah 2:8, Israel is the "apple of God's eye." Additionally, Ezekiel 39:7 declares the Lord intends to uphold His holy name through Israel, and according to Ezekiel 38:8, 16 this occurs in the end times.

The fact that the Lord loves Israel, and still has end time plans in place for the Jewish state, provides sufficient grounds for Him to be upset if Iran attempts to thwart those plans by decimating Israel. In fact, throughout all of Elam's history, it doesn't appear until recently that Elam, apart from being religiously pagan, has done anything to provoke the Lord to such a fierce anger.

## The Future of Iran

Since Jeremiah 49:34-39 appears to remain unfulfilled, the nine prophecies described could occur as follows:

### The Military Option

Iran's present enmity toward Israel has fiercely angered the Lord. As the Lord sits on His heavenly throne presently, He is extremely upset with the rogue state of Iran. This puts Iran in jeopardy of the severe judgments the prophet predicts.

The rogue state is about to be invaded militarily, by the *sword*, at the foremost center of its might. The target area is restricted to only the western central region of the nation; i.e., ancient Elam. The attack will be disastrous, witnessed and / or caused by Iran's enemies, and result in much dismay in Iran. As a result of the military invasion and wind patterns, the affected Iranians

COMMENTARY

disperse outside of the area into other nations. This suggests that nuclear fallout from Bushehr's nuclear facility occurs at the time.

Items listed in #7-9 above foretell that the Lord will set His throne in Elam, destroy their king and the princes, and in the latter days bring back their captives. This means the presiding Iranian leadership in the affected area is destroyed at the time of the breaking of the bow at the foremost of Elam's might.

Since Persia of Ezekiel 38:5 is not affected by the events in Elam, it remains in place to join up with Russia's coalition in the Gog of Magog invasion. This is regionally possible because when Ezekiel prophesied, Persia had not yet become a world empire and did not include Elam territorially. Thus, modern-day Iran was comprised of both Persia and Elam when the prophets wrote.

## The Natural Disaster Option

This option finds potential merit by chronologically ordering the events described in Jeremiah 49:34-38. It would probably play out similar to the military option above, but the military aspect comes after Elam's *bow is broken,* rather than before. The *military option* suggests that some *sword* invasion targets Elam's foremost point of might, but chronologically Jeremiah lists the *sword* subsequent to the breaking of the bow. Items #1-5 occur prior to the reference in #6 to a *sword.* In the *natural disaster option* the sword is a by-product of the disaster. The passage reads, "'For I will cause Elam to be dismayed before their enemies And before those who seek their life. I will bring disaster upon them, [Elamites] My fierce anger,' says the LORD; 'And [subsequently] I will send the sword [military campaign] after them Until I have consumed them.'"

Iran has a history of seismic activity. It has experienced a multitude of significant earthquakes, dating back as far as the 7.3 Silakhor quake on January 23, 1909, with an estimated 6,000 fatalities. At least 40,000 were killed in the 7.4 Mangil-Rudbar quake of June 20, 1990. Iran has experienced about ten 6.0 or greater quakes already in the twenty-first century.

Wikipedia states the following:

> Iran is one of the most seismically active countries in the world, being crossed by several major fault lines that cover at least 90% of the country. As a result, earthquakes in Iran occur often and are destructive.[63]

In light of Japan's Fukushima nuclear disaster, that resulted from the 8.9 quake and subsequent tsunami in March of 2011, it is possible that Iran could experience a natural disaster brought on by an earthquake, as well. Jeremiah says; "I will bring disaster upon them, My fierce anger," says the LORD."

*The Ezekiel 38-39 option* – Since Jeremiah's and Ezekiel's prophecy appear to be end-time's events, they could be part of the same episode. Ezekiel 38:18-39:7 clearly shows that the Lord is angry with the Magog invaders, which includes Iran, and as a result destroys them all. Perhaps the Jeremiah 49:34-39 prophecies simply add more detail to the fifty-two descriptive verses contained in Ezekiel 38-39. This would make sense and demonstrate a pattern in Scripture that other prophets have followed. Details of a prophecy are often given by more than one prophet.

However, this option doesn't address the logical question of "Why did Jeremiah allude to Elam, but Ezekiel to Persia?"

# The Lord Establishes Authority over Elam

Personally, I suspect Jeremiah and Ezekiel identify for us two differing last day's unfulfilled prophetic events, that are regionally specific to the time of their authorship. Perhaps addressing Jeremiah 49:38a, which declares "I will set My throne in Elam," holds a clue to our better understanding of his prophecy.

This is an interesting statement for two reasons. First, Elam is outside the Promised Land described in Genesis 15:18, which stops westward of Elam at the Euphrates River. This beckons the question: why would the Lord position His throne outside the Promised Land? Second, Isaiah 66:1 declares the Lord's literal throne is in heaven. This beckons the question: why would the throne be moved anywhere on Earth prior to the Messianic reign of Christ?

Jeremiah 49:38 does not describe an event characteristic of the messianic kingdom. It discusses the destruction of an Elamite king and his princes. The messianic kingdom is biblically presented to be a time of peace wherein swords are converted into plowshares, and the knowledge of the Lord covers the expanse of the earth.[64] Most of the killing of the world's bad kings and princes occurs prior to the establishment of the messianic kingdom at the end of Armageddon. Thus, Jeremiah 49:38 appears to happen before the return of Christ to establish His 1,000 year kingdom on Earth.[65]

Therefore, for these above reasons it is difficult to view this "throne" Jeremiah 49:38 alludes to as literal. The Hebrew word Jeremiah uses for throne is *kisse*, and it means a seat of honor, a throne, or authority.[66]

Jeremiah 49:38 states the throne gets set up in Elam, and then from that throne the king and princes are destroyed. Thus, who or whatever destroys the king and princes of Elam, probably occurs antecedent and is likely related to the throne in Elam. Jeremiah 49:37 talks about the sword used to consume the Elamites. Therefore, the sword and the throne seemingly find connection. The same prior verse notates that there are those who seek to kill the Elamites.

Hence the connection could be as follows: Because Iran has angered the Lord in that they plot the destruction of Israel, in turn the Lord gives authority (throne) and military empowerment (sword) to those who seek to destroy Iran. Listed above was an assortment of Iran's enemies, and any one of them could be empowered militarily to execute the Lord's will against Iran. It could be America, Israel, Saudi Arabia in conjunction with several other Sunni Arab States; or less likely, other members of the international community. It could be a combination of any of the above.

********

*Caveat to Jeremiah 49:34-39*: Unlike Ezekiel 38-39, Jeremiah's Elamite prophecies are less commonly taught. All of the above author comments are interpretive suggestions only of Jeremiah's prophecy regarding Elam. These interpretations are the result of a modicum of study performed by the author. Some possibilities border on classic newspaper exegesis, which the author attempts to avoid. Readers are encouraged to thoroughly research Jeremiah 49:34-39 carefully on their own for greater understanding of the text. If the prophecy can be proven to have found historical fulfillment then all of the author's comments regarded with the subject matter should be ignored.

*Read the next novel chapter now.*

COMMENTARY

# Chapter 7—
## Israel Attacks Iranian Nuclear Sites

*Topics covered:* Why Iran's Absent from Psalm 83; Iran is Persian and Psalm 83 is Arab; The Dual End-Time Prophecies of Iran; The Bleak Future of Islam

The prophecies regarding Elam in Jeremiah 49:34-39 have already been exposited upon in the commentary of the chapter titled *There's Trouble in Tehran, and Destruction in Damascus.* Jeremiah's Elamite prophecies were introduced before in order to set the potential stage for the events described in this chapter's novel section, which depicts an Israeli attack upon Iran's chief nuclear sites.

It is difficult to know whether or not Jeremiah 49 foretells of an Israeli air-strike upon Iran's nuclear sites resulting in nuclear fallout. The speculation of the novel chapter certainly borders on sensationalism and newspaper exegesis. However, if the prophets' predictions are about to find a modern-day fulfillment, then that could be exactly what he describes. Jeremiah says Elam gets attacked at the foremost of its might, and that the Elamites subsequently evacuate their homeland, and scatter amongst various world nations.

This is a plausible scenario because Israel has a history of attacking the nuclear sites of its enemies, Iran possesses several such sites, and Israel considers Iran to be an enemy.

Thus far in the novel story line, Israel has been defending itself against the aggressions of Iran, and its modern day proxies, Syria, Hezbollah, and Hamas. These three Iranian proxies all appear to be members of the Psalm 83 Arab confederacy. Surprisingly, Iran does not! Why not, considering the rogue nation is presently Israel's number one existential threat, and Psalm 83 appears imminent? Rather than expanding upon the theme of an Israeli attack against Iran, this chapter's commentary will discuss Iran's apparent absence in Psalm 83.

## Why Iran's Absent from Psalm 83

As the Psalm 83 confederates image in the images section (appendix 26) depicts, Syrians and Iraqis find association through Assyria, Hezbollah via Tyre, and Hamas connects with Philistia. However, there is no mention of Iranians by their three primary historical names, Elamites, Medes, or Persians. This is puzzling, considering Iran reportedly formed *bona fide* war-pacts in December, 2009, with this troublesome Muslim trio.[67] Some suggest Iran may be included in Psalm 83 as part of the Assyrians. The Assyrians seem to be among the stronger members in the psalm, because they support the Jordanian army referred to as the children of Lot (Moab and Ammon) in Psalm 83:8.

> Assyria also has joined with them; they have helped the children of Lot [Jordanians]. *Selah* (Psalm 83:8)

The pitfall of connecting modern-day Iran with Assyria is that during the psalmist's time, Assyria only comprised much of what is today northern Syria and part of Iraq. In order for Iran to be mentioned in Psalm 83, the psalmist would need to have included, Elam, Media, or Persia in the confederate lineup. At the time, Elam existed in what is now west-central Iran, Media existed in eastern Iran and far beyond, and Persia occupied primarily the northerly parts of today's Iran, a few centuries after the psalm was penned.[68] Thus, it is reasonably safe to exclude Iranians, which are primarily of Persian descent, from the predominately Arab confederacy of Psalm 83.

## Iran is Persian and Psalm 83 is Arab

The Persian verses Arab distinction made in the previous sentence may be part of the reason Iran doesn't participate alongside their Arab proxies in Psalm 83. The confederacy is dominated by Arab populations. Arabs and Persians have a longstanding history of warring against each other, dating as far back as the Persian conquest of the Babylonians around 539 BC. In modern history, Iraq and Iran fought against each other from 1980-1988.

Saudis, as the Ishmaelites, and Egyptians, as the Hagarenes, are members of Psalm 83 and they may feel threatened by any Iranian meddling in the Arab-Israeli war. Both of these Arab countries are deeply concerned about Iran's present nuclear aspirations, and fear Iran's greater goal is to subdue their respective nations in order to form a Shiite Crescent throughout the Middle East.

The Arab verses Persian argument is not the only possible reason Iran refrains from participating in the Psalm 83 War. Possibility number two is that part of Iran may be temporarily incapacitated at the time, according to a generally overlooked prophecy issued by Jeremiah.

# The Dual End-Time Prophecies of Iran

(Although some of this portion of commentary may seem redundant from previous portions of commentary, it is included because it is germane to the understanding of why Iran is apparently excluded from the Psalm 83 confederacy.)

Even though Iran appears absent from the climactic, concluding Arab-Israeli War, they are not excluded from two other significant end-time's events. The one most widely taught among eschatologists is the Ezekiel 38, Gog of Magog invasion of Israel. An overview of this prophecy is found in the commentary chapter called *The Russian – Iranian Nuclear Connection*. Persia is clearly identified militarily "with shield and helmet," in Russia's coalition.

> Persia, Ethiopia, and Libya are with them, all of them *with* shield and helmet; (Ezekiel 38:5)

Perhaps Persia's utter destruction in Ezekiel's prophecy prohibits Iran from fighting in Psalm 83. Although this would satisfactorily answer the question about Iran's apparent absence in the Arab war, the problem is that Psalm 83 seems to precede Ezekiel 38. If this is the case, then Iran's "shield and helmet," could still exist when the Arabs come against Israel.

The prophecy that may precede Ezekiel 38, and answer the question about Iran's mysterious absence in Psalm 83, is located in Jeremiah 49:34-39. As previously discussed, Jeremiah 49:35 predicts Iran gets struck at the foremost of its might, which could allude to its nuclear program. By way of review, the next verse says the Iranians will be scattered out of the immediate area into world nations.

> Thus says the LORD of hosts: "Behold, I will break the bow of Elam [Central Iran near the Bushehr nuclear facility], The foremost of their might. Against Elam I will bring the four winds From the four quarters of heaven [potentially causing the spread of nuclear fallout], And scatter them toward all those winds; There shall be no nations where

the outcasts of Elam will not go. For I will cause Elam to be dismayed before their enemies And before those who seek their life. I will bring disaster [potentially nuclear] upon them, My fierce anger," says the LORD; "And I will send the sword [military] after them Until I have consumed them." (Jeremiah 49:35-37)

Jeremiah and Ezekiel were contemporaries of each other. They both wrote around 2,600 years ago. Why did Ezekiel prophesy about Persia, and Jeremiah about Elam? Geographically, they occupied two adjoining territories at the time, and were distinct civilizations. Presently, Persia and Elam comprise greater Iran. A careful study suggests both Ezekiel's and Jeremiah's Iranian prophecies appear to be end time events, awaiting fulfillment.

The possible explanations of Jeremiah's prophecy given in this commentary in the chapter called *There's Trouble in Tehran and Destruction in Damascus*, makes one wonder if Iran's nuclear program comes under attack soon, rendering Iran of little military utility when Psalm 83 takes place. Additionally, perhaps nuclear fallout causes Iranians from the central west coast to evacuate into other nations, which would still leave Persia, (northern Iran) with some remaining *shields and helmets* to fight with in Ezekiel 38.

It is important to note that Ezekiel seems to intentionally omit Elam from the Gog of Magog invasion. This means that not all of modern-day Iran participates in the infamous Gog of Magog invasion of Israel. This conclusion can be drawn by recognizing that Ezekiel 32:24-26 identifies Elam and Meshech and Tubal. Meshech and Tubal are listed in the Magog invasion, but Elam is not. Why not? Why didn't Ezekiel list Elam alongside Persia to identify the entirety of modern-day Iran in his predicted invasion?

The fact that Ezekiel lists Persia in Ezekiel 27:10 and Ezekiel 38:5, and Elam in Ezekiel 32:24 implies that he recognized the territorial and ethnic distinctions between these two populations during his time. He probably omits Elam for the same reason that he omits the Arab populations identified in Psalm 83:6-8, which is because Elam and the Arabs of Psalm 83 do not participate in the Ezekiel 38 invasion.

The probable reason the Psalm 83 Arabs abstain is because they are dealt with in a prior separate war, won by the IDF. The reason Elam isn't listed is because Jeremiah 49:34-39 tells us the Elamites are also involved in their own separate prophecy. Thus, there appear to be three prophecies identified: Psalm 83 (Arabs), Ezekiel 38-39 (Persians), and Jeremiah 49:34-39 (Elamites).

In summary, it is important to note that clear territorial distinctions existed between Elam and Persia when Jeremiah and Ezekiel prophesied. It is doubtful that all of modern-day Iran participates in the Magog invasion of Israel in Ezekiel 38. More likely is the possibility that only northern Iran joins in with Magog (Russia); otherwise Ezekiel should have included both Persia and Elam in his prophecy. Since Elam is not part of Ezekiel 38, it suggests that Jeremiah's prophecy regarding Elam is a separate prophetic event. If Elam is struck at the foremost of its might prior to the fulfillment of Ezekiel 38, then this could be the reason Ezekiel omitted Elam from his prophecy.

# The Bleak Future of Islam

Both Psalm 83 and Ezekiel 38 involve predominately Muslim populations. The ten Arab populations of Psalm 83 and eight of the nine in Ezekiel 38 are unquestionably Islamic. The one exception in Ezekiel 38 is Russia. Although Russia's Muslim population remains a minority, that's expected to change by the year 2050. Vladimir Dergachyov, an advisor to Russian Prime Minister Vladimir Putin, said in 2007,

> Differences in growth rates of Christian and Muslim groups in Russia along with the arrival of Muslim immigrants from abroad will boost the percentage of Muslims there from 10 percent now to 50 percent by 2050.[69]

Regardless, if this boost occurs, the two invasions of Israel are characterized by Muslim attempts to destroy Jews, and the Jews win! Enmity toward Israel already existing in Iran, and rapidly incubating presently in Turkey, should mature into a fully-grown hatred for the Jewish state in the aftermath of the IDF defeat of the Arab Muslims in Psalm 83. Russia should have no problem coercing these two cohorts into its Ezekiel 38 coalition, subsequently.

When nineteen of Islam's most devout nations and terrorist populations are obliterated by the IDF in Psalm 83, and subsequently by the God of the Jews in Ezekiel 38, the public outcry of all remaining Muslims worldwide should be shouts of "Death to Israel!"—that is, the initial shouts.

It can be anticipated that sometime shortly after the Muslims digest the brevity of the two prophetic events, they will begin to question the power of their god Allah. First, they will be forced to wonder how a tiny state like Israel can defeat the Arabs. Many Muslims today are already asking that question in light of the fact that Israel still exists after past Arab attempts to destroy the Jewish state have failed.

Additionally, when world Muslims witness Israel receiving international esteem, which occurs when they bury the Muslim hordes of Gog, they

COMMENTARY

will inevitably be caused to question how the Jehovah of the Jews could successfully destroy the much more formidable Islamic forces.

> "For seven months the house of Israel will be burying them [the Muslim hordes of Gog], in order to cleanse the land. Indeed all the people of the land [a national Israeli effort] will be burying, and they will gain renown for it on the day that I am glorified," says the Lord GOD. (Ezekiel 39:12-13)

Zephaniah 2:8-11 suggests contextually that Allah's best days are behind him. His decline appears to be triggered by Psalm 83, and his final undoing appears to occur early in the tribulation period.

> "I have heard the reproach of Moab [central Jordan, a member of Psalm 83], And the insults of the people of Ammon [northern Jordan, a member of Psalm 83], With which they have reproached My [Jewish] people, And made arrogant threats against their borders. Therefore, as I live," Says the LORD of hosts, the God of Israel, "Surely Moab shall be like Sodom, And the people of Ammon like Gomorrah— Overrun with weeds and saltpits, And a perpetual desolation. The residue of My people [IDF] shall plunder them, And the remnant of My people shall possess them. This they shall have for their pride, Because they have reproached and made arrogant threats Against the [Jewish] people of the LORD of hosts. The LORD will be awesome to them, For He will reduce to nothing all the gods of the earth [Allah is the present god of these afore mentioned peoples]; People shall worship Him, Each one from his place, Indeed all the shores of the nations." (Zephaniah 2:8-11)

Zephaniah says the "Lord will be awesome to them," and that the gods of the earth will be "reduced to nothing." Who is "them," and what specific "gods," are in question? Consider that the previous passage refers to Moab and Ammon, who happen to be members of Psalm 83. And, they are threatening the Israelis and their borders; they must be "them." The Lord will be awesome to Moab and Ammon, which are primarily Jordanians today.

The Lord will prove He is awesome (in modern vernacular, "shock-and-awe") to the Jordanians by reducing their gods and ultimately "all the gods of the earth" to nothing. At Zephaniah's time, the god of Moab was Chemosh, and the god of Ammon was Milcom. Jeremiah, Zephaniah's contemporary, addresses the Jordanians and these two gods in the respective prophecies below.

For because you [Moab] have trusted in your works and your treasures, You also shall be taken. And Chemosh shall go forth into captivity, His priests and his princes together. (Jeremiah 48:7)

Woe to you, O Moab! The people of Chemosh perish; For your sons have been taken captive, And your daughters captive. "Yet I will bring back the captives of Moab In the latter days," says the LORD. (Jeremiah 48:46-47)

Against the Ammonites. Thus says the LORD: "Has Israel no sons? Has he no heir? Why then does Milcom inherit Gad, And his people dwell in its cities? Therefore behold, the days are coming," says the LORD, "That I will cause to be heard an alarm of war [probably Psalm 83] In Rabbah [near Amman Jordan] of the Ammonites; It shall be a desolate mound, And her villages shall be burned with fire. Then Israel shall take possession of his inheritance," says the LORD. "Wail, O Heshbon, for Ai is plundered! Cry, you daughters of Rabbah, Gird yourselves with sackcloth! Lament and run to and fro by the walls; For Milcom shall go into captivity With his priests and his princes together... But afterward I will bring back The captives of the people of Ammon," says the LORD. (Jeremiah 49:1-3,6)

Both instances above point out that the Jordanians and their gods go into captivity. But, in the "latter days" the captive Jordanians will be restored. This signals that these are end time events. Chemosh and Milcom are no longer the Jordanian gods. They, like most other Arab gods, submitted to Allah around the seventh century AD. Jeremiah wrote about 1,200 years earlier, before Islam came into existence. Thus, he appears to be suggesting the Jordanians will realize how awesome the Lord is when their current god, Allah, is reduced to nothing.

In my estimation, Psalm 83 is the punch to the gut of Islam. Subsequently, Islam receives an uppercut to the jawbone by Ezekiel 38-39. These two blows should decrease the world Muslim population dramatically, and begin the decline of Islam. By the time the Antichrist arrives on the scene, in the aftermath of the above, Islam should be in a serious state of disarray. The Muslim demographics below suggest about one-third of the Muslim population will be affected by these two wars.

Islam is the world's second largest religion after Christianity. According to a 2009 demographic study, Islam has 1.57 billion adherents, making up 23% of the world population.... Approximately 50 countries are a

Muslim-majority. Around 62% of the world's Muslims live in Asia, with over 683 million adherents in such countries as Indonesia, Pakistan, India, and Bangladesh. About 20% of Muslims live in Arab countries in the Middle East. The non-Arab countries of Turkey and Iran are the largest Muslim-majority countries; in Africa, Egypt and Nigeria have the most populous Muslim communities.[70]

Some suggest that the Antichrist will be a Muslim. However, by the time of his arrival Islam won't provide a very stable platform from which he can arise. Punched silly by these two pre-tribulation wars, by the time the first-half of the tribulation period begins, Islam should be knocked-out for the ten-count!

For more reading on this subject you can read my articles below:

"Does Daniel Debunk the Assyrian Antichrist," linked on the Internet at: http://prophecydepot.blogspot.com/2009/01/does-daniel-debunk-assyrian-antichrist.html

"Arguments Against a Muslim Antichrist," linked on the Internet at: http://www.prophecydepot.net/2011/arguments-against-a-muslim-antichrist/

"Operation Israeli Freedom," linked on the Internet at: http://www.prophecydepot.net/2008/operation-israeli-freedom-part-one-israel-expands-islam-expires-and-terror-ends/

"The Surrender of Allah's Akbar," linked on the Internet at: http://www.prophecydepot.net/2008/the-surrender-of-allahs-akbar-part-two-israel-expands-islam-expires-and-terror-ends/

"Jumping Jehoshaphat Judges Jihad," linked on the Internet at: http://isralestine-blog.blogspot.com/2008/06/jumping-jehoshaphat-judges-jihad.html

*Please read the next novel chapter now.*

# Chapter 8—
## Arabs Unite to Fight—
## Is it Psalm 83, Ezekiel 38 or Armageddon?

*Topics covered:* It's Not Armageddon, Yet; What is Armageddon, Anyway?; The Armageddon, Psalm 83 and Ezekiel 38 Distinctions; Why Satan Hates Jews; The Destruction of Damascus Creates a Harvest Field; Bible Prophecy is a Christian Witnessing Tool

This shortest novel chapter in *Revelation Road* addresses three important prophetic topics: Psalm 83, Ezekiel 38, and Armageddon. Furthermore, the chapter discusses the important role Bible prophecy is intended to have when witnessing to unbelievers.

## It's Not Armageddon, Yet

What is it, the Arab-Israeli war of Psalm 83 or the Russian-led invasion of Israel foretold in Ezekiel 38? This chapter concludes with George and Razz still stubbornly split on the controversial matter. Thus far, their prophetic tug-of-war has ended in a draw. Although this question remains unanswered, Razz' comment, "No, it's not Armageddon," was emphatically clear.

It is important to note Razz is correct. The scenario presented in this chapter is concerned with what appear to be pre-tribulation events. Therefore the response, "No, it's not Armageddon," which most scholars advocate occurs within the latter part of the tribulation period.

Armageddon ranks among the most popularized but misunderstood biblical terms in modern society's limited apocalyptic vocabulary. Even though most people lack a thorough knowledge about Armageddon, they are frightened by its end time implications. The mere utterance of the term can send shivers racing down one's spine. It seems whenever something significantly adverse happens in the world, Armageddon is the culprit.

## What is Armageddon, Anyway?

According to Dr. Arnold Fruchtenbaum, an expert on the subject, Armageddon involves much more than a massive apocalyptic battle; it consists of the following eight stages:[71]

- The Assembling of the Allies of the Antichrist,

- The Destruction of Babylon,

- The Fall of Jerusalem,

- The Armies of the Antichrist at Bozrah (modern day southern Jordan),

- The National Regeneration of Israel,

- The Second Coming of the Messiah,

- The Battle from Bozrah, and

- The Victory Ascent (of Christ) Up the Mount of Olives.

Importantly, Dr. Fruchtenbaum's teaching dispels the common misconceptions that every world crisis or catastrophe signals Armageddon has arrived. Since this book focuses primarily on what the author believes to be pre-tribulation (pre-trib) events, the details surrounding these eight stages of Armageddon will not be expounded upon at this point, other than to say it is extremely unlikely that any of these eight Armageddon stages apply to Psalm 83 or Ezekiel 38.

(More information on the eight-stages of Armageddon can be obtained in Dr. Arnold Fruchtenbaum's book, *The Footsteps of the Messiah*, available through Ariel Ministries at the website location of http://www.ariel.org.)

Although some eschatologists attempt to include the differing confederacies of Psalm 83 and Ezekiel 38 into the allies of the Antichrist in stage one above, Joel 3:2, 9-12, and elsewhere seems to nullify this possibility.

COMMENTARY

This is because thes passages informs us that the campaign of Armageddon involves all world nations. Neither Asaph, the author of Psalm 83, nor Ezekiel incorporated all world nations into their respective prophecies.

## The Armageddon, Psalm 83, and Ezekiel 38 Distinctions

This is one reason we can safely conclude Psalm 83, Ezekiel 38, and Armageddon are distinctly differing futuristic episodes. In contrast to all the nations of the world involved in Armageddon, the Psalm 83 and Ezekiel 38 images in the images section (appendix 26) evidence that only a select few nations participate.

Additional reasons we can draw this same conclusion are as follows:

*Psalm 83, Ezekiel 38 and Armageddon occur at different times.*

- Ezekiel 38 appears to be a pre-trib event. Psalm 83 seems to precede Ezekiel 38, making it likewise a pre-trib event. The arguments for Psalm 83 and Ezekiel 38 time placements are developed in the appendix entitled, *Psalm 83 or Ezekiel 38, Which is the Next Middle East News Headline*, and in the commentary chapter called *The Arabs Surrender!* The eight stages of Armageddon all occur during the trib-period, meaning Armageddon follows both Psalm 83 and Ezekiel 38.

*Psalm 83, Ezekiel 38 and Armageddon occur at different venues.*

- The Psalm 83 battlefield includes parts of Israel, Gaza, the West Bank, and portions of the territory inside the bordering Arab States of Syria, Lebanon, Jordan, Saudi Arabia, and Egypt.[72] Although the battlefield location is not specified within the Psalm, it can be determined from other connecting prophecies.

- The Ezekiel 38 invaders primarily swoop down like cloud cover from the north, upon the mountains of Israel. The battleground appears to include land inside Israel as well. The chapter called *Greater Israel Makes Plans for a Third Temple* illustrates that the land of Israel is probably greater in size and scope at the time Ezekiel 38 occurs.[73]

- The Armageddon battlefield spans from the Valley of Jezreel, where the armies of the Antichrist assemble, to Bozrah/Petra, modern day southern

Jordan. Due to its eight stages of development, it also incorporates Babylon (Iraq), Jerusalem, and the Kidron Valley, also known as the Valley of Jehoshaphat.[74]

*Psalm 83, Ezekiel 38 and Armageddon all suffer differing defeats.*

- The Arab forces in Psalm 83 appear to be defeated by the Israel Defense Forces in fulfillment of the prophecies found in Ezekiel 25:14, 37:10, Obadiah v. 18 and elsewhere. In Psalm 83:9-11, Asaph petitions God to empower the Israel Defense Forces (IDF) in a fashion similar to the way He did historically to Gideon over the Midianites, and Barak in his victory over the Caananites. Gideon and Barak were the generals of the IDF of their respective generations. These historical accounts are described in Judges chapters 4-8.

- The Ezekiel 38:1-6 invaders are not defeated by the IDF, as in Psalm 83. The Ezekiel invaders are defeated divinely by Jehovah, in accordance with the descriptions given in Ezekiel 38:18 to 39:6. In fact, the IDF does not appear to fulfill any significant military role in Ezekiel 38 or Armageddon. The armies of the Antichrist in Armageddon are defeated by Jesus Christ, as per Revelation 19:11-21.

*Psalm 83, Ezekiel 38 and Armageddon and are driven by differing motives.*

- Psalm 83 points out the bordering Arab populations want to destroy Israel, remove the name Israel from remembrance, and take the pastures of God as their possession. In essence, they want to commit Jewish genocide and confiscate the Promised Land.

- Ezekiel 38 says nine primarily non-Arab populations want to plunder Israel for spoil and great booty. In essence, they want to commit Jewish genocide and confiscate Israel's national wealth and livelihood.

- Armageddon is about the potential annihilation of the Jews. In essence, the Antichrist and his Armageddonite armies want to commit Jewish genocide to prove the God of Abraham, who promised he would have descendants forever, is a promise-breaking liar.

# Why Satan Hates Jews

Although these are three distinct events, they are all connected by a common thread, in that these events are all end time attempts at Jewish genocide. The extirpation of the Jew is no new phenomena. Hebrew history is plagued with extermination and first born male slaughter attempts. One must conclude that the annihilation of the Jew is an obsession of Satan's. But why is this? As emphasized in the previous paragraph, Satan desperately needs to discredit the Lord's covenant-making character. If Satan can destroy every last Jew, the obvious conclusion is that the Lord broke His promise to Abraham.

Scriptures like Genesis 13:15 and 22:17 clearly evidence Abraham would have biological descendants forever. Passages like Genesis 50:24, Deuteronomy 1:8, 34:4, Isaiah 41:8, Jeremiah 31:26 and elsewhere identify these descendants as being Israelis. Simply equated: 0 Jews on Earth = 1 flawed God in heaven. If the Lord's character is flawed, then His divine will is not perfect, and therefore, the fall of Satan would appear to have been justified.

However, the justification of his fall is not his only preoccupation in these end times. He is greatly concerned about the longevity of his current freedoms. Job 1:7 and 2:2 informs us Satan travels between heaven and earth seemingly at ease. 1 John 5:19 tells us Satan possesses enormous power over the world. Revelation 12:7-12 and 20:1-3 declare Satan's freedoms will be stripped from him because of his wrongdoings. Revelation 12 announces he will be cast out of heaven and Revelation 20 pronounces 1,000 years of judgment upon him.

Satan's thousand-year imprisonment directly correlates with the millennial reign of Christ, spanning the same duration according to Revelation 20:4-7. The millennial reign of Christ commences shortly after the final act of his glorious second coming, prophesied in Matthew 24:30 and elsewhere. Christ will not return until the nation of Israel says, "Blessed is He who comes in the name of the Lord," according to Matthew 23:37-39. Hosea 5:15 states this pronouncement will occur in the tribulation period, when the Jews are being afflicted by the Antichrist during Armageddon. Hosea says they will recognize their offense, and subsequently beckon His return.

> I will return again to My place [After resurrecting Christ ascended to heaven and presently sits at the right hand side of the throne of God] Till they acknowledge their offense [Jewish generational rejection of Christ as the Messiah]. Then they will seek My face; In their affliction [The great tribulation period] they will earnestly seek Me. (Hosea 5:15)

COMMENTARY

Satan utilizes the Antichrist in Armageddon to commit Jewish genocide. Zechariah 13:8 tells us that two-thirds of the Jews in Israel will be killed. But, a remnant will survive and will recognize Christ as the Messiah. Thus, the other primary reason Satan is obsessed with Jewish extirpation is to prevent any Jew from saying, "Blessed is He who comes in the name of the Lord." If Christ doesn't return and establish His messianic kingdom, then Satan will escape judgment. Simply equated: 0 Jews on Earth = 1 Messiah stranded in heaven.

## The Destruction of Damascus Creates a Harvest Field

Additionally, this chapter encourages believers to anticipate an increased harvest field of hungry souls in the aftermath of Damascus's ruination. The elimination of the world's oldest continuously populated city in recorded history will far surpass the horrors of the September 11, 2001, terrorist attacks on the World Trade Center towers. As it was then, it will undoubtedly be at the time of the destruction of Damascus, a perfect time to preach the gospel.

Isaiah emphatically announces that the destruction of Damascus will cause mankind to look toward its maker and question its idols. This point is exposited upon in the commentary chapter called *Isaiah 17 – The Destruction of Damascus*, located in the "Panic in Damascus" chapter. The pertinent Isaiah passage is below.

> In that day shall men look unto their Maker, and their eyes shall have respect to the Holy One of Israel. And they shall not look to the altars, the work of their hands; neither shall they have respect to that which their fingers have made, either the Asherim, or the sun-images. (Isaiah 17:7-8, ASV).

Believers are encouraged to familiarize themselves with the prophecies described throughout this book, like the destruction of Damascus, so when they occur they can be explained biblically. Non-believers are also encouraged to study these prophecies so their occurrence convinces them to convert to Christianity, if they haven't previously done so by then. Conversion is the most natural response one undergoes when they witness the fulfillment of Bible prophecy.

Pharaoh of Egypt was so impressed with Joseph's ability to foretell the future, he elevated him to ruler over all Egypt (Genesis 41:41). Babylonian King Nebuchadnezzar was so pleased with Daniel's prophetic interpretations that he extolled and honored God (Daniel 4:37). The Persian King Cyrus was so moved by prophecies written in Isaiah 44:28 and 45:1, he commissioned the rebuilding of the Jewish Temple (2 Chronicles 36:22-23 and Ezra 1:1-4).

These are the last days, and eschatologists and evangelists should be discerning the times and comparing notes like Razz and George in our story. In so doing, they exhibit intelligent faith before the watchful eyes of unbelieving humanity. The two stars of our story line realize that receptivity to biblical explanations of tragic world events increases when they adversely affect human lives.

# Bible Prophecy is a Christian Witnessing Tool

The terrorist toppling of the twin towers on September 11, 2011, is an excellent case in point. The surprise event shocked America and the world, and prompted many Christian leaders and pastors to travel to "Ground Zero." For many of them it became a ripened occasion to present the gospel. They were presented prime opportunities to inject the good news of Jesus Christ into an otherwise bad situation. As a result of their preaching, many came to the Lord.

That's the good news; but unfortunately, many of those pastors, when asked what the Bible had to say specifically about what happened, couldn't provide a sound prophetic answer. Why? Because many of them weren't studying or preaching prophecy for a variety of reasons. When asked point-blank what the Bible had to say about the towers falling, they didn't recognize the poignant prophecies. How many more could have been led to the Lord if they were told something like this below?

> **Question:** "Dear Pastor, I'm in shock; what has just happened? Do these September 11, terror events mean these are the last days of Armageddon? Does the Bible have anything to say about what just happened, and what America's future holds?"

> **Answer:** "Absolutely, the Bible has volumes to say about what has just happened, and yes, these events evidence that we are living in the last days. Fortunately friend, it's not Armageddon. At least, not yet anyway, which means there is still a short period of time to get saved and escape that coming period of the Antichrist and his unprecedented world tribulation.

> The Bible does predict the future. According to Isaiah the prophet, it is the only holy book that can. He declared in his forty-sixth chapter that only God knows the future. It is one of the ways the Lord authenticates His sovereign authority over all creation.

COMMENTARY

What the world just witnessed was a precursor to Armageddon. It was an act of terrorism, and terrorism is the ugly by-product of the Arab-Israeli conflict in the Middle East. This ongoing conflict between the Arabs and Jews was predicted in many places in the Bible, like Psalm 83, Ezekiel 25, Jeremiah 49, and elsewhere. In fact Ezekiel 38 and 39 present fifty-two verses of enormous detail about a coming major Mideast Muslim invasion of Israel, that will thoroughly shock the world.

Prophecy is a big deal in the Bible; about one-third of the Holy Scriptures are prophetic. There are about 31,373 passages in the Bible, and that means about 10,000 are tied to prophecy. And among them is Jeremiah 49:16, which seems to specifically address Palestinian terrorism. Israel has been facing off with this terrorism for decades now, but Al-Qaeda has elevated it to a dangerous new level by bringing it into America's backyard!

Hamas, Hezbollah, and maybe even Al-Qaeda appear to be identified in Bible prophecies written over 2,500 years ago. The prophecies they are involved in are powerful, world-changing events that are extremely unfavorable for America. And dear friend, they are stage-setting to happen soon, probably in our generation.

Yes, a loving God wants us to know what's headed our way, and that's why the Bible is filled with prophecies for our generation. Revelation 19:10 declares that the testimony of Jesus Christ is the very spirit of prophecy! Do you know Him? Would you like to?

He not only knows the future, but He also knows you. The Bible says He created you and loves you so much He knows the very number of hairs on your head.[75] Jesus died for our sins and rose from the grave[76] to prove He is alive and capable of saving our souls from the *pit of...* well, look around at all the rubble of the twin towers and you get my drift."

This type of informed response gives the sincere questioner something prophetically to sink his or her teeth into. It goes far beyond simply stating *Jesus loves you, this I know, for the Bible tells me so.* Of course, that is the message, but how the love of Christ gets introduced to the unsaved is all-important.

Prophecy as a witnessing tool works. It is how I personally got saved. Having wandered aimlessly in the world flirting with eastern religions and agnosticism, I was eventually captivated by a Chuck Missler Bible study on the book of Revelation. From that point forward, I devoted my life to Christ. For many, the splendor of God's creation or the call of a cancerous crisis causes them to consider Christ, but for me it was all about Bible prophecy.

For some, evangelizing the unsaved comes easy, but for others it is more difficult. However, for every Christian, witnessing is facilitated when world-changing events create a bountiful harvest field of hungering souls. The apocalyptic Middle East is coming soon, just as the Bible predicted, and when it does the world will want answers. If a Christian understands the pertinent Bible prophecies, they will be able to deliver the right responses.

*Please read the next novel chapter now.*

COMMENTARY

# Chapter 9–
## The Final Arab – Israeli War!

*Topics covered:* When Diplomacy Ends, War Begins; The Ancient Arab Hatred of the Jews; The Ezekiel 35 – Psalm 83 Connection; Ezekiel 35 and Author Commentary; Why the World Rejoices When Israel Wins; Who is Ezekiel 35 Identifying as Mount Seir?; Why Ezekiel 35 is Not an Armageddon Event; What is the Glorious Land of Daniel 11:41?

By this stage of the novel, Razz concedes to his best friend George that the Middle East war events occurring are related to Psalm 83, rather than Ezekiel 38-39. Presently, there are those who believe Ezekiel 38 precedes or incorporates Psalm 83. The appendix called *Is Ezekiel 38 Imminent?* argues against Psalm 83 as part of Ezekiel's prophecy. And, as pointed out in the appendix called *Psalm 83 or Ezekiel 38, Which is the Next Middle East News Headline?*, Psalm 83 probably precedes Ezekiel 38.

The secure dwelling and extremely prosperous end-times Israel described in Ezekiel 38:8-13 doesn't appear to exist as of the time of the authoring of this book in 2011. However, after Israel's surrounding Arab enemies identified in the Psalm are defeated, Israel should be able to at least temporarily dwell securely.

## When Diplomacy Ends, War Begins

Addressing the fact that war rather than peace resulted in the Middle East, this novel chapter declared, "Diplomacy had failed, staining the legacies of several US presidents and leaving all-out war as the only option."

Since the time of the Madrid Conference in October, 1991, to the present, a long list of US presidents have pressured Israel to make concessions for peace with the Arabs in general, and Palestinians specifically. In his article called the *Betrayal of Israel*, end-times expert Dr. David Reagan writes:

> Our nation's betrayal of Israel began in 1990 when the Communist government of Russia decided to open its doors to allow Jews to emigrate to Israel. . .Israel's Prime Minister, Yitzhak Shamir, applied to the World Bank for a loan of $10 billion to cope with the needs of the refugees. He was told that the loan would be granted only if the United States would guarantee it. When he then turned to the first Bush Administration, he was told that the guarantee would be supplied only if he agreed to start negotiating with the Palestinians. This resulted in the Madrid Conference in October of 1991. In short, we forced Israel to start down the suicidal path of trading land for peace. [77]

Since George H. Bush, each consecutive president has followed in the same vain footsteps, adding additional pressure along the way.

## October of 1991

US President George H. Bush invited Israel, Syria, Lebanon, Jordan, Egypt, and the Palestinians to a conference in Madrid, Spain. The goal was to model a broader Arab-Israeli peace patterned after the Egyptian-Israel treaty made in 1979. However, Prime Minister Shamir's plans for the $10 billion in US loan guarantees included expanding Jewish settlements in order to facilitate the influx of Jews flowing into Israel. The Arabs vehemently opposed Israeli settlement expansion, putting Bush in a precarious geopolitical *tug-of-war*.

The Arabs began questioning America's role as Mideast mediator at the time.[78] This troubled George H. Bush, because he had achieved high political marks for his handling of *Operation Desert Storm* against Saddam Hussein, in Iraq earlier that year.[79] For many, Bush's behavior at the time signaled the pro-Israel Ronald Reagan years had ended. As the list of failed attempts made by his successor's evidence below, their suspicions proved correct.

## July of 2000

US President Bill Clinton hosted the Middle East Peace Summit at Camp David. Unsuccessfully, he attempted to negotiate a final settlement status to end the Palestinian/Israeli conflict with Israeli Prime Minister Ehud Barak, and Palestinian Authority President Yasser Arafat. PM Barak was willing to concede land for peace. He generously offered to return about ninety percent of the West Bank to the Palestinians. His offer was rejected forcefully by Yasser Arafat. It was at that point many Israelis, liberal and conservative, began to question the true intentions of the Palestinians. It appeared Arafat wanted all, rather than part, of Israel.

## April of 2003

US President George W. Bush issued his three-phased Performance-Based Roadmap Plan to a Permanent 2-State Solution to the Israeli-Palestinian conflict. Bush's plan amounted to another land-for-peace deal, that didn't resolve the Middle East conflict. Phase one, calling for the cessation of Palestinian Terror, never got accomplished. His plan still sits on the shelf collecting dust.

## September of 2010

US President Barrack Obama hosted a meeting with Middle East leaders and foreign dignitaries. Former Egyptian President Hosni Mubarak, Jordan's King Abdullah II, Israeli Prime Minister Benjamin Netanyahu, Palestinian Authority President Mahmoud Abbas, and Quartet representatives Toni Blair and Hillary Clinton were all in attendance. Obama hosted this conference in order to jump-start direct peace talks between the Israelis and Palestinians. It didn't work, and by the end of that same year, all hopes for Mideast peace had again collapsed

## May of 2011

US President Barack Obama called upon Israel to forfeit lands acquired as a result of their victory over Jordan, Egypt, and Syria in the Six-Day war in June of 1967. It was another desperate American attempt to pressure Israel into a land-for-peace deal to resolve the Mideast conflict.

Just days after Obama's preposterous "real estate request," Israeli Prime Minister Benjamin Netanyahu declared before the US Congress, in a historic moment, that Israel would not comply with President Obama's wishes. He said Israel refused to give up the land it acquired in 1967, and furthermore specified the following:

- Jerusalem *will* be the undivided capital of the Jewish State,

- Millions of Palestinian refugees *won't* be returning inside Israel,

- The Palestinians *must* recognize Israel's right to exist as the sovereign Jewish State,

- The Hamas – Fatah unity agreement of 2011 *must* be abolished,

- Palestinian unilateral attempts at statehood through the United Nations *must* cease,

- Israel maintains the *right* to defensible borders,

- The Israeli demographic population changes since 1967 *must* be accepted, and

- Israel *will* monitor Palestinian organizations and operations for national security purposes.[80]

Simply stated, the summation of Netanyahu's declarations suggests that land-for-peace deals are over. They have run their two-decade course, to no avail. They have proven to be "fruitless" efforts, as expressed in this novel chapter, and Israel no longer possesses the luxury of pursuing the land-for-peace path further. This is because during the four presidential periods identified above, Israel's enemies have become armed and dangerous. They now possess the weapons and manpower to accomplish the mandate of Psalm 83:4, which is to destroy the Jewish state so that the name of Israel will be remembered no more.

*When diplomacy fails, war begins.* Diplomacy has failed and in the process America, apart from Israel's Arab enemies, has done more to pressure Israel to divide the Promised Land than any other country, since Israel became a nation on May 14, 1948. The futile efforts of these US Administrations have potentially put Americans in harm's way, according to prophecies like these below.

> I will also gather all nations, And bring them down to the Valley of Jehoshaphat; And I will enter into judgment with them there On account of My people, My heritage Israel, Whom they have scattered among the nations; They have also divided up My land. (Joel 3:2).

> And it shall happen in that day that I will make Jerusalem a very heavy stone for all peoples; all who would heave it away [divide the land] will surely be cut in pieces, though all nations of the earth are gathered against it. (Zechariah 12:3).

Although these prophecies are specifically addressing judgments that occur within the trib-period during the Armageddon Campaign, they should be a warning to Americans today. Suffice it to say, the Lord does not take kindly to those nations seeking to divide the Promised Land, or tear Jerusalem away from Jewish sovereignty. The overriding, divine rule-of-thumb is determined by Genesis 12:3, for America and all countries. This passage promises blessings to the nations that support Israel and curses those whose actions adversely affect the Jewish state.

Americans should recognize that the sun now sets on the British Empire. There was a time when it couldn't because British sovereignty extended into Australia, Asia, Africa, India, South America, and North America. However, when the British failed to implement Lord Balfour's declaration of 1917, which called for the restoration of the Jewish state, the sun began setting on one country after another as the empire collapsed. The US presidential timeline of meddling in Mideast matters above, explains why Americans over the past two decades have witnessed the sun begin to set on its superpower status.

## The Ancient Arab Hatred of the Jews

The Bible seems to predict that a climactic, concluding Arab-Israeli war, rather than political diplomacy, resolves the Arab-Israeli conflict. If correct, this war is primarily described in Psalm 83. Ultimately, a politically brokered peace-pact is confirmed, as recorded in Daniel 9:27, between the Antichrist and Israel, but that does not appear to apply in this case. That compact is made between Israel and the fourth horseman, *Death and Hades*, of the apocalypse in Revelation 6:7-8, according to Isaiah 28:15, 18. Isaiah alludes to *Sheol*, which is apparently the Hebrew word for the Greek *Hades*. The confirmation of this covenant is an event postponed until the Seal judgments are opened, in the book of Revelation. Psalm 83 likely occurs prior to this.

It's astounding to consider that the pent-up Arab anger against the Jews, that has plagued the Middle East for about 4,000 years, appears to be nearing a conclusion. The final Arab - Israeli war seems to close the final chapter on this ancient hatred. All present political attempts to resolve the conflict are destined for failure because they don't address this deep-seated hatred. Unless the historical biblical accounts and pertinent forthcoming Bible prophecies are appropriately aligned and understood, the geopolitics of the Middle East will remain a mystery to the international community.

The bottom line is that the preponderance of Middle East Arabs hates the Jews. There is no politically correct way to make this point. Most of those Arabs opposed to Israel's modern day existence are the product of an ancient hatred dating back to the time of the Jewish and Arab patriarchs and matriarchs.

Satan cleverly instigated this longstanding enmity and around the seventh century AD had Mohammed, the Muslim prophet, incorporate it into the Islamic religion. There are a plethora of Anti-Semitic Islamic scriptures, like Surah 5:51, which clearly instruct Muslims not to befriend Jews.[81] The fact that the preponderance of the twenty-two Islamic members of the Arab League won't recognize Israel's right to exist or conduct normal, national business relations with the Jewish State, testifies to this hatred.

Only Egypt and Jordan were willing to negotiate a temporary fragile peace with Israel. But, their respective treaties have seemingly become untenable as a result of the 2011 Arab Spring. These will prove to be temporary, fragile treaties, because Bible prophecy predicts these two Arab states attack Israel in the ten-member Arab confederacy of Psalm 83. Egypt in 1979 and Jordan in 1994 were motivated by the self-serving purposes of fear and greed to negotiate peace with Israel. They were tired of defeat in the Arab-Israeli wars of 1948, 1967, and 1973, and US financial aid came alongside to their rescue.

These two nations' cooperation, at a significant cost, set the false precedent for thinking that Mideast peace could be purchased. Failed land-for-peace deals have since evidenced this is an erroneous presumption. To understand the temporary fragile nature of Egypt's and Jordan's peace with Israel, read the attached appendices called *Jordan to Soon Sever Ties with Israel* and *Is Egypt in Psalm 83?*

The Bible refers to this perpetual enmity displayed by the Arabs against the Jews as an "ancient hatred!" The two Hebrew words for it are *olam ebah*. The prophet Ezekiel uses these two words in tandem twice, and by doing so describes, "A hateful condition stemming back long ago in ancient times, perpetuated throughout time, manifesting into hostility with no apparent end in sight."[82]

> Because you [Mount Seir] have had an ancient [*olam*] hatred [*ebah*], and have shed the blood of the children of Israel by the power of the sword at the time of their calamity, when their iniquity came to an end. (Ezekiel 35:5).
>
> Thus says the Lord GOD: "Because the Philistines dealt vengefully and took vengeance with a spiteful heart, to destroy because of the old [*olam*] hatred [*ebah*]." (Ezekiel 25:15).

Ezekiel 35 identifies the origin of the hatred to be the area of Mount Seir, and Ezekiel 25 demonstrates that long after its origination the disposition of hatred plagued Philistia. The Philistines embraced the *olam ebah* hundreds of years later. Mount Seir is the mountain range that ran the length of biblical Edom, which is where Esau settled around 1,900 to 1,800 BC. Mount Seir is located in modern-day southern Jordan.

The Philistines settled about 100 miles west of Mount Seir, near the Mediterranean seacoast. They were a seafaring people that invaded Egypt around 1,188 BC.[83] Shortly thereafter, Philistia became established in the proximity of today's Gaza Strip.

Genesis 36:8-9, Deuteronomy 2:5, and Joshua 24:4, clearly evidence that Mount Seir was home to Esau and his descendants, the Edomites (Genesis 36:1, 9). Esau was Jacob's twin brother, according to Genesis 25:23-34. We are informed that Jacob was renamed Israel in Genesis 32:28 and 35:10. Scripture says Esau coveted his brother Jacob's blessing. He desperately wanted to be heir to the messianic line passing through Abraham and Isaac. Esau's jealousy and covetousness fomented into a hatred of Jacob, and a desire to kill him.

> So Esau hated Jacob because of the blessing with which his father blessed him, and Esau said in his heart, "The days of mourning for my father are at hand; then I will kill my brother Jacob." (Genesis 27:41)

This hatred surfaces again over 400 years later, during the time of the Hebrew exodus out of Egypt, as recorded in Numbers 20. In fact, Ezekiel 35:5 predicts this hatred revives in the end-times. The American Standard Version translates Ezekiel 35:5 closing with the words "in the time of the iniquity of the end."

What Ezekiel prophesies is that the Arab hatred of the Jews survives until the end times, as evidenced by the Arab shedding of Jewish blood in the last days. The fact that the Arabs have fought against the Jews conventionally in 1948, 1956, 1967, and 1973, and in subsequent intifadas and terrorist jihads, evidences that the ancient hatred is still alive, in fulfillment of Ezekiel 35:5.

Ezekiel 35:6, the very next verse, cautions the Arabs to beware of their dangerous end-time's thirst for Jewish blood. Taking an in-depth look at Ezekiel 35 imparts a greater understanding of the present Middle East problem and how it culminates in the Psalm 83 war.

## The Ezekiel 35 – Psalm 83 Connection

Ezekiel 34:13, 36:24, 37:12, 38:8, and 39:27-28 all talk about the Jews being re-gathered out from the nations of the world back into the Holy Land of Israel. By the time one reads through Ezekiel 34-39 they are left with the indelible impression that in the last days, the Jews will be re-gathered into Israel. There is absolutely no way to draw any other conclusion!

Therefore, it stands to reason contextually that because Ezekiel 35 is huddled in the midst of the above chapters, it must have some association with the Jews, Israel, and the end times. As already demonstrated above, Ezekiel 35:5 is talking about a hatred that prompts Arabs to shed Jewish blood in the end times. So with this presupposition in mind, a study of Ezekiel 35 should underscore the present Arab-Israeli predicament in the Middle East.

# Ezekiel 35 and Author Commentary

(Ezekiel 35:1-4) Moreover the word of the LORD came to me, saying, "Son of man, set your face *against* Mount Seir and prophesy *against* it, and say to it, 'Thus says the Lord GOD: "Behold, O Mount Seir, I am *against* you; I will stretch out My hand *against* you, And make you most desolate; I shall lay your cities waste, And you shall be desolate. Then you shall know that I am the LORD. (emphasis added).

Ezekiel begins with the word "moreover," which implies a continuation from the previous chapter 34. Ezekiel 34, concluded with an end-times' depiction of the Jews being re-gathered into Israel, restored as God's people, and being blessed. From other Scriptures, we recognize that Israel becomes blessed during the messianic kingdom, but before this is re-gathered in a condition of unbelief in preparation for judgment.

Dr. Arnold Fruchtenbaum says the following in his book, *The Footsteps of the Messiah,* regarding this two-step process:

The Bible…speaks of two distinct worldwide regatherings (of the Jews). First, there is to be a worldwide regathering in unbelief in preparation for judgment; specifically the judgment of the Tribulation. That is to be followed by a second worldwide regathering in faith in preparation for blessing, specifically, the blessing of the Messianic Kingdom.[84]

The passages Dr. Fruchtenbaum uses to support this conclusion about the re-gathering in unbelief in preparation for judgment are contained in Ezekiel 20:33-38 and Ezekiel 22:17-22. Therefore, we are to recognize that the re-gathering of Jews into Israel occurs over time, and involves a two-step process.

The inference from Ezekiel 35:1-4 is that at some point during the two-step restoration process of the nation Israel, Mount Seir does something to aggravate the Lord. Four times the prophet uses the word "against," evidencing the Lord is provoked to anger to act *against* Mount Seir. Two times he uses the word desolate. Far beyond a divine disciplinary hand-slap, Mount Seir will experience desolation. The severity of punishment points out the seriousness of Mount Seir's crime.

As discussed earlier, Mount Seir finds connection with Esau and his Edomite descendants. However, we find out later in Ezekiel 35:15 that Mount Seir represents more Arabs than just the Edomites. Who exactly is the Mount Seir of Ezekiel 35? What are they guilty of? Lastly, at what point in the two-step regathering process does Mount Seir experience desolation?

> (Ezekiel 35:5) Because you have had an ancient hatred, and have shed the blood of the children of Israel by the power of the sword at the time of their calamity, when their iniquity came to an end.

Fortunately, we don't have to look farther than the next verse to find out what Mount Seir is guilty of. Because of their historical hatred of the Jews, the Arabs spitefully shed Jewish blood. The spilt blood angers the Lord; not just any blood, but Jewish blood. Furthermore, Ezekiel declares "the power of the sword" is used to shed this blood. This means the Arabs' war against Israel. This passage also identifies the timing of the Arab war. It occurs during the calamitous end times.

> (Ezekiel 35:6) therefore, as I live," says the Lord GOD, "I will prepare you for blood, and blood shall pursue you; [Arabs] since you have not hated [shedding Jewish] blood, therefore blood shall pursue you."

COMMENTARY

Arab blood for Jewish blood is the remedial requirement determined by the Lord. This is the curse-for-curse-in-kind specification in Genesis 12:3. The Arabs severely curse Israel, and in turn will be similarly severely cursed. The Lord preferred the Arabs would have abandoned their ancient hatred of the Jews. The inhumane treatment of the Jews by the Nazis during the Holocaust should have prompted empathy from the Arabs, but verse six informs they still hated the Jewish bloodline.

> (Ezekiel 35:7-9) Thus I will make Mount Seir most desolate, and cut off from it the one who leaves and the one who returns. And I will fill its mountains with the slain; on your hills and in your valleys and in all your ravines those who are slain by the *sword* shall fall. I will make you perpetually desolate, and your cities shall be uninhabited; then you shall know that I am the LORD. (emphasis added).

Again Ezekiel repeats the sentiment of verse three: Mount Seir will be "most desolate." The mountains, hills, valleys, and ravines will be filled with the slain and the cities will be abandoned. In the aftermath, the Arabs will realize that the Lord had His hand in the massive slayings. Ezekiel 35:3 declares the outstretched hand of the Lord causes the desolation, but here in verse eight we discover the Lord's weapon of choice is the "sword."

Ezekiel 25:14 may hold an important clue as to how the sword in the Lord's outstretched hand represents the IDF executing judgment upon Edom:

> "I will lay My vengeance on Edom by the hand of My people Israel [IDF] that they may do in Edom [Mount Seir] according to My anger and according to My fury; and they shall know My vengeance," says the Lord GOD. (Ezekiel 25:14).

This passage finds definite association with a military judgment upon the Edomites, who hailed from ancient Mount Seir. Esau's Edomite descendants will be forced to recognize the Lord's hand of judgment when the IDF takes vengeance against them.

It is important to note that the Edomites are listed first within the Psalm 83 Arab confederacy, as the "tents of Edom." In *Isralestine,* in the chapter called *Whodomites, Who are the Edomites Today,* I carefully connect the Palestinian refugees, through several historical waves of migration, with the tents of Edom. Today the Edomites have ethnic representation within the Palestinians.

It is additionally important to note that the massive slaying of Edomites described in Ezekiel 35:7-9 by the IDF has not occurred yet. After Ezekiel wrote, many Edomites were slaughtered by the Seleucid king Antigonus around 312 BC. However, this episode did not involve the IDF at the time, disqualifying it as a fulfillment of Ezekiel 25:14.

Subsequently, around 126 BC, the Jewish high priest John Hyrcanus fought and killed many Edomites. But, his IDF victory did not fill the mountains, hills, valleys, and ravines with the slain and cause the abandonment of the cities. To the contrary, Hyrcanus allowed the surviving Edomites, who were called Idumeans at the time, to remain and repopulate within their cities as long as they converted to Israel's religion of Judaism. In addition, neither of the Antigonus or Hyrcanus victories occurred in the end time's fulfillment of Ezekiel 35:5.

> (Ezekiel 35:10-13) "'Because you have said, "These two nations and these two countries shall be mine, and we will possess them," although the LORD was there, therefore, as I live,' says the Lord GOD, 'I will do according to your anger and according to the envy which you showed in your hatred against them; and I will make Myself known among them when I judge you. Then you shall know that I am the LORD. I have heard all your blasphemies which you have spoken against the mountains of Israel, saying, "They are desolate; they are given to us to consume." Thus with your mouth you have boasted against Me and multiplied your words against Me; I have heard them.'"

COMMENTARY

Ezekiel uses the word "because" three times in this chapter, and verse ten begins with the second usage. The first "because" dealt with the ancient hatred in verse five and the second now addresses the Arab motive. The Arabs seek to possess "two nations" and "two countries." Because the Arabs harbor an ancient hatred, they shed Jewish blood. The reason they shed this blood is to destroy the Israelis and possess Israel.

Ezekiel 35:10 says, "These two nations and these two countries shall be mine, and we will possess them." At the time Ezekiel wrote, approximately 2,600 years ago, Israel was a divided country. There was the northern kingdom, commonly referred to as Israel or Samaria, and a southern kingdom, commonly known as Judah. Prior to Ezekiel's time, in 722 BC, the northern kingdom was conquered by the Assyrians, and subsequently in 586 BC, the Babylonians conquered Judah.

The Hebrew word for nations is *goy*, and for countries is *erets*. *Goy* identifies Gentiles, nations, or peoples; whereas *erets* deals more specifically with the earth and its lands, territories, or regions. Ezekiel is probably declaring the Arabs seek sovereignty over the Jewish people and their divided lands.

Being omniscient and omnipresent, the Lord possesses the unique "fly on the wall" advantage of sitting in on all confidential Arab meetings, past, present, and future. Ezekiel summarizes the Anti-Semitic gist of these meetings for us by revealing the Arabs declare blasphemies against the mountains of Israel. Ezekiel notates the Arabs are angry, envious, hateful, and boastful people in their hatred of the Jews and their God Jehovah. They believe Israel's desolation evidences Israel's God is weak, and the land (mountains) of Israel belongs to the Arabs.

Below are some specific Arab quotes taken from the Bible, regarded with destroying the Jews and possessing the land of Israel;

- "Because you have said, 'These two nations and these two countries shall be mine, and we will possess them.'" (Ezekiel 35:10)

- "They [mountains of Israel] are desolate; they are given to us to consume." (Ezekiel 35:12)

- "Aha! The ancient heights have become our possession!" (Ezekiel 36:2)

- "Come, and let us cut them off from being a nation, that the name of Israel may be remembered no more." (Psalm 83:4)

- "Let us take for ourselves the pastures of God for a possession." (Psalm 83:12)

Jordan, identified by the Psalm 83 members of Moab and Ammon, has also made troubling comments along these lines. Zephaniah 2:8 informs us of the following;

> I [the Lord] have heard the reproach of Moab, and the insults of the people of Ammon, with which they have reproached My people, and made arrogant threats against their borders.

This disposition of Arab hatred and desire to dispossess Israel of their land was prophesied in Psalm 83. The Psalm warns that the Arabs will confederate, form a crafty plan, and attack Israel. Their mandate is to destroy the Jews and erase the name of Israel forever. Psalm 83:12 informs us the goal of the confederacy is possession of the land of Israel. They don't want a two-state solution, wherein Jews and Arabs co-exist side-by-side in peace; rather, they want one more Arab State of Palestine. Since Ezekiel 35:5 suggests the Arab war occurs in the calamitous end times, it appears that it could occur in the near future.

> (Ezekiel 35:14-15) "Thus says the Lord GOD: 'The whole earth will rejoice when I make you desolate. As you rejoiced because the inheritance of the house of Israel was desolate, so I will do to you; you shall be desolate, O Mount Seir, as well as all of Edom—all of it! Then they shall know that I am the LORD.'"

These verses, like Ezekiel 35:6 above, come out of the Genesis 12:3 foreign policy. The Arabs rejoiced when the Jews dwelt outside of their homeland in the Diaspora and Israel lay desolate. In turn, mankind will rejoice at the conclusion of the Arab – Israeli conflict.

## Why the World Rejoices When Israel Wins

Ezekiel proclaims "The whole earth will rejoice when I make you [Mount Seir] desolate." When the Arabs, represented by Mount Seir, are made desolate, humanity will be extremely pleased. This is peculiar, considering this desolation is characterized by a massive Arab slaughter by the IDF, according to Ezekiel 35:8, 25:14, and Obadiah v. 18. Considering most of the world presently believes Israel occupies Arab lands illegally, it is hard to imagine humanity would accept, let alone be comforted by, the massive slaughter of Arabs by the IDF. Yet, that is what Ezekiel predicts will occur. How can this be?

The picture painted in the novel aspect of *Revelation Road*, although fictitious, could resemble the turbulence created by the Psalm 83 Arab – Israeli War. Much

COMMENTARY

of mankind could be fearful of terrorism and oil-dependent world economies in dire straits, due to OPEC-induced oil shortages. Christians could certainly rejoice, because they will witness their God honor His foreign policy commitments in Genesis 12:3. But what about secular, unbelieving man?

Christians will be able to say the Arabs pursued Jewish blood and so Jewish blood retaliated according to Ezekiel 35:6. Believers will rejoice because fulfilled Bible prophecies reinforce their faith by proving the Bible is true, and the Lord remains in control of world events.

However, unbelievers won't see it that way. They will be more concerned with how Mideast events adversely affect their lives. The fact that they rejoice when the Arabs are desolated, evidences the Arab-Israeli War created severe problems for them. Exactly how humanity is aggravated by Mideast turbulence is speculation at this point; however, when the war is over and the Arabs defeated, the world rejoices. Apparently, a temporary regional stability of sorts occurs in the aftermath.

Somehow an IDF victory pleases the international community. Perhaps they fear a nuclear war might spill over into other places and are relieved the IDF victory eliminates that possibility. Or, perhaps the threat of international terror subsides, and Israel gets some OPEC oil flowing back into world markets as it mops up the war-zone. Somehow, Israel seems to strike it rich after Psalm 83, because Russia stops rejoicing shortly thereafter, and forms the Gog of Magog coalition, in fulfillment of Ezekiel 38-39. These invaders come to capture Israel's great spoil according to Ezekiel 38:13.

It appears that the Psalm 83 War is so devastating that the world rejoices when it ends. Maybe it has less to do with the world hating Arabs, and more to do with the world needing a respite from the past six decades of Mideast chaos.

# Who is Ezekiel 35 Identifying as Mount Seir?

Ezekiel 35:15 says "O Mount Seir, as well as all of Edom," and then repeats, "all of it," alluding to the entirety of Edom. This implies that Mount Seir represents more than Edom; something in addition to Edom. Ezekiel 36:1-5 identifies Mount Seir as the surrounding nations encircling Israel including "all Edom."

'Thus says the Lord GOD: "Because the enemy [Mount Seir] has said of you, 'Aha! The ancient heights have become our possession,'"' "therefore prophesy, and say, 'Thus says the Lord GOD: "Because they made you desolate and swallowed you up on every side, so that you became the possession of the rest of the nations, and you are taken up by the lips of talkers and slandered by the people"—'therefore, O mountains of Israel, hear the word of the Lord GOD! Thus says the Lord GOD to the mountains, the hills, the rivers, the valleys, the desolate wastes, and the cities that have been forsaken, which became plunder and mockery to the *rest of the nations all around*—'therefore thus says the Lord GOD: "Surely I have spoken in My burning jealousy against the rest of the nations and against all Edom, who gave My land to themselves as a possession, with wholehearted joy and spiteful minds, in order to plunder its open country."' (Ezekiel 36:2-5; emphasis added).

Ezekiel specifies, "the rest of the nations all around" with "all Edom," are the slanderous people that seek to make Israel desolate and possess it. The people all around Israel comprise the "inner circle" of Arab states and terrorist populations listed in Psalm 83:6-8. Refer to the images section (appendix 26) to identify confederacies described in Psalm 83 and Ezekiel 38.

The "inner circle" is a phrase coined in *Isralestine* to identify the Psalm 83 nations in contrast to the "outer ring," to identify the Ezekiel 38:1-5 Gog of Magog invaders. Refer to image titled "Outer Ring of Ezekiel 38." The pentagon in both the Psalm 83 and Ezekiel 38 images represents "the rest of the [Mount Seir] nations all around" with "all Edom."

Mount Seir seems to be the representative term for the Arab confederacy of Psalm 83. Although there was a literal Mount Seir that was home to the Edomites, the use of mount, or mountains, in Scripture can also identify rulers, governments, or hierarchies.[85]

# Why Ezekiel 35 is Not an Armageddon Event.

Verses connecting the powerful sword utilized to defeat the Arab confederacy of Mount Seir to the IDF have been provided above. However, during the Armageddon campaign, the Antichrist and his world armies wield a powerful sword, as well. How can we be certain that Ezekiel 35:8 is not identifying the Antichrist instead of the IDF? The answer is located in Daniel 11.

He [Antichrist] shall also enter the Glorious Land, and many *countries* shall be overthrown; but these shall escape from his hand: Edom, [Mount Seir] Moab, and the prominent people of Ammon. (Daniel 11:41; emphasis added).

Daniel declares the Antichrist enters into the "Glorious Land," and overthrows many countries. But, Edom escapes his siege. Edom is located in modern-day southern Jordan, where Mount Seir is located. Although Ezekiel 35:15 identifies

Mount Seir as an Arab confederacy, Ezekiel 35:7-8 suggests the literal Seir mountain range becomes the host location of the multitude of slain Arabs. Therefore, it makes no sense that the Antichrist slays Arabs upon Mount Seir, if Edom, Moab, and Ammon escapes his end times exploits.

## What is the Glorious Land of Daniel 11:41?

The Glorious Land identifies a much larger area than modern-day Israel encompasses. Daniel says countries are overthrown inside the Glorious Land. The fact Daniel calls it the Glorious Land identifies it with the Holy or Promised Land.[86] Genesis 15:18 describes its expanse as extending from the Nile River in Egypt over to the Euphrates in Iraq and Syria.

> On the same day the LORD made a covenant with Abram, saying: "To your descendants I have given this land, from the river [Nile] of Egypt to the great river, the River Euphrates—" (Genesis 15:18)

Daniel 11:42 locates Egypt inside the Glorious Land.

> He shall stretch out his hand against the countries, and the land of Egypt shall not escape.

Thus, Jordan, represented by Edom, Moab, and Ammon, and Egypt are part of the end-times Glorious Land. Other countries and / or territories, excluding Israel, that are probably incorporated at the time could include Syria, Lebanon, Iraq, Saudi Arabia, the Sinai, West Bank, and Gaza Strip. All or portions of these locations exist inside the land described in Genesis 15:18.

Presently, these locations are under Arab sovereignty, but according to Ezekiel 35:8 they experience a massive desolation. Since this slaughter is by the IDF and not the Antichrist, it's possible that after the IDF victory they become classified as the "Glorious Land." If so, this suggests that Israel might attempt to annex more territory after their IDF victory in Psalm 83. Obadiah v. 20, Isaiah 19:18, Jeremiah 49:2, and Zephaniah 2:4-9 lends credence to this possibility. I'm not suggesting that Israel acquires all of the Promised Land prior to the return of Christ, but perhaps a significant portion.

*Please read then next novel chapter now.*

# Chapter 10—
## The Russian-Iranian Nuclear Connection

*Topics covered:* Ezekiel 38-39 Overview; Where on Earth is the Church, God's People Presently, at the Time of this Event?

This chapter of the *Revelation Road* novel presents an alarming scenario that places missing Russian nuclear devices into the arsenal of the rogue state of Iran. Equally as suspenseful, is the earlier chapter called *Iran Prepares for the Apocalypse*, which depicts Iran's apocalyptically-minded President Zakiri seeking Israel's destruction. These scenarios are both realistic and troubling, because Russia and other former Soviet Union countries like Ukraine, are rumored to be missing nuclear weapons,[87] and Iran's present President Ahmadinejad believes Allah has anointed him to create a Mideast apocalypse in order to hasten the return of his Islamic messiah, called Muhammad al-Mahdi.

Adding additional credibility to the concerns expressed above, are the prophecies contained in Ezekiel 38-39. Most eschatologists concur that Ezekiel predicts these two powerful countries, Russia and Iran, someday invade Israel as part of a larger coalition, including Turkey, Libya, Tunisia, and several other nations.

In September of 1997, the CBS News program "Sixty Minutes" reported that perhaps 100 Russian 250 1KT tactical nukes were missing, based on a report by Russian General Alexander Lebed. It was uncertain if any of those missing found their way into Iran's arsenal.[88] Whether they did or not is a matter that now pales comparatively, in light of the fact that the International Atomic Energy Agency (IAEA) believes that Iran is well on its way to producing its own nuclear weapons.[89]

Missing Russian nukes in Iranian hands or manufactured Iranian nukes in their own hands gravely concerns Israel. Amidst the uncertainties of the Arab Spring of 2011, Israel continued to warn the world that Iran is its number one existential threat. Some speculate Israel or America, or maybe even both, may even launch a preemptive strategic strike against Iran's nuclear sites, in order to prevent Iran from developing a nuclear arsenal.

The consensus among many military analysts is that the world will have to accept a nuclear Iran unless some act of God or a military strike against its nuclear sites prevents this from occurring. They warn a nuclear Iran could create a regional arms race, as Saudi Arabia and others follow suit to maintain stability in the balance of Middle East power.

In fact, at the time of authoring this chapter (7/8/11) there are rumors abounding that Saudi Arabia is already attempting to procure its own nuclear weapons, and may already have two secured in hiding in northern Pakistan.[90] It is suspected that the generally poor country of Pakistan developed its nuclear arsenal, in large part, via Saudi oil riches. So Paki-nukes winding up in Saudi hands would be of little surprise.

COMMENTARY

Folks, we are talking about nuclear weapons in apocalyptically-minded Islamic fundamentalist hands soon shaping the direction of oil-rich Mideast events. Saudi Arabia is ranked number #1 in OPEC, and Iran number #2. OPEC presently possesses seventy-nine percent of the world's crude oil reserves and provides about forty-four percent of its daily crude oil needs.[91] Most of this oil travels through the Strait of Hormuz, the Gulf of Aden, and the Suez Canal. All these distribution venues can easily be closed-off during a significant regional conflict. In fact, Iran has previously threatened to do this very thing—close Hormuz—to discourage adversaries from attacking its nuclear facilities.[92] Historical Middle East precedent for this type of strategic behavior was exhibited during the six-day Arab-Israeli war, when Egypt closed off the Straits of Tiran.[93]

Complicating matters, Iran is predominately a Shiite Islamic country, and Saudi Arabia primarily Sunni. They feel threatened by each other due to their competing theologies. Although Shiites, or Shias, and Sunnis agree on the core fundamentals of the Islamic faith, like the Five Pillars of Islam, they have political differences. These two sects of Islam are divided over the leadership of Islam. Shias believe that following the Prophet Muhammad's death, leadership should have passed directly to his cousin/son-in-law, Ali. On the other hand, Sunni Muslims share the belief that leadership should have stayed within the Prophet's own family, among those specifically appointed by him.[94]

This political divide is significant, and sits at the core of Islamic controversy as to which sect should rule over the broader Middle East. In essence, a power struggle exists between Saudi Arabia, which is home to Islam's holiest city of Mecca, and Iran. If both countries acquire nuclear weapons, it makes for another Pakistan verses India nuclear face-off. Problematic for Israel is that Saudi Arabia refuses to conduct normalized national relations with Israel, and Iran has vowed to wipe the Jewish state off the map.

In a global economic crisis plaguing an oil-dependent world, this is an extremely dangerous prospect and one that appears to have been foretold in the Bible. Psalm 83 predicts Saudi Arabia (under the banner of the Ishmaelites) invades Israel as part of an Arab confederacy, and as stated above, Russia and Iran invade Israel in Ezekiel's prophecy.

Whether or not nuclear weapons are involved in these prophecies in large part depends on when they find fulfillment in relationship to the available weapons possessed by the invaders. Russia has nukes, and Israel supposedly does as well. Regarding Iran and Saudi Arabia, it appears they are on *fast-track* to possess some of their own.

Little tiny Israel, barely the size of America's fifth-smallest state of New Jersey, is facing the prospects of two coming massive nuclear invasions.[95] If so, the Holocaust could pale in comparison. Psalm 83 is covered extensively throughout much of *Revelation Road*. Below is an overview of the Ezekiel 38-39 "Gog of Magog" invasion.

## Ezekiel 38-39 Overview

A cruel Russian leader appears to be presiding at the time Ezekiel 38 occurs. Although he may not be as ruthless as Ziroski inside the novel, whoever he is, we are informed he devises a maniacal plan against Israel.

> Thus says the Lord GOD: "On that day it shall come to pass *that* thoughts will arise in your [Russian] mind, and you will make an *evil plan*: You will say, 'I will go up against a land of unwalled villages; I will go to a peaceful people, who dwell safely, all of them dwelling without walls, and having neither bars nor gates'—to take plunder and to take booty, to stretch out your hand against the waste places *that are again* inhabited, and against a people gathered from the nations, who have acquired livestock and goods, who dwell in the midst of the land." (Ezekiel 38:10-12; emphasis added)

This passage clearly evidences that the Russian leader forms an evil plan, which is to assemble a formidable strategic coalition in order to invade Israel for the sake of material gain. Ezekiel 38:12-13 points out that the invaders seek to take a spoil. I point out the strategic aspect of his evil plan in the commentary chapter entitled *Russia Forms an Evil Plan to Invade Israel*. For those of you not familiar with the official Old Testament identity of this Russian leader, he is referenced early on in Ezekiel's prophecy.

> Now the word of the LORD came to me, saying, "Son of man, set your face against Gog, of the land of Magog, the prince of Rosh, Meshech, and Tubal, and prophesy against him, and say, 'Thus says the Lord GOD: "Behold, I *am* against you, O Gog, the prince of Rosh, Meshech, and Tubal."'" (Ezekiel 38:1-3)

Gog, is the lead figure who hails from the land of Magog. And, at the time of the invasion he is also the prince of Rosh, Meshech, and Tubal. This means that whoever Gog is, he appears to achieve a princely stature within three additional places alongside Magog prior to, or during, the fulfillment of Ezekiel's prophecy. Some suggest Rosh is a title rather than a place, but contextually it appears to be a place much like Meshech (western Turkey), and Tubal (eastern Turkey).

Some scholars debate whether or not Gog is an individual or a location within the greater territory of Magog; however, Ezekiel calls Gog a prince and uses the pronoun "he" to identify him. The opinion among many scholars, like Dr. David Hocking, Dr. David Reagan, and others is that Gog represents a title of an individual, rather than a specific name or place. Gog, would be likened to a Caesar from ancient Rome, or a Czar from the former Soviet Union, or the Kaiser from Germany, prior to the Nazi era.

The connection between Magog and Russia runs partially through the Scythians. This association was made centuries ago, by the secular Jewish historian Josephus. He called them an "invading horde from the north."[96] During Ezekiel's time, Magog existed in the proximity of where Russia is today. Wikipedia states, "In the 17th and 18th centuries, foreigners regarded the Russians as descendants of Scythians. It became conventional to refer to Russians as Scythians in 18th century poetry."[97]

Because the name Russia only dates back to around the eleventh century AD, it makes the Magog-to-Russia connection a bit difficult, but most scholars point out that Ezekiel 38:15 declares that Gog personally comes out from the far north, which directionally to Israel is the location of Russia. Most scholars, including Dr. Arnold Fruchtenbaum, Chuck Missler, Dr. Ron Rhodes, Dr. David

Hocking, Dr. David Reagan, and Joel Rosenberg, subscribe to Russia being identified by Ezekiel.

Regarding Iran's involvement in the Ezekiel (or Gog of Magog) invasion, refer to Ezekiel 38:5, where Iran is identified as Persia. The Iranian-Persian connection is easily made, considering Persia was renamed Iran in 1935 AD.

For an exhaustive look at Ezekiel 38-39, I have footnoted my recommended readings on the subject.[98] Below is a nutshell outline of the Ezekiel 38-39 prophecies.

*Ezekiel 38:1-7* lists the nine-member coalition of Gog's hordes, consisting of armies from Magog, Rosh, Meshech, Tubal, Persia, Ethiopia (Cush), Libya (Put), Gomer, and Togarmah. To discover their modern-day identities, please refer to the *Ezekiel 38 Invaders* image (appendix 26).

*Ezekiel 38:8-10* appropriates the general timing and battlefield location of the invasion. The prophecy occurs in the latter years, upon the land of Israel. Prerequisites of the invasion require that the nation of Israel be reestablished, that the worldwide re-gathering of the Jews be underway, and that the Israelis live in a condition of national security.

It is safe to assume that the first two requirements have been met. Israel was restored as the Jewish State on May 14, 1948, and Jews have been returning steadily ever since. However, the last prerequisite does not presently exist, in my estimation. Israelis are not dwelling safely in their homeland. They live under constant threat by multiple surrounding enemies. To understand this argument better, read this book's appendix called *Psalm 83 or Ezekiel 38, Which is the Next Middle East News Headline?*

*Ezekiel 38:11-13* informs us that Russia's leader prepares an evil plan to invade Israel and capture great plunder. The plunder consists of agricultural and commercial goods, as well as gold and silver. At least four more populations are introduced into the prophecy, apparently as protestors. These are *Sheba* (Yemen), *Dedan* (Saudi Arabia), *the Merchants of Tarshish*, (Britain or Spain, or both), and *all their Young Lions*. (United States of America, and / or Central and South America)

*Ezekiel 38:14 through 39:6* informs us the attackers will be many, and they come against Israel primarily from the north. We are reminded the event finds fulfillment in the "latter days," and that the Lord warned of the event well in advance.

The invaders are destroyed by the Lord, through an Old Testament type of fire and brimstone battle. This is important to note, because it reminds us that the Israel Defense Forces (IDF) of today are not a factor in this battle. Forthcoming sections of this commentary evidence that today's IDF exist in

COMMENTARY

fulfillment of Bible prophecy and becomes the divinely empowered instrument to defeat the Arab confederacy of Psalm 83.

*Ezekiel 39:7-8* provides the Lord's purpose for personally defeating this massive Mideast invasion.

> "So I will make My holy name known in the midst of My people Israel, and I will not *let them* profane My holy name anymore. Then the nations shall know that *I am* the LORD, the Holy One in Israel. Surely it is coming, and it shall be done," says the Lord GOD. "This *is* the day of which I have spoken." (Ezekiel 39:7-9)

It is important to recognize the significance of what the prophet Ezekiel declares in these verses. They are the summation of the divine purpose surrounding this prophetic event. He is emphasizing that the God of his people, the Jews, is upholding His Holy Name in the end times through the nation of Israel. This beckons the question:

## Where on Earth is the Church, God's People Presently, at the Time of this Event?

COMMENTARY

Perhaps more importantly, it notifies the world that the God of the Jews is a promise keeper. The Magog invaders seek to annihilate the race that the Lord appointed virtually impossible to eradicate. One point made in the commentary's chapter one that is worth repeating, is that genocidal attempts of the Jews are all doomed to failure unless they meet the requirements specified below.

> Thus says the LORD, Who gives the sun for a light by day, The ordinances of the moon and the stars for a light by night, Who disturbs the sea, And its waves roar (The LORD of hosts is His name): "If those ordinances depart From before Me," says the LORD, "Then the seed of Israel shall also cease From being a nation before Me forever." Thus says the LORD: "If heaven above can be measured, And the foundations of the earth searched out beneath, I will also cast off all the seed of Israel For all that they have done," says the LORD. (Jeremiah 31:35-37)

*Ezekiel 39:9-10* clues us in to the types of weaponry the invaders possess. Israel will be able to convert the enemy weapons into fuel for at least seven years. The picture is of energy provision for the entire nation, rather than a few isolated households. Verse 9 says "those who dwell in the cities" utilize this converted weapons-grade fuel. The widespread use and lengthy seven year span suggests that the weapons must be far more sophisticated than wooden bows and arrows, which would undoubtedly only last a short while. I mention this because some expositors today limit the weapons to wooden ones. I doubt nuclear non-proliferation will reduce Russian arsenals to wood between now and then.

There may actually be more than seven years' worth of fuel provided by these weapons, but the possibility looms large that the events occurring at the mid-point of the tribulation period interrupts the continued usage of the weapons. At this critical *mid-trib* point on the end-time's timeline, three-and-one-half years into the tribulation period, Israelis come under genocidal attack by the Antichrist. Thus, they are preoccupied with survival and not weapons conversion. If so, then there could be eight-plus years of weapons fuel, but no Jews taking time to harness the additional energy.

These missiles and rockets probably include the ABCs of weaponry—atomic, biological, and chemical. We can presume this because these types of weapons already exist inside the arsenals of Russia and some of their cohorts. Additionally, the dead soldiers appear to require Hazmat (Hazardous Materials) teams to assist with their burial according to Ezekiel 39:14-16. The fascinating fact is that whatever the weapons configuration, Israel will possess the technological know-how to convert them into national energy. Today, whether it is cell phones or irrigation techniques, Israel is on the cutting-edge of technological advances.

*Ezekiel 39:11-16* describes the location of the mass burial grounds of the destroyed armies of Gog. A valley east of what is probably the Dead Sea is renamed the Valley of Hamon Gog, which means the "hordes or multitudes" of Gog, in Hebrew. Why I believe it refers to a valley in modern-day Jordan is explained in the commentary chapter called *Israel, the Next Emerging Market.*

In this section, we also find that the Israelis will be burying the dead in order to cleanse the land. This could imply two things. One, that the hordes of Gog's dead soldiers are contaminated, requiring a professional quarantined burial and two, that the Jews are adhering to their ancient Levitical Law. Concerning the latter, Dr. Ron Rhodes writes in his book *Northern Storm Rising*:

> From the perspective of the Jews, the dead must be buried because exposed corpses are a source of ritual contamination to the land (Numbers 19:11-22; Deuteronomy 21:1-9). The land must therefore be completely cleansed and purged of all defilement. Neither the enemies nor their belongings (their weapons) can be left to pollute the land![99]

COMMENTARY

COMMENTARY

*Ezekiel 39:17-20* is an invitation "to every sort of bird and to every beast of the field" to partake of the sacrificial meal of the "flesh" and "blood" of the invaders. This passage is not for the faint of heart. I remember hearing expert Joel Rosenberg, teach this topic at a Calvary Chapel Chino Hills prophecy conference and he brought tears streaming down from my eyes.

Additionally foretold, the creatures are instructed, "to drink the blood" of the defeated "princes." This implies that not only the Magog infantry, but their governments are destroyed.

Two questions come to mind when reading these three sobering verses: "How can the hordes of Gog's dead soldiers be contaminated," and "How can every sort of bird and beast get to Israel?"

Regarding the first question, we will have to assume that if some of the dead soldiers are contaminated, the birds and beasts will detect this and ingest those that aren't. Regarding the migration of every sort of vulture-type bird, the fact is they are already beginning to nest in Israel. Whereas, through the years they would make Israel a mere migratory pit-stop, they are now setting up shop in the Jewish state by the tens of thousands.

For more information on this phenomena listen to one of my most widely listened-to Prophecy Update Radio programs, with eschatologist Gary Fisher, called *Ezekiel's Birds Gather for the Gog of Magog Meal*, linked on the Internet at: http://isralestine-blog.blogspot.com/2010/02/ezekiels-birds-gather-for-gog-of-magog.html. A postscript program with Gary, offering far greater detail, called *The Ezekiel 35-39 Mideast War Prophecies,* can be listened to at this link: http://isralestine-blog.blogspot.com/2011/05/ezekiel-warned-in-end-times-israel.html.

*Ezekiel 39:21-29* concludes the chapter with a recap of some Jewish history and a promise to the faithful remnant of Israel that the Lord will pour out His spirit upon them in the end.

*Please read the next novel chapter now.*

# Chapter 11—
## Terrorists Attack America Again!

*Topics covered:* Will Terrorists Attack America Again?; Islamic Extremists Identify America as the Great Satan; America Slips from Super-Power Status, According to Bible Experts; The Primary Views about America's Location in the Bible; America Experiences Divine Remedial Judgments; If Remedial Warnings Go Unheeded, Divine Judgment Results

## Will Terrorist's Attack America Again?

Suicide bombers, airplane bombers, bus bombers, shoe bombers, and underwear bombers sit atop a developing list of modern-day methods of terrorism. One of the latest ill-conceived terror tactics is explosive breast implants in females.

"Bosom bombers: Women have explosive breast implants," writes Joseph Farah, the founder of World Net Daily, (February 2010).[100] The article points out that Muslim doctors trained at leading UK hospitals are fitting female Al-Qaeda suicide bombers with lethal explosives in techniques similar to breast enhancement surgery.

Because Al-Qaeda toppled the twin towers, Richard Reid smuggled triacetone triperoxide in his shoes, and Umar Farouk Abdulmutallab stitched a bomb into his under-britches, far too often Americans get groped by the Transportation Security Administration (TSA) at airports. Strict security measures seem like a minor price to pay to fly from point A to point B safely, but will it ever cease? Osama Bin Laden and his high ranking cohort, Anwar al-Awlaki, have both been assassinated; shouldn't the Department of Homeland Security (DOHS), which was established in response to the September 11 attacks, be shut down? That would save the struggling US economy about $100 billion dollars per year.[101]

Of course not, the DOHS should remain intact; the threat of terror has not subsided since Bin Laden's and al-Awlaki's death. In fact, the list of terror tactics above is almost laughable when compared to the sophisticated threats Americans may face in the future. This chapter's novel discusses a high-level, multi-pronged terror attack that puts the United States on virtual lock-down!

National threats like electromagnetic pulse (EMP) attacks, tactical nuclear weapons explosions in high profile places, and suicide germ bombers are of grave concern to the DOHS. In July 2011, the New York Police Department (NYPD) began testing a new technology intended to detect and thwart "dirty bombs."[102] The NYPD established a command center in lower Manhattan to monitor 2,000 mobile radiation detectors carried by officers *each day* around the city. *Each day* NYPD officers carry radiation detectors! That is a troubling reality.

More recently, during the weekend of the ten year anniversary of September 11, in September 2011, the NYPD was canvassing the streets of Times Square looking for cars containing potential dirty bombs. Fortunately, the credible Al-Qaeda terror threat they were acting upon turned out to be a false alert.[103]

Imagine several dozen imbedded jihadist cells intentionally infected with some incurable germ virus, roaming about densely populated city streets, purposing to create a widespread apocalyptic plague. These suicidal maniacs don't particularly care what poison they pick as long as it transports them to Jannah, the Muslim heaven, upon death. According to their misguided thinking, the more death and destruction they cause, the greater assurance they have of being received by Allah.

This type of plague campaign could be carried on undetected until it's too late, and hundreds of thousands of Americans are quarantined across the United States. Remember the H1N1 influenza virus scare, also called the "Swine Flu," in 2009? The US Centers for Disease Control (CDC), and World Health Organization (WHO) both elevated it to be a public safety emergency of pandemic proportions.[104] The British government ordered 90 million swine flu vaccines as a precaution.[105] At that time it equated to more vaccinations than citizens in the UK.[106] In Japan, Japanese citizens donned facial protection, causing the Japanese Trend Shop to sell out of surgical masks.[107]

Although the swine flu threat has temporarily subsided, there are other deadly diseases like ebola, bubonic plague, cholera, and typhoid fever to be concerned with, just to name a few.[108] Deadly famines and pestilences occur in the end times, according to Revelation 6:8, 18:8, and Matthew 24:7. When, why, how, and where these biblical catastrophes occur, may or may not be related to a terrorizing germ war within America, but the prospect for such a terrorist-induced plague exists today. It is at least plausible to think that an attack on America could serve as a trigger for a chain-reaction around the globe, thus fulfilling the prophecies concerning last days' plagues.

America could again become a target of terror for several reasons:

- Islamic extremists call America's the Great Satan,

- America seems to slip from superpower status, according to the Bible, and

- America is already experiencing divine remedial judgments.

# Islamic Extremists Identify America as the Great Satan

America is commonly called the Great Satan by many Muslim leaders and clerics. The term, first coined by former Iranian Ayatollah Khomeini in a November 5, 1979, speech, has resonated throughout many Mideast and world mosques ever since.[109] American freedoms of worship, speech, woman's rights, and more stand in strict contrast to rigid Sharia laws in many Islamic countries. Additionally, our nation's support for Israel, who many Muslims identify as the "little Satan," further fuels fundamentalist Islamic hatred toward America.

The goal of Islam is to conquer the world. Muslim's are called to convert, subjugate, or destroy non-Muslims. The holy book of Islam, known as the Qur'an, instructs Muslims that they are not to wage war with unbelievers until they are first preached to. But, if then they don't convert, they are to be fought.[110]

Below are a couple of Islamic scriptures that express this truth:

> "Slay the idolaters wherever ye find them, and take them captive, and besiege them, and prepare for them each ambush. But if they repent and establish worship and pay the poor-due, then leave their way free. Lo! Allah is Forgiving, Merciful." (Qur'an 9:5). The "poor-due" in this verse is *zakat*, which is one of the Five Pillars of Islam, and regulates religious tithes.

"Fight those who believe not in Allah nor the Last Day, nor hold that forbidden which hath been forbidden by Allah and His Messenger, nor acknowledge the religion of Truth, (even if they are) of the People of the Book, (Jews and Christians) until they pay the Jizya with willing submission, and feel themselves subdued" (Qur'an 9:29). The *jizya* was a tax inflicted upon non-believers.[111]

As long as Muslim extremists exist, employ tactics of terror, and consider America as Satan, Americans are subject to future terrorist attacks. Perhaps some devastating terror attack affects America, dethroning it from its superpower status.

## America Slips from Superpower Status, According to Bible Experts

Many Christian Americans are wondering if the United States can be identified in Bible prophecy. Seldom do my colleagues or I escape a question-and-answer session at a prophecy conference without being asked, "What is America's future according to prophecy?" This question is on the minds of many for three primary reasons:

- America is rapidly becoming less Christian,

- It's difficult to locate America in the Bible, and

- It's obvious that humanity is living in the last days.

When these three factors are all considered, one logically surmises that America's departure from the Lord in these last days brings forth divine judgment upon the United States, and that's why it's difficult to discover the USA in the Bible.

Fortunately, several respected prophetic voices have been burdened to research and write on this subject over the past couple years; Dr. Mark Hitchcock wrote *The Late Great United States*, Dr. David Reagan revised *America the Beautiful*, his third edition, and Terry James authored *The American Apocalypse*. All three books impart invaluable information related to the subject. I've had the privilege to interview each of these individuals over the radio about their books, and can report both *good* and *bad* news as a result.

The good news is that the three experts generally agree about America's future. Conversely, the bad news is that the news is not necessarily good for

Americans. They all agree that America is hard to locate in the Bible, and if it is identified it's probably not represented as a superpower.

Presuming America can even be found in the Bible, why is the world's greatest ever super-power, the United States of America, hard to locate in Scripture? The Bible lists countries, cities, and locations throughout its pages; Israel is listed approximately 2,302 times. Even the tiny Gaza Strip area, which encompasses approximately 140 square miles, is listed about forty-four times under Gaza, Philistia, or the land of the Philistines. But, where is America? How many times is it listed in the Scriptures?

# The Primary Views About America's Location in the Bible

Listed below are some prevalent views suggesting America can be located in the Bible. America could be identified:

- as the unnamed nation of Isaiah 18,
- as the Babylon of Revelation 18:9-11,
- within the ten lost tribes of Israel,
- the great eagle of Revelation 12:13-17,
- amongst the young lions of Tarshish in Ezekiel 38:13, or
- within the Armageddon nations of Joel 3:2.

*America as the unnamed nation of Isaiah 18*

> Woe to the land shadowed with *buzzing wings*, Which is *beyond the rivers* of Ethiopia, Which sends *ambassadors by sea*, Even in vessels of reed on the waters, saying, "Go, swift messengers, to a nation tall and smooth of skin, To *a people terrible* from their beginning onward, *A nation powerful* and treading down, *Whose land the rivers divide.*" (Isaiah 18:1-2; emphasis added.)

The buzz words causing some to consider America as this unnamed nation are, *buzzing wings, beyond the rivers, ambassadors by sea, a people terrible, a nation powerful, land the rivers divide.* The possible interpretations of these descriptions could be Americanized as follows:

COMMENTARY

- *Buzzing wings* – Advanced American commercial and military aircraft.

- *Beyond the rivers* (of Ethiopia) – America is far west of Ethiopia.

- *Ambassadors by sea* – Alludes to a great maritime and / or naval power, like America presently possesses. Because this armada floats on a sea beyond the rivers of Ethiopia, the Atlantic Ocean becomes a candidate for the sea described by Isaiah.

- *A people terrible* – Some translations, like the NASB and NIV, say "a people feared far and wide." America, as a superpower nation, is feared far and wide.

- *A nation powerful* – The United States military is ranked #1 in the world.

- *Whose land the rivers divide* – The United States has thousands of rivers; some say there are too many to count.

If only these two verses were considered when deciphering Isaiah 18, these above possible interpretations could identify America; however, contextually Isaiah 15-19 addresses burdens against regionally specific locations in the Middle East and Africa. Isaiah 15-16 is a burden against Moab (Jordan). Isaiah 17 is a burden against Damascus, the capital of modern-day Syria. Isaiah 19 is concerned primarily with Egypt, and remotely with Israel and Assyria at the end of the chapter. Sandwiched in between is Isaiah 18 and the prophet appears to be addressing "Cush."

Cush, the son of Ham and grandson of Noah, settled west of the Red Sea. His descendants spread across the proximity of what are today the African countries of Egypt, Sudan, Ethiopia, and possibly Eritrea and Somalia. Therefore, imposing the name of America upon the unnamed nation of Isaiah 18 would appear to be a mistake.

## America as Babylon of Revelation 18:9-11

The *kings of the earth* who *committed fornication* and *lived luxuriously* with her will weep and lament for her, when they see the *smoke of her burning, standing at a distance* for fear of her torment, saying, "Alas, alas, that *great city* Babylon, *that mighty city*! For in *one hour your judgment has come*." And the *merchants of the earth* will weep and mourn over her, for no one *buys their merchandise* anymore: (emphasis added)

This passage is filled with buzz-words likening end-times' Babylon to the United States of America. The theme is international commerce and the great city is supposedly New York, the iconic place of America's material abundance. Those advocating that America is identified in Revelation 18 have a field day with these verses, for a litany of reasons.

- Some suggest NYC because this American city is the central hub of global commerce.

- Babylon is represented as a "mighty city" similar to NYC.

- NYC is home to Wall Street and the World Trade Center (WTC).

- Babylon is a "harlot" in Revelation 17, and the Statue of Liberty in NYC is a *female.*

- When the WTC Twin Towers toppled, the "merchants of the earth mourned."

- The September 11th terrorist attacks suggested that "judgment" had come to America / Babylon.

- The towers toppled quickly, within "one hour" of each other.

- September 11 was a scene of "smoke" and "burning" witnessed by "standing at a distance."

To find America in Revelation 18 requires a lot of sensationalizing, as the list above demonstrates. Many *mighty cities* have come under siege over the past two millennia, since the apostle John inscribed this prophecy. In several instances, the same could have been thought about their disasters. For this and several other reasons it is difficult to conclude that the USA is identified as Babylon.

Revelation 18:11 concludes by saying "no one buys their merchandise anymore." Wall Street wasn't destroyed on September 11, 2011, and people are still buying and selling stocks and merchandise worldwide. Several remaining verses in Revelation 18 declare that Babylon's judgment is a permanent catastrophe.

Revelation 18:14 says all the materialism end-times Babylon characterizes can be found no more. Revelation 18:17 says all of her riches are brought to nothing. Revelation 18:19 says she is made desolate. Revelation 18:21 predicts that upon judgment, Babylon will not be found anymore. Revelation 18:23 says, "The light of a lamp shall not shine in you anymore, and the voice of bridegroom and bride shall not be heard in you anymore."

COMMENTARY

None of the declarations above can be said of New York City today. Additionally, Dr. Mark Hitchcock points out in the *Late Great United States* that Babylon appears about 265 times in the Bible by its actual or associated names, and almost always describes a literal location slightly west of the Euphrates in modern-day Iraq. The few exceptions are in Revelation 17 and in 1 Peter 5:13. In these instances it is believed Babylon represents Rome, rather than America.

## Within the ten lost tribes of Israel—(Anglo Israelism)

Some believe the ten lost tribes of Israel migrated throughout time into the UK and beyond into the USA. This theory is called *British Israelism* or *Anglo Israelism*. This hypothesis is rooted in the belief that the descendants of the ten Hebrew tribes of Reuben, Issachar, Zebulun, Dan, Naphtali, Gad, Asher, Ephraim, Manasseh, and Levi are primarily floundering about incognizant of their tribal identities in countries like America.

The brief background dates back to around 930 BC, when these ten tribes rejected Solomon's son Rehoboam as their king. They followed Jeroboam, who managed the laborers Solomon had conscripted for his huge building projects[112] instead, and in the process Israel became a divided kingdom. The split kingdom was generally identified as the northern kingdom of Israel, occupied by the ten tribes, and the southern kingdom of Judah, occupied by the remaining two tribes of Judah and Benjamin.

Both kingdoms were conquered at different intervals. Assyria conquered the northern kingdom in 722 BC, and Babylon conquered the southern kingdom around 586 BC. After the prophesied seventy years of Babylonian captivity, the tribes of Judah and Benjamin began making their way back into Israel.[113] However, tracking the migration of the ten tribes captured by the Assyrians has proven to be more difficult.

2,000 years ago, the Hebrews relied on handwritten records, rather than Facebook, to keep track of their tribal trees. These records were stored in the Jewish temple. In 70 AD, when the Romans destroyed the second Jewish temple, these important genealogical records were destroyed. Since there are no remaining accurate records readily available, the obvious conclusion the Anglo-Israelist draws is that America, being home to millions of Jews, must be where descendants of the ten lost tribes exist. Undoubtedly, there are Jews in America from an assortment of these ten tribes and genetic testing today is proving that.

A case in point is that of Bill Koenig, the founder of *World Watch Daily*. Recently Koenig, a red-blooded American citizen, discovered he was from the tribe of Levi. Bill recounted his story to me, how he was raised all his life thinking he was a Gentile, but his sudden love for Israel, after becoming a Christian, prompted him to trace his historical roots. Ultimately, Bill was genetically tested and found out that he wasn't a Gentile, but a Jew of Levite ancestry.

There are other Jews today finding themselves in Koenig's shoes. This is because at various points during the Diaspora, being a Jew was dangerously unpopular. For understandable reasons, many Jews shunned their natural identities over their 1,878 years of worldwide dispersion, between 70 – 1948 AD.

For instance, at the time of the Spanish Inquisition in the late 1400s, many Jews abandoned their heritages. They were coerced under duress to convert to Catholicism or be persecuted. Persecution often led to death or expulsion from Spain. Conversos and Marranos began springing up all over Spain. Conversos were true converts to Catholicism, but Marranos falsified their conversions. Some believe Christopher Columbus was a Jew, and that his three ships, the Pinta, Nina, and Santa Maria were filled with Jews attempting to flee persecution.[114]

During the Hitler holocaust, being a Jew in Europe turned out to be a death sentence for approximately six million Jews. It is believed that many Jews intentionally abandoned their heritage and became Gentile impostors, in order to escape Nazi extermination.[115]

This appears to be what happened at some point in Bill Koenig's family history. I'm informed that my grandfather shed his last name around the early 1900s, and opted for the name of *Salhus*. My author name is *Salus*, but my birth name is *Salhus*, which is a place located near a fjord in Norway. I have no idea why he changed his name. Perhaps I'll find out like Koenig someday, that I'm from some lost tribe of Israel.

The fact that Jews from the ten tribes of Israel may dwell in America, hardly clues us into America's future. Additionally, the ten tribes are not entirely lost, because passages like Ezra 7:7 tells us that many Levites migrated back to Israel after the Babylonian captivity. Furthermore, in the New Testament Luke 2:36 points out that the prophetess Anna was from the tribe of Asher. Also from the New Testament, it can be assumed that the assortment of Jews mentioned in the historical account of Acts 2 included members from the ten tribes.

Lastly, Revelation 7:1-8 informs us that the Lord has not lost track of the whereabouts of the ten tribes, as 12,000 members from each of those tribes show up in the end times among, the 144,000 Hebrew witnesses. However, the location of these ten tribes is not given, other than a clue that some angel

COMMENTARY

from the "east" is instrumental in sealing these witnesses for service to the Lord. But typically, *east* is not a term identifying America, which exists far *west* of Israel today.

Although there are likely members from the ten tribes of Israel residing in America today, their identities are not entirely lost, and their existence in America does not preclude that the United States exists in the Bible. More importantly, identifying the whereabouts of these ten tribes hardly offers any invaluable insights into America's future.

## The Great Eagle of Revelation 12:13-17

Dr. David Reagan addresses this argument as follows:[116]

> Another favorite passage for applied imagination is Revelation 12:13-17. These verses state that in the middle of the Tribulation God will provide a means of escape for the Jewish remnant in Israel. They will be carried into the wilderness to a hiding place on the "wings of a great eagle."
>
> Some people have seized on this imagery to teach that the U.S., whose national symbol is the eagle, will supply the end time airlift that will save the Jewish remnant.
>
> But the Bible is its own best interpreter. And when you look up the phrase, "wings of an eagle," you will find that it is the same one that God used in Exodus 19:4 to describe how He brought the Israelites out of Egypt. God is the eagle, not the United States (see Deuteronomy 32:11).

## Amongst the young lions of Tarshish, in Ezekiel 38:13

America appears to be identified in Bible prophecy as the young lions of Tarshish in Ezekiel 38:13. More and more respected eschatologists are beginning to believe Americans are these young lions. One of the best studies I have heard to date on this connection was delivered by Dr. David Hocking of *Hope for Today Ministries*. At the time, Dr. Hocking, Pastor Tom Hughes, and I were on a panel addressing questions about America in Bible prophecy on July 3, 2011. Hocking's teaching on the subject, and our overall program, can we viewed at this Internet link: http://www.ccsjonline.org/media/sunday-night/

Since the young lions—America tie is an important prophetic connection, and an integral part of the *Revelation Road* story line, this explanation is reserved for the commentary chapter, called *Russia Forms an Evil Plan to Invade Israel*. In this upcoming section of commentary, I point out the possibility that if America is these "young lions of Tarshish," that is encouraging for Americans.

Ezekiel 38:13 identifies a group of merchants of Tarshish and their young lions seemingly interested in conducting commerce with Israel. In stark contrast to Russia's coalition bent on wiping Israel off the map and confiscating great plunder, these merchants seemingly want to bless the Jewish State by participating in the spread of its prosperity.

### Within the Armageddon nations of Joel 3:2

> For behold, in those days and at that time, when I bring back the captives of Judah and Jerusalem, I will also gather *all nations*, and bring them down to the Valley of Jehoshaphat; and I will enter into judgment with them there on account of My people, My heritage Israel, Whom they have scattered among the nations; they have also *divided up My land*. (Joel 3:1-2; emphasis added)

This passage says all nations existing on Earth at the time will be gathered for judgment in the Valley of Jehoshaphat. The judgment of all nations occurs at the end of the end times, in the Armageddon campaign, as per Revelation 16:14-16. As Joel 3:1-2 points out, the Jews will have been previously re-gathered from world nations, and those nations are guilty of attempting to divide up God's land.

Since America is among all nations presently, the presumption is that America will be gathered alongside the other nations for judgment. The Jews are presently being re-gathered into Israel, and as pointed out in the commentary of chapter nine, *The Final Arab – Israeli War*, America is certainly guilty of attempting to pressure the Israelis to divide up their Promised Land.

## America Experiences Divine Remedial Judgments

One of the ways the Lord disciplines a nation is through remedial judgments, and giving them the political leadership they deserve. Israel's history is lined with good and bad kings that characterized the heart of the nation during their respective reigns. The goal of remedial judgments is to lead the affected nation to repentance and godliness. A classic historical example of this is found in the story of Nineveh. The prophet Jonah warned of Nineveh's imminent destruction, and it brought about a national repentance and a stay of execution for over 100 years, until the prophet Nahum proclaimed it subsequently.

Many end-times experts, including everyone mentioned in this chapter's commentary and myself, believe America is undergoing a period of remedial judgments. Since the turn of the century several big events, like the terrorist attacks of September 11 (2001), Hurricane Katrina (2005), the Mortgage Meltdown (2007), the BP oil spill (2010), and record–breaking, Bible Belt tornado seasons (2011), to name a few, have shaken the foundations of the United States. Additionally, political partisanship rose to an unprecedented high during the same periods.

Acts 17:26 declares the Lord establishes the times and boundaries of the nations. America appears to have been established for three primary purposes. First, *as a Christian nation*, America was established to become a beacon of Christianity for the nations.  Second, *as a Christian nation*, America was to become a safe-haven for the Jews during the Diaspora. Third, *as a Christian nation*, America was to be instrumental in the reestablishment of the nation Israel.

A careful tracking of history shows that America has fulfilled all three of its primary purposes. American Christian missionaries went forth into the nations and spread the gospel worldwide. Jews began arriving in America as far back as the 1600s, and more Jews ended up in America over time than anywhere else in the world. President Harry S. Truman was one of the primary world leaders used to reestablish the Jewish State in 1947-1948.

As a *Christian nation*, America accomplished all the above. However, in June, 2008, prior to being elected president of the United States, Barack Obama said the following about America's Christianity,

> Whatever we once were, we're no longer a Christian nation. At least not just. We are also a Jewish nation, a Muslim nation, and a Buddhist nation, and a Hindu nation, and a nation of nonbelievers.

Some pundits believe Barack Obama is the most anti-Israel, pro-abortion, and pro-homosexual president in American history. On January 20, 2009, did Americans inaugurate the president they deserved? One way to know is by honestly asking the following questions:

1.  Has money become America's god?

2.  Has greed become America's motivator?

3.  Has America kicked God out of its schools?

4. Has America legalized abortion?

5. Has America become the moral polluter of the earth?

6. Is America redefining the biblical meaning of marriage?

7. Are American states beginning to approve of same-sex marriages?

If the honest answer to all the above questions is yes, then why wouldn't Americans be experiencing serious remedial judgments and receiving the rulers they deserve?

With respect to bullet number 6 above; below is a quote from the *Huffington Post* on the Internet, that evidences a dramatic shift in US policy regarded with marriage. It pertains to the Defense of Marriage Act (DOMA). DOMA defines marriage as the legal union of one man and one woman.[117]

> "In a major policy reversal, the Obama administration said Wednesday (February 23, 2011) it will no longer defend the constitutionality of a federal law banning recognition of same-sex marriage."

> "Attorney General Eric Holder said President Barack Obama has concluded that the administration cannot defend the federal law that defines marriage as only between a man and a woman. He noted that the congressional debate during passage of the Defense of Marriage Act 'contains numerous expressions reflecting moral disapproval of gays and lesbians and their intimate and family relationships—precisely the kind of stereotype-based thinking and animus the (Constitution's) Equal Protection Clause is designed to guard against.'"[118]

The Bible defines marriage similar to DOMA.

> Therefore a man shall leave his father and mother and be joined to his wife, and they shall become one flesh. (Genesis 2:24)

This definition of marriage in the book of Genesis is confirmed by Christ, as in the gospel accounts of Matthew 19:5 and Mark 10:7, and elsewhere in the New Testament in Ephesians 5:31.

America has accomplished its three main purposes; and Israel is now in God's, not America's hands. Therefore, Americans need to repent of their immorality and stop pressuring Israel to divide its land. A fall from Christianity and failure to support Israel will evidence that America has stepped out of alignment with God's original intentions for the nation.

Two very famous historical figures echoed a timeless truth. First, about 2,000 years ago Jesus Christ said,

> If a kingdom is divided against itself, that kingdom cannot stand. And if a house is divided against itself, that house cannot stand. (Mark 3:24-25)

Subsequently on June 16, 1858, the then-Republican Senator Abraham Lincoln, thought to be a Christian, paraphrased Christ when he declared, "A house divided against itself cannot stand."

As it was during Lincoln's time, so it is again today in America; the nation is split over enslavement. Slaves to sin or bond-slaves to the Lord; that is the apropos question American Christians today must ask themselves.

America needs its own Nineveh moment and we are instructed in 2 Chronicles 7:14 how that can be brought about.

> If My people who are called by My name will humble themselves, and pray and seek My face, and turn from their wicked ways, then I will hear from heaven, and will forgive their sin and heal their land.

This passage states the Lord, not the politicians, possesses the ability to heal a nation's wounds. It declares the healing occurs as a direct result of God's people departing from wickedness in pursuit of godliness. Verses like this suggest American Christians can do more than call their congressman, or cast their vote at the ballot box; they can petition the Lord to respond favorably to their changed behavior.

However, on the flip-side, a country undergoing judgment beckons the question: why isn't God healing the land? Are His people pursuing wickedness rather than godliness?

## If Remedial Warnings Go Unheeded, Divine Judgment Results

The natural digression of God's interactions with a nation goes from blessings to remedial warnings, and finally to divine judgment if the warnings go unheeded. When a country finds favor with the Lord it is blessed, but when it falls from favor the nation undergoes disciplinary measures.

Since America is hard to locate in Bible prophecy, the possibility that America comes under divine judgment looms large. Dr. David Reagan points out in his book, and in his prophecy presentations about America, that several things could happen in a judgment sequence to the United States. Any one of the events listed below, or a combination of one or more, could occur as a form of judgment upon the nation.

- The rapture of the Christian church

- Economic collapse

- External nuclear attack, (including an electromagnetic pulse (EMP) attack)

- Internal terrorist attack

- Internal moral rot (Hedonism)

It is important to note that historically, dominant world empires usually fall from power within 200 to 250 years of their founding. At the time of the authoring of this book, America has existed for 235 years. Could the sun be about to set on America's superpower status? Is that why America is hard to find in the Bible?

*Please read the next novel chapter now.*

# Chapter 12—
## The Arabs Surrender!

*Topics covered:* The Timing of the Rapture; The Pre-Psalm 83 Rapture; The Pre-Ezekiel 38 Rapture; Why Ezekiel 38 is Probably Pre-Trib; Replacement Theology; Israel, God's Modern Day Miracle; More Psalm 83 Details

Brace yourself: this commentary section is a bit lengthy and begins where Razz left off at the end of the chapter. Regarding the timing of the rapture he opines, "I, also, believe it is an imminent event and think it might occur before Russia, Iran, Turkey, and the other Ezekiel 38 invaders confederate against Israel." Razz' reasons will be expounded upon further in this commentary. Additionally, Israel's decisive victory in Psalm 83 is explained at the end of this commentary, as more Psalm 83 details are revealed.

## The Timing of the Rapture

Like Harold Camping[119] found out the hard way, on May 22, 2011, the Bible doesn't predict the specific timing of the rapture. Mr. Camping, the widely listened-to broadcaster, president, and general manager of *Family Radio*, had previously predicted the Christian disappearance would occur the day prior, on May 21, 2011. However, when he and his followers woke up in their same beds the next morning, they all realized that his prediction was dead wrong.

The five primary views about the timing of the rapture are:  pre-trib, mid-trib, pan-trib, post-trib, and pre-wrath. Mid-trib and post-trib views are self-explanatory. A mid-tribber believes the rapture occurs in the middle of the seven years of tribulation. Post-tribbers believe the rapture occurs after the seven years are concluded. The pan-tribber doesn't take a view, but jests that it all pans out in the end.

I'm a pre-tribber, which means I don't eat Post-Toasties, buy green bananas, or drive in convertible cars unless the top is down. I believe the rapture could occur at any moment between now and the commencement of the trib-period. My arguments for a pre-trib viewpoint are explained in the subsequent rapture-related sections of commentary, and the *Old Testament Allusions to the Rapture* appendix.

The pre-wrather tends to favor the timing of the mid-trib view, because they believe the wrath Christians are promised to escape begins about midway through the trib-period. They often connect the wrathful events contained in the sixth seal in Revelation 6:12-17 to the relevant wrath Christians avoid via the means of the rapture. Because pre-wrathers tend to teach all the Seal judgments occur within the trib-period, they caution that the rapture could occur at the mid-trib point. As I hope to demonstrate in book two of this series, the pre-wrath view in many respects resembles the pre-trib view because it appears that the first five of the seven Seal judgments occur before the trib-period even commences. In the commentary of the next book, I will establish why the first five seals should probably be viewed as pre-trib events.

If I lost you somewhere between the pan-trib, Post Toasties and the green bananas, don't panic; the spell-check in my word document got confused also. I exhort you to just read the rest of this chapter's commentary, because the rapture and various views above become clearer in the later commentary and appendix.

I am often asked whether the rapture could occur before either Psalm 83 or Ezekiel 38 find fulfillment. Absolutely! It could occur before, during, or after either event. This is possible because, like the rapture, these events appear to conclude before the trib-period commences. To discover why I order Psalm 83 before Ezekiel 38, read the attached appendix entitled, *Psalm 83 or Ezekiel 38, Which is the Next Mideast News Headline.*

The appendix lists a flurry of reasons why Psalm 83 appears to precede Ezekiel 38. Since Ezekiel 38 appears to be a pre-trib event, Psalm 83 should certainly be so, also. A few reasons illustrating why Ezekiel 38 is probably a pre-trib event are included in this commentary.

Operating under the reasonable presumption that all three events occur prior to the trib-period, below are some views regarding a pre-Psalm 83 and a pre-Ezekiel 38 rapture.

# The Pre-Psalm 83 Rapture

Explained below are three differing perspectives addressing the timing of Psalm 83 in relationship to the rapture. They are, *Psalm 83 is now imminent, The church could be part of Psalm 83,* and *Israel, not the church, is called "my people" when Psalm 83 occurs.*

Before I begin this section let me state clearly, that I believe the rapture is a sign-less event. By that, I mean it is imminent and can happen at any time. Because I believe Psalm 83 could also happen immediately, some have assumed that I believe the rapture is not imminent, but that the Psalm event must occur prior to it. Although the Psalm event could occur prior to it, in no way do I advocate it must precede the rapture.

The fact is, we don't know which will come first; the timing of both events is unclear. All we know for certain is that Psalm 83 requires the existence of a nation called Israel. We know this because the goal of the confederates, as expressed in Psalm 83:4, is to destroy the Jewish state so that the name of Israel can be remembered no more.

*Psalm 83 is now imminent* – Some suggest Mideast signs of the times signal that Psalm 83 has become an imminent event. They don't see any further preconditions prohibiting its modern-day fulfillment. For instance, the Psalm calls for the destruction of Israel so that "the name of Israel may be remembered no more."[120] In order for the Jewish State to be destroyed, and the name of Israel banished forever, the nation had to first exist. On May 14, 1948, Israel regained its nationhood, fulfilling that precondition.

The Psalm also predicts that an Arab confederacy or league forms in order to destroy Israel. In Cairo, Egypt, on March 22, 1945, the Arab League was formed. Presently it is comprised of twenty-two members, and includes the prominent members of Psalm 83, like Egypt, Saudi Arabia, Jordan, Syria, Palestinian Authority, Iraq, and Lebanon. Originally, it was established to unite the newly forming Arab States by developing their fledgling economies, resolving their regional disputes, and coordinating their collective political aims.

At the time, there was no Palestinian refugee crisis competing for the league's agenda or resources. However, as a result of the Arab – Israeli conflict, some suggest the Arab League has become pre-occupied with the plight of the Palestinians. The Palestinian refugee crisis appears to be what motivates the prominent members of the league to confederate militarily against Israel, according to Psalm 83.

The first member listed in the confederacy is the "tents of Edom," which in large part appears to identify today's Palestinian Authority. Thus, it can be presumed that this League, which generally opposes Israel's existence, is also in place. Apart from fragile peace-pacts Israel has with Egypt and Jordan, the entire region is extremely volatile and war could break out between the Arabs and the Jews at any time.

Because the Psalm 83 Arab – Israeli war could occur without further preconditions and the church still occupies the earth, advocates of this argument believe the church could experience the fulfillment of Psalm 83. Although this is entirely possible, this assumption is primarily based upon logic and newspaper exegesis, rather than Scripture.

*The church could be part of Psalm 83* –Another reason some think the rapture can't occur until after Psalm 83, is because they believe the church is identified within Psalm 83. Subscribers to this reasoning point to Psalm 83:3 as their evidence.

> They have taken crafty counsel against thy people, and consulted against thy hidden ones. (Psalm 83, KJV)

They identify "thy hidden ones" as the church. To better understand their arguments and why I disagree with this possibility, read the appendices called *Is the Church Identified in Psalm 83* and *The Treasured ones of Psalm 83*. Interestingly, this camp is split on whether or not the rapture is a pre or post Psalm 83 event. Some suggest the church goes through Psalm 83, but are "hidden" or isolated from the event somehow, whereas others believe the church is previously raptured and therefore "hidden" in heaven from the earthly events of Psalm 83.

*Israel, not the church, is called my people when Psalm 83 occurs* – This argument is primarily based upon the description of Israel in Ezekiel 25:14, and secondarily supported by Obadiah v. 18. These passages seem to illustrate that the IDF becomes the instrument used by the Lord to defeat the Psalm 83 confederacy. Ezekiel 25:14 identifies the Jews as "my People Israel," during Psalm 83.

This "chosen people" classification suggests that Israel has been reinstated as God's client nation by the time Psalm 83 occurs. If this is the case, then the whereabouts of the church legitimately comes into question. Presently, believers in Jesus are considered to be God's chosen people. If the church is still present on the earth during Psalm 83, why is God calling the Jews "my People Israel?" This theme is developed thoroughly in the chapter called *My People Israel*, in my book *Isralestine*.

> "I will lay My vengeance on Edom [the tents of Edom in Psalm 83] by the hand of My people Israel, [the IDF] that they may do in Edom according to

My anger and according to My fury; and they shall know My vengeance,"
says the Lord GOD. (Ezekiel 25:14)

Obadiah's secondary passage below correlates with Ezekiel's passage, and
pictures the houses of Jacob and Joseph as today's IDF (my People Israel.)

"The house of Jacob [IDF] shall be a fire, And the house of Joseph [IDF] a
flame; But the house of Esau [tents of Edom] shall be stubble; They shall
kindle them and devour them, And *no survivor* shall remain of the house
of Esau," For the LORD has spoken. (Obadiah v. 18; emphasis added)

The startling comment made by Obadiah is that "no survivor" remains in
Esau's posterity. The IDF destroys them! Today's Palestinians have a remnant of
Esau's Edomite descendants inside their ranks. Not all Palestinians are Edomites,
but as pointed out in the "Whodomite" chapter inside *Isralestine*, Obadiah appears
to be alluding in large part to today's Palestinians.

Connecting verses in Jeremiah read,

But I have made Esau bare; I have uncovered his secret places, And
he shall not be able to hide himself. His [Palestinian] descendants are
plundered, His brethren and his [Psalm 83 Arab] neighbors, And he [Esau's
posterity] is no more. Leave your fatherless children, I will preserve them
alive; And let your widows trust in Me. (Jeremiah 49:10-11)

In the end analysis, it doesn't appear that any of these arguments provide
conclusive evidence that the church experiences a *pre-Psalm 83 rapture*. The
important thing for Christians to grasp is that if we are here to experience the
Arab-Israeli war of Psalm 83, it becomes our fantastic witnessing tool. Unbelievers
can be directed to the content of Psalm 83 and align it up to the Arab-Israeli war it
describes. By then, they will have witnessed the fulfillment of the prophecy, and
should appreciate the fact that the Bible predicted it accurately over 3,000 years
prior to its occurrence.

## The Pre-Ezekiel 38 Rapture

Razz' comments below, relative to this topic, were removed from the novel
section because they fit better in this commentary. Here is an excerpt from Razz
and George's parlor conversation that you were only partially privy to regarding the
pre-Ezekiel 38 rapture.

"I also believe it is an imminent event and think it might occur before Russia,
Iran, Turkey, and the other Ezekiel 38 invaders confederate against Israel. I believe

this because Ezekiel identifies the Jewish people as "My people Israel" three times within his fifty-two verses," Razz reported, as he opened up a nearby Bible and began reading.

> Therefore, son of man, prophesy and say to Gog, "Thus says the Lord GOD: 'On that day when *My people Israel dwell safely*, will you not know *it?*'" (Ezekiel 38:14; emphasis added.)

> You will come up against *My people Israel* like a cloud, to cover the land. It will be in the *latter days* that I will bring you against *My land*, so that the nations may know Me, when I am hallowed in you, O Gog, before their eyes. (Ezekiel 38:16; emphasis added.)

> So I will *make My holy name known* in the midst of *My people Israel*, and I will not *let them* profane My holy name anymore. Then *the nations shall know* that *I am* the LORD, *the Holy One in Israel*. (Ezekiel 39:7; emphasis added.)

"How do these verses suggest the Christian church is absent?" George queried.

Razz replied, "Because they illustrate the importance of God upholding His holy name by performing upon the unconditional promises given to Israel. The thrust of the Ezekiel 38 episode deals with the Lord proving He's a promise-keeper to the watchful eyes of the world at a crucial point in the end times. Shortly after the Ezekiel event concludes, humanity will have to choose between Abraham's blessed seed, the Messiah, Jesus Christ, or Satan's seed, the Antichrist."

"Impressive! How did you arrive at that conclusion from these mere three verses?" George inquired.

Razz explained, "First the 'promised people' are mentioned as 'My people Israel.' This indicates that when the invasion takes place the Jews will still exist! Considering the Jews have been targeted by repeated genocidal attempts, this is a crucial acknowledgement. The fact they are classified as 'My people' forces us to recognize that they exist because God personally preserved them throughout their centuries of dispersion. They have been safeguarded from complete extirpation, because the Lord is not done with them."

"Furthermore, verse 14 causes us to recognize that the Jews dwell securely somewhere at the time. This is equally as important, considering the Jews were without a homeland for about 1,878 years between AD 70 and AD 1948, and have been embattled with the Arabs ever since resuming nationhood. Reportedly, no other deported or dispersed ethnic group has ever survived without a homeland for more than 400 years. Now that Psalm 83 has occurred, (in the novel story line) the Jews can dwell securely."

"Second, the 'Promised Land' is discussed. The invaders march against God's land of Israel in verse 16. This passage compliments verse 14 by telling us *when* and *where* the Jews dwell securely. They exist and dwell securely inside the Promised Land of Israel in the latter days."

"Lastly, in the final usage of 'My people Israel' in Ezekiel 39:7, we are informed that the Lord uses the massive Mideast invasion to uphold His holy name through the Jews, in order to prove He's a covenant-keeping God."

"Slow down, you lost me while connecting all the dots." George confessed.

Razz clarified, "Let me summarize my thoughts. God promised Abraham 4,000 years ago that he would father a great nation, and through him all the nations of the earth would be blessed.[121] According to the account recorded in Genesis 15, we understand these promises to Abraham were unconditional. This age-old covenant is commonly referred to as the Abrahamic Covenant, and even though the preponderance of the international community is totally oblivious to it, it is still effectually intact."

"In order to have a great nation, you have to harbor a sizable population, and harness a significant piece of land for them to inhabit. God promised Abraham he would have both. In Genesis 13:15 Abraham was promised a family tree forever, and in Genesis 22:17 he was informed he would have a multitude of descendants. Then in Genesis 15:18, Abraham was granted land extending east of the Nile River in Egypt all the way to the Euphrates River that courses through modern-day Iraq and Syria."

"Several passages inform us that the great nation promised to Abraham would come through the lineage of his son Isaac and his grandson Jacob, and extrapolate down through the Jewish people of today. But, the Jews were promised more than the formation of a great nation, they were bestowed the honor of being a blessing to all the families of the earth. This is because the Messiah would be a Jew, according to Genesis 22:18 and 26:4."

"Abraham's Seed, the Messiah, would become the blessing to all the families. The Messiah is Jesus Christ, and although Christians are indeed spiritually blessed through faith in Him, the prophecy of blessings to the nations finds final fulfillment when he establishes His 1000-year messianic kingdom spoken about in Revelation 20:4, 6. At that time all the families of the earth, who make it through the trib-period will be blessed."

"Thus for the following two primary reasons I believe the rapture could be a pre-Ezekiel 38 event:

- The entire episode is connected with God's promises to Israel, which negates the need for the church to be present upon the scene at the time.

- The holy name of God is revealed to the nations through Israel, just before humanity has to make its final choices between Christ and the Antichrist."

"Doesn't the church need to preach the gospel before, during, and after Ezekiel 38? How can the believing church become negated at the time; because I don't believe the faithful remnant of Israel comes to faith in Christ until the end of the trib-period," George commented.

"You're right, Israel as a nation does not appear to recognize Christ through either Psalm 83, or Ezekiel 38. However, the gospel can still be preached and disseminated to the Jew first,[122] and then the Gentile in the aftermath via other means. Scripture informs us the gospel will go out through the following sources after the church is removed:

- The 144,000 Hebrew witnesses (Revelation 7:1-8)

- The martyred saints who come to faith after being left behind (Revelation 6:9-11, 20:4)

- Teaching materials, like articles, books, audios, videos, and movies produced by Christians before they are raptured (Inferred by martyred saints above)

- The Two Witnesses (Revelation 11:3)

- The angel with the everlasting gospel (Revelation 14:6)

George then questioned, "Can you elaborate on your second reason about the importance of pre-trib timing?"

## Why Ezekiel 38 is Probably Pre-Trib

Razz responded, "Gladly, but this gets a bit more complicated. It requires a better-than-basic understanding about the distinctions between the first and second halves of the trib-period. During the first half, Israel enjoys a temporary peace derived from the covenant confirmed by the Antichrist in Daniel 9:27. This peace ends abruptly at the mid-point of the seven-year trib-period when the Antichrist enters into the third Jewish temple, and fulfills the Daniel 11:31 and 12:11 prophecies Christ warned about in Matthew 24:15. From that point forward the Antichrist attempts a final genocidal attempt of the Jews."

COMMENTARY

"Now, with that understanding, here's why Ezekiel 38 is probably pre-trib. First, Israel burns Russian weapons for seven years, and second, the Antichrist causes people to lose their salvation by taking his mark."

"What? Come again?" George queried.

"Exactly, I thought that would pique your attention. Allow me to explain further," Razz said.

"Ezekiel 39:9-10 suggests Israel will possess the know-how to convert the weapons of mass destruction possessed by the Ezekiel invaders into fuel. They will utilize these weapons for fuel and energy consumption for a period of seven years. This will be no problem during the peaceful first half of the tribulation, but not likely during the perilous second half, because Jews will be fleeing for their lives, rather than harnessing this energy."

"Therefore, many scholars suggest that Ezekiel 38 must conclude, not commence, no later than three-and-one-half years before the tribulation even begins. This allows the Jews seven full years to burn the weapons before they begin fleeing for their lives. Realistically, it will probably take approximately a year to even collect, dismantle, and covert the weapons cache prior to that."

"Here's how this could break down incrementally in real time. If the rapture occurs, and the very next day Ezekiel 38 occurs, which is extremely unlikely, then allow about one year for the battle to occur and the weapons to be converted, subsequently. Remember, assembling a coalition and mobilizing an invasion of the scope described in Ezekiel 38 is no twenty-four hour undertaking. Then consider an additional seven-year span to burn the weapons. And lastly, add in the final three-and-one-half years of great tribulation, for a total of eleven-and-one-half years."

"If this hypothesis is correct, this means that at least (underscore *at least* because it's probably going to be longer) that from the time the Ezekiel 38 invasion begins until the second coming of Christ to set up His kingdom, there will exist approximately eleven-and-one-half years. I could be more technical on the timing, because Daniel 12:11-12 adds an additional seventy-five days to the equation. His infamous 'Seventieth Week' ends, and then the two-and-one-half month interval kicks in, at which time the sheep and goat judgment of Matthew 25:32-46 takes place."

"Now regarding the crucial timing of Ezekiel 38 I mentioned previously, the Lord utilizes Ezekiel 38 to uphold His holy name. In His infinite mercy, and omniscient foreknowledge, He wants mankind to know that He is the promise-keeping God of Abraham, Isaac, Jacob, and the believers in Christ. Not only does He want them to know this, but He wants to give them the opportunity to choose Christ before it's too late and they are offered the alternative Antichrist worship system."

"Without going into the supporting passages about the *mark of the beast* in Revelation 13, 14, 15, 16, 19, and 20, this mark condemns all who take it to hell. The Antichrist system appears to be established during the trib-period and therefore, the Lord opts to uphold His holy name through the Ezekiel invasion prior."

"Excellent explanation Razz, but what would you say to Catholics and Protestants that believe the church has replaced Israel?" George asked. "Many within their ranks teach that when the Jews rejected Jesus, that God rejected them, and that all their promises were bestowed to the church at that time."

"That's called Replacement Theology," Razz replied. "I have often refuted Replacement Theology by quoting these two chapters (Ezekiel 38-39). It is impossible to posit the church in place of Israel in this powerful prophetic episode. Israel, not the church, will be:

- Gathered from many people's upon the mountains of Israel (Ezekiel 38:8),

- In the latter years (Ezekiel 38:8),

- Dwelling securely in the midst of the land without walls, bars, nor gates (Ezekiel 38:11-12),

- Burying the dead in the Valley of Hamon Gog for seven months (Ezekiel 39:11-16), and

- Burning the invaders weapons for seven years (Ezekiel 39:9-10)."

"Furthermore, the invaders are marching into the Middle East to attack the mountains and land of Israel. This means the church would have to be performing all the above, and do so while being headquartered in the modern-day Jewish State."

George said, "That's an important point. It beckons the question, then: 'how can Replacement Theology even exist in the aftermath of Ezekiel 38?'"

# Replacement Theology

George concludes their discourse with an interesting question: "How can replacement theology even exist in the aftermath of Ezekiel 38?" I, the author, posed this very question to Dr. Arnold Fruchtenbaum during one of our past meetings, and his response went something like this,

> If replacement theology can exist after Israel became a nation in 1948, fulfilling numerous Bible prophecies, then it can and probably will exist even after Ezekiel 38.[123]

Of course, our conversation was predicated *only on the possibility* that the church experiences the fulfillment of Ezekiel 38. Dr. Fruchtenbaum teaches that Ezekiel 38 is probably a pre-trib event by citing the seven years of weapons burning scenario, referenced above. However, he refuses to predict the timing of the rapture, except to acknowledge that he believes it is a pre-trib event. Whenever I ask his opinion on the timing of the rapture, he says something humorous like this, "I'll go out on a limb and tell you this; today we are one day closer to the rapture than we were yesterday."

Replacement Theology is the belief in certain Christian circles that God is done with the Jews. Also called "Supersessionism," it teaches that when the Jews rejected Jesus as their Messiah approximately 2,000 years ago, God rejected the Jews. As such, the unfulfilled promises made to the Jewish people were inherited by the church. Thus, the church is the new Israel, according to most replacement theologians.

Wikipedia defines Supersessionism as follows:

> Supersessionism (also called fulfillment theology or replacement theology) is a Christian interpretation of New Testament claims, viewing God's relationship with Christians as being either the "replacement" or "fulfillment" or "completion" of the promise made to the Jews (or Israelites) and Jewish proselytes[124]

This erroneous teaching causes many Christians to think Israel's existence today resulted from nothing more than the moral obligation of the United Nations after the Hitler holocaust. They fail to see God's miraculous and conspicuous fingerprints upon the restored Jewish State. Clearly, Israel exists today in fulfillment of numerous Bible prophecies like, Ezekiel 36:22-24, Ezekiel 37:11-12, and Isaiah 11:11.

## Israel, God's Modern Day Miracle

In fact, in this author's estimation, Israel's existence today is a greater miracle than the parting of the Red Sea during the Hebrew exodus from Egypt, for the reasons listed below. In order for Israel to exist today, the Lord had to:

- Destroy the Ottoman Empire, which ruled over the Mideast from 1517 to 1917. This occurred during World War I, when the Entente Powers of Russia, France, and the UK defeated the Central Powers consisting of the Ottoman, German, and Hungarian empires.

COMMENTARY

- Create a Zionistic inclination in Jews scattered worldwide. This began in the late nineteenth century, around the time Theodor Herzl published his book *Der Judenstaat,* the Jewish State in German in 1896.

- Defeat the Nazi regime which attempted Jewish genocide in order to prevent the return of the Jews to their ancient homeland of Israel.

- Unite and empower the Allied Forces of the British Empire, the Union of Soviet Socialist Republic and the United States of America to stop Hitler's holocaust attempt.

- Reestablish the Arab and Persian States in order for many Arabs and Persians to vacate out of Israel: Afghanistan (1919), Egypt (1922), Saudi Arabia and Iraq (1932), Iran (1935), Lebanon (1943), and Syrian and Jordan (1946).

- Move the United Nations to legislate and approve the "Partition Plan of 1947," which called for the reestablishment of the Jewish State, so Jews could have a homeland again.

- Create and empower the Israel Defense Forces so that the Jews could survive Arab attempts in 1948, 1967, and 1973 to destroy the reestablished Jewish State.

- Preserve and prosper Israel, since the future Israel described in Ezekiel 38:8-13 turns out to be a very secure and prosperous Israel.

None of these above eight feats could have been accomplished single-handedly by the United Nations. They all required the Lord's divine providence in order for the Jewish State to exist today.

# More Psalm 83 Details

It is difficult to know if this chapter's novel scenario will play out as specified, regarding the Psalm 83 conflict, but there is Scriptural support suggesting in some respects it could. Take Egypt, as an example; Ezekiel 29:8-12 tells of a time a sword will come against Egypt and turn it into an utter waste and desolation. This passage teaches that Egypt, along with several other countries, becomes desolate. Egyptian and apparently other Arab cities are laid waste. Egypt's desolation causes many Egyptians to scatter among other nations not desolated at the time.

> And I will make the land of Egypt a desolation in the midst of the countries that are desolate; and her cities among the cities that are laid waste shall be a desolation forty years; and I will scatter the Egyptians among the nations, and will disperse them through the countries. (Ezekiel 29:12)

COMMENTARY

For more information about Egypt's forty years of desolation, read attached appendix called *Egypt's Forty Years of Desolation.*

Isaiah 19:18 states five cities in Egypt will speak Hebrew, and one will be called the "city of destruction." The city of destruction is probably one of the desolated cities in Ezekiel 29:12. However, which five cities embrace the Hebrew language is uncertain. We can presume it would be five located east of the Nile River, since this is land allotted to the descendants of Abraham, as per Genesis 15.

Some of these cities may be in the Sinai region, which is located east of the Nile River. For instance, Sharm el-Sheikh, a resort area attracting many Israeli and international tourists, is located on the southern tip of the Sinai Peninsula. On July 23, 2005, it was the site of a terror attack that left 200 injured and 88 people dead. It was considered Egypt's worst terror attack in recent history. Abdullah Azzam Brigades, a group tied to Al Qaeda, took credit for the attack and cited the war American war in Iraq as their motivation.[125]

Additionally, the Sinai has served as a primary battlefield in the Arab-Israeli wars of 1948, 1956, 1967, and 1973. As a result of the Arab Spring in 2011, the Sinai region has again seen some Egyptian and Israel troop build-up, as terrorists have attacked natural gas supply lines in the area, as well as other terror threats to Israel's southern border.[126] The Sinai Peninsula separates Israel from Egypt. As such, it can be expected to serve as the primary battlefield for any future confrontations between Egypt and Israel in Psalm 83.

Razz states Cairo, Suez, and Luxor come under attack as three of the five Egyptian cities. This scenario presumes Israel exclusively targets cities east of the Nile. This could be the case if the IDF strictly adheres to the mindset that northeastern Egypt ultimately belongs to Israel, as per the Abrahamic Covenant. However, since Israeli leadership today is more secular than orthodox, it is doubtful that religious reasons will guide the IDF military campaign in Psalm 83.

These cities were chosen for the purposes of this chapter because Cairo, the capital and most populated city of Egypt, is slightly east of the Nile. Suez is directly east of Cairo, and Luxor is south of Cairo, but slightly east of the Nile. Both Suez and Luxor rank among the top ten most populated cities in modern day Egypt.

Additionally, it is safe to presume that Amman, the capital of Jordan, will surrender sovereignty to Israel, since Jeremiah tells us:

> "Therefore behold, the days are coming," says the LORD, "That I will cause to be heard an alarm of war In Rabbah of the Ammonites; It shall be a *desolate mound*, And her *villages shall be burned with fire.* Then Israel shall take possession of his inheritance," says the LORD. (Jeremiah 49:2; emphasis added)

It appears Rabbah may also be among the Ezekiel 29:12 desolated cities. Rabbah was the capital city of ancient Ammon, which is comparatively Amman, Jordan today. Jeremiah says Rabbah and her villages will be destroyed. The Hebrew word for villages is *bath*, and can also mean surrounding towns. The inference is that the devastation extends beyond Jordan's capital city—possibly into other northern Jordanian cities.

The three most populated cities of Jordan are Amman, Az-zarqa' and Irbid, and they are all located in northern Jordan. Over two million people live in these three cities, comprising approximately one-third of Jordan's population, including many Palestinians. Presently, Palestinian refugees and their descendants comprise about seventy-percent of Jordan's overall population.

Additionally, Isaiah 17:1-2 implies the Damascus battlefield reaches as far as Aroer and its surrounding cities. Ancient Aroer was located near Rabbah. George points out above that Obadiah's verses offer some of the best clues as to the location and extent of lands taken over by Israel in the aftermath of the IDF victory over the Psalm 83 conspirators.

> But on Mount Zion there shall be deliverance, And there shall be holiness; The house of Jacob shall possess their possessions. The house of Jacob shall be a fire, And the house of Joseph a flame; But the house of Esau *shall be* stubble; They shall kindle them and devour them, And no survivor shall *remain* of the house of Esau, For the LORD has spoken. The South shall possess the mountains of Esau, And the Lowland shall possess Philistia. They shall possess the fields of Ephraim And the fields of Samaria. Benjamin *shall possess* Gilead. And the captives of this host of the children of Israel *Shall possess the land* of the Canaanites As far as Zarephath. The captives of Jerusalem who are in Sepharad Shall possess the cities of the South. (Obadiah vv. 17-20)

This passage informs us that Psalm 83 will fail because Mount Zion will experience deliverance and Israel, *the house of Jacob*, will maintain their possessions. Additionally, these verses instruct us that Israel will destroy Esau's Palestinian descendants, leaving "no survivor."

Then Obadiah says the mountains of Esau, located in modern-day southern Jordan and Philistia, which is where the Hamas operate out of Gaza, will be annexed as Israeli territory. Also the fields of Ephraim and Samaria, along with Gilead will be possessed by Israel. These lands primarily represent the West Bank today. Lastly, Israel extends the land grab as far as Zarephath, which is located in southern Lebanon. The acquisition of these lands would enlarge Israel's borders. The theme of a Greater Israel is picked up in the next chapter.

Regarding Allah's Akbar being questioned in the aftermath of Psalm 83, it is reasonable to conclude that many Muslims will wonder why their god Allah was unable to reign victorious over tiny little Israel. Throughout Middle East history it was, and still is, commonly understood that the deity of a people displayed its strength and superiority by leading its subjects to victory in battle. They would often pray to their god or goddess for deliverance in wars. This is still the case today. Take an Islamic terrorist for example, the last words uttered from his lips before he commits a suicidal terror attack is Allah Akbar ("god is great"). This utterance is made to call upon Allah to plead for the success of the act of terror, and guarantee the perpetrator receives deliverance in heaven immediately after his jihadist attack. The IDF conquest over the Psalm 83 confederacy will be an enormously embarrassing defeat for the Muslim god Allah.

Considering the Psalm 83 and Ezekiel 38 nations are predominately Muslim, apart from Russia, I quote Zephaniah 2:11 below, and posit the following with regards to Islam's longevity.

> Psalm 83 will be a punch to Islam's gut, Ezekiel 38 an uppercut to Islam's jaw, and the events during the first half of the trib-period, should knock Islam down for the final ten-count.

> "The LORD will be awesome to them, For He will reduce to nothing all the gods [including Allah] of the earth; People shall worship Him, Each one from his place, Indeed all the shores of the nations." (Zephaniah 2:11)

*Please read the next novel chapter now.*

COMMENTARY

# Chapter 13—
## Israel, the Next Emerging Market

*Topics covered:* Arab War Casualties from Psalm 83; The Post-Psalm 83 Greater Israel; Israel's Great Booty Includes Arab Spoils of War; Jordan Surrenders Sovereignty to Israel; The Faithful Jewish Remnant Flees to Southern Jordan; The Protesters of Ezekiel 38:13

This chapter of the novel section begins by addressing the possibility that there may be "collateral damage on both sides of the Arab – Israeli fence," during Psalm 83. A previous chapter's commentary addressed the potential harm to Israelis, and this section's commentary discusses the Arab casualties of war. Several Scriptures suggest the Arabs will suffer severely from their bitter defeat. Numerous Arab refugees, prisoners of war (POWs), deaths, and injuries can be expected.

As you read about the Arab losses, be reminded that the Lord so loves everyone that He desires none should perish. That's the gospel message of John 3:16 and the reason Jesus Christ, the only begotten son of God, died sacrificially and rose again for all sinners; Arabs, Jews, and all of humanity alike.[127] Proverbs 8:31 states that the Lord rejoices in His inhabited world and delights in mankind.

The Lord's "druthers" are to have a personal relationship with the Arabs through the sacrificial blood of Jesus Christ, rather than witness their demise during Psalm 83. But, He has longstanding divine foreign policy in place, as outlined in Genesis 12:3. This policy mandates the cursing of those who oppress Abraham and his Israelite descendants; i.e., the Jews today. Psalm 109:17 confirms this by stating, "As he [the Arabs in the case of Psalm 83] loved cursing, so let it come to him; As he did not delight in blessing, so let it be far from him."

The Psalm 83 Arab confederates "love cursing" Israel. According to Ezekiel 35:5 and Ezekiel 25:15, the Arab hatred toward the Jews is deeply steeped in ancient roots. The very mission of the confederacy in Psalm 83:4 is the total destruction of the Jewish State, that "the name Israel be remembered no more."

Psalm 68:30b says, "Scatter the peoples who delight in war." Scattering often occurs as a result of war. The citizens are reduced to refugees, and the soldiers become POWs. This inhibits them from waging further war, and hopefully humbles them and inclines them to the God of the victors, which in the case of Psalm 83 is the Lord Jehovah of the Bible.

"Scattering the peoples who delight in war" to the end that they incline themselves toward the Lord, is what the Psalmist appears to request:

> O my God, make them like the whirling dust, Like the chaff before the wind! (Psalm 83:13)

Whirling dust and chaff blown about by the wind is a picture of dispersion. Then in the last verse, after he requests in Psalm 83:13-17 that the Arab confederates become shamed, and made like the whirling dust and the chaff before the wind, and as the flame that sets the mountains on fire, he closes with the following imprecation:

> That they [the Arab confederates] may know that You, whose name alone is the LORD, Are the Most High over all the earth. (Psalm 83:18).

In the case of the Jordanians (Moab and Ammon, in Psalm 83), that's what happens, according to the passages below:

> "Woe to you, O Moab! The people of Chemosh [former Moabite god, now replaced by Allah] perish; For your sons have been taken captive, And your daughters captive. "Yet I will bring back the captives [POWs and refugees] of Moab In the latter days," says the LORD. Thus far is the judgment of Moab. (Jeremiah 48:46-47)

> "Behold, I will bring fear upon you," Says the Lord GOD of hosts, "From all those who are around you; You shall be driven out, [scattered] everyone headlong, And no one will gather those who wander off. But afterward I will bring back The captives [POWs and refugees] of

the people of Ammon," says the LORD. Thus says the LORD of hosts. (Jeremiah 49:5-6)

Moab and Ammon were the children of Lot, Abraham's nephew. In Psalm 83 they are depicted as one of the weaker military members taking part in the Arab confederacy. We know this, because the Psalmist declares, "Assyria also has joined with them; They have helped the children [Moab and Ammon] of Lot. *Selah.*" (Psalm 83:8)

The Hebrew word for helped is *zeroa,* and in this instance it suggests Assyria shoulders much of Jordan's military burden, or otherwise attempts to compensate for the general insufficiencies of the Jordanian Armed Forces (JAF). Whereas the other members of Psalm 83 have world-class armies, the JAF doesn't even rank within the military top forty.[128] The primary function of the JAF is to prevent the overthrow of the ruling Hashemite Kingdom. They have performed well against the PLO, but miserably against Israel in their 1948, 1967, and 1973 wars.

Jeremiah says fear comes upon Jordan from all around. Those around Jordan today are Israel to the west, Hezbollah to the northwest, Syria to the north, Iraq to the east, and Saudi Arabia to the south. All of the above, including Jordan, are part of Psalm 83. Assyria, at the time of the Psalm's issuance, was comprised of parts of modern-day Syria and Iraq.

The above suggests that Jordan gets drawn into the Psalm 83 conflict and at some point witnesses fearful events on all sides of its borders. Interestingly, Jordan's King Hussein I was pressured by Egyptian president Gamal Abdel Nasser to join in the 1967 Arab-Israeli war. Damascus, which ceases to be a city according to Isaiah 17:1, is 109 miles north of Amman, Jordan. The destruction of Damascus could be one of the reasons fear befalls Jordan. Jordan is clearly an enemy confederate member against Israel, but whether they are a voluntary or involuntary member is uncertain. At present, Jordan possesses a fragile peace treaty with Israel, but that will be abandoned when Jordan enlists in Psalm 83.

In the chapter called *The Arabs Surrender!*, George and Razz discuss the POWs and some of the harder hit Arab cities and territories in Jordan and Egypt. The fact that these and many other important Arab cities are lethally struck, implies Arab losses will be numerous and their sufferings severe.

# Arab War Casualties from Psalm 83

As the commentary in the chapter called *The Arabs Surrender!* pointed out, there will probably be hordes of Arab casualties resulting from Psalm 83.

COMMENTARY

Before identifying several more supporting Scriptures that deal with the Arab human losses and associated sufferings, please be informed that Dr. Arnold Fruchtenbaum does an outstanding job in his *Footsteps of the Messiah* (revised edition) book approaching this subject from a somewhat different angle, when he writes about the Arab States in Bible prophecy. He points out how the Arabs are dealt with for their aversion to Israel either through *occupation, destruction, or conversion.*[129]

Listed below are some of the Scriptures that I believe identify the Arab casualties suffered as the apparent result of the Psalm 83 war.

## The Killed and Wounded:

- *Jordan* – Primarily alluding to passages about Ammon, Moab, and Edom. Ammon represents modern-day northern Jordan, Moab—central Jordan, and Edom—southern Jordan. Ezekiel 25:13, and Ezekiel 25:9-10; Jeremiah 48:8,42, and 49:2; Isaiah 15:4; and Amos 2:2-3.

- *Egypt* – Isaiah 19:18; and Ezekiel 29:5,8, and 30:4,8.[130]

- *Syria* – Isaiah 17:1,14; Jeremiah 49:26-27; and possibly Amos 1:3-5.

- *Saudi Arabia* – Primarily alluding to passages about Dedan, which is modern–day, northwestern Saudi Arabia. The Saudis are represented under the banner of the Ishmaelites in Psalm 83. Ezekiel 25:13.

- *Palestinians* – Primarily alluding to passages about Gaza, Philistia, Philistines, and the Edomites. Jeremiah 49:10; Ezekiel 25:16; and Obadiah v.18.

- *Lebanon* – Primarily alluding to passages about Tyre and Sidon. Ezekiel 28:13; Amos 1:10; and Joel 3:4 (possibly).

## The POWs and Refugees:

- *Jordan* – Isaiah 11:14; Jeremiah 48:7, 44-47, 49:3, 5-6; Ezekiel 25:3-4; and Amos 1:15.

- *Egypt* – Ezekiel 29:12-13.

- *Syria* – Isaiah 17:3, 9, 11:16; and Amos 1:5.

- *Saudi Arabia*- Jeremiah 49:8.

- *Palestinians* – Jeremiah 49:11, 20; Obadiah vv. 19-20; and Amos 1:8.

- *Lebanon* – Obadiah v. 19 alludes to captives as far as Zarephath, which would be located in modern-day southwestern Lebanon.

# The Post-Psalm 83 Greater Israel

In the aftermath of their decisive IDF victory over the Psalm 83 Arab confederacy, Israel temporarily becomes a safer place. Temporarily, because looming in the shadows of Psalm 83 appears to be an even more formidable offensive foretold to follow in Ezekiel 38-39. Ezekiel 38:11-13 informs us that Israel is extremely prosperous at the time of this subsequent invasion. These verses seem to describe a "Greater Israel" than presently exists. For the purposes of this book, Greater Israel identifies a safer, wealthier, and larger nation than the modern-day Jewish State.[131]

How Israel amasses its great wealth prior to the Ezekiel 38 invasion is a subject of some debate. Many believe that Israel strikes it rich someday from its own commercial endeavors and natural resources. In addition to the relatively recent sizable natural gas and shale oil discoveries, many believe Israel soon locates a significant surplus of crude oil under its soil.

Most of the proponents of this theory don't include Psalm 83 into the greater Israel equation. Factoring out the Arab threats, riches, and lands, they gravitate toward thinking that Israel already dwells securely and its coming prosperity is entirely self-made.

Additionally, they generally believe that the lesser Israel of today, which measures approximately 9,000 square miles, becomes extremely wealthy within its modern-day (pre-Psalm 83) borders. The menu of reasons that they don't include Arab spoils into the national treasures of Israel, include the following:

- Psalm 83 is only an imprecatory prayer and not a *bona fide* Bible prophecy.

- Psalm 83 found historical fulfillment according to 2 Chronicles 20.

- Psalm 83 occurs at the same time as the Ezekiel 38 Gog of Magog invasion.

- Psalm 83 occurs during the battle of Armageddon.

The second reason listed above is refuted in the appendix called *Psalm 83 – Has it Found Final Fulfillment*. The third reason is debated in the appendix called *Is Ezekiel 38 Imminent*. These appendices should also dispel the first reason, illustrating that Psalm 83 is much more than a prayer.

Regarding the fourth reason, it is doubtful that either Psalm 83 or Ezekiel 38 is part of the Armageddon nations of the Antichrist. Prophecies in Joel 3:2, Zechariah 12:3, 9, and elsewhere inform us that "all (world) nations" are part of

COMMENTARY

Armageddon. However, the caveat is that not "all nations" as we know them today, may remain intact by the time Armageddon unfolds. Psalm 83 involves only ten populations, and Ezekiel 38 lists nine entirely different ones. Neither prophecy alludes to "all nations," in their prophetic description. There are approximately 195 recognized nations in the world, and presently they include those spoken of in Psalm 83 and Ezekiel 38. However, by the time Armageddon comes, the Psalm and Ezekiel invasion should be concluded and the world will probably have morphed into a ten-division state, as per Daniel 7:24, Revelation 17:12, and elsewhere.

In essence, the world as we presently identify it will not likely be the same at that time. The fact that neither Psalm 83 nor Ezekiel 38 allude to "all nations," along with other reasons given throughout this book, strongly suggests that Psalm 83, Ezekiel 38, and the battle of Armageddon, are three different prophetic events.

## Israel's Great Booty Includes Arab Spoils of War

COMMENTARY

Conversely, many others, myself included, believe a greater Israel becomes a reality in the aftermath of Psalm 83. We believe that Israel, in addition to its own resources, captures Arab spoils of war through Psalm 83.

Additionally, the Jewish nation seems to capture more of their Promised Land identified in Genesis 15:18, which extends between northeast Egypt and portions of Iraq and Syria.

> On the same day the LORD made a covenant with Abram, saying: "To your descendants I have given this land, from the river of Egypt to the great river, the River Euphrates." [132]

The Jews have both an ancient and a modern history of expanding their borders in the aftermath of achieving military victories over the Arabs. Joshua started this trend about 3,500 years ago, when he led the Hebrews out from their forty years in the wilderness. [133] King David followed suit about 500 years later in the aftermath of his conquests, and Israel continued this precedent in June 1967 after the IDF victory in the infamous "Six Day" war against primarily Egypt, Syria, and Jordan.

Some Arab lands Israel might acquire from defeating the Psalm 83 Arab confederacy would be at least five cities in Egypt, parts of Lebanon, the Gaza, West Bank, Syria, and most all of Jordan. Isaiah 19:18 states five cities in Egypt will speak the language of Canaan, which is Hebrew. Obadiah v. 19 appropriates the Gaza, West Bank, and probably the Golan Heights. Obadiah v. 20 describes Israel possessing portions of southern Lebanon up to ancient Zarephath.

# Jordan Surrenders Sovereignty to Israel

Listed below are a few passages which teach that the modern-day nation of Jordan surrenders sovereignty to Israel.

> "Therefore behold, the days are coming," says the LORD, "That I will cause to be heard an alarm of war In Rabbah of the Ammonites [northern Jordan]; It shall be a desolate mound, And her villages shall be burned with fire. Then *Israel shall take possession* of his inheritance," says the LORD. (Jeremiah 49:2; emphasis added)

> But they shall fly down upon the shoulder of the Philistines [Gaza] toward the west; Together they shall plunder the people of the East; They shall lay their hand on Edom [southern Jordan] and Moab [central Jordan]; And the people of Ammon [northern Jordan] *shall obey them.* (Isaiah 11:14; emphasis added)

> "Therefore, as I live," Says the LORD of hosts, the God of Israel, "Surely Moab shall be like Sodom, And the people of Ammon like Gomorrah— Overrun with weeds and saltpits, And a perpetual desolation. The residue of My people shall plunder them, And the remnant of *My people shall possess them.*" (Zephaniah 2:9; emphasis added)

Today, Jordan rests within the Promised Land, as allotted to Abraham in Genesis 15:18. Many eschatologists believe that Jordan, along with the rest of the Promised Land, will be given to the Jewish descendants of Abraham by Christ at His second coming.[134] I disagree with this assessment, and suspect that the Jews capture parts of Jordan prior to this, as a result of winning in Psalm 83. For the following two reasons, I believe the Jews annex Jordan before Ezekiel 38 occurs:

- The Valley of Hamon Gog is probably located in central Jordan.

- The faithful remnant of Israel flees to southern Jordan.

*The Valley of Hamon Gog is probably located in Central Jordan.* Hamon Gog in Hebrew means the multitudes or hordes of Gog. It is a place that presently doesn't exist, and won't exist until it becomes necessary. It is necessitated when the Lord destroys the Ezekiel 38 invaders. As mentioned earlier, the Lord destroys the Ezekiel invaders through an Old Testament fire, hailstone, and brimstone episode.

> And I will bring him to judgment with pestilence and bloodshed; I will rain down on him [Gog of the land of Magog], on his troops, and on the many peoples who *are* with him, [the other Ezekiel invaders including Iranians, Turks, and more] flooding rain, great *hailstones, fire,* and *brimstone.* (Ezekiel 38:22; emphasis added)

(On a side note, please recognize that the IDF does not appear to serve an instrumental military role in the defeat of the Ezekiel invaders, described in Ezekiel 38:18-39:6. This is another issue that separates both prophecies from one another.)

In the aftermath of the Lord's victory, there will likely be death and destruction second only to the flood of Noah. These dead must be buried promptly, in order to prevent the plague potentials associated with the decomposition of dead soldiers. In Ezekiel 39:11-16, we are given a detailed account of the burial instructions.

The process begins with seven months of burial in a designated location, in order to cleanse the land. The cemetery is in a valley east of some sea. The valley is called Hamon Gog. As stated earlier, no such place presently exists. However, it will when the multitudes of Gog's dead soldiers lay stricken dead across parts of the Middle East.

What sea could the prophet be alluding to, that has a large enough valley on its east side to accommodate the burial of potentially millions of dead contaminated soldiers? There are only four primary choices to choose from: the Mediterranean, the Sea of Galilee, the Red Sea, or the Dead Sea.

## The Mediterranean Sea

The Mediterranean Sea can probably be ruled out because the candidate valleys in Israel, like the Jezreel, Kidron, Hula, Beit Netofa, Beracah, and Valley of the Cross are inside of modern-day Israel. Logically, since Ezekiel 39:14 declares the Jews are "cleansing the land," it doesn't make sense that they would contaminate their own fertile Israeli soil, given other options.

Contamination is an appropriate term in this instance, considering Ezekiel 39:14-15 appears to involve the resemblance of a hazmat (hazardous materials) team. Additionally, some of us believe the Jews are cleansing the land in compliance with requirements specified in the Mosaic Law. (Numbers 19:11-

22; Deuteronomy 21:1-9). If so, this implies the supernatural defeat of the Magog invaders inclines the Jews to revert to orthodoxy, and resulting in their seeking to rebuild their temple, reinstate Levitical Law, and resume their animal sacrifices.

## The Sea of Galilee

The Sea of Galilee is likewise unlikely, because candidate valleys to the east are located primarily in southern Syria or northern Jordan. Occasional southwesterly wind patterns blow through these areas into Israel, which could cause the contamination referenced above to spread into the world's most heavily populated Jewish area of Gush Dan.[135]

Another negative is that presently both Syria and Jordan are under Arab rule. The Syrians and Jordanians would prohibit Israel from burying the multitudes of Gog under their sovereign soil. However, if Israel captured these valleys during Psalm 83, perhaps they would gain the option of someday burying the dead in one of their valleys.

But, what about Damascus, the capital city of Syria, which is approximately sixty miles northeast of the Sea of Galilee? Isaiah 17:1, 9, 14 predicts it will someday be destroyed (v. 1), probably overnight (v. 14), and probably by the IDF (v. 9). Damascus may be a desolate and contaminated place, due to its possible prior destruction. This could also dissuade the use of some valley east of the Sea of Galilee.

For these above reasons the Sea of Galilee drops low on the list of choices. However, even if it is the referenced Sea, eastward Arab valleys can only be used by Israel for mass burial purposes if Israel negotiates either politically or militarily, the use of the land. Politically, this is improbable, but as a result of an IDF military victory in Psalm 83, it becomes possible.

## The Red Sea

The Red Sea option is unfeasible due to the logistics of transporting multitudes of dead and probably contaminated soldiers so far southward. The Red Sea is over 400 miles to the south of Israel's capital city of Tel Aviv.[136] Valleys east of the Red Sea are currently under Saudi sovereignty, inhibiting Israel's ability to bury the dead there, as well. Additionally, Saharan winds that could potentially blow contaminants into Israel should be considered.

COMMENTARY

*The Dead Sea*

The Dead Sea presents the best option for the creation of a place called the Valley of Hamon Gog. Satellite topography shots of the Middle East clearly picture central Jordan as the perfect location for the mass burial site of the multitudes of Gog. Unlike northern Jordan, where most Jordanians live, and portions of southern Jordan that are mountainous, much of central Jordan is flat, barren, and home to Bedouins.

Regional wind patterns favor this location as well. For instance, the hot, dry, dusty desert wind called a "Sirocco," an Arab word for "easterly," often blows in the eastward direction of Europe. Sirocco is also known as the Sharkiye in Jordan, Sharav in Israel, and Simoom in Arabia.[137]

If the central Jordanian land, formerly called ancient Moab, becomes captured by the IDF during Psalm 83, then Israel would possess the unrestricted ability to establish the Valley of Hamon Gog there. Thus, when the hordes of Gog need a burial location, one already exists, requiring Israel to simply use it and rename it.

Moab is one of the ten members listed in the Psalm 83 Arab confederacy. Because the Valley of Hamon Gog is probably going to exist in Jordan, and Ezekiel 38 precedes Christ's second coming, this is one reason I believe Israel annexes all or part of Jordan in the aftermath of Psalm 83 and prior to Christ's return.

Interestingly, the Balfour Document of 1917 intended to create a Jewish state inclusive of modern-day Israel and Jordan, but in 1922 the League Nations passed the Transjordan memorandum, which essentially excluded modern-day Jordan from the proposed Jewish territory.[138] On May 25, 1946, the United Nations recognized Jordan as an independent sovereign Arab kingdom. Two years later, on May 14, 1948, Israel was officially established as the Jewish State. It is my opinion, fashioned from Jeremiah 49:2, Zephaniah 2:8-9, and several other verses which I connect with the Psalm 83 prophecy, that after the Psalm 83 war Israel captures all, or part of Jordan.

# The Faithful Jewish Remnant of Israel Flees to Southern Jordan

Zechariah 13:8-9 informs us that a remnant of Israelis emerges from out of the Antichrist's final genocidal attempt of the Jews. This horrific holocaust episode takes place during the final three-and-one-half years on the earth's timeline, in a period commonly called the "great tribulation" (great-trib). Zechariah says this remnant will ultimately become believers and say, "The Lord is my God." (Zechariah 13:9). Thus, they are often referred to as the "faithful remnant of Israel." They are the saved Israel, described in Romans 11:26-27.

> And so all Israel will be saved, as it is written: "The Deliverer will come out of Zion, And He will turn away ungodliness from Jacob; For this is My covenant with them, When I take away their sins."

In Matthew 24:15 Christ instructs this group of survivors to flee to the mountains without delay, when they witness the "abomination of desolation" spoken of by the prophet Daniel (Daniel 9:27, 12:11). We glean from connecting passages in Isaiah 63 and elsewhere that the specific mountains Christ alludes to are located in ancient Edom, which is modern-day southern Jordan. According to Hosea 5:15, this Jewish remnant recognizes Christ as their Messiah during their great tribulation. Subsequently, they plead for Him to return and rescue them from the onslaught of the Antichrist. Isaiah 63:1 tells us that He first touches down at their location in Edom. Isaiah's verses go on to declare that Christ's garments are stained with the blood of Antichrist and his Armageddon armies. Christ wins the war and then makes His victory ascent up to the Mount of Olives, as per Zechariah 14:3-4.

The point of all the above is that no faithful remnant would presently be permitted unrestricted passage into Jordan, as southern Jordan is under Arab rule. Thus, should a remnant of approximately several million Jews attempt to cross the Israeli borders for refuge in the Jordanian mountains, the Jordanian government would undoubtedly protest. Under current pre-Psalm 83 conditions the historical account inscribed in Numbers 20, would likely repeat itself.

> Then Edom said to him, "You [Moses and the Hebrews at the time of their exodus out of Egypt] shall not pass through my *land,* lest I come out against you with the sword." So the children of Israel said to him, "We will go by the Highway, and if I or my livestock drink any of your water, then I will pay for it; let me only pass through on foot, nothing *more.*" Then he said, "You shall not pass through." So Edom came out against them with many men and with a strong hand. Thus Edom refused to give Israel passage through his territory; so Israel turned away from him. (Numbers 20:18-21)

However, unrestricted passage could come under future conditions when Edom, a member of Psalm 83, is conquered by Israel. This is the second reason I believe Jordan surrenders sovereignty in advance of Christ's second coming. The faithful remnant, refuged in Edom, crying out, "Blessed is He who comes in the name of the Lord," in fulfillment of Matthew 23:39, is a prerequisite requirement of Christ's return.

> For I say to you, you shall see Me no more till you say, "Blessed is He who comes in the name of the Lord!" (Matthew 24:39)

## The Protestors of Ezekiel 38:13

In Ezekiel 38:13 we find a group of nations that seem to be protesting the intentions of the Ezekiel invaders. In fact, their declaration of protest clues us into the primary motive of the Ezekiel invaders.

> Sheba [modern-day Yemen], Dedan [modern-day Saudi Arabia], the merchants of Tarshish [possibly Britain], and all their young lions [possibly America] will say to you, "Have you come to take plunder? Have you gathered your army to take booty, to carry away silver and gold, to take away livestock and goods, to take great plunder?" (Ezekiel 38:13)

The Russian-Iranian led coalition is coming to strip Israel of "great plunder," or in other Bible translations, "great spoil." Hence, here is yet another reason we realize that Israel someday becomes extremely prosperous. Russia would not go to great lengths to form its massive coalition to come collect some chump change from Israel. No, Israel someday possesses the spoil that the Russian coalition covets.

In 2009, approximately ninety kilometers due west of the port of Haifa, in the Mediterranean Sea, Israel discovered a large supply of natural gas. The drilling site is called *Tamar-One*, and the gas supply is estimated to be worth about $15 billion.[139] Subsequently in 2010, Israel located another sizable natural gas supply near *Tamar-One,* called *Leviathan.* This gas field reserve is estimated at $90 billion.[140] To learn more about the Bible predictions concerning Israel's future prosperity, read the appendix called *Israel Strikes it Rich Someday.* This appendix explains how the great spoil Israel possesses probably includes the Psalm 83 spoils of war. More information about the Ezekiel 38-39 prophecy is contained in the commentary chapter called *Russia Forms an Evil Plan to Invade Israel.*

To conclude this commentary, below you will find a part of the conversation between retired general George and his best friend Razz, that was omitted from the novel portion. It is a pertinent discussion about the Ezekiel 38 protestors. In order to appreciate their discourse, I recommend a previous reading of the corresponding novel chapter by the same name, *Israel, the Next Emerging Market.* Their conversation begins with:

"Ezekiel 38 teaches that Israel will garner 'great spoil' just before Russia invades," Razz reminded. "It must be referring to spoils of war from the Arab conflict."

"Razz, do you still believe America shows up as merchants wanting to conduct commerce with Israel in the Ezekiel 38 prophecy?" George inquired.

Razz replied, "Absolutely, the theme of 'merchants' has definite application to Israel's great spoil, and implies some nation is interested in conducting international commerce with a prosperous Israel. Additionally, by alluding to Dedan in verse 13, Ezekiel tells us Saudi Arabia has concerns about Russian motives."

Pondering the implications, George asked, "Do you think the remaining Saudi remnant will also want to participate in Israel's oil exploitation program?"

Razz responded with a resounding "Yes! After undergoing the destructiveness of Psalm 83 by the IDF, the Saudis will want no part in the nine-member Russian coalition. They will be overwhelmed by Israel's miraculous ability to survive against overwhelming odds. As a matter of national survival, they appear to join in sideline protests with Sheba (Yemen), the merchants of Tarshish, and their young lions."[141]

Razz continued, "Saudis working alongside Americans will be a great asset to Israel's oil exploitation program. The Saudis were the number one producer of OPEC oil and are most familiar with internal OPEC production and exportation policies. Additionally, America offers Israel expertise in oil drilling, distribution, and will undoubtedly consume all the oil Israel can export."

*Please read the next chapter of the novel now.*

# Chapter 14–
## Greater Israel Makes Plans for a Third Temple

*Topics covered:* Israel Expands Territorially into Arab Lands; Israel Dismantles the West Bank Barrier Wall; Millions of Jews Return to Israel; Israel Constructs Third Jewish Temple; Israel Reinstates Animal Sacrifices

(The appendix called *Israel Strikes It Rich Someday* is a recommended reading alongside this chapter's commentary. Also, the theme of "Greater Israel" identifies a safer, wealthier, and larger nation than the modern-day Jewish State.[142])

On September 14, 2008, then Israeli Prime Minister, Ehud Olmert was quoted as saying, "The notion of greater Israel no longer exists."[143]

On September 18, 2008, in a display of antagonistic one-up-man's-ship, Iranian president Mahmoud Ahmadinejad deviously echoed harsher sentiments by declaring, "A lesser Israel has expired, too."[144]

The apocalyptically-minded Ahmadinejad had three years earlier, in October 2005, declared his intentions to expunge a lesser Israel when he was quoted at the *World Without Zionism* conference in Tehran as saying that Israel, "Must be wiped off the map."[145]

At the time Ahmadinejad announced his intentions to wipe the Jewish State off the map, Iran was developing its nuclear weapons program. Although this program began several years earlier, it was officially christened in August, 2010, when their Bushehr nuclear facility went "red hot," meaning nuclear fuel began loading into the facility.[146] The fueling of Bushehr signaled that Iran was nearer to possessing the nuclear weapons capability to accomplish the dastardly deed of obliterating Israel.

One of Israel's most liberal prime ministers, Ehud Olmert, had eleven months prior to his statement, left the November, 27, 2007, Annapolis Summit with renewed optimism about peace between his people and the Palestinians. Hosted by US President George W. Bush, Olmert met alongside Palestinian Authority President, Mahmoud Abbas to hash out the terms of the two-State solution. As expected, nothing was realized out of their overrated summit, and as Olmert's prime ministerial term neared its end, he made his above-mentioned frustrated statement that greater Israel no longer exists.

Since Olmert's departure from office his replacement, Benjamin Netanyahu, has adopted a much more conservative policy toward the two-State, land-for-peace solutions. Netanyahu has drawn a seemingly immovable line in the Middle East sand opposing present land for peace proposals. For more clarification of Netanyahu's requirements for Mideast peace, read the appendix called *Is the Arab Spring Setting Up for Winter War?*

What is it? Is a Greater Israel soon to transpire, or a lesser Israel about to expire?

Certainly Israel's enemies are working toward the accomplishment of the latter. However, the God of Israel promises otherwise. Numerous Bible passages predict an everlasting Israel that possesses great wealth and much more land. Israel's modern-day enemies are putting the Lord's covenantal promises and Bible prophecies to task. Who, the Lord or Israel's surrounding foes, will have the final word in this matter?

Ahmadinejad is not the only one seeking the destruction of Israel. The preponderance of Arab States refuse to recognize Israel's existence as the Jewish State, evidencing a similar Anti-Semitic sentiment. This chapter's novel and commentary sections discuss:

- Israel Expands Territorially into Arab Lands

- Israel Dismantles the "West Bank Barrier Wall"

- Millions of Jews Return to Israel

- Israel Constructs Third Jewish Temple

- Israel Reinstates Animal Sacrifices

# Israel Expands Territorially Into Arab Lands

About 4,000 years ago, recorded in Genesis 15, the Lord promised Abraham an enormous amount of land. This land extended from the Nile River in Egypt to the Euphrates in modern- day Iraq and Syria. Through his son Isaac, rather than Ishmael, and through his grandson Jacob instead of Esau, the Promised Land became the heritage of the Israelites. Jacob was renamed Israel in Genesis 32:28 and 35:10. Thus, the Israelites, or Jews today, are named after their patriarch Jacob / Israel.

However, Abraham was informed, as recorded in the passage below, that at least 400 years stood between the promise and the possession of the land.

> Then He [the Lord] said to Abram [Abraham]: "Know certainly that your [Hebrew] descendants will be strangers in a land [Egypt] that is not theirs, and will serve them, [Egyptians] and they will afflict them [Hebrews] four hundred years. And also the nation [Egypt] whom they serve I will judge; afterward they shall come out with great possessions. Now as for you, you shall go to your fathers in peace; you shall be buried at a good old age. But in the fourth generation they shall return here, [to the Promised Land] for the iniquity of the Amorites is not yet complete." (Genesis 15:13-16)

After the 400 years of exile elapsed and the exodus of the Hebrews out of Egypt ensued, Joshua brought the Israelites into some of the Promised Land. The division of the land is described in the book of Joshua chapters 13-21. At the time, the Israelites possessed more land than their modern-day equivalents.

About 500 years later, around 3,000 BC, King David and subsequently his son King Solomon, expanded into an even greater Israel. For the first time, Israel annexed lands to the northeast extending to the River Euphrates in Syria, as promised in Genesis 15:18. Unfortunately, King Solomon's reign was followed by "two bums...," as eschatologist Jacob Prasch humors; Rehoboam (Rehobum) and Jeroboam (Jerobum).[147] Their struggle for power split the Israelite kingdom in two. Rehoboam was Solomon's son, but Jeroboam was not kin to the king; Solomon appointed him to be the superintendent over his vast labor forces. Jeroboam used this position of authority to gain support for eventual quest for rulership over Israel.

That was as good as the Israelite land-grab got, because Jeroboam took ten of the twelve tribes into the northern kingdom, and Rehoboam ruled over the remaining two in the southern kingdom. Assyria conquered the northern kingdom in 722 BC, and Babylon conquered the southern kingdom in 586 BC.

The Jews began returning to their homeland over a period of time after the Babylonian captivity, but they never grew back into the landmass Solomon previously possessed. Then in 70 AD, the Romans conquered Israel, sacked Jerusalem, and destroyed the second Jewish temple. The Romans brought down the Jewish rebellion at that time, and in 135 they defeated the final rebellion, led by Bar Kokhba.

The Jewish leadership at the time had reached a condition of irreversible apostasy. According to Leviticus 26:31-34, this required a desolation of the land and a dispersion from the land. The Roman Empire was empowered to execute this disciplinary duty of the Mosaic Law. At the time, the world thought the God of the Jews was a weak god, because He couldn't sustain His chosen people in the land. However, they didn't understand this disciplinary clause in Leviticus.

If they'd read on further to Leviticus 26:44-45, they would have realized that the Diaspora of the Jews and the desolation of the Promised Land was only a temporary scenario. Albeit 1,878 years elapsed between Israel's desolation in 70 AD and her restoration on May 14, 1948, Israel's existence today proves their God is anything but weak. In fact, part and parcel with the prophesied return of the Jews into Israel is the promise to expand the borders of Israel to accommodate their massive aliyah. Someday, the Jews will occupy all of the territory defined in Genesis 15:18. But when?

Many eschatologists believe the full spectrum of the land will be deeded over to the faithful Jewish remnant upon the return of Christ during the 1,000-year messianic kingdom period. However, I believe Scripture supports the premise that some of the land will be captured by the IDF, prior to the second coming of Jesus Christ.

The Promised Land includes parts of Jordan, the Gaza Strip and the West Bank, and portions of Egypt, Saudi Arabia, Lebanon, Syria, and Iraq. Coincidentally, all of these Arab populations are listed in the Psalm 83:6-8 confederacy that someday seeks to destroy the Jews and rob them of their homeland. As pointed out in "Israel's Exceedingly Great Army," chapter six of *Isralestine*, the IDF wins this war!

Like they did during the time of Joshua, King David, and in June of 1967, the Jews will probably repeat the pattern of capturing portions of conquered Promised Land. Listed below are several Scriptures that suggest this could be the case. These passages appear to find association with the Psalm 83 war scenario.

COMMENTARY

## Jordan

Jordan was addressed extensively in the previous chapter's commentary, but below are the pertinent passages relating to Israel's capture of Jordan.

Jeremiah 49:1-2. Jeremiah seems to predict the surrender of Jordanian sovereignty to Israel after a devastating Arab – Israeli war in these verses.

Isaiah 11:14. Isaiah says Israelis will lay their hands on Jordan, and Jordanians will obey them. (Jordan is represented by Edom, Moab, and Ammon in this passage.)

Isaiah 17:2. Isaiah possibly predicts the cities of Aroer Gad become rezoned as agricultural lands by Israel, after the destruction of Damascus, Syria. These cities could be located in between modern-day northern Jordan and southern Syria. It is interesting to note that, although Isaiah 17:1 predicts the destruction of Damascus, Ezekiel 47:16-18 uses Damascus as a future boundary line for dividing the tribal territories for the Jews.

Zephaniah 2:9. Zephaniah clearly evidences the plundering of Jordan by the IDF leads to its annexation by Israel.

## Egypt

Isaiah 19:16-18. Isaiah declares that after Egypt becomes terrified of Israel, five cities inside Egypt begin speaking the language of Hebrew. One of these cities is named the "City of Destruction."[148] This implies Egypt surrenders at least five cities to the Jews upon destruction. For more commentary on these verses refer to appendix called *Is Egypt in Psalm 83*?

Isaiah 11:15. Isaiah points out the men will walk over dried-up streams connected to the Nile River. Contextually, it appears as though these are Israelis, when compared to Isaiah 11:14-16.

## Gaza

Obadiah v. 19. Obadiah suggests the lowland inhabitants of Judah will possess the coastal areas near Gaza. The preceding verse 18 discusses an Arab – Israeli conflict between the house of Jacob (Israel) and the house of Esau (Arabs).

Zephaniah 2:4. Zephaniah correlates with Obadiah v. 19 and emphasizes that the seacoast of the Mediterranean near Gaza will be designated for the flocks of Judah.

## Saudi Arabia

Jeremiah 49:8. Jeremiah warns the Saudis to abandon the area once called Dedan. Dedan was located in what is today northwest Saudi Arabia and appears to be located within the Promised Land parameters.

Ezekiel 25:13. Ezekiel says the Saudis will experience casualties of war apparently for their involvement in Psalm 83.

## Lebanon

Obadiah v. 20. Obadiah prepares us to recognize that Israel will expand its borders at least up to Zarephath, in the aftermath of the Arab – Israeli war in Obadiah v. 18. Zarephath was located in what is today part of southern Lebanon.

## West Bank

Obadiah v. 19. Obadiah says the Jews will possess the fields of Ephraim and fields of Samaria, in addition to Gilead. These are all areas associated with today's West Bank and slightly beyond.

## Syria

Obadiah v. 19. Similar to the West Bank, Obadiah says Gilead becomes the possession of the tribe of Benjamin. According to *Parson's Bible Atlas* there are several candidates for Gilead, including, Gilead (Transjordan), Gilead (Jezreel), and Gilead (City). Gilead (Transjordan) was a territory east of the Jordan River, which places it in modern-day Jordan, and possibly a small portion of southern Syria.

Isaiah 11:16. Isaiah points out there will be a remnant of Jews in Assyria. At the time Isaiah wrote, approximately 2,850 years ago, Assyria encompassed much of modern-day Syria. Although there are a few Jews still residing in Assyria today, the point Isaiah seems to make is that there could eventually be more, requiring a highway to facilitate their future travel to Israel.

# Israel Dismantles the West Bank Barrier Wall

In his speech of September 20, 2001, President George W. Bush declared "War on Terror." In so doing, Israel was given a temporary respite. Finally, the world put a face on the masked marauders Israel had fought for decades: "Islamic Terrorists!" Israel promptly seized the opportunity to step-up its war on terror internally, while the US fought terrorism in Afghanistan and Iraq externally.

Momentum had shifted to Israel's side, so the State of Israel began constructing what is called the West Bank Barrier Wall, in 2002. The wall is approximately 403 miles, and extends well beyond the Armistice Green Line, established in 1949 between Israel and the West Bank. Since its construction, Palestinian terrorism inside of Israel has significantly decreased. Looking backward in time, this wall served its purpose; it kept Palestinian terrorism outside of Israel proper.

In the novel section, the Israeli Minister of Defense decrees "Tear Down This Wall," reminiscent of former US President Ronald Reagan's petition to tear down the Berlin Wall. After the IDF defeats the Arab confederacy of Psalm 83, such a decree might be forthcoming; one of the reasons being, that Israel should experience a deepened sense of national security in the war's aftermath and feel this separation wall is unnecessary. The IDF will have proven to be the "Exceedingly Great Army" of Ezekiel 37:10, and the Arab propagators of terrorism will have been severely defeated.

Additionally, Israel will probably be seeking to entice more Jewish aliyah by promoting an atmosphere of calm in the Holy Land. Increased manpower could become vital to Israel in its bid to recover from the war and become a "Greater Israel." Reparations and exploitations from the war should prompt Israel to encourage a mass migration of Jews from the nations of the world into the greater, safer, and wealthier Jewish state.

In the aftermath of the war, events in Israel could resemble what the novel chapter eleven suggests about the "*Tzion Levav*" (heart of Zion) campaign. Israel's slogan could read something like, "Escape Anti-Semitism, Experience Religious Freedom, and Enjoy Economic Opportunity! Come Home to the Holy Land!"

All of the above predictive comments may seem imaginative, but they are not that far-fetched, considering what Ezekiel 38:8-13 foretells. In these informative verses Ezekiel establishes eight important facts about the conditions inside of Israel at the time the Gog of Magog invasion takes place. Israel must be:

- Regathered from the nations,
- In the "latter years,"
- Brought back from the "sword," (Inquisition / Holocaust)
- Dwelling in the "midst" (center) of land long desolate,

- A peaceful people dwelling securely in unwalled villages,

- Dwelling without "walls," "bars" or "gates,"

- Possessing gold and silver, and acquired livestock and goods,

- A wealthy nation having booty and "great plunder."

A detailed explanation of these requirements is located in the appendix called *Psalm 83 or Ezekiel 38, Which is the Next Middle East News Headline?* This appendix strongly suggests that Israel needs to undergo something significant, like Psalm 83, in order to meet some of these requirements. Presently, Israel is not dwelling securely without walls, bars, or gates.

Freed from further Arab torment and terror after the Arab-Israeli war, the Jews could dwell securely in Israel, tear down the West Bank Barrier Wall, and eliminate all the bars, gates, and security checkpoints simultaneously. They have already proven to be quite efficient in dismantling such structures during lulls in terror activity.

Additionally, Israelis could "acquire" livestock and goods from the Arabs in fulfillment of Ezekiel 38:12. The Hebrew word for acquired is *asah*, and it is translated appropriately in the New King James Version. The Jews seemingly acquire, rather than develop, much of the prosperity Russia and its allies pursue in the Magog invasion. Ezekiel says:

> To take plunder and to take booty, to stretch out your [Gog of Magog] hand against the waste places *that are again* inhabited, and against a [Jewish] people gathered from the nations, who have acquired [*asah*] livestock and goods, who dwell in the midst of the land. (Ezekiel 38:12).

Perhaps when Ezekiel 38:11 states that Israel will be "dwelling without walls, and having neither bars nor gates," he is speaking figuratively to describe a safer Israel. Maybe after Psalm 83, the minister of defense won't call for the dismantling of the West Bank Barrier Wall. But, if Ezekiel 38:11 is to be understood literally, the expansive West Bank Barrier Wall will need to come down before the Gog of Magog invasion can occur.

## Millions of Jews Return to Israel

As referenced above, a greater and safer Israel is conducive to more wide-scale Jewish aliyah. Presently, many Jews residing outside of Israel would like to move there, but have refrained for various reasons. One primary concern is Israel's national security. Israel presently lives under constant existential threat.

COMMENTARY

In the aftermath of Psalm 83, this threat should be minimized; especially if Iran's nuclear program somehow becomes neutralized concurrently.

Although Iran doesn't appear to play an active role in Psalm 83, they remain as one of Israel's main existential threats. However, the prophecies of Elam in Jeremiah 49:34-39 previously exposited upon in *Revelation Road* appear to somehow neutralize Iran. Presuming Psalm 83 concludes about the same time the prophecies of Elam find fulfillment, Israel will undoubtedly become a safer place temporarily.

Understandably, these are "what-if" propositions; however, the Lord has miraculously implanted a Zionistic inclination into the hearts of Jews worldwide. This desire dates at least back to 1896, when Theodor Herzl published his book called *Der Judenstaat*, which means *The Jewish State* in German. Herzl's book was one of the pioneering texts concerning Zionism. His book emphasized that the best way to avoid mounting Anti-Semitism in Europe and elsewhere in the world, was to return to a designated Jewish state. In fulfillment of Bible prophecy, that State was miraculously created in 1948.

Over the past six decades, millions of Jews have made aliyah into Israel. Out from persecution, poverty, and occasionally prosperity, Jews have made Israel their permanent home. They clearly evidence the Lord has indelibly impressed upon them a need to come back to the historical land of their heritage.

Amongst a planet presently populated by nearly seven billion people, estimates are that about 14 million cohabitants are Jews. Israel hosts about six million, and America is home to about five million.[149] Many American Jews, like my good friend Jonathan Bernis of *Jewish Voice Ministries*, voice concerns that growing persecution inside the US will someday force American Jews to finally flee to Israel. Although I agree that persecution may be the catalyst for many, I shared with Jonathan that a greater, safer, post-Psalm 83 Israel might entice Jews to make aliyah, as well.

Scriptures like Romans 11:26, Ezekiel 37:11, and Ezekiel 39:25, 28 suggest that someday "all" or the "whole house of" world Jewry return to Israel. Almost half of them already have. I suggest to you the strong possibility that in the aftermath of Psalm 83, many more will make their move back to the homeland of their ancestry.

What an amazing spectacle that would be. Not over a span of decades, but months or maybe a few years, millions of Jews could flock to the Holy Land. Such a massive aliyah would certainly precipitate the need for the modern-day Jewish State to expand its borders into Arab lands, in order to facilitate their return. If the Christian church has not been raptured beforehand, then they will experience this miracle and have opportunity to evangelize about it.

# Israel Constructs Third Jewish Temple

Daniel 9:26 predicted approximately 550 years prior to its occurrence that the second Jewish temple would be destroyed. Christ also pre-confirmed this would occur in Matthew 24:2, Mark 13:2, and Luke 21:6. Both of their predictions proved accurate when the Romans destroyed the second Jewish temple in 70 AD.

This left the Jews without an official place to perform future animal sacrifices as prescribed in their Mosaic Law. Christians realize the sacrificial system of the Mosaic Law was rendered inoperative when the Lamb of God, Jesus Christ, made final atonement for all sins by His crucifixion.

> The next day John [the Baptist] saw Jesus coming toward him, and said, "Behold! The *Lamb of God* who takes away the sin of the world!" (John 1:29; emphasis added).

> For such a High Priest was fitting for us, *who is* holy, harmless, undefiled, separate from sinners, and has become higher than the heavens; who does not need daily, as those high [Levitical] priests, to offer up sacrifices, first for His own sins and then for the people's, for this He did once for all when [at the crucifixion] He [Christ, the Lamb of God] offered up Himself. For the [Mosaic] law appoints as high priests men who have weakness, but the word of the oath, which came after the law, *appoints* the Son [of God, Jesus Christ] who has been perfected forever. (Hebrews 7:26-28; emphasis added).

For approximately 1,941 years, from 70 AD to 2011 AD, the Jews have been without their temple. In fulfillment of Hosea 3:4 the Jews have lived "many days," approximately 700,000 days, without animal sacrifice.

> For the children of Israel shall abide *many days* without king or prince, *without sacrifice* or sacred pillar, without ephod or teraphim. (Hosea 3:4; emphasis added)

However, Daniel 9:27 predicts the future construction of a third Jewish temple. This coming Jewish temple is confirmed elsewhere in Matthew 24:15, Mark 13:14, Daniel 12:11, Revelation 11:1-2, and 2 Thessalonians 2:4.

COMMENTARY

The Temple Institute has already posted blueprints for this temple on their website.[150]

Additionally, many of the holy vessels and vestments are already created to perform temple-related functions.[151] The Sanhedrin, that formerly embodied the ultimate ruling authority over Jewish laws and customs, reconvened in 2005.[152] Official priestly garments are presently being tailored.[153] The traditional high priest's crown has also been created.[154] There is a lengthy list of evidences supporting the possibility that this temple could be constructed and become operational in relatively short order.

Many believe because Jerusalem hosted the first and second Jewish temples that the future third temple will likewise be built there. However, it is unclear if the relative prophecies specifically identify Jerusalem as its location. Most eschatologists believe Jerusalem will be the site of the third temple. Some of the best clues about its future whereabouts are given by Christ in Matthew 24:16, and Mark 13:14, and the apostle John in Revelation 11.

As recorded in both Matthew and Mark, Jesus warns those in Judea to flee to the mountains when the Antichrist enters into this temple and performs the "abomination of desolation" fulfilling Daniel's prophecy. Jerusalem existed within the province of Judea when Christ issued this prophetic warning.

In Revelation 11:1-8 John seems to identify two witnesses with the location of the temple. He says these two are killed and subsequently miraculously resurrected in the city where the Lord was crucified. He is alluding to the crucifixion of Christ in the city of Jerusalem.

Although it can be argued that neither of these above instances conclusively places the third temple in Jerusalem, they, along with historical temple precedent, seem to strongly identify Jerusalem as the host city of the coming temple.

Preventing the construction of this temple today is the controversy over the status of Jerusalem. The IDF captured West Jerusalem in 1948 and East Jerusalem in June, 1967, but the Palestinians dispute claims of Israeli sovereignty over the area. Muslims treat Jerusalem as Islam's third holiest city, behind Mecca and Medina. This understandably bolsters Muslim support for Palestinian claims over the city. Existing sacred Islamic structures, like the Dome of the Rock and the Al Aqsa Mosque inside Jerusalem, present an obstacle to constructing this coming temple.

Some believe that the temple can be built around these sites, but *Revelation Road* novel chapter ten presents another possible scenario, suggesting these Muslim sites could be captured by the IDF during Psalm 83. The present Palestinian attempts to establish dominion over the Temple Mount may be eliminated, according to Obadiah v. 18. The prophet predicts Esau's Edomite descendants won't survive the coming war with Israel. Obadiah appears to be alluding to the Edomite remnant currently existing within the Palestinians. If the Palestinians don't survive, neither will their claims over Jerusalem. Today, it is primarily the drive of the Palestinians laying claim to the site that interests neighboring Arab states, all of whom primarily look to Mecca and Medina as their main holy sites.

Some, subscribing to the idea that the coming temple will be built around the Dome of the Rock and Al Aqsa Mosque, point to Revelation 11:1-2 as their proof.

> Then I was given a reed like a measuring rod. And the angel stood, saying, "Rise and measure the temple of God, the altar, and those who worship there. But leave out the court which is outside the temple, and do not measure it, for it has been given to the Gentiles. And they will tread the holy city underfoot for forty-two months." (Revelation 11:1-2).

In this instance, they believe Muslims represent a large contingency within the "Gentiles" in these verses. However, this requires Muslims to be treading the holy city underfoot for three and one-half years during the trib-period. Since Islam should be almost non-existent after the pre-trib prophecies of Psalm 83 and Ezekiel 38 occur, these Gentiles may not be predominately Muslims.

The Gentiles being referred to in Revelation 11:2 appear to be those identified with the harlot world religion of Mystery Babylon in Revelation 17. This world religious system exists during part of the tribulation period and is comprised primarily of Gentiles, rather than Jews. We can safely presume this, because the Jews at the time seem to be reverting back to traditional forms of temple worship prescribed in their ancient Mosaic Law.

Although remaining Muslims will probably become part of this end-times world religious system, they will not likely be its ruling majority. More about this harlot religious system is discussed in the commentary's chapter called *The Christian Exodus Into the Clouds*.

## Israel Reinstates Animal Sacrifices

The emergence of a Jewish temple should prompt the reinstatement of the animal sacrifices that took place in the prior Jewish temples, and are required under the antiquated Mosaic Law. It appears that winning the wars of Psalm 83 and Ezekiel 38 moves Israelis to become more religious. Even today, secularists in Israel, particularly in the military, are nevertheless aware that something greater than themselves has assisted in modern miraculous victories on the battlefield. The ridding of their Psalm 83 Arab adversaries against overwhelming odds by the IDF will probably prompt many Israelis to recognize that their Old Testament God, Jehovah, had a supernatural hand over the matter.

Those that refuse to make the connection after Psalm 83 will be hard-pressed not to do so after the hordes of Magog invaders are devastated, during Ezekiel 38-39. Ezekiel 38:18-39:6 orders the events as follows:

- A massive earthquake occurs in Israel, causing mountains to be thrown down, and walls to collapse. The magnitude of the event will force humanity to realize the earthquake was caused by the Lord. If the West Bank Barrier Wall hasn't been dismantled prior to this, it appears to be toppled at this juncture. If the Dome of the Rock is still standing at that time, this earthquake could level it to the ground. (per Ezekiel 38:18-20).

- Then a bloody war scene commences, resulting in massive military casualties. The battlefield spans throughout all the surrounding mountainous areas—probably the same mountains damaged by the significant earthquake of the preceding verses. Ezekiel states "Every man's sword will be against his brother," suggesting many of those slain are victims of friendly fire. (Ezekiel 38:21).

- The battlefield rapidly metastasizes into a scene of pestilence and bloodshed, as flooding rain, great hailstones, fire, and brimstone rain down upon the invaders. Like the initial earthquake in verse 19, these events will also evidence the Lords supernatural involvement. (Ezekiel 38:22-23).

An overview of the devastation is presented in Ezekiel 39:1-6. This passage informs us that all the invaders are destroyed in the battle, and their carcasses are left for the birds of prey and beasts of the field to devour. Additionally, Ezekiel says the battlefield expands back into Mother Russia (Magog) and other coastlands, otherwise thought secure.

These twelve Ezekiel verses descriptively give evidence that the God of the Jews miraculously protects the nation of Israel from the most massive armed and dangerous Middle East invasion of all time, through supernatural means. Ezekiel clearly indicates that humanity realizes the Lord has had a hand in the war-torn events. This doesn't necessarily mean that all of mankind become believers, but that they begin to fret about the fact that because of their God, the Jews have become a really big deal on the world scene. Ezekiel 39:13

declares the Jews gain renown after the episode. By that future point of the timeline, the whole world should be a much more spiritual place, especially if the rapture has already occurred.

In the aftermath of the destruction we are told even Israel recognizes the Lord protected them from genocide. Ezekiel says the Lord's holy name is made known in the midst of the Jewish people.

> So I will make My holy name known in the midst of My people Israel, and I will not *let them* profane My holy name anymore. Then the nations shall know that *I am* the LORD, the Holy One in Israel. (Ezekiel 39:7).

Furthermore, Ezekiel 39:11-16 pictures the Jews involved in a national campaign of cleansing the land of the dead invaders. Three times in this passage (vv. 12, 14, 16) he says the Jews will work together in order to "cleanse the land." Certainly, burying the hordes of the dead helps to prevent the pestilences and plagues that can emerge from masses of dead and potentially contaminated corpses, but it also indicates the Jews are acting in compliance with requirements of the Mosaic Law.

According to the ancient "Law," the Jews were to bury the dead expeditiously to prevent defilement of the land.

> If a man has committed a sin deserving of death, and he is put to death, and you hang him on a tree, his body shall not remain overnight on the tree, *but you shall surely bury him that day, so that you do not defile the land* which the LORD your God is giving you *as* an inheritance; for he who is hanged *is* accursed of God. (Deuteronomy 21:22-23; emphasis added).

The fact that the Jews launch a national campaign to cleanse the land after they witness the Lord supernaturally protect them against insurmountable odds in the Ezekiel invasion, strongly suggests the Jews are operating in compliance with the Mosaic Law. This means that the Jews gravitate toward their Old Testament forms of worshipping in accordance with the Law, rather than investing their faith in Christ as their nation's Messiah.

This likelihood, coupled with the fact that the Bible predicts the Jews will construct an end times temple, implies they will operate under the Law and reinstate animal sacrifices. Daniel 9:27 and 12:11 both confirm the Jews will be offering animal sacrifices in the third temple. He says the Antichrist will end the sacrifices at the midpoint of the tribulation period when he sets up the "abomination of desolation."

COMMENTARY

Presently about twenty-seven percent of Israeli Jews are orthodox, and far less are messianic, meaning they believe Jesus is the Jewish Messiah.[155] Zechariah 12:10-11, Matthew 23:39, Romans 11:25-27, and elsewhere remind us that someday Israel will someday produce a faithful remnant of Jewish believers in Christ, but Hosea 5:15 informs us that won't occur until they go through the affliction of the great tribulation period.

For now, most Jews are repeating the problematic patterns of their idol worshipping ancestors and forgetting the importance of the *Shema* prayer in Deuteronomy 6. Many of them have returned to the land with the same mindset their ancestors departed with back in 70 AD. This is not surprising, since we were informed in Ezekiel 36:22-24 that the Jews would return to Israel in a condition of unbelief. The *Shema* prayer recites:

> Hear, O Israel: The LORD our God, the LORD is one! You shall love the LORD your God with all your heart, with all your soul, and with all your strength. "And these words which I command you today shall be in your heart. You shall teach them diligently to your children, and shall talk of them when you sit in your house, when you walk by the way, when you lie down, and when you rise up. You shall bind them as a sign on your hand, and they shall be as frontlets between your eyes. You shall write them on the doorposts of your house and on your gates. (Deuteronomy 6:4-9).

*Please read the next chapter of the novel now.*

COMMENTARY

# Chapter 15—
## Russia Forms an Evil Plan to Invade Israel

*Topics covered:* Gog's Evil Plan; Gog Gathers Formidable Friends; Gog's Plan is Strategic; Boycott Israel by Blockading Important Waterways; The Lord Proves He is a Promise Keeper

## Gog's Evil Plan

Thus says the Lord GOD: "On that day it shall come to pass *that* thoughts will arise in your [Gog's] mind, and you will make an evil plan:" (Ezekiel 38:10)

This passage advises that Gog devises an evil plan. Previous commentary has already identified Gog as a title for the ruler of Magog. It also connected ancient Magog with modern-day Russia. We gather from Ezekiel 38:8 and 16 that the evil plan is formulated in order to invade Israel in the end times. Thus, in this section of commentary we treat Gog, represented by Mad Vlad Ziroski in our story line, as an evil, Anti-Semitic Russian ruler who plots to invade Israel in the last days. But why? What compels Russia to strategize against Israel?

Sheba [Yemen], Dedan [Saudi Arabia], the merchants of Tarshish, [UK?] and all their young lions [America?] will say to you, "Have you [Gog] come to take plunder? Have you gathered your army to take booty, to carry away silver and gold, to take away livestock and goods, to take great plunder?" (Ezekiel 38:13)

This passage reveals, through the inquiry of several apparent protestors, that Gog covets the "Greater Israel" prosperity and assembles an army to capture it. Although the gist of Gog's sinister plan is outlined in Ezekiel 38:11-13, the entire plot is contained throughout Ezekiel 38:1-16. These opening sixteen verses contain important clues detailing the framework of Russia's invasion campaign. They reveal that Russia, covetous of Israel's prized plunder, schemes a multi-pronged strategy to seize it.

## Gog Gathers Formidable Friends

Ezekiel 38:1-5 lists those that join Russia's alliance against Israel. The coalition members are identified on a map in the images section (appendix 26). The map illustrates how the consortium of nations dwarf the present-day Jewish state by comparison.

At first glance the question naturally arises, "Why does Russia need so many big friends to invade tiny little Israel? It would be like America aligning with Canada and Mexico to attack New Jersey, which is about the same size as modern-day Israel." The word "overkill" would seem like an "understatement" in characterizing the scene! Something must have happened in the Middle East for this massive invasion campaign to make sense. Presently, Russia has enough nuclear weapons to wipe Israel off the map on its own; why call for reinforcements? Why not go it alone and keep the spoil for Russian coffers, rather than split it amongst a large coalition?

Setting the geopolitical stage at the time demonstrates why Russia probably goes to exorbitant lengths to form this formidable strategic alliance, which appears to include Iran, Turkey, Libya, Ethiopia, Sudan, Somalia, Algeria, Morocco, Tunisia, and several former Soviet Union Republics. Aligning prophecies sequentially beginning with Psalm 83, paints a potential Middle East picture like this below.

- At the time, a "Greater Israel" exists, prompting Russia to covet its possessions. The IDF will have previously eliminated the Arab threats to its borders by winning the Psalm 83 war. Possibly having displayed nuclear power during the war, the IDF world army ranking should leap from number ten upward into the top five, leaving Turkey, France, and UK in its dust.

- As a nation, Israel should be reaping the benefits of Arab spoils of war. Remember, in the ten years Israel controlled the Sinai after the Six Day War, a whole host of oil wells and other energy infrastructure gave the tiny state renewed independence. The new and improved Jewish state will probably be burgeoning into a viable emerging market, offering abundant oil and natural gas resources to America, Europe, and China. World Jews will probably be flocking into Israel at an unprecedented rate, in order to capitalize on accelerating economic growth opportunities. As this commentary is being written, amid unprecedented global economic crises, Israel's credit rating was upgraded by the S&P to A+!

- Greater Israel should present those returning Jews with better prospects for a future, than the nations they abandon. This is because world markets will probably be reeling at the time. Recent years of tough global economic times, compounded by the Psalm 83 Mideast war, should have governments moving to embrace a global banking system and one-world government as predicted in Daniel 7:23. World Jews should seek security in Israel, in contrast to uncertainty in an insecure global environment.

- Greater Israel will probably be expanding beyond its 2011 borders into conquered Arab lands. As such, Israel's coffers could be overflowing with additional natural gas and OPEC oil reserves, creating competition for Russia's gas and Iran's oil.

- Muslims worldwide will detest Israel for decisively defeating and displacing the Syrians, Saudis, Jordanians, Egyptians, Lebanese, Iraqis, Hezbollah, Hamas, and Palestinians. Russia should have no problem harnessing the Islamic hatred into its predominately Muslim coalition. Eight of the nine coalition members are predominately Muslim. Russia is the only exception, and that trend is changing as Islam actively spreads its tentacles throughout parts of Russia.

COMMENTARY

These few paragraphs predicting the geo-political scene at the time, suggest that Russia reaches out to many allies because Israel will be maturing into the primary regional superpower at the time. Israel will represent a much more formidable threat as a result. In the New Jersey example above, it would be as if middle America had been wiped out by New Jersey in a war. Arsenals, police departments, and natural resources of the defeated states become captured, causing the remaining Americans concern about the emergence of a "Greater New Jersey."

If such a scenario occurred inside the United States, it would justify remaining America seeking to ally with Canada and Mexico to wipe out a greater New Jersey. The USA-Canada-Mexico coalition would invade New Jersey to recapture the spoils gathered from the former American war. The invaders would hope to liberate the losing states from New Jersey's jurisdiction.

Although this American scenario is a far-fetched fairly-tale, the Greater Israel scenario is not. The Arabs of Psalm 83 want to destroy the modern-day Jewish state, leaving the IDF no choice but to fight back for Israel's national survival. The Bible seemingly predicts an IDF victory and the coming of a Greater Israel.

# Gog's Plan is Strategic

Summarizing the above, stage one of Gog's evil plan is to form a formidable coalition of Muslim populations religiously driven to despise Israel for defeating their Psalm 83 Muslim brothers. The ten-member Arab confederacy of Psalm 83 is Islamic. The Ezekiel invaders should abhor Israel with renewed hatred at the time.

Additionally Russia, the world's number one oil producing country, seems to stir up its coalition by raising concerns over Israel's newfound ability to compete for international commercial interests. Already upset because the IDF destroyed hordes of Arab Muslims, OPEC nations like Iran, Algeria, and Libya won't want to lose market share to Israel. With Saudi Arabia adversely affected in Psalm 83, Iran likely becomes OPEC's leading oil exporter. Along with Russia, these three OPEC providers stand to gain increased demand after Psalm 83, and possibly for that reason enlist as part of Russia's coalition.

Ezekiel 38:11-13 describes a wealthy Israel. Israel has been discovering sizable deposits of natural gas and shale oil, and they are also drilling for oil. Some believe they will discover it. The appendix called *Israel Strikes it Rich Someday* develops the theme of Israel's prophesied prosperity in the last days.

By the time the Ezekiel 38 invasion occurs there are legitimate grounds for believing Israel has burgeoned into a viable international exporter. Not only does Ezekiel inform us that Israel will possess great plunder enabling them as an exporter, he inserts a group of "merchants from Tarshish" along with "all their young lions," into the prophetic equation. Who these groups represent is debatable, but what is clear is that merchants are appalled by Gog's evil intentions to plunder Israel.

The Hebrew word used by Ezekiel for merchants is *sachar* and it classifies these merchants as commercial traders. Ezekiel uses the word five times in Ezekiel 27 to identify customers of Tyre.[156] In fact, in Ezekiel 27:12 he specifically identifies Tarshish as one of Tyre's most prolific customers.

> Tarshish was your customer because of the abundance of all *kinds* of wealth; with silver, iron, tin and lead they paid for your wares. (Ezekiel 27:12, NASB).

COMMENTARY

The point the prophet appears to make is that some large international contingent is interested in doing business with Israel at the time Russia forms its coalition. Rather than joining Russia's team to steal Israel's spoil, these customers want to exploit it commercially—probably to re-start their struggling economies. Although Ezekiel doesn't squarely say they come from struggling economies, it can be presumed that they could be if the Middle East had just experienced the Psalm 83 war; especially, if Psalm 83 and Ezekiel 38 occur soon before global economies recover from the current financial crisis (2007 to present).

Many believe Tarshish represents the UK, while others suggest Spain as an alternative. Most agree that "young lions" identify the offshoot countries from either the UK or Spain. In the case of the UK, that would include the US, Canada, and Australia, and in Spain's case, Central and South America. The best argument I've heard for the US as these young lions came from Dr. David Hocking of *Hope for Today Ministries.* You can watch his presentation on the subject at this Internet link posted on 8/2/11: *http://www.prophecydepot.net/2011/prophecy-panel-tom-hughes-david-hocking-bill-salus/*

If the young lions represent America in Bible prophecy, and I'm inclined to believe they do, this could be a good sign for Americans. It implies that the United States is attempting to bless Israel by becoming one of its international customers. Genesis 12:3 promises to bless those that bless Israel. Doing business with a prosperous end-times Israel could prove to be the shot in the arm the struggling American economy needs to recover from its mortgage meltdown and financial crisis.

COMMENTARY

## Boycott Israel by Blockading Important Waterways

Stage two of Gog's evil plan can be inferred by the geographic location of each of its allies. As *Ezekiel 38 Invaders* points out, each coalition member borders a critical waterway Israel needs to export its commerce into international markets. This is probably strategic. Ultimately, Gog's evil plan involves a military invasion in order to capture Israel's great spoil, but first it appears Russia may attempt to boycott Israel's goods through its coalition members. A small-scale boycott of Israeli products has been underfoot for years, driven, ironically, by mainline American church denominations; so there is a precedent.

Positioned strategically on the important waterways, Russia's allies could easily attempt to blockade the waterways in an attempt to prohibit Israel's ability to export its great spoil. For more information on how this could occur, and why this could be part of Gog's evil plan read the  appendix entitled, *Blockade the Waterways: Gog of Magog's "Evil Plan"*.

# The Lord Proves He is a Promise Keeper

It is important to note that Ezekiel 38:7 and 10 clearly indicates that Gog champions this campaign against Israel. He is the one going to exorbitant ends to form a formidable strategic alliance. Ezekiel 38:10 says evil thoughts emanate from Gog's mind, but Ezekiel 38:16 and 39:2 declares the Lord uses the occasion to inform the nations that He is *"the Lord, the Holy One in Israel."*

> So I will make My holy name known in the midst of My people Israel, and I will not *let them* profane My holy name anymore. Then the nations shall know that *I am* the LORD, the Holy One in Israel. (Ezekiel 39:7).

Why does the Lord choose such a David and Gog-liath end-times episode to uphold His holy name?

There appear to be a few reasons for this. First, after centuries of character defamation, restoring His holy name requires a spectacular event. Ezekiel 36:20-23, in tandem with 39:7, teachs that during the Diaspora the Jews profaned God's holy name. Second, during the Diaspora, the Gentiles, to their detriment, conveniently forgot about the Abrahamic Covenant. Lastly, the timing of the invasion "in the latter years" is intended as a wake-up call to humanity.

In the aftermath of the invasion, Ezekiel 39:21-29 explains that the nations receive a rude awakening about the historical plight of the Jews.

> The Gentiles shall know that the house of Israel went into captivity for their iniquity; because they were unfaithful to Me, therefore I hid My face from them. I gave them into the hand of their enemies, and they all fell by the sword. (Ezekiel 39:23).

This verse corrects the centuries-old, misguided mindset of mankind regarding the reason for the Jewish Diaspora. It instructs that the Jews were dispersed for 1,878 years into the nations of the world from 70 – 1948 AD, as a disciplinary duty of the Law, as per Leviticus 26:31-34. While the Jews experienced Diaspora, the Gentiles reckoned their God was weak. Hence, God's holy name became profaned amongst them, and the Jews did nothing notable to reverse the defamation process. Far from feeble, their God Jehovah preserved them outside their homeland because He had previously promised to Abraham a nation of descendants through Isaac forever.[157]

By re-gathering the Jews into Israel and protecting them from Gog's genocidal attempt, God earns the right to be called a promise keeper. Additionally, He should receive accolades for preserving them through an unbelievably lengthy time outside of their homeland. No other ethnic population ever maintained their identity away from home for so long.

Not only were they preserved, but guarded from the most serious genocidal attempt in recorded history. Nothing compares to the size and scope of the Nazi Holocaust. Then they returned to Israel in 1948; not as an army, but as beleaguered refugees. And they returned, not to banners and balloons, but to Arab bullets and bombs. Out of necessity, they matured from refugees into a world-class army. That, too, was predicted thousands of years ago by Ezekiel.

> So I prophesied as He commanded me, and breath came into them, and they lived, and stood upon their feet, an exceedingly great army. (Ezekiel 37:10)

Equally as important as the nations knowing the Lord keeps His promises, they get to realize at a critical point in the end times that the God of the Bible exists. The timing of the Magog invasion is everything. Since it appears to be a pre-tribulation period event, humanity is given advance notice that there is a promise-keeping God. This is extremely important because shortly thereafter, they will be invited to sell their souls to the devil by worshiping the Antichrist and receiving his mark in either their right hand or forehead.[158]

The proof that the God of the Bible exists will be evident within the prophetic pudding at that time. The fulfillment of events described in the fifty-two verses of Ezekiel 38-39 will prove that they were foreknown. When the war is over, and the Jews are burying the dead and burning the weapons as predicted in Ezekiel 39:9-16, humanity will be hard-pressed to deny that the Lord saw the whole thing coming over 2,500 years beforehand. That should catch attention, and is probably why such an enormous end-times episode has been chosen by God to prove He keeps all His promises, including those made to Abraham and to Christians.

*Please read the next novel chapter now.*

COMMENTARY

# Chapter 16—
## The Christian Exodus into the Clouds

*Topics covered:* Christians Are Caught Up into the Clouds; Christians Escape the Wrath of God; The Bride of Christ and the Jewish Wedding Models; Is the Rapture Pre-Trib or Pre-Wrath?

This novel chapter introduces the rapture amidst the backdrop of a mysterious canopy of worldwide cloud cover. This tapestry enveloping the troposphere is primarily comprised of a combination of vapor and volcanic ash clouds. Just moments before millions of believers vanish into these clouds, a majestic Marian apparition hovers over the Vatican.

The apparition was inserted in the story line as a reminder that after the rapture a counterfeit world religious system surfaces. Revelation 17:5 calls it "Mystery Babylon the Great, the Mother of Harlots and of the Abominations of the Earth." Some believe demonically inspired apparitions posing as Mary, will increase after the rapture in order to deceive people into following her pagan religious system. Revelation 17:9, 18, appears to identify the Vatican as the headquarters of this counterfeit religion. Although many Catholics will undoubtedly be raptured, Revelation 2:22 promises an apostate remnant experiences the great tribulation.

This harlot world religion is revealed more exhaustively in book two of this series. Meanwhile, expert information on this religious system is currently available through Jim Tetlow's website, http://www.eternal-productions.org/ and Mike Gendron's website, http://www.pro-gospel.org/. Additionally, the appendix called *The Fallible Assumption of Mary* addresses this subject and should be read alongside this section of the commentary.

# Christians Are Caught Up into the Clouds

An important note to the novel reader is that the abnormal universal cloud cover clued Satan to consider the rapture could occur at any moment. Although Matthew 24:36 and Mark 13:32 reveal Satan can't know the timing, for story line purposes Satan anticipates the rapture from the inexplicable cloud mass. This is because of what's known from 1 Thessalonians 4:17.

> For this we say to you by the word of the Lord, that we [believers] who are alive *and* remain until the coming of the Lord will by no means precede those [deceased believers] who are asleep. For the Lord [Jesus Christ] Himself will descend from heaven with a shout, with the voice of an archangel, and with the trumpet of God. And the dead in Christ will rise first. Then we who are alive *and* remain shall be caught up together with them in the *clouds* to meet the Lord in the air. And thus we shall always be with the Lord. Therefore comfort one another with these words. (1 Thessalonians 4:15-18; emphasis added).

Realizing believers will be caught up into the clouds, Satan instigated the apparition sighting in an attempt to steal some thunder from the impact of the rapture. Additionally, the Queen of Heaven apparition sighting was intended to set the stage for explaining the Christian disappearance to a startled world. It can be safely assumed that the devil realizes the spiritual nature of the rapture will force humanity to seek a viable supernatural explanation for it. Thus, the Marian manifestation was not the cause of the planetary cloud cover, but a preparatory, strategic satanic response to it in the novel story line.

In the novel, the rapture occurs unexpectedly within the span of a nanosecond, "in the twinkling of an eye." When the apostle wrote, the blinking of an eye was the fastest-known measurement of time. The expedient departure of believers into the clouds is predicted in 1 Corinthians 15:52.

> Behold, I tell you a mystery: We shall not all sleep, but we shall all be changed—in a moment, *in the twinkling of an eye*, at the last trumpet. For the trumpet will sound, and the dead will be raised incorruptible, and we shall be changed. (1 Corinthians 15:51-52; emphasis added).

The intent of this chapter's commentary is not to legitimize the rapture. The 1 Thessalonians and 1 Corinthians passages cited above clearly declare that there will be an instantaneous departure of Christians into the clouds, to be with Christ forever. Even though some argue the Bible doesn't technically use the word rapture, there are volumes of articulate works refuting this concern, and validating the reality of the event. Recommended websites offering scholarship in this area are duly footnoted here.[159]

Regarding the word rapture, Christian author Jim Tetlow writes,

> Rapture is an English word derived from the Latin word raeptius, taken from the Latin Vulgate translation, which in turn is a translation of the Greek word harpazo. Harpazo is found 13 times in the New Testament. Harpazo means to seize, catch away, caught up or taken away by force. The clearest passage describing the Rapture is found in 1 Thessalonians 4. In this chapter the Apostle Paul describes the "catching away" of the believers to meet the Lord in the air.[160]

There are prolific arguments addressing the timing of the event. Some believe it occurs before the trib-period (pre-trib), while others place it at the midpoint, (mid-trib) or at its end (post-trib). Rather than address the competing views about the timing of the rapture, I will explain why I believe it is an imminent pre-tribulation event. Additionally, I hope to demonstrate why the pre-wrath argument closely resembles the pre-trib viewpoint.

## Christians Escape the Wrath of God

There are several Scriptures that teach believers are not to experience the wrath of God coming upon sinful humanity. Some of them are listed below.

> But God demonstrates His own love toward us, in that while we were still sinners, Christ died for us. Much more then, having now been justified by His blood, we shall be saved from wrath through Him. (Romans 5:8-9; emphasis added).

> And to wait for His Son from heaven, whom He raised from the dead, even Jesus who delivers us from the wrath to come. (1 Thessalonians 1:10; emphasis added).

> For those who sleep, sleep at night, and those who get drunk are drunk at night. But let us who are of the day be sober, putting on the breastplate of faith and love, and as a helmet the hope of salvation. For God did not appoint us to wrath, but to obtain salvation through our Lord Jesus Christ, who died for us, that whether we wake or sleep, we should live together with Him. (1 Thessalonians 5:7-10; emphasis added).

Revelation calls it an hour of trial that comes upon the entire world, which believers are kept from.

> Because you have kept My command to persevere, *I also will keep you from the hour of trial* which shall come upon the whole world, to test those who dwell on the earth. Behold, I am coming [rapture] quickly [in the twinkling of an eye]! Hold fast what you have, that no one may take your crown. (Revelation 3:10-11; emphasis added).

These verses above teach that believers are *saved*, *delivered*, and *kept* from the wrath of God; but how and when? The rapture is the logical explanation for how. 1 Thessalonians 1:10 specifies that Jesus personally "delivers us from the wrath to come." 1 Thessalonians 5:10 instructs that "whether we wake or sleep, we should live together with Him."

These passages closely parallel the events described above in 1 Thessalonians 4:17-18, that state, "And the dead [asleep] in Christ will rise first. Then we who are alive and remain [awake] shall be caught up together with them in the clouds to meet the Lord [Jesus] in the air. And thus we shall always be with the Lord. Therefore comfort one another with these words."

Believers are to comfort one another with this unique understanding. This is because Christians seemingly *escape*, rather than *endure*, the wrath of God. There are several reasons to argue that believers escape the wrath poured out during the tribulation period.

*First*, the fact believers are instructed to comfort one another by reminding each other about the rapture implies they won't endure the upheavals of the trib-period. How can one be comforted when they are concerned about experiencing the wrath of God? It is impossible! Therefore, the comfort comes when believers remind each other that an escape route exists. *Parakaleo*, the Greek word used for comfort, can be translated to mean encourage. In essence, the apostle Paul exhorts believers to encourage one another with reminders of the rapture.

*Second*, the tribulation judgments are worldwide, leaving believers no safe-haven from wrath anywhere on Earth. Revelation 6 contains a vivid description of the worldwide danger-zone.

> I looked when He opened the sixth seal, and behold, there was a great earthquake; and *the sun* became black as sackcloth of hair, and *the moon* became like blood. And *the stars* of heaven fell to the earth, as a fig tree drops its late figs when it is shaken by a mighty wind. Then *the sky* receded as a scroll when it is rolled up, and *every mountain and*

*island* was moved out of its place. And the kings of the earth, the great men, the rich men, the commanders, the mighty men, every slave and every free man, hid themselves in the caves and in the rocks of the mountains, and said to the mountains and rocks, "Fall on us and hide us from the face of Him who sits on the throne and from the wrath of the Lamb! *For the great day of His wrath has come, and who is able to stand?"* (Revelation 6:12-17; emphasis added).

The *sun, moon, sky, stars, mountains,* and *islands* are all disturbed. These environmental disorders are evidence the wrath of God has come. Everyone from king, to slave, to free man are at a loss to find suitable refuge from the catastrophes of the "great day of His wrath." Unless Christians are somehow gathered into some unaffected place beforehand, they will not be *saved, delivered, kept,* nor *comforted* from the perilous planetary events.

There were Christians that died on September 11, 2001, when the twin towers toppled, and there are Christians struggling today in the global financial crunch. But, there doesn't appear to be any Christians on Earth hiding out in caves alongside all the unbelievers in Revelation 6:12-17, witnessing God's wrath descend upon mankind.

It is important to note that many left behind unbelievers will become believers during the tribulation period, when the wrath of God is poured out. But, believers up to the point of the rapture seem to escape just under wrath's wire. The church, which is analogous with the bride of Christ,[161] appears to be fetched by Christ, the Bridegroom, before the wrath begins.

The promise to escape the wrath of God is unique to believers that are raptured. Those who accept Christ after the rapture are instructed to be patient even to the pain of death for their rewards in heaven. These last days, post-rapture believers exist in a period the book of Revelation appears to identify as "the patience of the saints."

If anyone has an ear, let him hear. He who leads into captivity shall go into captivity; he who kills with the sword must be killed with the sword. Here is *the patience* and the faith *of the saints*. (Revelation 13:9-10; emphasis added).

Here is *the patience of the saints*; here *are* those who keep the commandments of God and the faith of Jesus. Then I heard a voice from heaven saying to me, "Write: 'Blessed *are* the dead who die in the Lord from now on.'" "Yes," says the Spirit, "that they may rest from their labors, and their works follow them." (Revelation 14:12-13; emphasis added).

# The Bride of Christ and the Jewish Wedding Models

*Third*, the Bridegroom (Christ) and bride (Christian church) analogy given several times in the New Testament, also infers believers *escape* the wrath. It is doubtful that Christ would come for a bride that has been battered, bruised, and tarnished from seven years of tribulation. Contrarily, it makes more sense that Jesus would return to rapture His believers before they are ravished by those judgments, that are specifically intended for unbelievers.

The bride's worthiness is based solely upon her genuine faith in the Bridegroom, and not courageous works performed amidst the backdrop of tribulation judgments. Believers have nothing further to prove. They are not obligated to undergo the fiery trials taking place in the trib-period.

> For by grace you [believers] have been saved through faith, and that not of yourselves; *it is* the gift of God, *not of works*, lest anyone should boast. (Ephesians 2:8-9; emphasis added).

Many Christian expositors compare the Bridegroom example to the traditional Jewish wedding model. What could be more appropriate, considering Christ was a Jew? The following brief outline of the process was partially taken from notes provided within a related Chuck Missler article called *The Wedding Model*.[162]

### Betrothal

The groom negotiated a fair price (*mohair*) for his bride. In the case of believers, the price was paid by the Lord's precious sacrificial blood upon the cross for the sins of believers.

### Separation

The engagement period was actually a time of separation usually lasting about twelve months. While the bride-to-be stayed home, the groom returned to his father's house to make preparations for their future lives together. This gave the bride time to prepare her trousseau, and the groom to construct a place for the two of them to live happily ever after. Presently, Christ and the bride are separated. He is in

COMMENTARY

heaven while she is on Earth preparing her wedding garments, which according to Revelation 19:8 are her righteous acts.

## Preparation

The groom utilized the separation period to return to his father's house to construct the couple's new home on the premises. John 14:1-4, listed below in this commentary, points out this is a function Christ is presently performing in heaven. John 14 says Christ is building mansions at His Father's house for His followers. Believers can expect to inhabit spectacular heavenly abodes because several Scriptures point out that Christ is no novice when it comes to carpentry.

> Is this [Jesus] not the carpenter, the Son of Mary? (Mark 6:3a).

This question was asked by Jesus' local countrymen who were astounded by His teaching in the neighborhood synagogue. They had identified Him as a carpenter in the past, rather than the prophet He had become.

> He [Jesus] is the image of the invisible God, the firstborn over all creation. For by Him all things were created that are in heaven and that are on earth, visible and invisible, whether thrones or dominions or principalities or powers. All things were created through Him and for Him. And He is before all things, and in Him all things consist. (Colossians 1:15-17).

The major premise that can be drawn from these Colossians verses is that Jesus can create anything, including thousands of stars, species, varieties of vegetation, and much more. Thus, the minor premise is, He can construct spectacular mansions for his faithful followers.

## Fetching

At the appropriate time, after the construction was completed, the groom came to fetch his bride. Although the bride knew the time would come, she didn't necessarily know precisely when. This is the case with believers today; they know Christ is coming, but don't know the day or hour. Also, the groom's arrival was usually accompanied by the best man and several friends. When the party arrived to fetch the bride, there was often a shout from the friends to announce the groom had arrived. 1 Thessalonians 4:16 declares there will be a shout from His friend the archangel announcing Christ's return.

## Consummation

Once fetched, the two returned to the groom's father's house where they were secluded in a bridal chamber (*huppah*). While inside the chamber they consummated their marriage by entering into physical union for the first time. They remained secluded in the chamber for seven days while the wedding guests enjoyed the wedding feast at the groom's father's house. This will be the similar case with Christ and his believers. Together they will be secluded somewhere in heaven consummating their union, while the seven years of tribulation take place on Earth. The seven-days seem to represent these seven years of tribulation.

## Celebration

After the seven days had elapsed, the groom brought his bride out of the chamber to greet the wedding guests and partake of the celebration. This will be the case after the trib-period; Christ will reign in His messianic kingdom and His bride will co-reign faithfully by His side.

This Jewish wedding model suggests that believers escape the seven years of tribulation, by being safely secluded somewhere in heaven.

*Fourth*, believers are promised by Christ to escape the trib-period.

> But take heed to yourselves, [bride / believers] lest your hearts be weighed down with carousing, drunkenness, and cares of this life, and that Day come on you unexpectedly. For it will come as a snare on all those who dwell on the face of the whole earth. Watch therefore, and pray always that you may be counted worthy to *escape all these things* that will come to pass, and to stand before the Son of Man. (Luke 21:34-36; emphasis added).

Christ warns His bride to be sober, watchful, and prayerful while she prepares her trousseau (righteous acts). The promise is that she will be worthy to "*escape all these things that will come to pass*," alluding to the wrath that is to come. She is not being invited to *endure* all these things, nor is she being informed that she will escape *only some* of these treacherous things. No, none of the above; Christ's bride gets a honeymoon suite specially prepared in heaven according to John 14, where she goes to escape the wrath of God.

Let not your heart be troubled; you believe in God, believe also in Me. In My Father's house are many mansions; if *it were* not *so,* I would have told you. I go to prepare a place for you. And if I go and prepare a place for you, I will come again [in the rapture] and receive you to Myself; that where I am, *there* you may be also. And where I go you know, and the way you know. (John 14:1-4).

Christ comes again in the clouds to fetch His bride and take her to heaven, where His Father's house exists. And, the bride supposedly knows the way to get there, "And where I go you know, and the way you know." Believers "know" the only way to escape all these wrathful things coming is through faith in Jesus Christ. They know this from the two passages above.

Thomas said to Him, "Lord, we do not know where You are going, and how can we know the way?" Jesus said to him, "I am the way, the truth, and the life. No one comes to the Father except through Me." (John 14:5-6).

With all that has been written above, I would be remiss not to remind you that the way to say "I Do" to such a glorious wedding proposal is given in Romans 10. The apostle Paul writes;

That if you confess with your mouth the Lord Jesus and believe in your heart that God has raised Him from the dead, you will be saved. For with the heart one believes unto righteousness, and with the mouth confession is made unto salvation. For the Scripture says, *"Whoever believes on Him will not be put to shame."* For there is no distinction between Jew and Greek, for the same Lord over all is rich to all who call upon Him. For *"whoever calls on the name of the Lord shall be saved."* (Romans 10:9-13).

The bride of Christ realizes that it's a matter of saying her "I do" wedding vows; "I do, confess my faith in Lord Jesus, and I do believe in my heart that God raised Him from the dead." Dear reader, if you haven't said your "I do" wedding vows as of yet, then you run the risk of *enduring,* rather than *escaping,* the wrath of God, by missing out on Christ's return to fetch His bride. Time is of the essence, since these are the last days and the rapture could occur at any moment. You can claim your passport to heaven by reading the appendix called *The Sinner's Salvation Prayer*, and accepting Christ through this prayer.

## Is the Rapture Pre-Trib or Pre-Wrath?

Now that we know the rapture is the probable reason believers are *saved, delivered, kept,* and *comforted* from "the great day of His wrath;" knowing *when* they are rescued becomes critical. At what point on the end-time's timeline do believers disappear? This question is partially answered by allocating the starting point of God's wrath. At some time pre-wrath, *before God's wrath begins*, Christians should be caught up into the clouds.

As stated above, nobody knows the exact day or hour of the event according to Matthew 24:36, but the rapture is imminent. This means no preconditions exist in Scripture that would delay it from taking place instantly. It could happen at any split second, before the opening of the sixth seal in Revelation 6:12.

Revelation 6:12-17 quoted previously appears to announce the commencement of the wrath of God. These verses inform us that divine judgment begins upon the opening of the sixth seal of the heavenly scroll, introduced in Revelation 5. Thus, the rapture should occur before seal six is opened. This means that believers of today's church could be present on Earth up to just moments before that seal is revealed.

This possibility has caused some to adopt the "pre-wrath" position about the timing of the rapture. Many pre-wrathers believe the seven seal judgments occur during the seven-years of tribulation. The general consensus among many of them is that the sixth seal of Revelation 6:12 describes events that occur around the middle of the trib-period, or at least sometime within the first half of the trib-period. They suggest the first five seals of Revelation 6:1-11 also occur during those first three-and-one-half years.

Ordering the chronological events contained in seals one through six reveals that the first five seals appear to be opened before the seven years of tribulation begin. If it can be proven that they do, then pre-wrathers, believing these seals occur during the trib-period, are mistaken. If they base their view upon the premise that the wrath contained in the sixth seal occurs at the mid-trib point, then they should be willing to consider the pre-trib view equally valid.

For the sake of abbreviating this section of commentary at this point, the ordering of the first five Seal judgments will be accomplished in the *Companion's Commentary* of book two in this series. However, in conclusion, be reminded that the sacrificial price Christ paid on the cross, enabling believers to be saved, pleased the heavenly Father. This is important information to possess, since believers will soon be caught up into the clouds to be with Christ forever.

Yet it pleased the LORD to bruise Him; [Jesus Christ] He [God] has put *Him* to grief. When You make His soul an offering for sin, He shall see *His* seed, He shall prolong *His* days, And the pleasure of the LORD shall prosper in His hand. He shall see the labor of His soul, *and* be satisfied. By His knowledge My righteous Servant shall justify many, [believers] For He shall bear their iniquities. (Isaiah 53:10-11; emphasis added).

*Please read the next novel chapter now.*

# Chapter 17—
## After the Rapture, the World Gets Religious

*Topics covered:* After the Rapture, the World Gets Religious; The Coming Counterfeit Religions; The Strong Delusion of 2 Thessalonians 2:11; The Three Competing Wills: *God's, Satan's,* and *Man's*; The Counterfeit Gospel—The Lie; The Rapture Profoundly Affects America

This corresponding chapter of the novel begins by briefly addressing the worldwide distress that likely occurs in the aftermath of the rapture. The unannounced, instantaneous vanishing of millions of believers worldwide will be an unprecedented phenomenon. Extra-biblical Marian apparitions, and isolated biblical examples, like Christ's resurrection (Matthew 28:1-8), Enoch's rapture (Genesis 5:24), Elijah's rapture, (2 Kings 2:11), Philip's catching away (Acts 8:39), the Mount of Transfiguration (Matthew 17:1-9), and some unexplainable angelic-human interactions in the Bible, should all pale inter-dimensionally to what the world witnesses at the rapture.[163] Both gravity and the grave will lose their grasp upon the departing believers.

The miraculous event will defy all scientific logic and reason, and demand a reasonable explanation. Some scholars speculate extra-terrestrials (ETs) may claim responsibility for the Christian disappearances. This postulation is based upon the premise that humanity is primed to receive "Official Disclosure" that the UFO phenomena is a reality, and that advanced intelligent life exists elsewhere in the universe. Examples of the ET explanations are given below.

# After the Rapture, the World Gets Religious

COMMENTARY

Either the "rapture" of millions of Christians or "Official Disclosure" of alien life (or both!), should serve to throw the world headlong into an entirely spiritual direction, which appears to be where Bible prophecy suggests it is heading.

I have often said, a time is coming, when there will be no more atheist, agnostics, or naturalists,[164] but a world filled with religionists. At that time, people won't be asking if there is a god, rather they will be choosing which one, or ones, they feel compelled to serve. In the end analysis, after the ten kings destroy the interim harlot world religious system, the choice will ultimately be between Christ and Antichrist! (Revelation 17:16-17 predicts ten kings will destroy the harlot.)

To some, all this supernatural discourse may sound far-fetched; perhaps like another Hollywood *Star Wars* episode. Even believers have to admit, the prophecy of the rapture almost sounds like an episode from the old Rod Serling science fiction TV program called *The Twilight Zone*.[165] But, the Bible clearly promises Christ is coming to catch up believers in the clouds. After all, He did resurrect and is alive today, validating the possibility for the rapture.

Meanwhile the UFO phenomenon enjoys the privilege of being protected by the highest level of governmental security classification known to exist. In 1950, Wilbert Smith, a Canadian Department of Transport engineer, wrote in a Top Secret memo to the Canadian government, that the subject of flying saucers "was the most highly classified subject in the United States."[166]

End-times expert Chuck Missler is very familiar with this fact, and the way classified information is treated by the government. His aerospace background and involvement in the intelligence community for the Department of Defense afforded him high levels of security clearance throughout his career.[167] As such, he became aware that the UFO phenomenon was indeed, *the most highly classified subject in the United States*.

Chuck informed me of this fact when we spoke together at a prophecy conference in southern California in September, 2010. He said Jimmy Carter, known as the UFO president, wept because he couldn't honor a presidential campaign promise, which was to make UFO information more transparent to the public.[168]

Why is the UFO phenomena so highly classified? If the UFO researchers are merely a bunch of kooks, why is all the pertinent ET information so heavily classified, especially at a time when the UFO phenomenon is burgeoning worldwide?[169] Interestingly, a Google word search for "rapture" provided almost

45 million results. Even more interesting, a Google word search for "UFO" can come up with about 210 million results! These significant findings suggest that the rapture and UFO scenarios are weighing on the minds of many, and are perhaps not that far-fetched after all. It is ironic however, that the idea of UFOs is seen as credible by many, including media, but the Bible's presentation of the rapture is commonly mocked.

Some end-times researchers believe one explanation the world might receive for the disappearance of Christians has something to do with an alien gospel scenario that morphs out of the "Panspermia" theory. Panspermia is the theory that life exists and is distributed throughout the universe in the form of germs or spores that develop, and eventually evolve into advanced life forms, in the right environment.[170] By the way, this idea was advanced by the Nobel Prize winner Francis Crick, who made no secret of the fact that he loathed the Bible.[171]

Some eschatologists believe that based upon this theory, gullible humanity could be convinced that it was neither created by God, nor the result of evolution, but was seeded by a higher alien intelligence. In essence, aliens, or perhaps fallen angels masquerading as ETs, might deceive mankind into believing they were its creators. The Bible makes it clear that there are fallen angels.

> For we do not wrestle against flesh and blood, but against principalities, against powers, against the rulers of the darkness of this age, against spiritual hosts of wickedness [fallen angels and demons] in the heavenly places. (Ephesians 6:12).

Whatever the response, or responses, the world receives for the disappearance of millions of Christians, undoubtedly Satan already has his explanation prepared. If full disclosure has been given prior to the rapture, the devil's answer to the rapture might possibly be like that which is already circulating among some "New Age" sources. The examples below are alleged messages from extra-terrestrials.

> "The people [Christians] who leave the planet during the time of Earth changes do not fit in here any longer, and they are stopping the harmony of Earth. When the time comes that perhaps 20 million people leave the planet at one time [in the rapture] there will be a tremendous [benevolent] shift in consciousness for those who are remaining." (This is supposedly a message from extra-terrestrials from the Pleiades.

COMMENTARY

Barbara Marciniak, "Bringers of the Dawn," bracketed material added by author).[172]

# The Coming Evacuation!

"Our rescue ships will be able to come in close enough in the twinkling of an eye to set the lifting beams in operation in a moment. And all over the globe where events warrant it, this will be the method of evacuation. Mankind will be lifted, levitated shall we say, by the beams from our smaller ships. These smaller craft will in turn taxi the persons to the larger ships overhead, higher in the atmosphere, where there is ample space and quarters and supplies for millions of people." (A message from extraterrestrials of the Ashtar Command, Project World Evacuation, 1993).[173]

An interesting read on this subject is available in the book called *Alien Encounters,* by Dr. Chuck Missler and Dr. Mark Eastman. Especially recommended is chapter nine, entitled, *The Coming Evacuation.*

Some eschatologists believe that these types of messages indicate that Satan is so concerned the rapture is about to happen, that he has already begun channeling misinformation in advance through these types of New Age sources. For what other reason than the rapture, could these bizarre explanations exist? Why are these individuals pre-explaining a peculiar event that simulates the biblical rapture?

# The Coming Counterfeit Religions

In his bid to be like the "Most High" God, which is exposed in Isaiah 14:12-15, Satan cunningly devises a false replica of God's biblical model, replete with a counterfeit trinity and religion. The Bible actually seems to identify two pagan world religions that surface sequentially in the end times. Both appear to commence in the spiritual vacuum created by the rapture.

One is identified in Revelation 17 as a New Testament mystery called "Babylon the Great, the Mother of Harlots and of the Abominations of the Earth." Revelation 17:1-5 portrays it as an adulterous brand of false religion that prostitutes itself throughout the earth. However, Revelation 17:16 explains that eventually this harlot religion exhausts its usefulness, and gets destroyed by ten kings, in order to pave the way for the second religious system of the Antichrist. Revelation 13 informs of his religious system.

COMMENTARY

Several prophecies suggest that alongside these counterfeit religious systems, Christianity revives, and Judaism survives, and both co-exist independent of these coming world religions. Those professing Christians that never truly accepted Christ as their savior will be left behind with other unbelievers after the rapture. Some of them, along with others that have never heard the gospel prior, will keep true Christianity intact by becoming *bona fide* believers, after the fact.

The reader might be surprised to hear that there are a minority of Bible teachers today that believe people having heard the gospel prior to the rapture can't get saved after the rapture. I strongly disagree with this teaching and intend to exposit further on this topic in book two of this series. The teaching that follows in this section of commentary regarding 2 Thessalonians 2:7-12 should not be interpreted to apply to only those who have heard the gospel prior to the rapture. I believe this 2 Thessalonians passage applies to everyone left behind. Everyone left behind is perishing and has a chance to accept Christ, except those who willingly accept the "mark of the Beast," addressed in Revelation 13:16-18.

We recognize from Revelation 6:9-11, 7:9-17, 20:4 and elsewhere, that after the rapture, many will come to Christ. However, these passages point out their conversions are characterized by end-times Christian martyrdom. The Bible labels their time of existence as the "Patience of the Saints" period in Revelation 13:10, and 14:12.

Chapter fourteen of this commentary, *Greater Israel Makes Plans for a Third Temple*, points out that the nation of Israel seemingly reinstates their ancient Mosaic system of Jehovah worship in response to their overwhelming victories in Psalm 83 and Ezekiel 38. Ultimately, they construct a third Jewish temple and conduct the animal sacrifices required by Old Testament Levitical Law.

Regarding the two satanically inspired end-times religions, greater details about their counterfeit systems will be discussed in the subsequent books of this series, but it appears that until the rapture occurs, they remain under restraint. This we conclude from a passage in 2 Thessalonians.

> For the mystery of lawlessness is already at work; only He who now restrains will do so until He is taken out of the way. (2 Thessalonians 2:7).

Once the restraint is removed, which many believe occurs at the time of the rapture,[174] the Antichrist is revealed, and humanity is subjected to *additional* mind-boggling supernatural phenomena like the rapture. However, unlike the rapture, the ensuing paranormal activity is intended to deceive, rather than benefit, those left behind.

> And then the lawless [Antichrist] one will be revealed, whom the Lord [Christ] will consume with the breath of His mouth and destroy with the brightness of His [second] coming. The coming of the lawless one is according to the working of Satan, with all power, signs, and lying wonders, and with all *unrighteous deception among those who perish*, because they did not receive *the love of the truth*, that they might be saved. And for this reason God will send them strong delusion, that they should believe the lie, that they all may be condemned who did not believe the truth but had *pleasure in unrighteousness*. (2 Thessalonians 2:8-12; emphasis added).

Excluded from the rapture and subsequently left behind, are those that did not receive the "love of the truth." This is what disqualified them from being caught up into the clouds to be with Christ. They are identified above as "those who perish." If the restraint is removed via the rapture, then this can be simply stated as follows: because those left behind lacked the love of the truth, they missed out on the rapture, and thus, became included among those perishing.

The New Testament book of John informs us that this critical "truth" separating those "saved," from "those who perish," is Jesus Christ. Jesus said to him, "I am the way, *the truth*, and the life. *No one comes to the Father except through Me.*" (John 14:6; emphasis added).

Correspondingly, John 3:16 respectively taught that God so loved the world that He sent Jesus, so that those who believed in Him would not *perish*, but be saved. Some of those perishing in 2 Thessalonians are not doing so because they failed to know the truth, rather because they chose indifferently not to possess a love of the truth; i.e., a love for Jesus Christ. This infers they knew the truth, but because of their "pleasure in unrighteousness," they decided not to embrace it. In essence, they rejected the "good news gospel of Jesus Christ."

As is the case today, and will continue to be the case after the rapture, some of those perishing believe the message of Christ crucified for the sins of man is foolishness.

> For the message of the cross is foolishness to those who are perishing, but to us who are being saved it is the power of God. (1 Corinthians 1:18).

I allude to "some of those perishing" two times above. This applies to individuals that have heard the gospel before the rapture occurred, but outright rejected its claims. This caveat does not apply to those who have heard the gospel, but remained undecided about Christ, or those who never heard the gospel prior to the rapture. Everyone left behind will fall into at least one of these three categories:

- *Rejecters:* This could include someone who hears and understands the gospel of Christ, but outright rejects it and chooses to be an atheist, which is someone who denies the existence of God.

- *Resisters:* This segment could include those that heard and understood the gospel, but were agnostics—which means they were skeptical about the existence of God. Perhaps they were conducting more research into the gospel, like reading sections of the Bible for instance, before reaching a final decision.

- *Unenlightened:* These represent people that have not yet heard the gospel, such as a person that is geographically isolated from missionaries and all other means of hearing the gospel.

This is an important distinction to make, because, as I stated earlier in this section of commentary, some Bible prophecy teachers believe that 2 Thessalonians 2:7-12 condemns all who have heard the gospel prior to the rapture and then get left behind. They teach that those left behind after hearing the gospel, forfeit their shot at salvation. They believe there is no "second chance" for them to accept Christ after the rapture. The proponents of this view suggest that these "no second chancer's" are not among the multitudes that get saved after the rapture. Although this is a minority view, it is important to note.

Some eschatologists, including me, disagree with this no second chance teaching, and hold to the belief that there is hope for everyone left behind to receive Christ, as long as they don't accept the mark of the beast in Revelation 13:16-17. According to Revelation 14:9, 11, Revelation 19:20 and contextually throughout Revelation 20, receiving this mark condemns those left behind. In book two of this series I explore this "no second chance" topic in greater detail.

Below are links to articles by Dr. Thomas Ice and Jack Kelley that suggest everyone left behind after the rapture, except those receiving the "mark of the beast" in the trib-period, has a chance to receive Christ after the rapture.

Dr. Ice's article is linked on the Internet here as of 11/3/11: *http://www. pre-trib.org/articles/view/salvation-in-tribulation-revisited*.

COMMENTARY

*Jack Kelley's article is linked on the Internet here as of 11/3/11:* http://gracethrufaith.com/ikvot-hamashiach/is-there-a-second-chance/

Central to Christianity is God's love for those being saved, who believe in the message of the cross. However, this is only part one of the good news gospel of truth. Part two of the gospel is the resurrection of Christ. The resurrection displayed that God possessed the power over death, to prevent those who believed in Christ from perishing. The entire gospel is explained in the appendix called *The Sinner's Salvation Prayer*. However, in a nutshell the good news gospel of truth declares that God:

- Loves us (John 3:16),

- Sent His son Christ to die on the cross for our sins (1 Peter 3:18, 1 John 4:10),

- Raised Christ from the grave (Matthew 28:6-7),

- Proved He possesses the power over death in the process (Revelation 1:18, 1 Corinthians 15:5),

- Plans to use that power to prevent us who believe in Christ from perishing (Hebrews 9:28), and

- Promises to give believers in Christ, eternal life! (John 3:15-16, Matthew 19:29).

## The Strong Delusion of 2 Thessalonians 2:11

In essence, the full gospel is highlighted in these above 2 Thessalonians 2:7-12 verses to explain why those who reject it will be turned over to a coming strong delusion. Because many of mankind will have heard and rejected the gospel of Christ, they will be given a taste of what transpires beyond the spiritual scene within the angelic conflict. Those supernatural powers, presently being restrained and thereby enabling people to acquire "the love of the truth," are about to be unleashed upon unsuspecting mankind after the rapture. Those perishing didn't receive the truth, so they receive the opportunity to experience the counterfeit alternative.

The series of supernatural events that ensue will cause the preponderance within humanity to conform to Satan's will. This is because after the rapture, the paranormal becomes the normal. Man's futile attempt to understand the *power, signs, and lying wonders* through his frail faculties of logic and reason will quickly falter, as Satan orchestrates unexplainable events intended to deceive him. The apostle John informs us the whole world is presently swayed by Satan, but after the rapture, the satanic sway matures into forced worship of Satan and his seed, the lawless one (Antichrist) according to Revelation 13.

> We know that we [believers] are of God, and the whole world lies under the sway of [Satan] the wicked one. (1 John 5:19)

Today's humanist may think that the universe revolves around him, and that mankind possesses the power to control its own destiny, but after the Christians are raptured and the restraint is removed, the Bible predicts otherwise. A counterfeit gospel, that which 2 Thessalonians 2:11 calls "The Lie," gets presented to humankind. It becomes believable because it is empowered by Satan with *all power, signs, and lying wonders*.

Remember, the first biblical reference to Satan is as the serpent in Genesis 3:1, and that he is "more cunning than any beast of the field, which the Lord God had made." If he could convince Adam and Eve to disobey God in the garden, and can presently sway the whole world without *all power, signs, and lying wonders*, imagine the influence he can exert over man, once he is permitted unhindered use of his supernatural powers.

# The Three Competing Wills: God's, Satan's, and Man's

Before discussing this lying gospel, empowered by strong delusion, it is important to note that there are primarily three competing wills in the universe. Donald Grey Barnhouse writes: "God, man or the devil: these are the three sources of hope."[175] Although man has free will, Barnhouse goes on to explain that it is ultimately subservient to the dominant will of God and competing will of the devil.

Created with free choice, mankind indeed possesses a self-governing, independent will of its own. The humanist believes that man's will is all-important. However, taking on the role of a man to die for the sins of men, Christ acknowledged the subservient nature of man's will when he conceded to God's will below.

> And He [Jesus Christ] was withdrawn from them about a stone's throw, and He knelt down and prayed, saying, "Father, if it is *Your will*, take this cup away [representing the crucifixion] from Me; nevertheless *not My will, but Yours*, be done." (Luke 22:41-42; emphasis added).

Christ's prayer in this instance acknowledged two of the three primary existing wills. In addition to the will of man, Christ also confirmed the existence of God's will. Christ makes clear in His prayer that man's will is subservient to God's. This understanding is reinforced in the Lord's Prayer. Teaching His disciples how to pray, Christ preaches,

> In this manner, therefore, pray: Our Father in heaven, Hallowed be Your name. Your kingdom come. *Your will be done On earth as it is in heaven.* Give us this day our daily bread. And forgive us our debts, As we forgive our debtors. And do not lead us into temptation, But deliver us from the evil one. *For Yours is the kingdom and the power and the glory forever.* Amen. (Matthew 6:9-13; emphasis added).

This prayer, echoed throughout tens of thousands of churches over the past two thousand years, instructs that in heaven God's is the operative will, and that Earth will be benefited when God's kingdom descends upon the planet, and His will prevails. Importantly, Christ didn't teach the disciples to pray that man's will be performed in heaven like it is on Earth. This is partially because man's will has become self-centered and short-sighted, due to his sin nature. But more so, it is because God's will holds the best interests of His entire creation in hand.

God's will is that no man, woman, or child, should perish, but that all should have eternal life. In His wisdom, He realized the only genuine way to demonstrate His love was to give His only begotten Son, Jesus Christ, as a sacrifice for sin, rather than sending forth a razzle-dazzle spectacle of powerful signs and wonders. At the time Christ came, the Jews asked for a sign, but no sign was given but the resurrection.

> Then some of the scribes and Pharisees answered, saying, "Teacher, we want to see a sign from You." But He [Christ] answered and said to them, "An evil and adulterous generation seeks after a sign, and no sign will be given to it except the sign of the prophet Jonah. For as Jonah was three days and three nights in the belly of the great fish, so will the Son of Man be three days and three nights in the [grave] heart of the earth." (Matthew 12:38-40).

The religious leaders of the time hungered for a sign because they were *an evil and adulterous generation*. Satan, who possesses a powerful will of his own, realizes this. He recognizes that *an evil and adulterous generation*, like that which exists after the rapture occurs, will seek signs and wonders.

Additionally, we know from the story of Job, that Satan has supernatural power. Job 1:12 acknowledges that Satan possesses power and is capable of:

- Provoking men into war – Job 1:15,17,

- Manipulating atmospheric conditions – Job 1:16,19,

- Dispossessing people from their prosperity – Job 1:14-15,17,

- Destroying families – Job 1:19, and

- Causing diseases and thus, potentially spreading pestilences Job 2:7.

These are a few of the powers known to be exerted by the devil, but when he is given clearance to introduce *the lie* through *strong delusion*, he may display a flurry of other supernatural powers, and they may not all seem negative to the naked eye. Perhaps he will demonstrate illusionary power over death, and miraculous healing. These things would encourage people to believe in his counterfeit gospel. This appears to be what takes place as one of the signs and wonders empowering the rise of the Antichrist.

> And I saw one of his heads as if it had been mortally wounded, and his [Antichrist] deadly wound was healed. And all the world marveled and followed the beast. [Antichrist] So they worshiped the dragon [Satan] who gave authority to the beast; and they worshiped the beast, saying, "Who is like the beast? Who is able to make war with him?" (Revelation 13:3-4).

These verses depict that the devil possesses the power to heal and resurrect, and that they are used to encourage the subservient will of man to worship and obey the will of the dragon. Humanity marvels, "Who is like the beast? Who is able to make war with him?"

Technically, only Christ possesses the power of the resurrection; however, 2 Thessalonians 2:9-10 reminds us that Satan will be performing his deceptive dog and pony show, *with all power, signs, and lying wonders, and with all unrighteous deception among those who perish*. This devilish deception will no doubt be far superior to a Criss Angel magic act in Las Vegas.

> Jesus said to her, "I am the resurrection and the life. He who believes in Me, though he may die, he shall live. And whoever lives and believes in Me shall never die. *Do you believe this?*" (John 11:25-26; emphasis added).

COMMENTARY

Germane to the gospel point, Jesus asks in these verses: "Do you believe this?" Those perishing in 2 Thessalonians do not believe this. They reject Christ, illustrating that they refuse to believe that He represents the only means of entering into eternal life with Him and the heavenly Father. As such, they will be subjected to the coming unrighteous deception, and strong delusion, outsourced by Satan in order that those perishing will believe in "the lie."

## The Counterfeit Gospel—The Lie

The nature of "the lie" is a subject of some controversy among eschatologists. Most concede that at its core it represents a counterfeit gospel. This reasoning fits perfectly within the false biblical replica characterizing the end times. Satan's counterfeit model includes the false trinity, with Satan as would-be God the father, Antichrist as fake messiah, the son, and the false prophet as the imitation Holy Spirit. The harlot religious system becomes the counterfeit bride of the Antichrist, falsely replicating the church as the bride of Christ. And, the lie emulates the erroneous gospel.

The scholarly consensus is that the lie is something specifically intended to deceitfully detract from the true gospel of Jesus Christ. It could be as simple as satanically fabricated evidences that evolution is more than a theory, but perhaps a reality. This would mean that creationism is a lie and that there is no God the Creator, with a Son as a savior. However, one of the relatively recent arguments worthy of mention is the ET scenario, which forwards an "alien gospel."

Some, like Christian author L.A. Marzulli, believe it could take the shape of an alien gospel intended to convince humanity that it is the product of extra-terrestrial origin. Marzulli suggests that the fallen angels or demons referenced in the Bible manifest themselves to mankind, masquerading as ET impostors, in the end times.

Marzulli suggests their showmanship could come complete with large spacecraft of unknown origins, that hover above major world cities. He is concerned these fallen angelic ranks, masked as extra-terrestrials, perform paranormal feats that dupe humanity into thinking that they, rather than Christ, represent truth. Thus, since Christ is the truth, these alien intelligent beings forward a dissenting anti-Christ message; i.e., "the lie."

Marzulli's not alone in this line of thinking; other respected end-times experts present similar possibilities, like authors Chuck Missler, Tom Horn, and Terry James. Although none of these individuals are dogmatic in their views, they have all provided important research through their bestselling books and widely read articles on this subject. Of particular interest in this area is an audio drama I highly recommend, which was released in the summer of 2011 by Jim Tetlow and Brad Myers, called *The Coming Global Transformation.* This drama contains twenty-one scenes of riveting information, addressing the Psalm 83 war, rapture, Marian Apparitions, ETs, and more.[176]

It is interesting to do a Greek word study into the pertinent 2 Thessalonians verse about the lie. "And for this reason God will send them strong delusion, that they should believe the lie." (2 Thessalonians 2:11). The definitions of *send, strong, delusion,* and *lie* are taken from *Strong's Hebrew and Greek Dictionaries* and the *New American Standard Hebrew and Greek Dictionaries.*

* *Pempo* – to send, or dispatch, notably in an orderly motion.

* *Energeia* – operative power - efficiency ("energy"):—operation, strong, (effectual) working – influence.

* *Plane* – a wandering, deceitful, objectively fraudulence; subjectively a straying from orthodoxy or piety:—deceit, to deceive, delusion, error.

* *Pseudos*—a falsehood, untruth, lie.

A possible translation of these words, used to send a strong delusion to cause unbelievers to believe in the lie, could read like this: Satan, with all power, signs, and lying wonders, will present to humanity *a deceitful wandering, which is dispatched in an orderly motion, that is characterized by an operative power capable of influencing them to falsely believe in an untruth.*

If this passage is interpreted in this manner, it would add credence to the argument that the strong delusion revolves around a cleverly orchestrated extra-terrestrial campaign. But, if so, why? Why would Satan, who spearheads this powerful campaign, containing signs and lying wonders, utilize a UFO smokescreen?

The answer to this question could be answered by first posing the question, "Why wouldn't he?" Why wouldn't the devil costume his campaign in an extra-biblical fashion, if the means were available to him? Considering that the strong delusion appears to occur without restraint in the aftermath of the miraculous rapture, it is doubtful that Satan would want to add any credence to a biblical view of the Christian disappearances.

Why would Satan send his fallen angelic cohorts to delude humanity, professing to be angels from the heavenly realm? The existence of angels tends to validate the teachings of the Bible. Thus, if the Bible correctly taught about angels from heaven, then maybe it also correctly taught about Jesus

Christ and the rapture? This would not appear to be the thought process the devil would want those left behind after the rapture to begin contemplating. Rather, alien-looking, intelligent beings, defying the laws of known science, breaking through the veils of dimensionality unexplainably in other-worldly spacecraft, makes more sense.

These are just a few speculative thoughts about the potential deception in store for those left behind after the rapture. Although the "alien gospel" explanation is interesting, it is difficult to know exactly what the actual "lie" of 2 Thessalonians will be. However, one thing that is reasonably certain to occur after the rapture is that America will be profoundly affected by the event.

## The Rapture Profoundly Affects America

This corresponding novel chapter announces, "The disappearance of Christians profoundly affected America and portions of Europe, whereas in Muslim dominated countries like Turkey and Iran, life went on relatively unchanged."

The three largest Christian populated countries of America, Brazil, and Mexico will probably be catapulted into chaos, as millions of their citizens depart from the planet. Many first responders (policemen and firemen), political leaders, plumbers, janitors, soldiers, nuclear power plant operators, etc., will go on eternal sabbatical from their jobs. In their absence, important societal functions will undoubtedly be disabled.

The world population is presently about 6.8 billion, and approximately 2 billion of them are professing Christians.[177] Additionally, there are reportedly about 38,000 Christian denominations worldwide. Supposedly, America hosts 224,457,000 Christians, Brazil—139,000,000, and Mexico—86,120,000.[178] It is highly likely that not all professing Christians are true believers, but even if half of them are, these three countries, and many other predominately Christian nations like Australia, South Africa, Britain, France, and Germany, will likely never fully recover from the impact of the loss of so much citizenry.

Whereas predominately Christian countries will undoubtedly be reeling from the effects of the rapture, Muslim dominated countries like Turkey and Saudi Arabia probably won't realize the disappearance occurred until they learn about it in the world news. China, mainly Buddhist, and India, primarily Hindu, have a growing number of citizens becoming Christians, but it is doubtful their societies will be irreparably damaged, either.

The caveat to this idea is the possible occurrence of millions of children getting raptured out of these predominately Islamic, Buddhist, or Hindu countries. Some believe all children under an age of accountability get raptured. Author Terry James, the co-founder of *Rapture Ready*, believes there could be such a cut-off age. The age of accountability means that at some point an individual is accountable to make his or her own decision to accept or reject Christ, but prior to that point the youth receives a waiver of spiritual accountability and is automatically saved.

During a radio interview with Terry, I asked him to elaborate on his views about what might happen to children during the rapture, and Terry explained that he believes all children under the age of accountability, including infants in their mother's womb will be raptured with believers. He even goes so far as to suggest the wombs of Muslim mothers and other non-Christian mothers could be emptied during the rapture. This fascinating interview can be listened to at this Internet link: *http://www.prophecydepot.net/2010/expert-discusses-the-rapture-departure-of-christians/*

Conversely, other Christian scholars, like Dr. Arnold Fruchtenbaum, remind us that the Bible doesn't seem to stipulate a specific age of accountability, and that children, especially from unbelieving households, could be left behind in the rapture. Examples of this would be the children that perished in the flood at Noah's time, described in Genesis 7 and 8, or, the youth killed during the destruction of Sodom and Gomorrah, in Genesis 19.

Regardless, families will be separated, because unbelievers are not sanctified by their believing family members. Only those who claim Christ personally as their Lord can be raptured.[179]

Even worse than all the implications above, everyone left behind will be unbelievers that have been forced into somewhat of a survival mode because of the chaos. It can be expected that looting, rioting, and plundering will occur afterward throughout various parts of the world, at unparalleled levels. That thought alone should make one want to become a Christian today, before the event happens.

*Please read the final chapter of the novel now.*

COMMENTARY

# Chapter 18—
## Left Behind, the Heavenly Love Letter

*Topics covered:* Many Left Behind Will Receive Christ; The Righteous Sheep Gentiles; Introducing the 144,000 Witnesses of Revelation; The 144,000 Witnesses Are Post-Rapture Saints; The 144,000 Witnesses Are Jews for Jesus; The Message of the 144,000 Future Jews for Jesus; The New Testament Mystery of Grafting in Jews and Gentiles

## Many Left Behind Will Receive Christ

Inside the story line, Nathan Severs receives Christ as his Lord and Savior. All the one-on-one preaching his best friend Robert Rasmussen had presented throughout the years finally clicked when the rapture occurred. In turn, Nathan's conversion helped lead to the conversions of Lisa and Jami in this final novel chapter. All three had heard the gospel prior to the rapture. For the trio, the supernatural rapture event served as the prophetic "proof in the pudding" that the good news of Jesus Christ was genuine. As such, they acquired the critical *love of the gospel truth*, alluded to in 2 Thessalonians 2:10.

Some readers may struggle with the fact that these characters in the story line receive a second chance at salvation after the rapture. This topic was briefly addressed in the commentary chapter called *After the Rapture, the World Gets Religious*.

By way of review, the "no second chance" after the rapture advocates teach that only those having never heard the gospel before the rapture, have an opportunity to receive Christ and be saved after the rapture. They generally acknowledge that many people get saved after the rapture, but do not believe this includes those that heard the gospel before. Many of these teachers come from a pre-trib viewpoint of the rapture. Thus, in their estimation, *Revelation Road* characters like Nathan Severs, and Lisa and Jami Thompson can't get saved after the rapture. As the novel story line suggests, I disagree with this no second chance thinking.

It is not my intent to belabor this topic here. However, in preparation for the discussion of this topic in the next book, please consider that the no second chance view generally assumes the following:

- The 144,000 witnesses of Revelation 7:1-8 never hear the gospel before the rapture. They only hear the good news about Christ afterward, because if they heard the gospel before they couldn't have a second chance to accept Christ. Since they are sealed for godly service in Revelation 7:3, they obviously accept Christ. Thus, the inference is that they must hear the gospel for the first time after the rapture occurs.

- In addition to these 144,000 witnesses, more Jews get saved, including the faithful remnant of Jews that go through the trib-period. The no second chance view means, that none of these Jews hear the gospel prior to the rapture, either.

- Any of the reader's family members, friends, neighbors, associates, or strangers—be they Jew or Gentile—that have already been exposed to the gospel, but not made a decision to accept Christ as of yet, should be warned that after the rapture occurs, they cannot receive Christ. Since the rapture is imminent and could occur at any moment, these individuals should promptly be told to accept Christ now, or else be condemned forever.

These are just a few inferences that can be safely made by those who subscribe to this no second chance teaching. Several more will be identified when this topic is explored in book two of this series.

Presumably, the most relevant verses in the Bible for those that get left behind are found in 2 Thessalonians 2:7-12. These verses point out what happens after the rapture. The Antichrist will be revealed according to the supernatural workings of Satan, and mankind will be confronted with strong delusion, causing many to believe what the Bible calls "the lie."

For anyone left behind that wonders what the Bible says happens after the rapture, they will probably read these specific verses, and possibly some related articles and commentaries expounding upon them. This is why their accurate interpretation is critically important. Many no second chance advocates use these verses to teach that God sends strong delusion upon those left behind, who had previously heard the gospel, but neglected to accept Christ for whatever the reason. In essence, God purposes that they perish because they neglected to accept Christ when they had the opportunity.

John 3:16 informs us that God desires that none should perish, but the no second chance teachings suggest that rule-of-thumb does not apply to those left behind, who neglected to accept Christ when they heard about Him before the rapture occurred.

Nathan Severs, and Lisa and Jami Thompson represent a crop of true believers that emerge from those who were left behind. Like them, many will recognize that Jesus Christ, the only begotten Son of God, is the way, the truth, and the life, and that no one is received by the heavenly Father apart from possessing a genuine faith in Christ.[180] The commentary chapter entitled *The Arabs Surrender!* discusses the primary ways people left behind in the rapture recognize this truth, which then will prove to be a costly and unpopular decision. It will be considered costly, because for many it comes at a martyr's price, and unpopular because the preponderance of humanity will be captivated by strong delusion, according to 2 Thessalonians 2:9-12. Those that receive Christ after the rapture will have undoubtedly considered the consequences. *Apocalypse Road*, book two of this trilogy, explores their fate.

By way of reminder, the primary means the gospel is dispensed after the rapture is through: the 144,000 Hebrew witnesses, the martyred saints who come to faith after being left behind, teaching materials—like articles, books, audios, videos and movies produced by Christians before they are raptured, the Two Witnesses, and the angel with the everlasting gospel. Along with these means, the rapture itself should convince many to accept Christ as their Savior.

The DVD alluded to in this concluding novel chapter is an example of the types of materials left behind that potentially lead people to Christ. The informative and predictive content of the DVD, which will establish chronologically the prophetic events that should follow the rapture, will be revealed in book two of this series. This DVD is guaranteed to cover additional eschatological insights.

Presently, many end-times experts are preparing websites and materials intended to bless those left behind. *Rapture Ready*, www.raptureready.com on the web, is one such site. The founders, Todd Strandberg and Terry James, have posted thousands of articles that speak about the subject of the rapture specifically, and the end times in general. In a radio interview with Todd

Strandberg, that can be heard at this link: http://prophecyupdateradio.blogspot. com/2009/04/are-christians-google-yahoo-rapture.html, he informed me of the elaborate means *Rapture Ready* has taken to ensure the longevity of their web information after the rapture.

Other works include the *Left Behind* book series authored by Tim LaHaye and Jerry Jenkins and an excellent video available through Dr. David Reagan's *Lamb and Lion Ministries*, produced by Nathan Jones, called *Jesus Came, What's Next?*[181]

The problem those left behind will likely encounter is that invaluable resources like these listed above, will be short-lived. Soon after the rapture, these Christian-witnessing elements should be eradicated by the Antichrist in a hasty effort to indoctrinate the world into his deceitful global order and cashless society.[182]

# The Righteous Sheep Gentiles

Subsequent to his Christian conversion, Severs embarked upon a crash study course of end-times Bible prophecy. This prompted him to become a sort of last days Oskar Schindler, and move to Israel. The previous novel chapter says, "Nathan understood [from prophecy], that the Antichrist would soon attempt a final Jewish genocidal campaign that would make the Hitler holocaust seem like a walk in the park." Realizing this, Nathan patterned his life as a righteous (sheep) Gentile in Matthew 25:31-46. The Antichrist's campaign to exterminate the Jews is discussed in the subsequent book(s).

> When the Son of Man [Jesus Christ] comes in His glory, and all the holy angels with Him, then He will sit on the throne of His glory. All the nations will be gathered before Him, and He will separate them one from another, as a shepherd divides his *sheep* from the goats. (Matthew 25:31-32; emphasis added)

Matthew 25:31-46 points out that those helping the Jews to survive the final genocidal attempt of the Antichrist are rewarded for their righteous behavior. Conversely, the indignant Anti-Semitic "goat" Gentiles receive harsh condemnation for mistreating the Jews. The righteous Gentiles are blessed for blessing Christ's Jewish brethren in their deepest, end-time of need. The rewards of the righteous Gentiles in the end times evidences the foreign policy of Genesis 12:3 remains in effect, even in the trib-period. Sheep Gentiles will be blessed for helping Jews, but goat Gentiles will be cursed for cursing Jews. Both responses are executed in accordance with Genesis 12:3.

COMMENTARY

More specifically in this Matthew passage, Christ appears to allude to the faithful remnant of Jews that recognize Jesus as Messiah during the great tribulation period. The faithful remnant will somehow survive the final three-and-one-half years of unprecedented persecution of the Antichrist, that Zechariah 13:8 declares will kill two-thirds of all Jews in the land. The sheep Gentiles are credited for being part of the reason for this, and as such they are duly rewarded.

*Revelation Road* explains at various points that many will become believers after the rapture. The righteous sheep Gentiles represent a segment within this post-rapture harvest of converts. However, not all of those who accept Christ at that time survive to become Oskar Schindler sorts of sheep-like Gentiles. Unfortunately, many will die sometime after the rapture, but before the great tribulation (second-half of the trib-period) begins. This is because the post-rapture period is characterized by Christian martyrdom. This statement above speaks about the true, post-rapture Christianity, in contrast to the counterfeit religious system that develops simultaneously as discussed in the commentary of the previous chapter. The prophecies pertaining to the last days' Christian martyrs and the faithful Jewish remnant are addressed in the subsequent book(s).

# Introducing the 144,000 Witnesses of Revelation

One of the primary means that people come to hear the gospel of Christ after the rapture is through the 144,000 witnesses of Revelation 7. The previous chapter of the novel alludes to them as "Royal Jews from the Twelve Tribes of Israel." Although this is not an official name attributed to them within the Bible, they are clearly descendants from the tribes of Israel. Due to their prophetic significance they are represented in thirteen verses in Revelation 7:1-8 and 14:1-5.

# The 144,000 Witnesses Are Post-Rapture Saints

We can safely conclude the ministries of these 144,000 commences after the rapture, by ordering the book of Revelation as follows:

Revelation 2 and 3 identify the church on Earth, and Revelation 4 and 5 pictures the church raptured and residing in heaven. The appendix called *The Final Century—Christian Survival versus Pagan Revival,* summarily explains the prophetic application of the letters to the seven churches in Revelation 2 and 3.

The appendix presents a brief outline of church history and demonstrates how the seven letters predicted important aspects of the church age when they were written; thus, suggesting Revelation 2 and 3 represents the church on Earth, is a qualified assessment.

After the church age is completed, Revelation 4 begins with the Greek words *meta tauta*, which means "after these things," and pictures the church being raptured into heaven. In other words, after these things pertaining to the church on Earth, it is caught up to heaven in Revelation 4 and 5.

> After these things [*meta tauta*] I looked, and behold, a door standing open in heaven. And the first voice which I heard was like a trumpet speaking with me, saying, "Come up here, [representing the rapture] and I will show you things which must take place after this." (Revelation 4:1; emphasis added).

The absence of the Christian church on Earth segues into Revelation chapter 6, which addresses the seal judgments. These judgments are unleashed on Earth when Christ opens the scroll in Revelation 6:1, that He received in Revelation 5:7.

> Then He [Christ] came and took the scroll out of the right hand of Him who sat on the throne [in heaven]. (Revelation 5:7).

> Now I saw when the Lamb opened one of the seals; and I heard one of the four living creatures saying with a voice like thunder, "Come and see." (Revelation 6:1)

The seals opened in Revelation 6:1-17 reveal the infamous four-horsemen of the apocalypse (6:1-8), the martyred fifth seal saints (6:9-11), and the wrath of God (6:12-17). Many believe these seal judgments occur within the first-half of the seven-year trib-period, but for reasons that will be explained in book two of this series it appears the first five seals are opened in the post-rapture gap period, prior to the trib-period. Regardless of this possibility, the events described in Revelation 6 occur after the rapture.

Correlating events that occur on Earth after the church is removed, begin in Revelation Chapter 7. Revelation 7:1 also begins with the Greek words *meta tauta*, meaning after the church is raptured the 144,000 witnesses enter onto the world scene.

> After these things [*meta tauta*] I saw four angels standing at the four corners of the earth, holding the four winds of the earth, that the wind

should not blow on the earth, on the sea, or on any tree. (Revelation 7:1).

In summary, during Revelation 2 and 3 the church is on Earth. Revelation 4 and 5 portrays the church raptured, and residing in heaven. Revelation 6 and 7 identify events taking place on Earth after the rapture occurs.

## The 144,000 Witnesses Are Jews for Jesus

These are individuals of Hebrew descent from the tribes of Judah, Reuben, Gad, Asher, Naphtali, Manasseh, Simeon, Levi, Issachar, Zebulun, Joseph, and Benjamin. There are 12,000 divinely selected from each of these twelve tribes, totaling 144,000 witnesses. Revelation 7:1-8 clearly identifies their Hebrew pedigree. They are Jesus-believing Jews that are sealed for godly servitude.

> Then I saw another angel ascending from the east, having *the seal of the living God*. And he cried with a loud voice to the four angels to whom it was granted to harm the earth and the sea, saying, "Do not harm the earth, the sea, or the trees till we have *sealed the servants of our God* on their foreheads." And I heard the number of those who were *sealed*. One hundred *and* forty-four thousand of all the tribes of the children of Israel *were sealed*: (Revelation 7:2-4; emphasis added).

We infer they believe in Jesus, from Revelation 7:9-17. These verses describe the multitudes that convert to Christianity after the 144,000 witnesses' minister on the world scene. They are preaching the gospel and many receive Christ as a result of their message. Moreover, Revelation 14 infers that they are probably male virgins.

> They sang as it were a new song before the throne, before the four living creatures, and the elders; and no one could learn that song except the hundred and forty-four thousand who were redeemed from the earth. These are the ones who were *not defiled with women*, *for they are virgins*. These are the ones who follow the Lamb wherever He goes. These were redeemed from among men, being firstfruits to God and to the Lamb. (Revelation 14:3-4; emphasis added).

These Revelation verses state they are *not defiled with women, for they are virgins*, meaning that they are literally male virgins, or that they are individuals that are not defiled by the idolatrous world religious system established in the aftermath of the rapture, or both. Revelation 17 and elsewhere pictures an idolatrous global religious system personified by a harlot.

> Then one of the seven angels who had the seven bowls came and talked with me, saying to me, "Come, I will show you the judgment *of the great harlot* who sits on many waters, [peoples, multitudes, nations, and tongues][183] with whom the kings of the earth committed fornication, and the inhabitants of the earth were made drunk with the wine of her fornication." Revelation 17:1-2; emphasis added).

# The Message of the 144,000 Future Jews for Jesus

The specific ministry of these Jews for Jesus may be encoded in the ordering of their names in Revelation 7:5-8. This concluding portion of commentary will explore this possibility. The book of Romans exclaims that the gospel message is important to both Jews and Gentiles.

> For I am not ashamed of the gospel of Christ, for it is the power of God to salvation for everyone who believes, for the Jew first and also for the Greek. (Romans 1:16).

Since the formation of Israel on May 14, 1948, Christians worldwide have stepped up efforts aimed at getting the gospel message out to the Jewish people. Many of these "good news" recipients are hearing for the first time fundamental facts such as, Jesus was a Jew, and the current outpouring of Christian support for the nation Israel is biblically based. Over six decades of sincere evangelism has Jews flocking to Jesus in record numbers. Yet scores more remain undecided, or uninformed, about the messianic claims of Christ.

Among this latter grouping are 144,000 Jews destined for spiritual greatness. They will witness the Christian church vanish from the earth in a twinkling of an eye,[184] which is the likely event prompting many of them to realize that Jesus Christ was, is, and will always be the Messiah! Left behind,[185] these individuals will commence to administer the gospel of Christ in a perilous period of time.

Revelation 7:5-8 identifies these future evangelists by their ancient tribal origins. From each of the twelve previously identified tribes, come 12,000 members who commit themselves to godly service. As previously mentioned, these 144,000 witnesses turn out to be instrumental in escorting many end-time souls to salvation.

Curiously, these twelve tribal patriarchs are not listed in their chronological birth order. Since the Bible normally identifies genealogies chronologically, this contrast demands our attention. Judah, listed first, was actually the fourth son of Jacob and his wife Leah, and Manasseh, Joseph's son, is listed before his father. Similarly the other names are not listed in any apparent order, or are they? Conspicuous Scriptural abnormalities like this compel a deeper analysis. A standard starting point of exploration is to discern the meaning of the names to see if they are message-formatted. This method apparently finds application in the case of the 144,000 witnesses.

> *The Meaning of the Names*: *Judah*- Praise God; *Reuben*- behold a son; *Gad*- good fortune; *Asher*- happiness; *Naphtali*- my wrestling or struggle; *Manasseh*- God has caused me to forget; *Simeon*- hearing; *Levi*- joining or grafting in; *Issachar*- God hath given me my hire, or has reinstated me; *Zebulun*- elevated or elevated position; *Joseph*- adding or increasing; *Benjamin*- son of the right hand.[186]

> *The Message of the Names*: Praise God! Behold a Son of good fortune and happiness. My struggle, God has caused me to forget. Hearing of our grafting in, God has reinstated me into an elevated position, increased by the Son of the right hand.

> *The Mission Statement*: Inherent in these oddly ordered names, appears to be the ministerial message of the 144,000 witnesses. Their "Mission Statement" should read as follows: Praise God for the gospel of Christ, a Son of good fortune and happiness. My struggle with sin and the Mosaic Law, God has caused me to forget. Hearing of the *mystery of our grafting*[187] *in* with the Gentiles, God has reinstated me into an elevated position of ministry once again, and is increasing those being saved through Christ, the Son of the right hand.

## The New Testament Mystery of Grafting in Jews and Gentiles

The *mystery* alluded to in the mission statement is that the Gentiles were to be *partakers* alongside the Jews of the blessings of God via being *grafted in* through faith in Jesus Christ, the Jewish Messiah. Because of the unconditional covenant God made with Abraham, the Jews were never to be entirely dismissed from the Lord's prophetic program. The relevant passages regarding *the mystery* and Gentile *grafting in* are found below. A New Testament mystery is a new revelation not contained in the Old Testament.

> How that by revelation He made known to me [the apostle Paul] *the mystery* [as I have briefly written already, by which, when you read, you may understand my knowledge in *the mystery of Christ*], which in other ages [the Old Testament] was not made known to the sons of men, as it has now been revealed by the Spirit to His holy apostles and prophets: that *the Gentiles should be fellow heirs* [with the Jews] of the same body, and partakers of His promise in Christ through the gospel. (Ephesians 3:3-6; emphasis added).

*The Grafting In and Partaking* – The olive tree symbolisms in the verses below represents the spiritual blessings of God contained in the Abrahamic Covenant. Namely, the New Covenant of Jeremiah 31:31-34, whereby the Holy Spirit indwells those who receive Christ as their Savior.[188] The shed blood of Christ at the crucifixion serves as the seal of the New Covenant,[189] just as circumcision was the seal of the Abrahamic Covenant. Circumcision indicated that a descendant of Abraham was under the covenant that God had made with Abraham.[190]

> And if some of the [Jewish] branches were broken off, and you [Gentiles], being a wild olive tree, were *grafted in* among them [through Christ], and with them became a partaker of the root and fatness of the olive tree, do not boast against the branches. But if you do boast, *remember that* you do not support the root, but the root supports you. [Romans 1:16, to the Jew first]...You will say then, "Branches were broken off that *I might be grafted in*." Well *said*. Because of unbelief [in Christ] they [the Jews] were broken off, and you stand by faith. Do not be haughty, but fear. For if God did not spare the natural [Jewish] branches, He may not spare you [Gentiles] either. Therefore consider the goodness and severity of God: on those who fell, severity; but toward you, goodness, if you continue in *His* goodness. Otherwise you also will be cut off... *And* they also, if they do not continue in unbelief [in Christ], will be grafted in, for *God is able to graft them in again.* For if you were cut out of the olive tree which is wild by nature, and were *grafted* contrary to nature into a cultivated olive tree, how much more will these [Jesus believing Jews], who *are* natural *branches,* be grafted into their own olive tree?[the Abrahamic Covenant]... *For I do*

C
O
M
M
E
N
T
A
R
Y

*not desire, brethren, that you should be ignorant of this mystery*, lest you should be wise in your own opinion, that blindness in part has happened to Israel until the fullness of the Gentiles has come in. And so all Israel will be saved, as it is written: *"The Deliverer will come out of Zion, And He will turn away ungodliness from Jacob; For this is My covenant with them, When I take away their sins."* (Romans 11:17-27; emphasis added)

These post-rapture Jews will be among the "Firstfruits"[191] of the restored "My people Israel" period. This is a future point in time, wherein the Jewish people regain their former "Client Nation" status. For over 2,000 years, in fulfillment of Hosea 1:9, the Jews existed in a "not My people" condition. The rebirth of the nation Israel in 1948 set the stage for their entitlement reclassification process. They are soon to be reinstated as "My people Israel."[192] Forthcoming events that occur during this period of time are detailed in my book, *Isralestine, The Ancient Blueprints of the Future Middle East*. In the chapter called "My People Israel," explanations are provided for when the Jews became "not My people," and when they become reinstated as "My people Israel."

Briefly stated, with the sudden disappearance of the Christian church, God's people Israel, formerly recognized as the "chosen people" take center-stage once again. Performing in the main arena at the time, will be the 144,000 Jewish evangelists. Their faith in Christ, understanding of the Bible, and Christian artifacts like books, commentaries, tapes, videos, songs, and other assorted teachings, will undoubtedly escort them through their end-time's gospel campaign.

Corresponding with the mysterious exit of Israel's greatest fan club, the evangelical church, dawns the daunting realization that the Jewish State is left behind to fend for itself. If not fulfilled beforehand, the Arabs of Psalm 83, and then the Russian – Iranian led coalition of Ezekiel 38-39, will each advance against Israel for their piece of the chosen pie.

Against this amazing backdrop, these 144,000 witnesses accomplish one of the greatest worldwide revivals in history. At the cost of a martyr's death, many people will come to accept Christ as their Savior. Therefore, the good news today is that the gospel continues on tomorrow, through the faithful efforts of the 144,000 future Jews for Jesus.

# End Notes—Commentary

1 Deuteronomy 18:21-22

2 Deuteronomy 18:20; Jeremiah 14:14-15

3 Deborah was a prophetess, Judges 4:4

4 *Isralestine* is available at www.prophecydepot.com, or through Amazon

5 More information about the Iranian, Syrian, Hezbollah, and Hamas war-pacts of 2009 is available over the Internet as of 9/20/11 at this link: http://prophecydepot.blogspot.com/2009/12/is-middle-east-about-to-go-ballistic.html

6 Information supporting that Israel passed out gas masks in 2010 can be obtained over the Internet as of 9/20/11 at this link: http://www.eutimes.net/2010/01/israel-to-issue-gas-masks-to-entire-population/

7 Asaph is called a seer in 2 Chronicles 29:30. The Hebrew word for seer is *chozeh*, which according to the *Strong's Hebrew and Greek Dictionaries* means a beholder in vision; also a compact (as looked upon with approval):—agreement, prophet, see that, seer, [star-] gazer. *The New American Standard Hebrew and Greek Dictionaries* defines *chozeh* as a seer:—pact, prophets, seer, seers.

8 The definition of Hebrew was located in *Easton's Bible Dictionary*.

9 John 14:1-4 discusses the mansions in heaven awaiting those true believers of Christ.

10 The Bible often refers to believers in Christ that have previously died, as those who have "fallen asleep." Examples are located in 1 Cor. 15:18,20 and 1 Thess. 4:13,15.

11 Eschatologists are those who study eschatology, which is a combination of the Greek words, *eschatos* and *ology*. *Eschatos* means last or final, and *ology* means the study of. Thus, an eschatologist is one who studies the prophecies relating to the end times.

12 Daniel 9:24-27 alludes to seventy weeks of years totaling a span of 490 years. Most scholars agree that 483 of those years have already found fulfillment, but the final seven years occur during the tribulation period.

13 Gapper is a neologism created for the purposes of this book to describe an individual(s) or event(s) that emerge(s) in fulfillment of Bible prophecy in the post-rapture pre-tribulation gap period.

14 The "seed of Satan" is the very first reference of the Antichrist in Genesis 3:15.

15 David Dolan's commentary on Psalm 102, in connection with the Holocaust, can be read over the Internet as of 9/4/11 at this link: http://juchre.org/nor/psalm102.htm

16 Noah's testimonial actions are described in Hebrews 11:7, 1 Peter 3:20, 2 Peter 2:25.

17 The quote was taken from the Internet on 9/4/11 at this link: http://www.konig.org/wc24.htm

18 This Scripture teaches that God pre-appointed the time a nation would exist and its national boundary. It also implies that the citizens of those nations have been pre-appointed a time to live within that nation.

19 The five stages of grief were first introduced by Elisabeth Kübler-Ross in her 1969 book, *On Death and Dying.* She orders the five stages as follows: Denial, Anger, Bargaining, Depression, Acceptance.

20 These events are described in 2 Thessalonians 2:8-12.

[21] Numbers 14:29-30.

[22] http://www.allaboutworldview.org/definition-of-religion.htm (Internet accessed 12/16/10)

[23] http://en.wikipedia.org/wiki/Nuclear_Non-Proliferation_Treaty (accessed 11/19/10)

[24] http://timesofindia.indiatimes.com/world/pakistan/Paks-new-nuclear-reactors-will-increase-weapon-production-7-fold-SIPRI/articleshow/6003825.cms (Website accessed 12/15/2010)

[25] Dr. Hitchcock authored *The Late Great United States*. Dr. Reagan authored *America the Beautiful*. Terry James authored *American Apocalypse*.

[26] "The heart *is* deceitful above all *things,* And desperately wicked; Who can know it? Jeremiah 17:9

[27] Reference to this mark can be found in Revelation 13:16-17, 14:9-11, 16:2, 19:20, 20:4.

[28] Information about Syrian President Assad's threats against Tel Aviv were obtained over the Internet on 10/16/11 at this link: http://www.ynetnews.com/articles/0,7340,L-4131259,00.html

[29] Internet accessed on 6/15/2011 at http://www.washingtontimes.com/news/2010/apr/22/hezbollah-may-have-scud-type-missiles/

[30] Internet accessed on 6/15/2011 at http://www.haaretz.com/news/report-chemical-weapons-in-hezbollah-arms-cache-blast-1.8552

[31] Joel 3:2 and Zechariah 12:9 use the phrase "all nations" alluding to the battle of Armageddon.

[32] Internet accessed on 6/15/2011 at http://geography.about.com/cs/countries/a/numbercountries.htm

[33] *Viva la* is French for long live. In this usage it should read "long live Palestine."

[34] Internet accessed on 6/15/2011 at http://www.jewishvirtuallibrary.org/jsource/History/1948_War.html

[35] Internet accessed on 6/15/2011 at http://www.jewishvirtuallibrary.org/jsource/myths2/1967war.html

[36] Internet accessed on 6/15/2011 at http://users.erols.com/mwhite28/warstat4.htm

[37] 2 Chronicles 29:20 identifies Asaph, the author of Psalm 83, as a seer. The Hebrew word used is *chozeh* and can also be translated as, prophet, or a beholder in vision, according to *Strong's Hebrew and Greek Dictionaries* as per H2374.

[38] 300 of Gideon's men destroyed 120,000 Midianites, according to Judges 8:1-10.

[39] Gary Fisher's website is http://lionofjudahministry.org

[40] *International Standard Bible Encyclopedia* states this under Assyrian Invasions section 8.

[41] Internet accessed on 6/16/2011 at this link: http://topicalBible.org/c/carchemish.htm

[42] *Parsons Bible Atlas* under Carchemish.

[43] *International Standard Bible Encyclopedia* states this under "Assyrian Invasions section 8". "Soldiers of the Hatti had seized the cities of Sumasti (probably Samosata), but the Assyrian conqueror made his soldiers swim the Euphrates on skin bags, and so attacked "Carchemish of the land of the Hittites." http://books.google.com/books?id=rH0PAAAAYAAJ&pg=PA1398&lpg=PA1398&dq=Euphrates+on+skin+bags,+and+so+attacked+%E2%80%9CCarchemish+of+the+land+of+the+Hittites&source=bl&ots=2t9WYINBkR&sig=v17JzJlc7H4nTFalG1XpQfOWu4g&hl=en&ei=VzHUTt_zIqeqiAKlx6SnDg&sa=X&oi=book_result&ct=result&resnum=1&ved=0CB0Q6AEwAA#v=onepage&q=Euphrates%20on%20skin%20bags%2C%20and%20

so%20attacked%20%E2%80%9CCarchemish%20of%20the%20land%20of%20the%20
Hittites&f=false

[44] Definition of *azab* gathered from *New American Standard Hebrew and Greek Dictionaries*.

[45] *Parsons Bible Atlas* – Aroer (GAD) A town near Rabbah, capital of Ammon, that was assigned to Gad. (Numbers 32:1) "Now the children of Reuben and the children of Gad had a very great multitude of livestock; and when they saw the land of Jazer and the land of Gilead, that indeed the region *was* a place for livestock. Also the *Holman Bible Dictionary* says, "GAD At the conclusion of the period of wilderness wandering, when the Israelites were preparing to occupy Canaan, the tribe of Gad requested permission, along with the tribe of Reuben and half the tribe of Manasseh, to settle east of the Jordan. Their reason was that they owned large numbers of livestock and the territory east of the Jordan was particularly suitable for raising livestock (Num. 32). This territory became known as Gad (Jer. 49:1)."

[46] *Holman Bible Dictionary* gives the span of Isaiah's ministry.

[47] Valley of Rephaim – is the location of two historic battles fought between King David and the Philistines. 2 Samuel 5, 1 Chronicles 11, and 14. The Philistines are listed in Psalm 83 as a member of the Arab confederacy. They would appear to be partially represented by Hamas today. It is remotely possible that the Valley of Rephaim, the Philistines, and Psalm 83 have some association here.

[48] John 14:6, and Acts 4:10-12, informs us that Jesus is the only way of salvation.

[49] Revelation 13:1 an example of sea connecting with Gentile nations.

[50] Jeremiah 31:35-36, teach that Israel cannot be destroyed.

[51] Definition of *Leom* taken from the *Strong's Hebrew and Greek Dictionaries*.

[52] The definition of *Leummiym* was taken from two sources. 1) Arabian: *Strong's Hebrew and Greek Dictionaries*, and 2) as Dedan in the *New American Standard Hebrew and Greek Dictionaries*. The latter spells the word *Leummim*.

[53] Syrian Armed Forces information accessed over the Internet on 7/16/11 at http://en.wikipedia.org/wiki/Military_of_Syria

[54] http://www.nationsencyclopedia.com/Asia-and-Oceania/Syria-POPULATION.html Information accessed over the Internet on 12/14/2010.

[55] BBC interview with Syrian president Assad can be read on the Internet as of 9/4/11 at this link: http://www.bbc.co.uk/news/10337041

[56] Lieberman quote gathered from the internet on 9/4/11 at this link: http://www.informationclearinghouse.info/article24599.htm

[57] Syrian Scud Missile potential gathered from a *Prophecy Update Radio* interview between white house correspondent Bill Koenig and the author, and can be heard as of 7/14/11 at this Internet link: http://isralestine-blog.blogspot.com/2011/07/big-squeeze-against-israel.html

[58] Information gathered from *Parson's Bible Atlas* under "Susa." *Quickverse Bible Software 6.0*.

[59] *International Standard Bible Encyclopedia* in the "Temperament of the Inhabitants of Elam" identifies the Elamites as a war like people.

[60] Notes found in Jeremiah 49 commentary inside *The Bible Knowledge Commentary* written by John Walvoord and Roy B. Zuck (Old Testament).

[61] Dates gathered from the *Parson's Bible Atlas* under "the Persian Empire" in *Quickverse Bible software 6.0*.

[62] *The Footsteps of the Messiah* book, section C-6 pages 510-511. By Dr. Arnold Fruchtenbaum

[63] Quote taken from the Internet on 7/18/2011 at this link: http://en.wikipedia.org/wiki/List_of_earthquakes_in_Iran: all the earthquake information was gathered at this web link.

[64] Isaiah 2:4, Micah 4:3, and Isaiah 11:9

[65] Matthew 24:30-31, Revelation 20:4

[66] *New American Standard Hebrew and Greek Dictionaries*

[67] More on the war pacts between Iran, Hezbollah, Syria, and Hamas can be accessed over the Internet as of 7/10/11 at this link: http://www.worldviewweekend.com/worldview-times/article.php?articleid=7021

[68] It is difficult to know if Persia technically occupied modern-day northern Iran at the time of the Psalm, about 3000 years ago. The Persian Empire was at its height around 500 BC. By the time Ezekiel included Persia in his Ezekiel 38 prophecy, Persia existed in this location. Ezekiel wrote about 500 years after the Psalm was penned.

[69] Information about Russia's growing Muslim population accessed from the Internet on 7/10/11 at this link: http://windowoneurasia.blogspot.com/2007/08/window-on-eurasia-russia-to-have-muslim.html

[70] Quote from Wikipedia and was accessed from the Internet on 7/11/11 at this link: http://en.wikipedia.org/wiki/List_of_countries_by_Muslim_population

[71] *The Footsteps of the Messiah,* by Dr. Arnold Fruchtenbaum pages 315-361

[72] Psalm 83 battlefields—Further information about the expanse of the Psalm 83 battlefield can be gathered from the book called *Isralestine, The Ancient Blueprints of the Future Middle East,* by this author.

[73] Ezekiel 38 battlefield—Ezekiel 38:8-9, 14-16, 21; Ezekiel 39:1-4

[74] Information gathered from chapter 14 of Dr. Arnold Fruchtenbaum's book called *The Footsteps of the Messiah.*

[75] Matthew 10:30 and Luke 12:7.

[76] 1 Corinthians 15:3-4, and John 3:16.

[77] Dr. Reagan article, "Betrayal of Israel" is posted on the Internet as of 7/20/11 at this link: http://www.lamblion.us/2011/07/betrayal-of-israel.html

[78] Information about the Madrid Conference gathered from the Internet on 7/20/11 at this link: http://en.wikipedia.org/wiki/Madrid_Conference_of_1991

[79] *Operation Desert Storm* was also called the Persian Gulf War and occurred between (8/2/90 – 2/28/91).

[80] These eight specifications have been paraphrased by the author, and published in an internet article on 5/26/11 linked here: http://prophecynewsstand.blogspot.com/2011/05/is-arab-spring-headed-for-mideast.html

[81] More Islamic scriptural quotes that are Anti-Semitic can be found as of 7/22/11 at this Internet link: http://prophetofdoom.net/Quotes_Overview.aspx

[82] Quoted from *Isralestine, The Ancient Blueprints of the Future Middle East,* by author, in the chapter called "The Ancient Arab Hatred of the Jews (Olam Ebah)" on pages 109-110.

[83] *Holman Bible Dictionary* – under the Philistines says they were a sea people that invaded Egypt around 1188 BC.

[84] Quote taken from Dr. Arnold Fruchtenbaum's book, *The Footsteps of the Messiah*, chapter 4 page 99, available through Ariel Ministries or on the web at http://www.ariel.org.

COMMENTARY

85 Biblical examples of mount, mountain, or mountains alluding to leaders, governments or hierarchies: Daniel 2:35, 45, Micah 4:7, Zechariah 4:7, Revelation 17:9-10.

86 Other references to the Glorious Land are located in Daniel 8:9, 11:16.

87 Information about Ukraine's missing nuclear weapons accessed on the Internet on 7/9/11 in an article called "Iranian Nuclear-Capable Cruise Missile Threat." Linked on the web at http://theneinblog.blogspot.com/2008/05/iranian-nuclear-capable-cruise-missile.html

88 Articles about Russia's missing nuclear devices were accessed via the Internet on 7/10/11 at the following links: http://nuclearweaponarchive.org/News/Lebedbomb.html, http://www.freerepublic.com/focus/news/747969/posts

89 Reuters article called "IAEA Gets Info on Possible Iran Military Work," points out IAEA concern about Iran's nuclear aspirations. Article accessed on the Internet on 7/9/11 at this link: http://www.reuters.com/article/2011/02/25/us-nuclear-iran-idUSTRE71O4RC20110225. http://www.eurasiareview.com/25112011-iaea-report-on-iran-storm-before-the-lull-analysis/ accessed as of 12/2/11 over the Internet

90 Information accessed over Internet on 7/9/11 at this link http://www.freerepublic.com/focus/f-news/2649457/posts "Pakistan Makes 2 Nuclear Weapons Available to Saudi Arabia.

91 OPEC members collectively hold 79% of world crude oil reserves and 44% of the world's crude oil production, affording them considerable control over the global market. Information accessed over the Internet on 7/9/11 at this link: http://en.wikipedia.org/wiki/OPEC

92 Strait of Hormuz information gathered from the Internet on 7/911 at this link: http://www.freerepublic.com/focus/f-news/2056412/posts

93 Information about Egypt closing off the Straits of Tiran was accessed from the Internet on 8/31/11 at this link: http://en.wikipedia.org/wiki/Six-Day_War

94 More information regarding the different theologies between Shias and Sunnis can be obtained over the Internet as of 9/1/11 at this link: http://islam.about.com/cs/divisions/f/shia_sunni.htm

95 U.S. States Area and Ranking accessed on the Internet on July 8, 2011 at this link: http://www.enchantedlearning.com/usa/states/area.shtml

96 Information about Josephus connecting Magog with the Scythians was collected from "The Old Testament Volume" of the *New Commentary on the Whole Bible*—Based on the classic commentary of Jamieson, Fausset, and Brown. It can be located in the commentary regarded with Ezekiel 38.

97 Information accessed from the Internet on 7/8/11 at this link: http://en.wikipedia.org/wiki/Scythians

98 Author recommended books and / or articles, and / or videos presentations covering Ezekiel 38 are *Northern Storm Rising* by Dr. Ron Rhodes; *Epicenter* by Joel Rosenberg; *The Magog Invasion and the The Alternative View to the Magog Invasion* by Dr. Chuck Missler; and *The Footsteps of the Messiah* by Dr. Arnold Fruchtenbaum.

99 *Northern Storm Rising* – Russia, Iran, And the Emerging End-Times Military Coalition Against Israel - Page 159 under "The Burial of Enemy Bodies for Seven Months (Ezekiel 39:11-12,14-16) Published by Harvest House - Copyright 2008. Authored by Dr. Ron Rhodes.

100 WND article accessed from the Internet on 7/26/11 at this link: http://www.wnd.com/?pageId=123758#ixzz1TEQE1McS

101 The DOHS operating budget for 2011 was $98.5 billion according to this Internet link accessed on 7/27/11: http://en.wikipedia.org/wiki/United_States_Department_of_Homeland_Security

COMMENTARY

102 "NYPD Pioneers New Dirty Bomb Detection System" article accessed on the Internet on 7/29/11 at this link: http://apnews.myway.com/article/20110729/D9OP0RTG0.html

103 "Dirty bomb threat reported on the Internet by CBS New York on September 9, 2011" at this link: http://newyork.cbslocal.com/2011/09/09/times-square-could-be-target-of-dirty-bomb-sources-say-police-on-heightened-alert/

104 Read more about CDC and WHO concerns about the Swine Flu of 2009 at this internet link accessed on 7/26/2011 at: http://www.cdc.gov/h1n1flu/

105 Information gathered over the Internet on 7/26/11 at this link: http://news.sky.com/skynews/Home/UK-News/Swine-Flu-Vaccines-Hampton-School-Closes-As-Govt-Orders-90-Million-Vaccines-To-Fight-H1N1-Virus/Article/200905315282480

106 The UK has approximately 61,838 million residents, according to this Internet website accessed on 7/26/11 at: http://www.google.com/publicdata/explore?ds=d5bncppjof8f9_&met_y=sp_pop_totl&idim=country:GBR&dl=en&hl=en&q=population+of+britain

107 Japanese Trend Shop information collected from the Internet on 7/26/11 at this link: http://www.japantrendshop.com/japanese-face-mask-protect-against-swine-flu-in-fashion-p-503.html

108 List of top ten deadly diseases can be accessed on the internet as of 7/26/11 at this link: http://www.toptenz.net/top-10-deadly-viruses.php

109 Khomeini coined the term for America as the Great Satan. Information gathered from the Internet on 7/26/11 at this link: http://en.wikipedia.org/wiki/Great_Satan

110 More information on the fundamental tenets of Islam can be obtained from the Internet at this link, which was accessed by author on 7/26/11. http://www.vexen.co.uk/religion/islam_unbelievers.html

111 Quote taken from Internet on 7/26/11 at this link: accessed by author on 7/26/11. http://www.vexen.co.uk/religion/islam_unbelievers.html

112 Regarding Jeroboam's superintendent position appointed by Solomon see 1 Kings 11:26-28.

113 Jeremiah 25:10-11, and 29:10 predicted that seventy-years of Babylonian captivity would burden the Jews.

114 Chuck Missler writes about the subject of Christopher Columbus's possible Jewish heritage at this Internet link, which was author accessed on 7/30/11 here: http://www.khouse.org/articles/1996/109/print/

115 This information was gathered from the Internet on September 14, 2011 at this link: http://www.jewishfederationpittsburgh.org/page.aspx?id=148359

116 Dr. David Reagan comments copied from an article accessed on 7/30/11 from the Internet at this site link: http://www.raptureready.com/featured/reagan/dr10.html

117 DOMA definition taken from the Internet on 10/22/11 at this link: http://en.wikipedia.org/wiki/Defense_of_Marriage_Act

118 *Huffington Post* quote about DOMA was taken from the Internet on 10/22/11 at this link: http://www.huffingtonpost.com/2011/02/23/obama-doma-unconstitutional_n_827134.html

119 The widely listened to Christian radio broadcaster named Harold Camping predicted the rapture would occur on May 21, 2011. Accessed on the Internet on 6/18/11 at http://en.wikipedia.org/wiki/Harold_Camping

120 Psalm 83:4 says, They have said, "Come, and let us cut them off from being a nation, That the name of Israel may be remembered no more."

121 Genesis 12:1-3

122 Romans 1:16

123 This Fruchtenbaum interview was hosted by the author and can be accessed on the web at http://prophecyupdateradio.blogspot.com/2010/01/by-bill-salus-fruchtenbaum-salus.html as of 2/4/2011.

124 Wikipedia definition accessed on the Internet on 6/22/11 at this link: http://en.wikipedia.org/wiki/Supersessionism

125 Internet sites researched on Sharm el-Sheikh terror attack as of 9/14/11 were: http://news.bbc.co.uk/2/hi/middle_east/4709491.stm. And http://newsone.com/newsone-original/casey-gane-mccalla/10-terror-attacks-post-911/. And http://en.wikipedia.org/wiki/2005_Sharm_el-Sheikh_attacks

126 Information gathered from the internet regarding the natural gas line attack in the Sinai was retrieved on 9/14/11 at this link: http://articles.cnn.com/2011-02-05/world/egypt.pipeline_1_gas-pipeline-natural-gas-sabotage?_s=PM:WORLD. And regarding the credible threat to Israel's border, see this internet site: http://www.cbn.com/cbnnews/insideisrael/2011/August/Israel-Oks-Deployment-of-Egyptian-Troops-in-Sinai/

127 The full gospel requires the sacrificial death and the resurrection. This is explained in 1 Corinthians 15:3-4 "For I delivered to you first of all that which I also received: that Christ died for our sins according to the Scriptures, and that He was buried, and that He rose again the third day according to the Scriptures.

128 Rankings of Middle East armies accessed from the Internet on 7/6/11 at this link: http://www.globalfirepower.com/ Israel ranked #11, Pakistan #15, Egypt #17, Iran# 18, Saudi Arabia #24, Syria #34, Iraq #38, Afghanistan #40, Lebanon #42.

129 This section is located in Chapter 20 "The Gentiles in the Messianic Kingdom." Specifically read pages 497-515 of Dr. Fruchtenbaum's book called the *Footsteps of the Messiah*, revised edition.

130 The Ezekiel 30 usages regarding the Egyptian war casualties, may apply to the timing of the Antichrist when he invades Egypt later in Daniel 11:42-43.

131 The modern day Jewish State refers to the Israel existing as of the authoring of this statement on July 4, 2011.

132 The Genesis 15:18 quote was taken from the New King James Version.

133 Joshua chapters 15-17.

134 Christ returns to set up His 1,000 year messianic kingdom as per Revelation 20:4, Matthew 24:30.

135 Gush Dan is the world's most populated Jewish area, according to information gathered from the Internet on 7/5/11 at http://en.wikipedia.org/wiki/American_Jews

136 Distance between Red Sea and Tel Aviv is 422 miles according to this (True Knowledge) Internet site accessed on 7/5/11 http://www.trueknowledge.com/q/distance_between_tel_aviv_and_red_sea

137 Internet information accessed on 7/5/11 at this link: http://www.weathernotebook.org/transcripts/2005/06/02.php

138 Information about the Transjordan memorandum can be researched at this Internet site as of 9/14/11http://en.wikipedia.org/wiki/Transjordan_memorandum

139 *Tamar One* value estimate obtained from the Internet on 9/14/11 at this link: http://www.businessweek.com/globalbiz/content/jan2009/gb20090119_996007.htm

[140] Estimated value of *Leviathan* natural gas reserves was obtained from the Internet on 9/14/11 at this link: http://www.haaretz.com/print-edition/news/leviathan-natural-gas-reserve-said-worth-90-billion-1.334143.

[141] These populations are all listed in Ezekiel 38:13. Some believe the "merchants of Tarshish" represents Great Britain, and their "young lions," the United States, Canada, and Australia. These are countries that were once colonized by Great Britain.

[142] The modern day Jewish State, refers to the Israel existing as of the authoring of this statement on July 4, 2011.

[143] Quote accessed from the Internet on 7/6/11 at this link: http://www.ynetnews.com/articles/0,7340,L-3596428,00.html

[144] Quote accessed from the Internet on 7/6/11 at this link: http://www.ynetnews.com/articles/0,7340,L-3598705,00.html

[145] Quote accessed from the Internet on 7/6/11 at this link: http://www.nytimes.com/2005/10/26/world/africa/26iht-iran.html

[146] Information accessed from the Internet on 7/6/11 at this link: http://abcnews.go.com/US/wireStory?id=11450601

[147] Jacob Prasch is the founder of Moriel Ministries. He and I occasionally speak at prophecy conferences together.

[148] Isaiah 19:18 calls one city in Egypt the "City of Destruction," in the New King James Version.

[149] Data rounded from the Internet on 8/1/11 at this link: http://www.jewishvirtuallibrary.org/jsource/Judaism/jewpop.html

[150] Temple Institute blueprints for temple located on Internet as of 8/2/11 here: http://www.templeinstitute.org/blueprints-for-the-holy-temple.htm

[151] Temple vessels and vestments can be viewed on the Internet as of 8/2/11 at this link: http://www.templeinstitute.org/gallery.htm

[152] Sanhedrin reconvened in 2005 can be researched on the Internet as of 8/2/11 at this link: http://www.heisnear.com/Sanhedrin.html

[153] Information about priestly garments accessed from the Internet on 8/2/11 at this link: http://www.templeinstitute.org/archive/03-07-08.htm

[154] Information about high priest's crown accessed from Internet on 8/2/11 at this link http://www.templeinstitute.org/archive/07-12-07.htm:

[155] Information on percentage of orthodox Israeli Jews collected on 8/2/11 at this Internet link: http://en.wikipedia.org/wiki/Orthodox_Judaism

[156] *New American Standard Exhaustive Concordance* translates the Hebrew word of sachar to mean "customers" in Ezekiel 27:12,16,18, 21.

[157] Genesis 12 2-3, 15:18, and 22:17 discuss Abraham's great nation and eternal descendants.

[158] Revelation 13:16 says "He causes all, both small and great, rich and poor, free and slave, to receive a mark on their right hand or on their foreheads."

[159] Rapture Ready (www.raptureready.com), Rapture Forums (www.raptureforums.com), and The Pre-Trib Research Center (www.pre-trib.org).

[160] Jim Tetlow's entire article about the rapture can be read at this Internet site as of 8/15/2011, http://www.eternal-productions.org/PDFS/articles/Rapture.pdf

[161] The church as the bride of Christ is identified in Matthew 25, Ephesians 5, and Revelation 21 and 22.

[162] Chuck Missler article accessed from the Internet on 8/12/11 at: http://www.khouse.org/articles/2003/449/.

[163] Definition of inter-dimensional can be found over the Internet as of 8/16/11 at this link http://en.wikipedia.org/wiki/Interdimensional_hypothesis. The definition of inter-dimensional is from the interdimensional hypothesis (IDH or IH), also called the extradimensional hypothesis (EDH), and is an advanced theory by Jacques Vallée that says unidentified flying objects (UFOs) and related events involve visitations from other "realities" or "dimensions" that coexist separately alongside our own.

[164] *Merriam-Webster's* online dictionary defines naturalism as: a theory denying that an event or object has a supernatural significance; specifically: the doctrine that scientific laws are adequate to account for all phenomena. This definition was accessed over the Internet on 8/22/11 at http://www.merriam-webster.com/dictionary/naturalism.

[165] More information on the twilight zone found on the Internet on 8/17/11 at this link http://en.wikipedia.org/wiki/Rod_Serling

[166] Quote ascertained from the Internet on 8/15/11 at this site http://www.checktheevidence.co.uk/Disclosure/Web%20Pages/www.presidentialufo.com/jimmy.htm

[167] Regarding Chuck Missler's background in the intelligence community, read on the Internet as of 8/11/11 at this link http://www.worldviewweekend.com/worldview-times/bio.php?authorid=88

[168] Missler also talks about the highly classified UFO subject on the "Watchers Two" DVD, which was produced by L.A. Marzulli in 2011. Watchers Two is available over the Internet as of 8/11/11 at www.lamarzulli.net

[169] Information about UFO classification can be gathered over the Internet as of 8/14/11 at this link: http://www.checktheevidence.co.uk/Disclosure/Web%20Pages/www.presidentialufo.com/jimmy.htm

[170] Panspermia definition gathered from the Internet on 8/11/11 at this link http://dictionary.reference.com/browse/panspermia.

[171] Francis Crick on Panspermia was referenced from the Internet on 10/10/11 at this link http://en.wikipedia.org/wiki/Panspermia:

[172] New Age explanation for the rapture copied from the Internet on 8/17/11 at: http://www.redmoonrising.com/newage.htm. Barbara Marciniak is an internationally acclaimed trance channel. Information about her was obtained from the Internet on 8/16/11 at: http://www.pleiadians.com/

[173] Quote was copied on 8/17/11 from the Internet link: http://www.eternal-productions.org/PDFS/articles/Rapture%20-%20A%20Counterfeit%20Explanation.pdf. (Taken from Chapter Nine of *Alien Encounters*, by Chuck Missler and Mark Eastman, Koinonia House, Coeur d'Alene, ID, 1997). Used with permission.

[174] Dr. Thomas Ice, the co-founder of the Pre-Trib Research Group writes about this and his article can accessed on the Internet as of 8/17/11 at this link: http://www.according2prophecy.org/hsrap.html

[175] Quote taken from page 94 of *The Invisible War* authored by Donald Grey Barnhouse and accessed from the Internet on 8/21/11 at this link: http://books.google.com/books?id=7QKfVvCeXe8C&pg=PA94&lpg=PA94&dq=invisible+war+three+wills+god+satan+man+barnhouse&source=bl&ots=t0glaaJu8X&sig=8PBO8PEvO3XIisTrv7RImzPZBxo&hl=en&ei=vJFRTuXDBO

COMMENTARY

TiAKeoJht&sa=X&oi=book_result&ct=result&resnum=3&sqi=2&ved=0CCsQ6AEwAg#v=one page&q&f=false

[176] Information about the Jim Tetlow and Brad Myers audio drama, *The Coming Global Transformation*, can be obtained as of 8/25/11 on the Internet at this link: http://www.eternal-productions.org/

[177] World and Christian statistics gathered from the Internet on 8/15/11 at: http://en.wikipedia.org/wiki/List_of_religious_populations

[178] Christian statistics taken from the Internet on 8/15/11 at this link: http://christianity.about.com/od/denominations/p/christiantoday.htm.

[179] Scriptures supporting the statement that unbelievers are not sanctified by believing family members are: Matthew 12:48-49, 19:29, Mark 3:32-34, 10:29-30, Luke 12:51-53, 14:26, 18:29-30.

[180] John 3:16 and John 14:6 substantiate this statement.

[181] Nathan Jones video is available at http://www.lamblion.com/articles/articles_rapture2.php as of 9/26/2011.

[182] Supporting passages attesting to this claim are, Daniel 7:23, Revelation 13: 7, 16-18, and 1 John 5:19.

[183] Revelation 17:15 identifies the many waters as peoples, multitudes, nations, and tongues.

[184] 1 Corinthians 15:51-52 and 1 Thessalonians 4:15-18.

[185] Left behind is a term popularized for those remaining on Earth after the rapture, in the apocalyptic fiction series by Tim LaHaye and Jerry Jenkins.

[186] Name definitions primarily collected from *Easton's Bible Dictionary*, and *Holman Bible Dictionary*.

[187] Regarding the mystery: Romans 11:25, Ephesians 3:3-6. Regarding the grafting in: Romans 11:17-24.

[188] Some Scriptures connecting the indwelling of the Holy Spirit with believers in Christ in relationship to the New Covenant are: 1 Corinthians 6:19, Romans 8:9-11.

[189] Luke 22:20 connects the blood of Christ with the New Covenant.

[190] More information about the connection of circumcision and the Abrahamic Covenant can be obtained over the Internet as of 10/1/11 at this link: http://www.thirdmill.org/files/english/html/th/TH.h.Glodo.Signs.1.html

[191] Revelation 14:4 identifies the 144,000 as "Firstfruits."

[192] Pertinent "My people Israel" passages are Ezekiel 38:14,16, Ezek. 39:7, Ezek. 25:14, Ezek. 36:8,12, Hosea 1:10, Romans 9:26

# Revelation Road

# Appendices

# Appendix 1
## The Final Century—Christian
## Survival versus Pagan Revival

Behold, I stand at the door, and knock: if any man hear my voice, and open the door, I will come in to him, and will sup with him, and he with me. (Revelation 3:20, KJV)

This appendix opens with the well-known quote from Christ to the "lukewarm" Christian church of Laodicea.[1] Christ warns of a time when the professing church will position Him outside its door as an ordinary stranger rather than its extraordinary Savior. This precarious end-times placement outside church confines causes Christ to long from His exterior location for either a soothing "cold" drink, be it a hot day, or a "hot" meal should a cold night be in store—both equally satisfying. Conversely, He receives a lukewarm reception, which neither quenches His thirst nor satiates His appetite. As this final twenty-first century commences, do we see Christianity simmering down to this undesired temperature? Will a "lukewarm" Christian condition push Christ outside its door, making room for a pagan spiritual revival?

Three themes are developed in this opening paragraph that will characterize the content of this appendix. First is the possibility that this is likely the final century on this present earth's timeline. Second is the genuine concern that Christianity is faltering toward apostasy in these last days. Lastly is the likelihood that a "lukewarm" Christian religion invites the revival of paganism, which is loosely defined as the practice of false, polytheistic religious practices by humanity's heathen populations.

## Part 1—The Final Century

The Bible, in addition to several other religious books, identifies an expiration date on this present earth's timeline. Like the Bible, these other books tend to profess that divine judgment is forthcoming and that a new era filled with a brighter future will ensue in the aftermath. Could this be the final century? Are all the prophetic signs falling into place, encouraging end-time apocalyptic thinking?

Judaism, Christianity, and Islam, listed in the order of their religious origin, advocate that world judgment is coming on the nearby horizon and that this reckoning will commence and conclude at the end of time. These three predominant world religions believe in the monotheistic worship of a God, which separates them from Hinduism, Buddhism, and other alternative New Age religions that generally encourage the worship of self as a god among other gods. (These latter types of polytheistic religions will be dealt with in Part 3 of this appendix, since they will likely also play a predominate part in the ecumenical religious embrace of the end times.)

Christian eschatologists like me are becoming increasingly convinced that humanity has been thrust beyond the point of no return into the last days. The prophetic signs reinforcing our views are abundantly clear. Scholars today are hard-pressed to locate even a single prophecy—out of the myriad of Bible prophecies remaining to be fulfilled—that couldn't occur in the very near future. A few examples are listed below.

- *A climactic concluding Arab-Israeli war.* Psalm 83 foretells of an Arab confederacy comprised of Palestinians, Syrians, Saudis, Egyptians, Lebanese, Jordanians, and likely their terrorist bedfellows, the Hezbollah, Hamas, Al-Qaeda, and more. In my book, *Isralestine, the Ancient Blueprints of the Future Middle East*,[2] I write extensively about this prophecy and its fulfillment. This prophecy could easily be fulfilled in the next one to two decades.

- *An invasion of Israel.* Ezekiel 38 and 39 tell of the last-days, Russian-Iranian led, nuclear equipped consortium of nine populations that comes to invade the Jewish State of Israel. Today, Russia and Iran have become the best of national friends. Russia has helped Iran develop nuclear technologies and Iran has expressed a desire to "wipe Israel off the map"![3] (Joel Rosenberg has written an excellent book, *Epicenter 2:0: Why Current Rumblings in the Middle East Will Change Your Future*,[4] detailing the Ezekiel invasion.) This prophecy will likely occur in the aftermath of the Psalm 83 event, according to my assessments, and it could also easily occur in the early decades of this twenty-first century.

- *The mark of the Beast.* Revelation 13 issues the infamous "666" prophecy, which is also referred to as the "mark of the Beast" (Antichrist). This prophecy declares that no one will be able to buy or sell unless he or she receives a mark upon the right hand or forehead. Many eschatologists believe that about 2,000 years ago the apostle John attempted to describe a type of advanced computer technology that exists today. This prophecy, which seems to predict humanity's ability to conduct cashless commerce, was impossible at the time it was written, but is a definite possibility today. A one-world order, coupled with a one-world banking system, could evolve out of the current world economic crisis and such a system could effortlessly segue into the fulfillment of this prophecy.

- *Two witnesses.* Revelation 11 informs us that a day will come when two evangelical witnesses will be crucified by the Antichrist in Jerusalem for their Christian testimony. We are told that they will lie dead in the streets, on full visual display, for a period of three and one-half days. The prophecy declares that the entire world will see their dead bodies lay waste in the street. In the nineteenth century, atheists would argue that this prophecy could never happen and that therefore, the Bible must be errant. However, in this century—with satellite television technologies—the whole world will be able to witness this prophetic spectacle. To international astonishment, these two witnesses will rise from the dead and ascend into heaven outside the range of television viewing.

These prophetic examples are just a few among a litany of others that suggest biblically these are the last days, and that this is likely the final century. Extra-biblical sources suggest similar apocalyptic scenarios are about to occur, such as the growing number of those who believe the end of the world will occur in the year 2012, with the conclusion of the Mayan calendar. Many Muslims, like Iran's President Mahmoud Ahmadinejad, are predicting the nearby coming of the Mahdi, the Islamic Messiah who is foretold to arrive at the end of time. Furthermore, as the world entered its first threshold decade of this century it was greeted by turbulent events sequenced in fairly rapid succession, evidencing the disturbing possibility that this is the concluding century. Listed below are a few examples:

- The Al-Qaeda terrorist attacks of September 11, 2001, that toppled the twin towers of the World Trade Center in New York City.

- The Asian tsunami of December 26, 2004, which was generated by a magnitude 9.1 earthquake in the Indian Ocean and which estimates suggest killed 225,000 people in eleven countries. This was the deadliest natural disaster in recorded history.

- Hurricane Katrina in August 2005, which ranks as the costliest hurricane in American history.

- The financial crisis of 2007-2009 that caused the collapse of numerous major banking and financial institutions worldwide.

- The 7.0 magnitude Port-au-Prince, Haiti earthquake on January 12, 2010, which according to Haitian government reports killed an estimated 316,000, injured 300,000, and left about 1,000,000 people homeless.[5]

- The British Petroleum (BP) *Deep Water Horizon* oil spill on April 20, 2010, that lasted until July 15, 2010, and was considered the world's largest oil spill.

- The 9.0 magnitude Japan earthquake off the Pacific coast of Tohoku on March 11, 2011. This quake generated a tsunami that killed approximately 20,000[6] and severely damaged several nuclear reactors. Japan said the cost of the earthquake and tsunami could hit 25 trillion yen ($309 billion), double the Kobe quake (1995) and nearly four times more than Hurricane Katrina.[7]

- The 2011 Arab Spring, which witnessed Arab protests morph into revolts in many Middle East and North African countries. Several governments collapsed, leaving the regional geopolitics extremely volatile.

Add to this list the 2006 Israeli-Hezbollah conflict, the 2008-2009 Israeli "Operation Cast Lead" campaign into Gaza, and the burgeoning UFO phenomena, and we have further cause to consider this century as the time of the end. When asked to "tell us when these things will be" in Matthew 24:3, alluding to the end of this present world as we know it, Jesus replied, "For nation will rise against nation, and kingdom against kingdom, and there will be famines and earthquakes in various places: all this is but the beginning of the *birth-pangs*" (Matthew 24:7-8, RSV; emphasis added).

Eschatologists tend to agree that "nation" already rose "against nation" in World Wars I and II, fulfilling the first part of this prophecy. It is also commonly understood that "kingdom" coming "against kingdom" refers to regionalized conflicts[8] and those also have been and are still occurring in the aftermath of the world wars. Lastly, significant earthquakes spontaneously shaking assorted world locations have become an increasingly regular phenomenon. Jesus said these events would characterize creation in convulsion as it nears the time of the end. By labeling these events as "birth pangs," Christ leaves humanity with an all-important clue: like the pregnancy of an expectant mother who experiences more intense and frequent contractions the closer she comes to her time of delivery, the closer this present world comes to its end point will be characterized by intense and frequent military conflicts and natural calamities. As stated earlier, two major Middle East war prophecies, Psalm 83 and Ezekiel 38-39, are likely to occur in rapid succession soon.

# Part 2—Christian Survival

If this is the final century, then what role will Christianity play within it? Will it survive and thrive in these final few decades, serving as a vibrant venue by which humanity can come to Christ, or is it destined for a less fertile future? According to prophecy, there appears to be both a yes and no answer. Yes, it survives and thrives through a sincere, Bible-believing base that will be "hot" on fire for the Lord. Purportedly, this Christian contingency continues to preach the good news fervently from Jerusalem unto the uttermost parts of the world! However, against the backdrop of this evangelistic component emerges an increasingly lackadaisical, "lukewarm" element that spirals deeply downward into apostasy.[9]

These two groups seem to coexist up until the point of the rapture, after which only the latter group remains. For the purposes of this appendix, these two groups will be called Philadelphia and Laodicea, in association with two of the seven churches described in the book of Revelation. Philadelphia, which means "brotherly love," represents—again, for the purposes of this appendix—true, born-again Christian believers who overcome the last-days tendency toward the lukewarmness that will characterize the Laodicean faction of the Christian church.

For readers not familiar with the powerful rapture event, it is described in the passages that follow, which tell of a time when Jesus Christ returns in a nanosecond to *retrieve* His true, born-again believers miraculously in the air, and to *receive* them into the heavenly abode:

> Behold, I tell you a mystery: We shall not all sleep, but we shall all be changed in a moment, in the twinkling of an eye, at the last trumpet. For the trumpet will sound, and the dead will be raised incorruptible, and we shall be changed. For this corruptible must put on incorruption, and this mortal *must* put on immortality. So when this corruptible has put on incorruption, and this mortal has put on immortality, then shall be brought to pass the saying that is written: "*Death is swallowed up in victory.*" (1 Corinthians 15:51-54)

> For this we say to you by the word of the Lord, that we who are alive *and* remain until the coming of the Lord will by no means precede those who are asleep [deceased Christian believers]. For the Lord Himself will descend from heaven with a shout, with the voice of an archangel, and with the trumpet of God. And the dead in Christ will rise first. Then we who are alive *and* remain shall be caught up together with them in the clouds to meet the Lord in the air. And thus we shall always be with the Lord. Therefore comfort one another with these words. (1 Thessalonians 4:15-18)

There are conflicting opinions as to the timing of this event. Some suggest this event is imminent, which means it will occur at any moment and likely before the tribulation period; others teach that it will occur either at the end or mid-point of the tribulation period.[10] Regardless of the reader's perspective, the event will likely occur in this final century, and in the aftermath the "lukewarm" Laodicean apostates will likely be those left behind. Furthermore, the occurrence of this event should severely impact the way the world thinks and operates in the minimal time remaining in this final century.

One of the several ways scholars confidently predict the condition of the Christian church in its final stage of development is through the prophetic interpretation of the seven letters to the seven churches in Revelation 2 and 3. Many eschatologists teach that these letters were partially intended to chronologically order the seven stages of church development throughout its earthly existence.[11] In essence, these letters include an intrinsic prophetic value intended to offer more than just contemporary instruction to the specific seven churches existing at the time of issuance. Fortunately, today's experts have the opportune advantage of looking back upon church history, which enables them to accurately make this association.

Below is an outline of the chronological development of the Christian church in accordance with the blueprints of the seven letters in Revelation.[12] This outline reveals that we are living in the final days of church development, the "days of Laodicea."

## Ephesus (Revelation 2:1-7; AD 40-150)

The first stage of Christianity was primarily an apostolic period. Christians operated in compliance with Matthew 28:18-20. It was a time of reconciliation wherein the disciples successfully preached the good news gospel of Jesus Christ outwardly from Jerusalem into the surrounding Gentile populations of the world. This was Christianity in its infancy, and as a religion it was rapidly spreading throughout the broader Middle East region and into the greater Roman Empire.

## Smyrna (Revelation 2:8-11; AD 100-312)

This segment of church history was characterized by a period of persecution. Rome was conducting wide-scale Christian executions in an attempt to prevent the growth and spread of the religion. Martyrdom was the unfortunate predicament forced upon the church by the Roman Empire during the Smyrna era. However, to Rome's chagrin, the persecutions actually bolstered the growth of Christianity. Christians dying for their faith caught the attention of multitudes that in turn fixated their focus upon Christ as their Savior.

## Pergamos (Revelation 2:12-17; AD 300-600)

The period of Pergamos, meaning "mixed marriage" in Greek, is associated with the paganization of the church. As the Roman Empire began its decline, it embraced Christianity as its state religion. This served two primary purposes. First, it began to fill deepening political rifts developing in the deteriorating Roman government; and secondly, it facilitated the survival of faltering pagan religious practices by cleverly integrating and incubating them into Christianity. Also, the martyrdom period of Smyrna that experienced Christianity flourishing became problematic for Rome. Each martyr's death brought new and renewed strength among fellow Christians. Thus, Rome adopted the attitude, "If you can't beat them [kill all the Christians], join them." As time passed this Roman attitude eventually led many Christians to reciprocate and romanticize Romanism, and to believe that "when in Rome, do as the Romans do."[13]

During the Pergamos period, Christianity essentially was asked to compromise itself—and in so doing, create an end to the persecutions occurring during the Smyrna stage. By marrying up with Roman paganism, Christianity was insured its survival. Shortly thereafter, ancient Roman religious practices began to permeate and adulterate the church. Christian traditions, such as Christmas trees and Yule logs, can likely be traced to this Pergamos period of church history.

## Thyatira (Revelation 2:18-29; AD 600-Tribulation)

This church is commonly thought to represent the Roman Catholic Church, which evolved out of the Pergamos period. Thyatira tends to be a works-based, rather than a faith-based church. In so doing it emphasizes the religious rather than relational importance between God and humanity. Revelation 2:22 declares that an apostate element within Thyatira will exist in the end times and be cast into the "sickbed" of the great tribulation period. (More on this topic is explored in the appendix called *The Fallible Assumption of Mary*).

## Sardis (Revelation 3:1-6; AD 1500-Tribulation)

This period is best described as the Protestant Reformation; however, it lacked true transformation. Salvation through faith rather than works was here reintroduced within Christianity; however, the Reformation continued to be more about religion than about a personal relationship with God.

## Philadelphia (Revelation 3:7-13; AD 1800-Rapture)

Powerful, worldwide missionary movements beginning in the mid-1600s characterize the period of Philadelphia. In accordance with Matthew 28:18-20, this church answered the call to the "Ministry of Reconciliation." The Philadelphian period concludes with the rapture. (More will be said about this church later in this appendix.)

## Laodicea (Revelation 3:14-22; AD 1900-Tribulation)

This church began in the twentieth century and will continue on into the seven-year tribulation period. This last-days church is guilty of preaching a social rather than a spiritual gospel. (More on this church later in this appendix.) Many eschatologists believe that the world hourglass has made its final turn and that the church, alas, has entered into the "days of Laodicea." However, they also believe that up until the rapture, the Philadelphian component still will preside in the Christian equation. As such, it is important to interpret through the prophetic lens the key passages contained in the pertinent sixth and seventh letters to the seven churches that validate this scholarly viewpoint.

## Philadelphia–The Sixth Letter

> And to the angel of the church in Philadelphia write, "These things says He who is holy, He who is true, *He who has the key of David, He who opens and no one shuts, and shuts and no one opens*: I know your works. *See, I have set before you an open door, and no one can shut it; for you have a little strength, have kept My word, and have not denied My name.* Indeed I will make *those* of the synagogue of Satan, who say they are Jews and are not, but lie—indeed I will make them come and worship before your feet, and to know that *I have loved you.* Because you have kept My command to persevere, *I also will keep you from the hour of trial* which shall come upon the whole world, to test those who dwell on the earth. Behold, I am coming quickly! Hold fast what you have, that no one may take your crown. He who overcomes, I will make him a pillar in the temple of My God, and he shall go out no more. I will write on him the name of My God and the name of the city of My God, the New Jerusalem, which comes down out of heaven from My God. And *I will write on him* My new name." (Revelation 3:7-13; emphasis added)

Definite contrasts are observable between the sixth and seventh letters. This letter to the church of Philadelphia evidences that it is a beloved contingent within Christianity that has an open missionary door to the international community. Furthermore, it is a believing population that will escape "the hour of trial which shall come upon the whole world." It is commonly taught that this "hour of trial" refers to the final seven-year tribulation period that concludes this present earth's timeline. Thus, this group will be removed sometime prior to the tribulation period. Its departure will likely be the result of the rapture event previously referenced.

As listed above in the chronological outline of church history, this group still effectively espouses the gospel today, throughout the nations of the world. Whereas the church of Philadelphia is loved and will escape the hour of trial, the church of Laodicea does not seem to share the similar blessings or the same fate. The seventh church letter below, to Laodicea, reveals a church component in need of repentance that disconnects from Christ, causing Him to vomit it out of His mouth.

## Laodicea—The Seventh Letter

> And to the angel of the church of the Laodiceans write, "These things says the Amen, the Faithful and True Witness, the Beginning of the creation of God: 'I know your works, that you are neither cold nor hot. I could wish you were cold or hot. So then, because *you are lukewarm, and neither cold nor hot, I will vomit you out of My mouth.* Because you say, "I am rich, have become wealthy, and have need of nothing"—and do not know that *you are wretched, miserable, poor, blind, and naked*—I counsel you to *buy from Me*

*gold refined in the fire*, that you may be rich; and white garments, that you may be clothed, *that* the shame of your nakedness may not be revealed; and anoint your eyes with eye salve, that you may see. *As many as I love, I rebuke and chasten.* Therefore be zealous and repent. Behold, *I stand* [outside] *at the door and knock.* If anyone hears My voice and opens the door, I will come in [from outside the door] to him and dine with him, and he with Me. To him who overcomes I will grant to sit with Me on My throne, as I also overcame and sat down with My Father on His throne. 'He who has an ear, let him hear what the Spirit says to the churches.'''" (Revelation 3:14-22; emphasis added)

As we can decipher from these telling passages, this last-days church component is deceived into thinking it is something that it is not. Laodicea believes that it is a prosperous church having need of nothing; conversely, Christ considers it "wretched, miserable, poor, blind, and naked." Furthermore, Christ encourages this church to abandon its prevailing problematic practices and purchase gold from Him that is refined through the fire. By the reference to gold refined through fire, Christ says that Laodicea is an impure and undisciplined church in severe need of repentance—a point further emphasized in the statement "*As many as I love, I rebuke and chasten.* Therefore be zealous and repent." (emphasis added)

This last-days group appears to dethrone Christ as Savior, minimize the value of the inerrant word of God, and enthrone itself instead. This makes the resurrected Jesus Christ ill, provoking Him to step outside of its confines in order to "vomit" this element of the church out of His mouth, after which He makes His way back to knock upon its door for one last salvation altar call to humanity. Christ located outside of the church is a severe positional change, as noted in Revelation 1:12-20, which describes the Savior as clearly located in the midst of the Christian church at its point of inception.

This illness illustration infers that unlike the church of Philadelphia, the preponderance of the church of Laodicea will not escape the tribulation period. Thus, this represents a relatively large portion within end-times Christianity that is not truly born again, which according to John 3:3-7 is a prerequisite condition of true belief and eternal salvation. This group professes to represent Christianity, but apparently ignores the required relationship between Christ and a true, born-again believer. Instead, members of this group likely turn Christianity into an emotional religious experience rather than a personal relationship between the individual soul and its Creator, which is the essence of true Christianity.

The prescription for eternal salvation is contained in the following passages and elsewhere in the Bible:

But what does it say? *"The word is near you, in your mouth and in your heart"* (that is, the word of faith which we preach): that if you confess with your mouth the Lord Jesus and believe in your heart that God has raised Him from the dead, you will be saved. For with the heart one believes unto righteousness, and with the mouth confession is made unto salvation. For the Scripture says, *"Whoever believes on Him will not be put to shame."* For there is no distinction between Jew and Greek, for the same Lord over all is rich to all who call upon Him. For *"whoever calls on the name of the LORD shall be saved."* (Romans 10:8-13; emphasis added)

Homosexual bishops, lesbian Methodist ministers, name-it-claim-it prosperity teaching pastors, and mega "emergent church" congregations further evidence that we have entered into the final period of Laodicea. Many of today's prominent preachers refuse to deliver sermons purposed to take sinners to the foot of the cross where Jesus died for their sins. Furthermore, God's greatest twentieth-century miracle, the reinstatement of the Jewish State of Israel, hardly gets an honorable mention from church pulpits any more.

In these turbulent, terror-filled times, the world ponders legitimate evangelical and eschatological questions about the significance of the sacrificial death and subsequent resurrection of Christ and the biblical relevance of modern-day Israel. Unfortunately, the Laodicean church component provides warm and fuzzy, feel-good-about-yourself teachings that fail to adequately address either of these sincere secular concerns. Instead, the Laodicean component favors a social gospel and agenda in an attempt to win humanity over. This is becoming epidemic and reveals that Christianity today often feels the need to take pew-filling matters into its own carnal hands, rather than modeling the Acts 2:46-47 church-building format.

Christianity is rapidly succumbing to the belief that it best grows through self-subscribed means whereby carnal methods of sustaining its congregational health and wealth are acceptable. It has indoctrinated the view that its survival is proportionate to its ability to successfully serve humanity's emotional rather than spiritual needs. This turnabout of church thinking segues well into Part 3 of this appendix, which is paganism—Christianity's recently revived competitor.

# Part 3—Pagan Revival

> Now the serpent [Satan] was more cunning than any beast of the field which the LORD God had made. And he said to the woman, "Has God indeed said, 'You shall not eat of every tree of the garden'?" And the woman said to the serpent, "We may eat the fruit of the trees of the garden; but of the fruit of the tree which *is* in the midst of the garden, God has said, 'You shall not eat it, nor shall you touch it, lest you die.'" Then *the serpent said* to the woman, "*You will not surely die*. For God knows that in the day you eat of it *your eyes will be opened*, and *you will be like God*, knowing good and evil." (Genesis 3:1-5; emphasis added)

When we discuss paganism, a safe starting location is in the garden of Eden about six thousand years ago. In the above Genesis 3 account we find that Satan encourages humanity to achieve its own godhead condition. He tells Eve that she can "be like God." Furthermore, he accuses God of being a liar; God had told Eve that should she be disobedient she would die, but Satan declared she "surely" would not "die." This episode lays the foundational groundwork for recognizing a fundamental difference between the monotheistic worship of God, the claimant creator of the universe, and the polytheistic worship of self as a god among a host of other gods.

Ultimately God was right, and Adam and Eve both died, and so has all of humanity since (barring the biblical exceptions of Enoch and Elijah, who were translated from

Earth into heaven without experiencing death). Therefore, Satan turns out to be the liar, which Christ poignantly clarifies in John 8:42-44.

In keeping with his lying persona, Satan had to continue along the same deceitful path and create concepts like karma, reincarnation, and Christ consciousness in order to cover up his original lie in the garden of Eden. Certainly humans die, but cleverly this most cunning serpent Satan had a logical explanation for the death phenomena. Eastern religions like Hinduism echo another ancient spiritual lie: that people reincarnate, rather than cease to exist, upon dying.

The cover-up lie probably sounded something like this: "You will not surely die; you shall reincarnate and come back again in another life." The truth according to Hebrews 9:27 is that man is appointed to die only once, not multiple times, as the theory of reincarnation espouses. Furthermore, the Hebrews passage declares that upon death man subsequently experiences judgment. To counteract this truth, the devil injected the "karmic clause" into his reincarnation fantasy.

As the web of lies became more deceptively complex, one lie building upon another, the ensuing cover-up likely went something like this: "You will not surely die and subsequently face God in final judgment; you will temporarily cross over and be evaluated by your good or bad previous life's deeds, at which point you will return to live and do better the next time." This is how karmic law correlates with reincarnation, according to Hinduism and several other offshoot New Age religions.

The goal of these polytheistic pagan religions like Buddhism, Hinduism, or their New Age counterparts is obtaining a utopian state of consciousness through a multitude of good works, compiled through a series of reincarnated lives. Buddhism's nirvana, Hinduism's bliss, or the New Ager's Christ consciousness is the end game of these spiritual sojourners. The prevalent teaching inherent in these assorted religions is the age-old garden lie that "you will be like God."

According to most of these religions, Jesus Christ obtained this utopian state of consciousness, and therefore so can you. This theology that nirvana, bliss, or Christ consciousness, which has become the modernized term for the godhead condition, is available to anyone and everyone plays well into Satan's end game. We are told in Isaiah 14:13-14 that Satan himself seeks to someday exalt his throne above all the stars (angels in biblical typology) of God and be like the most high, alluding to God. Furthermore, we are informed in Daniel 11:36 that Satan's seed, the Antichrist, will ultimately attempt to magnify himself above every god.

It is obvious that Satan is the primary source of inspiration for paganism and that the old "you will be like God" garden lie is resurfacing again in a New Age format. A quick query on your Internet's search engine for "New Age religions" coupled with "Christ consciousness" yields pages of evidence that the predominant New Age belief is that humanity can strive to obtain the utopian mental state of godhead. However, humanity's quest for spiritual satisfaction can be only be obtained via Jesus' statement, "I am the way, the truth, and the life. No one comes to the Father except through Me" (John 14:6).

The monotheistic religion of Christianity clearly teaches that there is a distinct difference between sinful humanity and its righteous Creator. According to the Bible, Adam and Eve and their offspring of humanity were created to worship God, not to become God. Jesus Christ declares that only through His personage, not His consciousness, can one even come to the heavenly Father, let alone worship Him. Thus, there are foundational differences between Christianity and paganism.

Part and parcel of the revival of paganism are the concerns that numerous end-times Bible prophecies allude to a strong, deluding deception that overtakes humanity, causing it to believe in what Scripture calls "the lie."[14] Mankind apparently becomes overwhelmed by powerful signs and lying wonders. Since Satan is a liar, these lying wonders should have his fingerprints all over them. Some writers and researchers, including Tom Horn, I.D.E. Thomas, Patrick Heron, L.A. Marzulli, Terry James, David Flynn, and a host of others have connected the UFO phenomena to this coming great deception.

All of the above is further complicated by the coming rapture and the harlot prophecy of Revelation 17. The rapture will be a powerful, world-changing event removing millions of born-again evangelical Christians from the earth. In the aftermath, the world will demand prompt and logical answers about what will have happened. This should open the door for the pagan perspective to be powerfully delivered. Many New Age channelers are already suggesting that the earth is about to be purged of the Christians by the gods and/or the aliens.

A common teaching about the harlot of Revelation 17 says she represents a one-world religious system that emerges onto the international scene during the lifetime of the Antichrist. This system ecumenically embraces all religions and amalgamates them into one universalistic format. With all true born-again Christians likely being previously raptured, this suggests that a pagan free-for-all will manifest about the time the world is deluded into believing "the lie" previously discussed.

# Summary

This century appears to be the final one, and it will be filled with powerful, prophetic, world-changing events. The rapture will likely occur; removing millions of Christians—and in the aftermath a pagan revival could easily overtake humanity. Remaining world religions such as Islam, Hinduism, Buddhism, New Ageism, and "lukewarm" Christianity will be invited to ecumenically embrace a similar spiritual vision. About that time, the dreaded Antichrist will emerge upon the world scene. Signs and lying wonders will accompany his beastly rise to power; ultimately, mankind will be overtaken by some great deceptive "lie." Powerful Middle East wars will be occurring prior to this or simultaneously, and humanity will be swept into the eye of the last-days storm.

Currently, the world appears to be going through a preparatory period for the above events. Christians should be watchful of the prophetic signs and utilize them to witness to a world that is about to be overwhelmed by pagan deception. God issued prophecy for this important purpose. By accurately foretelling the future, God has authenticated His sovereignty and equipped humanity with invaluable information. Twenty-first century Christians should be on the alert for the return of Christ in the rapture, the rise of paganism on the horizon, and every opportunity to preach the good news gospel to anyone who will listen in these days.

Time is of the essence and is running out. These are the last days, and the harvest field is increasingly bountiful. Christians can be certain that souls are searching for spiritual answers in these troubling times and that Satan is lifting up pagan systems with deceitful theologies to satiate their growing appetites.

Mankind tends to prefer the possibility that its individuals can obtain godhead over the reality that it is a collection of sinners in need of a Savior. Thus, Christianity has to know thoroughly, and deliver powerfully, the good news of Christ. These are the days of Laodicea, and the tendency to simmer the gospel message down to a lukewarm temperature must be resisted. The world is filled with itching ears seeking pleasing, socially spun, spiritual answers; however, Christians must rise to the occasion and take sinners back to the cross of crucifixion, where they can repent and receive forgiveness through the shed blood of Christ.

# Appendix 2
## The Three Types of Tribulation

Christ warned His disciples about three different types of tribulation in the world. He declared there would be General Tribulation, Christian Tribulation, and Great Tribulation.

## General Tribulation

> In the world you will have tribulation; but be of good cheer, I have overcome the world. (John 16:33)

Simply stated, general tribulation is the natural by-product of sinful people interacting with each other. Billions of non-Christians roaming about worldwide in pursuit of their own self-interests, independent of any input from the Bible or obligation to God's will, is, and has always been, a recipe for disaster. Take Adolph Hitler for example; he imposed his will upon Europe and six million Jews died in the process. He is one example inside an endless list of selfish others who caused many to suffer as a result of their own pursuits.

Child molesters ruin children's lives in pursuit of their sexual perversions. Adulterers destroy marriages and families. Thieves rob merchants of their livelihood. Islamic terrorists impose their will upon humanity by committing heinous acts under the banner of religion. These are a just a few examples of general tribulation. Christ instructed His believers to face general tribulation cheerfully as over-comers through faith in Him. Scripture teaches believers the following in that regard.

> I can do all things through Christ who strengthens me. (Philippians 4:13)

## Christian Tribulation

> And to the angel of the church in Smyrna write… "Do not fear any of those things which you are about to suffer. Indeed, the devil is about to throw *some* of you into prison, that you may be tested, and you will have tribulation ten days. Be faithful until death, and I will give you the crown of life." (Revelation 2:8,10)

> Then they will deliver you up to tribulation and kill you, and you will be hated by all nations for My name's sake. (Matthew 24:9)

The first passage in Revelation addressed to the church in Smyrna demonstrates the devil can create tribulation for Christians. The Merriam - Webster's online dictionary defines tribulation as "distress or suffering resulting from oppression or persecution;" also, "a trying experience." Satan and his fallen angelic cohorts intentionally create havoc for Christians in order to discredit and eliminate their witness in the world.

The apostle Paul described this process in Ephesians when he wrote;

> Finally, my brethren, be strong in the Lord and in the power of His might. Put on the whole armor of God, that you may be able to stand against the wiles of the devil. For we do not wrestle against flesh and blood, but against principalities, against powers, against the rulers of the darkness of this age, against spiritual *hosts* of wickedness in the heavenly *places*. (Ephesians 6:10-12)

The Matthew 24:9 passage above also evidences Christian tribulation. Christ warned that His disciples would be martyred and hated by the world because of their religious affiliation with Him. The growth and spread of Christianity was rooted in martyrdom during its first three centuries. Persecution continued to plague the church throughout various stages of its history. Even today, in places like Sudan, China, and much of the Islamic world, Christian tribulation and martyrdom continues to occur. For post-rapture believers accepting Christ in the gap or later during the tribulation period, this condition worsens worldwide, according to Revelation 6:9-11, 7:9-17, 20:4.

## Great Tribulation

This term shows up several times in the Bible to describe a specific period of time inside the seven-year tribulation period. Most scholars teach it is confined to the events contained in the second-half of the seven-years of tribulation. The final three and one-half years of great tribulation commence when the Antichrist enters into the Jewish Temple in Jerusalem and violates it causing a full cessation of Jewish worship.

> Therefore when you see the *'abomination of desolation,'* spoken of by Daniel the prophet, standing in the holy place" [Jewish Temple] (whoever reads, let him understand), then let those who are in Judea flee to the mountains. (Matthew 24:15-16)

> For then there will be *great tribulation*, such as has not been since the beginning of the world until this time, no, nor ever shall be. And unless those days were shortened, no flesh would be saved; but for the elect's sake those days will be shortened. (Matthew 24:21-22; emphasis added)

In Matthew 24:15-16 Christ issues a severe warning to the Jews living inside of Judea at the time the Antichrist enters into their temple and abominates it. He instructs them to flee to the mountains immediately when they witness this because "there will be great tribulation." By stating, "when you see the 'abomination of desolation,' spoken of by Daniel," He intentionally draws their attention to Daniel 9:27, expecting them to grasp the diabolical significance of the abominable event.

Christ alludes to an event that occurs in a future third Jewish temple. Although this temple doesn't presently exist, the priests are being identified and trained, their garments are being sewn, and the temple implements are being prepared. These facts suggest many religious Jews today eagerly anticipate the creation of this prophesied temple. The construction of this temple is presently hindered by the Arab – Israeli conflict.

Daniel 9:24 references seventy weeks comprised of seven-year periods. Daniel 9:25 tells us that sixty-nine of these seven-year cycles would exist between the command to restore and build Jerusalem until the Messiah would arrive. Jerusalem had been destroyed by the Babylonians in 586 BC.

Founder of Calvary Chapels, Chuck Smith, writes the following commentary regarding the historical understanding of Daniel's sixty-nine weeks:

> In the year 445 B.C., the commandment was finally given by Artaxerxes to Nehemiah to restore and rebuild Jerusalem. Earlier, Ahasuerus and the other Persian kings had given commandments to Ezra to go back and to rebuild the temple. But this prophecy was to be from the commandment to restore and rebuild Jerusalem.

> March 14, 445 B.C.... (The specific date) is an important date in history because according to the promise (Daniel 9:25)...from the time that commandment goes forth to restore and rebuild Jerusalem unto the Messiah the Prince will be seven sevens and sixty-two sevens, or sixty-nine seven-year cycles, or 483 years. And so from the year March 14, 445 B.C., according to the prediction here, the Messiah should have come in 483 years from the time of this commandment.

> And transposed into days, 483 times 360 would give you 173,880 days. And if you take and then work that out on our calendar, you find it comes out to the date April 6, 32 A.D.

Smith concludes that the 173,880 days ended on April 6, 32 AD, when Jesus presented Himself as the Messiah in Matthew chapter 21.[15] Some other scholars suggest the 173,880 days began at different times, but most agree that these days concluded during Christ's first advent. Regardless of the exact timing, the prevalent teaching among many dispensational Bible teachers today, including myself, is that the first sixty-nine weeks of years have passed and Daniel's final Seventieth week commences with the confirmation of the false covenant between the Antichrist and Israel described in Daniel 9:27.

> Then he [Antichrist] shall confirm a covenant with many [including Israel] for one [seven-year] week; [starting the tribulation period]. But in the middle of the week He shall bring an end to [animal] sacrifice and offering [which will be occurring inside the coming Jewish Temple at the time]. And on the wing of abominations shall be one who makes desolate, Even until the consummation, which is determined, Is poured out on the desolate. (Daniel 9:27)

Although Daniel 9:24 tells us the entire seventy weeks are for Daniel's Jewish people and their holy city of Jerusalem, it is the confirmation of the covenant that initiates the final seven-year clock ticking. Additionally, Daniel 9:27 describes the abominable event Christ alluded to in Matthew 24:15 and places its timing at the midpoint of his Seventieth week. Christ vociferously warned that "great tribulation" would occur in the aftermath of the "abomination of desolation."

The book of Revelation also references the "great tribulation" in two prophetic passages.

> Indeed I will cast her into a sickbed, and those who commit adultery with her into great tribulation, unless they repent of their deeds. (Revelation 2:22)

> So he said to me, "These are the ones who come out of the *great tribulation*, and washed their robes and made them white in the blood of the Lamb. Therefore they are before the throne of God, and serve Him day and night in His temple. And He who sits on the throne will dwell among them. They shall neither hunger anymore nor thirst anymore; the sun shall not strike them, nor any heat; for the Lamb who is in the midst of the throne will shepherd them and lead them to living fountains of waters. And God will wipe away every tear from their eyes." (Revelation 7:14-17; emphasis added)

# Appendix 3
## When Will Damascus be Destroyed?

elow is one of two appendices written by author Jim Tetlow that has been included inside Revelation Road. I obtained permission from Jim Tetlow to include his study about Damascus because he presents a fascinating non-dogmatic overview of what he believes the Bible declares about the future of Damascus.

## When Will Damascus be Destroyed? by Jim Tetlow

Damascus is the oldest continuously inhabited city in recorded history, dating back four thousand years to the time of Abraham (Genesis 14:15). It is Syria's capital, housing about four million people in or around its metropolitan areas. It is a strategic target for Israel because every known terrorist organization has a hub or headquarters located there. God's Word declares that Damascus will be destroyed in the last days. Will this occur before, during, or toward the end of the seven year tribulation period?

> Isaiah 17:1, 9: "The burden against Damascus. 'Behold, Damascus will cease from being a city, and it will be a ruinous heap.' . . . *In that day* his strong cities will be as a forsaken bough and an uppermost branch, which they left because of the children of Israel; and there will be desolation."

In the Bible, the expression "in that day" usually refers to "the day of the Lord" – a common phrase for the last days and specifically the tribulation period.[16] Sometimes though, the expression "in that day" or "the day of the Lord" encompasses the period from Israel's end-times re-gathering and extends all the way to the end of the Millennium (Isaiah 11; Micah 4; etc.). Therefore we need to look for additional clues to see if Scripture reveals the timing of Damascus's destruction.

> Isaiah 17:4 provides this insight: "In that day it shall come to pass *that* he glory of Jacob [Israel] will wane [diminish], and the fatness of his flesh grow lean."

We know from several passages that Israel will be very strong and prosperous at the beginning of the tribulation period (Ezekiel 38; Zechariah 12; Micah 4:11-13). It is not until the final three and one-half years of the tribulation that Israel will diminish

(Matthew 24:15-22; Daniel 7:25; 9:26; 11:36-45; Zechariah 14; etc.). Of course, if "in that day" is just a general expression for the last days, then the Holy Spirit may be giving us a panoramic picture of the entire period. However if "in that day" refers specifically to the time when Israel weakens, then Damascus may be forsaken during the final three and one-half year period. This would place the destruction of Damascus during the final three and one-half year period – either when Antichrist attacks the king of the north (Daniel 11:40) or at the very end during Armageddon (Revelation 16:13-16), when Christ returns.

On the other hand, Isaiah 17:9 explains that Damascus will be destroyed "because of the children of Israel." This would certainly place Damascus's destruction either before the tribulation or during the first half of it, when Israel is still militarily strong.

> Jeremiah 49:26-27 provides this insight: "'Therefore her [Damascus's] young men shall fall in her streets, and all the men of war shall be cut off in that day,' says the LORD of hosts. 'I will kindle a fire in the wall of Damascus, and it shall consume the palaces of Ben-Hadad.'"

Jeremiah uses the same expression: "in that day." If this refers specifically to the seven-year tribulation period, then Jeremiah's prophecy also suggests the destruction of Damascus during the great tribulation rather than before it. However, he adds this provocative clue: "*There is trouble on the sea*...Damascus has grown feeble" (Jeremiah 49:23-24, emphasis added). "There is trouble on the sea" is an interesting expression when we consider that Israel has never had a significant naval presence until our generation. But today, for the first time in history, Israel has both nuclear weapons and submarines positioned in the Mediterranean, capable of turning Damascus into "a ruinous heap" in one day. Furthermore, in 2007 "Israeli officials vowed to wipe Syria off the map if it is attacked with chemical weapons."[17]

Combine this insight with Isaiah's reference to quick destruction: "Then behold, at eventide, trouble! And before morning, he is no more." (Isaiah 17:14), and nuclear weapons appear to be in view here. If this refers to Damascus,[18] then this would indicate Israel will be forced to use its nuclear arsenal against this terrorist regime. It also indicates Israel will deal with Damascus before the seven-year peace covenant is confirmed (Daniel 9:27).

> Amos 1:3-5 adds additional insight: "Thus says the LORD: '*For three transgressions of Damascus, and for four*, I will not turn away its punishment, Because they have threshed Gilead with implements of iron. But I will send a fire into the house of Hazael, Which shall devour the palaces of Ben-Hadad. I will also break the gate bar of Damascus, and cut off the inhabitant from the Valley of Aven, and the one who holds the scepter from Beth Eden. The people of Syria shall go captive to Kir,' Says the LORD." (emphasis added)

Since the reestablishment of Israel in 1948, the fledgling nation has been attacked by Arab/Muslim armies in three major wars (War of Independence in 1948, Six-Day War in 1967, and Yom Kippur War in 1973) and several smaller wars. In each of the three major battles, Syria was an offender – violently attacking Israel to take over her land and destroy the Jews. God declares Damascus will be punished on the fourth transgression.

This could very well point to the Psalm 83 war – which appears imminent and almost certainly prior to the tribulation.

Interestingly, in the book of Amos, the Lord does not say that Damascus is utterly destroyed, but that He will send fire into the house of Hazael, break the gate bar (power) of Damascus, cut off some of the inhabitants, destroy the king and/or rulers, and they will go captive to Kir (in Jordan likely).

Syria is one of the ten threatening nations/groups in Psalm 83 (v. 8 – Assyria encompassed much of present day Syria). Furthermore, during the Psalm 83 war part of Syria, Jordan, southern Lebanon and Gaza will be annexed (Obadiah v. 1; Ezekiel 39:11). Therefore, it is possible Israel will set up detention camps in Jordan for those who survive the Psalm 83 war. Amos's passage would place at least a partial destruction of Damascus during the Psalm 83 war.

> More clues are found in Zechariah 9:1-2, 8: "The burden of the word of the LORD against the land of Hadrach, And Damascus its resting place (For the eyes of men and all the tribes of Israel are on the LORD); Also against Hamath, which borders on it, and against Tyre and Sidon, though they are very wise. … I will camp around My house [Jerusalem] because of the army, because of him who passes by and him who returns. No more shall an oppressor pass through them [Israel], for now I have seen with My eyes."

In this passage we are told, "No more shall an oppressor pass through them [Israel], for now I have seen with My eyes." This will only happen when Jesus returns to the Mount of Olives, suggesting that Damascus may not be utterly destroyed until Armageddon. However, Zechariah 9 may simply provide a broad-scope prophetic picture of the last days.

Taking all the clues together, here is one possible scenario: Damascus and the surrounding terrorist organizations will be brought to their knees, with many killed and many survivors placed in detention camps during and after the Psalm 83 campaign. Damascus may not be completely destroyed at this time, but significantly subdued (their power broken).

Though Damascus is not specifically listed in the Magog invasion, we are told that "many people are with" Gog, the leader of Magog, and they come "from the far north" (Ezekiel 38:6). Therefore, it is possible that Damascus – which is north of Israel – will be a staging area for the Magog coalition. God says He will rain down fire on Gog, "on his troops, and on the many people who are with him" (Ezekiel 38:22; 39:6). So it is possible that whatever is left of Damascus will be utterly destroyed during the Magog invasion described in Ezekiel 38-39.

There are two final possibilities. Syria may be part of the king of the north's army that battles Antichrist (Daniel 11:40-45). Or it may be destroyed at the very end – during Armageddon (Revelation 16:14; 19:11-21). Personally, I believe the Scriptural clues indicate that Damascus will likely be destroyed by nuclear weapons, or at least greatly humbled and subdued, during the Psalm 83 war. If any remnant remains, they will be destroyed during the Magog invasion. Rather than Syria, the king of the north listed in Daniel 11:40-45 may refer to one of the ten kings of the tribulation and his region (Daniel 7:24).

Though we should not be dogmatic concerning the exact timing, we know Damascus will be destroyed in these last days.[19] May this fact and God's repeated warnings cause all those who would threaten His people to repent and trust in Christ while there is still time.

In the midst of these tragic events, there is good news: "In that day a man will look to his Maker, and his eyes will have respect for the Holy One of Israel" (Isaiah 17:7) and "In that day Israel will be one of three with Egypt and Assyria– a blessing in the midst of the land" (Isaiah 19:24). Many will be saved! May we as believers be praying for the people of the Middle East and warning whosoever to trust in Jesus Christ as Creator, Lord, and Savior, while there is still time.

# Appendix 4
## Is Ezekiel's Army About to Face Off with the Arabs?

*(Appendix is based upon an article from the author written on 5/19/2011 Linked at: http:// prophecynewsstand.blogspot.com/2011/05/psalm-83-icegesis.html)*

Approximately 2,500 years ago the prophet Ezekiel envisioned a future valley filled with dry bones and is described in Ezekiel 37:1-13. It appears the dry bones represent the Jews in a holocaust condition, dispersed throughout the nations of the world. This conclusion can be safely suggested, because Ezekiel 37:11-12 says,

> Then He said to me, "Son of man, these bones are the whole house of Israel. They indeed say, 'Our bones are dry, our hope is lost, and we ourselves are cut off!'" Therefore prophesy and say to them, " Thus says the Lord GOD: 'Behold, O My people, I will open your graves and cause you to come up from your graves, and bring you into the land of Israel.'"

These verses clearly evidence that these bones represent the "whole house of Israel." Furthermore, it pictures the Jews in a desperate condition. Their "hope is lost," and they "are cut off." Lastly, they are being restored "into the land of Israel," meaning they were outside of the land of Israel during the vision.

Dr. Arnold Fruchtenbaum, Dr. David Reagan, and I, conclude that Ezekiel's dry bones vision pictures the Jews during the Diaspora, and that Hitler's holocaust caused their condition of hopelessness. Thus, Ezekiel sums up the metric of time that the Jews would be without a homeland; not in years, decades, or centuries, but in their helpless concluding condition. History testifies to the accuracy of Ezekiel's prediction, because shortly after the Holocaust the reestablishment of the nation Israel officially occurred on May 14, 1948. It is important to note that Ezekiel prophesied that the Jewish people would arise from their hopeless condition as refugees and emerge into an "exceedingly great army."

> So I prophesied as He commanded me, and breath came into them, and they lived, and stood upon their feet, an exceedingly great army. (Ezekiel 37:10)

The ongoing Arab – Israeli conflict has forced Israel to form a great army. The Israel Defense Forces (IDF) have had to become the superior military in the Middle East as a matter of national survival. In my book, *Isralestine, The Ancient Blueprints of the Future Middle East*, I devote an entire chapter to the existence of today's IDF in fulfillment of Bible prophecy. In addition to Ezekiel 37:10, prophecies written in verse 18 of Obadiah, Ezekiel 25:14, Zechariah 12:6, and elsewhere also seem to identify today's IDF.

Based upon the above premises, the remainder of this article discusses the debate among scholars as to whether or not Ezekiel 37:10 describes an exceedingly great army. Some scholars believe Ezekiel describes an army; whereas others believe Ezekiel is predicting a great multitude or host will emerge out of the dry bones.

## Point 1

The Hebrew word Ezekiel uses in verse 10 for army is *chayil* and it is used twelve times elsewhere by Ezekiel, and over 225 times throughout the Old Testament. All of Ezekiel's usages, and many Old Testament renderings clearly depict it as either an army, or riches acquired via the spoils obtained by an army, in the aftermath of a war. Nowhere else in the book of Ezekiel can it possibly be translated as a multitude or host. This establishes precedent that an army, rather than a multitude, is being described by Ezekiel.

- Ezekiel's twelve specific usages of the word *chayil* are as follows:
- Ezekiel 17:17 – describing Pharaoh's army,
- Ezekiel 26:12 – depicting the Babylonian army taking "riches" or spoil from victory over Tyre,
- Ezekiel 27:10-11 – alluding to the armies of Tyre,
- Ezekiel 28:4-5 – picturing the riches acquired by the ruler of Tyre,
- Ezekiel 29:18-19 – describing Nebuchadnezzar's Babylonian army,
- Ezekiel 32:31 – alluding to Pharaoh's army,
- Ezekiel 37:10 – describing Israel's "exceedingly great army,"
- Ezekiel 38:4, 15 – predicting the coming armies of Gog of Magog.

## Point 2

Further supporting the proper interpretation being an army, the following Bible translations interpret *chayil* to be an "army": *King James Version, New King James Version, American Standard Version, New American Standard Bible, New International Version, New Living Translation, New Century Version,* and *The Living Bible.* Conversely, the *Revised Standard Version* translates the word as "host." *The New Revised Standard Version* calls it a "multitude."

*Conclusion*—Obviously the above reasons overwhelmingly favor the interpretation of Ezekiel 37:10 as an army, rather than a host or multitude. *Isralestine* points out that the purpose of this army is to protect Israel from its surrounding enemies, who someday confederate in a final attempt to destroy the Jewish State of Israel, according to Psalm 83.

In light of the 2011 "Arab Spring," I believe the Psalm 83 Arab-Israeli war could occur soon, and that today's IDF is fit for the challenge.

# Appendix 5
## Divine Vengeance—The Israel Defense Forces in Bible Prophecy

*(Taken from an article authored by Bill Salus on 7/14/09. Linked at: http://www.prophecydepot.net/2009/divine-vengeance-the-israeli-defense-forces-in-bible-prophecy/)*

will lay My vengeance on Edom [Palestinians] by the hand of My people Israel, that they may do in Edom according to My anger and according to My fury; and they shall know My vengeance," says the Lord GOD. (Ezekiel 25:14)

From shovels to Sherman tanks, pitchforks to Patriot missiles, and knifes to nuclear warheads, the resilient Israel Defense Forces (IDF) have managed to defend a nation that for all intents and purposes should have been wiped off the map a few decades ago. Coming out of 1,878 years of worldwide dispersion and the Holocaust, the Jews have managed to muster-up a mighty military machine that in just sixty-one years now threatens to send Iran's nuclear program back to the "stone-age."

Many experts, like eschatologist Hal Lindsey and former US/UN Ambassador John Bolton, are suggesting that may happen someday. Israel appears ready to knock the nuclear bow temporarily out of Iran's hand and from my prophetic vantage point this could be a primary reason why Iran, formerly Persia until 1935, isn't listed in the upcoming Psalm 83 confederate invasion of Israel. Persia is omitted from the Psalm 83 Bible prophecy, but oddly they bare their banner in the Russian invasion of Israel described in Ezekiel 38-39, which is an event some scholars, myself included, sequence subsequent to Psalm 83. It could be that a strategic Israeli strike on Iran's nuclear sites renders Iran of little utility to the Psalm 83 confederates destined to someday assemble and conspire to destroy Israel according to Bible prophecy.

Amazingly, against all odds, the nation of Israel continues to survive. The Arabs, who for the most part refuse to recognize Israel's right to exist, have attempted to destroy the Jewish nation conventionally in 1948, 1967, and 1973. When conventional attempts failed the Arabs persuaded the Palestinian refugees to formulate terrorist organizations like the PLO, Fatah, and Hamas, to antagonize the restoration of the Jewish nation via unconventional methods of warfare. These terrorist groups, many now-turned political parties, enabled the Arab nations to maintain clean hands while busloads of Jewish blood poured into the streets of Jerusalem.

In the summer of 2006, the Hezbollah terrorist organization performed a feat the Arab states had never been able to accomplish; they successfully fought against and embarrassed the Israel Defense Forces. The Arabs walked away with a sense of victory in the aftermath of that month-long conflict. The Hezbollah proved that the unconventional method of warfare called terrorism worked!

The Hezbollah do not comprise an Arab state; rather they are thugs turned terrorists, processed into militant politicians. Presently, they have veto power in the Lebanese legislature and, according to some estimates possess about 60,000 advanced rockets, some perhaps chemically charged, that are strategically positioned for the opportune time to take out Tel Aviv and other strategic sites inside Israel. The present Israeli leadership is so concerned about the current Hezbollah threat that they recently completed the largest civilian defense drill in their nation's history. Turning Point 3 (in 2009), as it was labeled, was a societal, top-to-bottom shake-down of all facets of Israeli civilian life in preparation for the possibility of a multi-front war with Iran's proxies: the Hezbollah, Syrians, and Hamas.

Why them and why now? Is Israel expecting President Obama's dangerous Rodney King "can't we all just get along" style of Mideast foreign policy, called "engagement," to fail? Apparently so; Ehud Barak, the Israeli Defense Minister, has all of the IDF and IAF (Israeli Air Forces) combat ready for the same scenario anticipated in the Turning Point 3 exercise. Is something of biblical proportion about to erupt in the epicenter of the Middle East? It appears so and from the prophecy buff's perspective it fits perfectly into the present prophetic timetable. The international community has had sixty-one years to step up to the plate and promote Israel's right to exist, and to call Jerusalem its holy capital city! Instead they are encouraging the Jews to give back east Jerusalem as part of a two-state solution to the Palestinian refugees. This is contrary to God's plan and warnings, contained in passages like Genesis 12:3, 15:18, Jeremiah 12:14-17.

No my brothers and sisters, it appears the time has come for the fulfillment of prophecies that demonstrate today's Israel Defense Forces exist in Bible prophecy. Prophecies like Ezekiel 25:14 and verse 18 of Obadiah which announce the IDF will destroy the Palestinians, likely leaving few survivors behind, and passages like Isaiah 17:1 and Jeremiah 49:2, and Jeremiah 49:23-27 that declare the doom of Damascus and the transfer of Jordanian sovereignty into Israeli hands.

These passages and a flurry of others highlighted by Ezekiel 37:10, which declares that someday the IDF will be called an "exceedingly great army," appear about ready to adorn the prophetic pages of modern-day history. The only thing standing between the crowning achievements of the IDF becoming classified as exceedingly great are a few decisive victories over Israel's modern-day nemeses; victories that may begin with a surgical strategic strike upon Iran's nuclear sites and conclude with a massive, domino-effect Israeli conquest over the Hezbollah, Syrians, Hamas, and other members of the Psalm 83 confederates.

# Appendix 6
## Ezekiel: Israel's Dry Bones Can Fight

*(Appendix taken from an article written by the author on 6/17/2008. Linked at: http:// www.prophecydepot.net/2008/ezekiel-can-israels-dry-bones-fight/)*

Lining bookstore shelves today are numerous books foretelling the coming invasion of Israel by a nuclear equipped, Russian – Iranian led coalition. Relations between Russia and Iran have never been stronger, causing the serious spectator to wonder if this assault is about to commence. Prescribed in Ezekiel 38:18 - 39:6 is Israel's survival and the confederacy's demise.

Turning a few pages back to Ezekiel 37:10, we discover that Israel someday produces an "exceedingly great army." This army, the Israel Defense Forces (IDF), exists today. Although it would appear this army has emerged to engage in the coming Russian – Iranian led conflict, IDF participation in the battle is minimal. Instead, as per Ezekiel 39:3-6, divine events collapse this Russian led coalition. Justifiably, this beckons the question: what future military event earns the IDF "exceedingly great" esteem?

Clues deposited in Ezekiel 37:1-9 help us to discover what necessitated the existence of the IDF. These passages inform us that about 2,600 years ago the Hebrew prophet was fast-forwarded in time to the 1940s, wherein he envisioned the holocaust. He saw a valley full of dry bones, which represented the Jewish people in a horrifically grave condition. He was asked, "Can these bones live?" or simply put, can the Jewish race survive? Not only will they survive, he was told, but they would be restored to their ancient homeland of Israel, and emerge into an "exceedingly great army." By alluding to this army, he causes humanity to ponder its purpose. Why would the surviving Jews need to graduate from refugees to soldiers? Amazingly, we see that one failed Arab war upon another has caused the creation of the IDF. The enemies of Israel have quickly learned that Ezekiel's "dry bones" can fight!

By strategically inserting the prophecy of Psalm 83 somewhere between the events of Ezekiel 37:1-13 and Ezekiel 38, we come to recognize the primary purpose of Ezekiel's emerging army. Psalm 83 tells us that the Arabs are going to follow on the heels of the Germans with a genocidal attempt of their own. This Psalm foretells the future development of a predominately Arab confederacy that will soon seek to destroy the Jewish state and erase the name of Israel from the map forever.

Although the Israel Defense Forces do not play a major role in Ezekiel 38-39, they will face-off with an Arab confederacy comprised of Syrians, Saudis, Palestinians, Jordanians, Egyptians, Iraqis, Lebanese, and their associated terrorist entities, like the Hezbollah and Hamas. Coincidentally these populations are not listed in the Russian – Iranian coalition of Ezekiel 38. As a modern-day map of the Middle East depicts, they have Israel surrounded. According to numerous Scriptures, Israel will go ballistic and soundly defeat this confederacy. In victory, the Jewish army achieves the title of becoming "exceedingly great"! Greater detail can be obtained about the coming Arab – Israeli war in my book *Isralestine – The Ancient Blueprints of the Future Middle East*, available at http://www.prophecydepot.com. Passages depicting the expansion of Israel, destruction of Damascus, surrender of Jordanian sovereignty, final fate of the Palestinians, and many other related events are detailed within the book.

Destiny designed the emergence of the IDF to prevent the destruction of modern-day Israel. Ezekiel foretold the arrival of these Israel Defense Forces. Now the only thing that stands between Ezekiel's dry bones army and its "exceedingly great" title is the Israeli conquest over the Psalm 83 Arab confederacy.

# Appendix 7
## Those Surrounding Israel
## to be Devoured!

*(Appendix drawn from an article written by author on 6/9/11. Linked at: http:// prophecynewsstand.blogspot.com/2011/06/those-surrounding-israel-to-be-devoured.html)*

The prophet Zechariah informs us in chapter 12 that those peoples surrounding Israel will someday be devoured by Israel. The key to understanding portions of his prophecy rests in recognizing the direct correlation between Zechariah 12:2 and Zechariah 12:6.

> Behold, I will make Jerusalem a cup of drunkenness to all the surrounding peoples, when they lay siege against Judah and Jerusalem. (Zechariah 12:2)

Someday Jerusalem will become a cup of *raal* in the Hebrew, which is commonly translated as reeling, trembling, or drunkenness. This occurs when the *surrounding peoples* lay siege against both Judah and Jerusalem. This cup of *raal* should not be confused with the "heavy stone" classification of Jerusalem in the following passage.

> And it shall happen in that day that I will make Jerusalem a very heavy stone for all peoples; all who would heave it away will surely be cut in pieces, though all nations of the earth are gathered against it. (Zechariah 12:3)

Jerusalem becomes a heavy stone for all peoples, from all nations, rather than a cup of trembling to the surrounding peoples sharing common borders with Israel. Certainly, Jerusalem will feel like a burdensome stone and a cup of trembling to Israel's bordering nations, when they lay siege upon Judah and Jerusalem, but the heavy stone application applies to a much broader worldwide audience.

Zechariah 12:6 informs us that the Israel Defense Forces devour those sharing common borders with them like a fiery torch consumes sheaves or rows of fallen grain.

> In that day I will make the governors of Judah like a firepan in the woodpile, and like a fiery torch in the sheaves; they shall devour all the surrounding peoples

on the right hand and on the left, but Jerusalem shall be inhabited again in her own place—Jerusalem. (Zechariah 12:6)

The differing imageries of a cup of trembling verses a burdensome stone seems to represent different prophetic events. Although they are somewhat interrelated due to their connection with Jerusalem, the first event describes the IDF causing their surrounding enemies to tremble because they retaliate against them for laying siege upon Judah and Jerusalem. As a result of a decisive IDF victory, Jerusalem is inhabited again by Israelis.

Continued Israeli claims of exclusive sovereignty over Jerusalem meet with ongoing resistance throughout the world. From Joel 3:2, Psalm 2:1-3, and elsewhere we realize anti-Semitism spreads throughout the world and ultimately causes all peoples from all nations to assemble against Israel in the final stages of the Armageddon Campaign.

# Clues

The main clues given to separate the two Jerusalem-centered prophecies are:

* The Surrounding Peoples
* The Fiery Torch
* The Heavy Stone

*The Surrounding Peoples*—appears to identify those sharing common borders with Israel at the time Jerusalem becomes a cup of trembling. The Hebrew word used for the surrounding peoples is *sabiyb*. This same word is used to describe the enemy Arab nations encircling Israel in Ezekiel 36:3, 4, and 7. It is doubtful Zechariah was loosely identifying all peoples from all nations by using this specific Hebrew word. If he was, why didn't he repeat the same word again in Zechariah 12:3?

*The Fiery Torch*—the illustration of a torch devouring a swath of sheaves is a clear picture of a military conquest. Since it is the governors (also translated as clans or captains) of Judah that wield the torch, rather than the Lord single-handedly, like in Isaiah 63:3 and Ezekiel 38:18-39:6, it must be regarded with a prophecy involving the Israeli military.

Ezekiel 25:14, Obadiah v. 18, Isaiah 11:13-14, Zephaniah 2:9 and elsewhere describe the Israel Defense Forces in end-time military action. However, the IDF is not instrumental in Isaiah 63:3 or Ezekiel 38:18-39:6. These events involve the destruction of Israel's enemies solely by the Lord. In Isaiah's prophecy it is the Messiah that is "mighty to save" that fights against the Antichrist and his armies. In Ezekiel's account, it is the Lord that destroys the Ezekiel 38 invaders. In neither Isaiah's nor Ezekiel's scenarios is the IDF influential in the battle.

Thus, there must be at least three end-time battles over Israel; two of which the IDF plays no decisive role whatsoever. If Zechariah 12:2 and 12:6, which both identify surrounding peoples, is not part of Armageddon or Ezekiel's Gog of Magog invasion, then what battle remains? The only logical conclusion is that described in the Psalm 83 prophecy. The Psalm identifies the surrounding peoples, sharing common borders with Israel, that want to destroy Israel.

*The Heavy Stone*—although some allegorical correlation to the stone of Daniel 2:34-35, 45 could be made with Zechariah 12:3, the illustration appears to deal with disputed territory. Sovereign Israeli claims over Jerusalem become a burden to all peoples from all nations, and Jerusalem is pictured as an immovable stone. Due to its weight it can neither be heaved away nor cut into pieces, to be removed fractionally. Even though the international community continuously attempts to heave it out of Israel's real estate portfolio, it falls back in its same location, injuring those attempting to cast it away.

The prophet Joel predicts this matter's final resolution as an end time event occurring after the Jews return from the nations of the world into the reestablished State of Israel.

> For behold, in those days and at that time, When I bring back the captives of Judah and Jerusalem, I will also gather all nations, And bring them down to the Valley of Jehoshaphat; And I will enter into judgment with them there On account of My people, My heritage Israel, Whom they have scattered among the nations; They have also divided up My land. (Joel 3:1-2)

The nations of the world are guilty of attempting to divide the land of Israel, including Jerusalem. This is occurring now, and will probably continue to occur after the Psalm 83 conflict. Ultimately, the Lord gathers all the nations to a final battle against the Jews, which appears to be when Zechariah 12:3 finds its final, literal fulfillment. Partial geo-political fulfillment has been occurring since Israel was reestablished on May 14, 1948.

# Appendix 8
## Palestinians to be Forced to Israel's Borders!

*(Appendix taken from an article written by the author on 5/31/2011. Linked at: http://prophecynewsstand.blogspot.com/2011/05/prophecy-palestinians-to-be-forced-to.html)*

All the men in your confederacy Shall force you to the border; The men at peace with you Shall deceive you and prevail against you. Those who eat your bread shall lay a trap for you. No one is aware of it. (Obadiah v. 7)

The prophet Obadiah had a prophetic vision regarding the Edomites. Today, the Edomites have ethnic representation inside the Palestinians. The 7th verse of Obadiah declares that the Edomites enlist in a future confederacy that ultimately forces them to a border. The 10th and 18th verses of Obadiah make it clear that the confederacy forms to fight Israel. Thus, we can deduce that the border in question must be Israel's.

Verse 7 of Obadiah says—"your" confederacy, "you" to the border, peace with "you," deceive "you," prevail against "you," "your" bread, and a trap for "you." The fact that Obadiah uses "you" or "your" seven times in combination suggests the Palestinians play a key role within the confederacy.

However, even though the Palestinians are an integral part of the confederacy, they appear to be a subservient member. This is indicated by Obadiah's statement that the other members "prevail" against them. The Hebrew word for prevail is *yakol*, and in this usage it implies the other confederate populations possess power or influence over the Palestinians. As we witness Palestinian protesters marching against the borders of Israel, and recognize they are supported by a conglomeration of Arab states sharing common borders with Israel, we are caused to consider the possibility that Obadiah's vision finds real-time prophetic application.

The "Arab Spring" has seemingly morphed into the liberate Palestine Summer. Nakba, Naksa, or whatever other Arab name given in association with a day of Palestinian protests, is incubating into a potentially dangerous summer scenario for

Israel that could soon prove disastrous for the Middle East. On May 15, 2011, thirteen Palestinian protesters were killed as they marched against the borders of Israel on Nakba day. Nakba commemorated the anniversary of the creation of the Palestinian refugees on May 15, 1948, when the Arab states told the Arabs residing inside former Palestine to vacate for a few days so they could confederate against Israel to destroy it.

History evidences this was a terrible miscalculation, as Israel won the war, and the Arabs who left Palestine became refugees. Thus, two important Bible prophecies occurred in May, 1948. First, the reestablishment of the nation Israel in fulfillment of prophecies in Ezekiel 36:22-24, 37:11-12, Isaiah 11:11 and elsewhere; and second, the creation of the "tents of Edom" in fulfillment of Psalm 83:6.

Tents in the Bible typically represent refugee conditions, or military encampments. In Psalm 83, Esau's descendants, the Edomites, become tent-dwellers. A close study of Edomite history demonstrates that they have an ethnic contingency inside the modern-day Palestinian refugees. Additionally important, the Edomite refugees are listed first inside a confederacy of Arabs. This likely identifies these refugees as lead instigators of the Arab confederacy. In essence, the Palestinian refugee plight unites the Arabs to fight against Israel. Psalm 83:3-5 tells us this, and Psalm 83:12 informs us the goal is the liberation of Palestine from Israeli sovereignty.

A new protest is being called for on Naksa day to commemorate the Arab defeat by Israel in the Six-Day war in June, 1967. The organizers are being quoted as declaring "The process of empowerment and liberation, which started in Tunisia and Egypt, should end with the liberation of Jerusalem and Palestine. Palestine will be liberated from the river to the sea, and the sea to the river." The inflammatory rhetoric streaming across the social networks about the Naksa day protests is more regarded with liberating Palestine, than creating a Palestinian state. This is troublesome; raising legitimate concerns that the protesters prefer one final Arab state called Palestine, rather than a two-state solution whereby Israel and Palestine coexist peacefully side-by-side. The organizers are pressing the Palestinians to forcefully march against Israel's borders with the goal of liberating Palestine. Additionally, they are calling for widespread protests throughout the Arab countries, including Tahrir Square in Egypt. Meanwhile, in preparation for the demonstrations Israel has stepped up security and fortified its borders with IDF troops, in an attempt to avert a potential crisis.

Upon a careful review of Psalm 83, this plan to reclaim Palestine for the Palestinian refugees seems to have prophetic implications. However, there's more to the prophetic story. It might be timely to dust off an ancient Bible prophecy that seemingly connects with the Psalm 83, written by Obadiah. Both Psalm 83:4 and Obadiah v. 7 identify an Arab confederacy involving the Edomites (Palestinians). They appear to be discussing the same confederacy in their respective prophecies. Greater detail on this subject is available in the chapter called "The Palestinian Confederacy" contained in my book, *Isralestine, The Ancient Blueprints of the Future Middle East.*

# Appendix 9
## Psalm 83 or Ezekiel 38: Which is the Next Middle East News Headline?

*(Appendix based upon an article from the author written on 6/17/08. Linked here: http:// isralestine-blog.blogspot.com/2008/06/raiders-news-feature-print-story-email.html)*

These days there is much talk centered upon the future timing of the Russian and Iranian-led invasion of Israel, foretold in the Bible prophecies of Ezekiel 38-39. Due to the newsworthy events that are presently occurring, wherein Russian and Iranian relationships are ever strengthening, prophecy buffs are appropriately attempting, with godspeed, to connect the prophetic dots.

For those of you who are not familiar with today's most prevalent prophetic news pervading the Christian and Jewish scholarly communities, you should study Ezekiel 38-39, with the understanding that it probably alludes to a nuclear-equipped, Russian – Iranian led confederacy, which forms to invade the nation of Israel in the end times.

Although scholars are somewhat split as to who all the other enjoining coalition member nations are, they all tend to agree that no explicit reference is made to the inclusion of Palestinians, Syrians, Egyptians, Lebanese, or Jordanians. Furthermore, Saudi Arabians apparently abstain from enlisting themselves in the fight alongside Russia, Iran, Turkey, and the additional consortia of nations. The absence of these above listed, predominately Arab populations tends to perplex the scholars, often causing them to postulate, rather than promulgate as to the reasons why.

In their zeal, have the prophecy buffs managed to put the colloquial cart before the proverbial horse? Certainly the events described in Ezekiel 38-39 are slated to arrive soon, but are they indeed scheduled next? There exists a litany of questions that should be appropriately answered before any scholar dare flip the pages of the prophetic calendar forward to the date of this Goliath Ezekiel event. Newspaper exegesis makes for sensational reporting, but has no inherent ability to accelerate the final fulfillment of a Bible prophecy.

Before we list the flurry of questions, let's ponder the most obvious one, which is: why are the Palestinians, and their Arab neighbors from Saudi Arabia, Syria, Lebanon, Egypt, and Jordan not declared by Ezekiel to be enlisted members in the Russian – Iranian led coalition? These are the nations that have proven to be the most observable opponents of the Jewish State, since its inception in 1948. It is through much of their Arab soil that Russia, Iran, and their cohorts intend to travel in order to invade Israel. This question will be answered further in this article, but for now let's explore the following additional questions.

Is Israel:

- A people dwelling securely, *yashab betach* in the Hebrew language? (Ezekiel 38:8)

- A people dwelling without walls? (Ezekiel 38:11)

- A nation at peace in the Middle East? (Ezekiel 38:11)

- One of the wealthiest nations in the world? (Ezekiel 38:13)

- A people who have acquired "great plunder"? (Ezekiel 38:13)

- Recognized as a sovereign nation, by the international community? (Ezekiel 38:8)

These questions address some of the prerequisite conditions required for the stage to be appropriately set for the Russian – Iranian led, nuclear equipped invasion of Israel. Furthermore, Ezekiel 38:8 describes the Jewish people as being re-gathered from the nations of the world and returning to the mountains of Israel, which had long been desolate. Though the Jewish people are being restored back to their ancient promised land, the honest answers to the above questions are in each case, No!

Israel is not dwelling securely; in the summer of 2006 there were over 4,000 Hezbollah rockets launched into Haifa and other northern Israeli locations from Lebanon. Additionally, the Hamas are still a constant threat from the Gaza area. Then, of course, there were the wars of 1948, 1956, 1967, and 1973. Likewise, Israel is not a people dwelling without walls; to the contrary, they have constructed a huge 25-foot-high, soon to be 403 miles long, wall in the midst of their land, intended to partition Palestinian terrorists away from Israel proper.

No, it does not appear as though Israel is presently a nation at peace in the Middle East, whose sovereignty is officially recognized by all their Arab neighbors. Neither has Israel become one of the wealthiest nations in the world, as a result of acquiring "great plunder," which biblically alludes to the spoils obtained as the result of a war. In fact, Israel continues to forfeit land, their most valuable asset, in an attempt to obtain peace with their Arab neighbors.

So then, if the prerequisite conditions are not yet come into alignment for the final fulfillment of the Ezekiel 38-39 prophecies, what is the next major ground shaking prophetic event foretold to unfold in the Middle East? What dare the Bible say will happen in the most perplexing region on planet Earth? Will it be an event that serves to bring Israel into appropriate alignment with the stage-setting requirements that facilitate the fulfillment of Ezekiel's Russian – Iranian-led invasion?

Now we have some Yes answers to introduce. Yes, something else of epic proportion is foretold in the Bible to occur in the Middle East! Yes, its conclusion will bring forth the announcement that the world theater is now readied for the nuclear-equipped advance of the Russian – Iranian led invasion. Yes, it does adequately answer the fundamental question of why the Arab populations listed above are nowhere to be found in the Russian – Iranian coalition. Are you ready?

> There is destined to be an Arab – Israeli war, as per Psalm 83. An Arab confederacy consisting of Palestinians, Syrians, Saudi Arabians, Lebanese, Egyptians, Jordanians, and all their associated terrorist bedfellows, is destined to form with the explicit mandate of, and I quote: "They have said, Come, and let us [Arabs] cut them [Jews] off from being a nation, That the name of Israel may be remembered no more." (Psalm 83:4)

These Arab peoples referred to by their ancient territorial names in Psalm 83 come together in one last crazed attempt to destroy the Jewish State of Israel. This will prove to be a fatal mistake for these Arab confederates. They will meet up with the technologically advanced arsenal of weapons possessed by the powerful army of Israel. It will be a matter of Israel's survival, and their army will prevail. In victory, Israel finds itself fulfilling numerous prophecies such as:

- They have become an "exceedingly great army". (Ezekiel 37:10)
- The execution of judgments on those who despise them. (Ezekiel 28:25)
- They will then dwell securely (*yashab betach*). (Ezekiel 28:26)
- They will acquire Arab lands and great plunder. (Obadiah v. 19, Jeremiah 49:2)
- Sovereign International acclaim as "My People Israel". (Ezekiel 25:14, 38:14, 16)
- They will become one of the wealthiest nations on Earth. (Zephaniah 2:7, 9; NRSV)

These and many more prophecies find there fulfillment as a result of the Arab – Israeli war, which is certain to come, and is most likely the next major Middle East headline event, according to Scripture. A more exhaustive understanding of this major event can be found in my book, *Isralestine, The Ancient Blueprints of the Future Middle East*.

Why are the Palestinians and their Arab cohorts not enjoined in the Ezekiel 38-39 prophecies? Today's most observable Arab opponents to the restoration of the nation Israel collectively abstain due to the fact, that they are soon to be decimated by the might of the Israel Defense Force. How does Israel achieve peace in the Middle East and obtain international recognition as the sovereign Jewish state? It is through military means, rather than politically brokered real estate deals such as "The Roadmap Plan." When will the partition wall in Israel come down and the Jews dwell securely in the Middle East? This will occur when the Jewish state expands territorially, acquires great plunder, and becomes regionally superior.

Digesting the above, Russia and Iran become threatened by what will then be the new and improved, enlarged and fully in charge future Israel. As a result of the Israeli conquest over the inner circle of the core Arab nations that most closely border Israel today, the Russians and Iranians will promptly invite an outer circle of nations to join their coalition in an attempt to destroy the Jewish state, and capture Israel's newfound fortunes. It is then, and not before, that the prophecy buffs can safely turn the next page of the prophetic calendar forward and warn the world, that the events of Ezekiel 38-39 are about to reveal themselves.

APPENDICES

# Appendix 10
## Psalm 83: Has It Found Final Fulfillment?

*(Appendix based upon an article from the author written on 3/18/2009 . Linked at: http://prophecydepot.blogspot.com/2009/03/psalm-83-has-it-found-final-fulfillment.html)*

Currently many prophecy buffs are discussing the Psalm 83, petition-formatted prophecy written by the seer Asaph approximately 3,000 years ago. This prophecy enlists a ten-member population whose goal is nothing short of wiping Israel off of the map. Their confederate mandate is:

> They have said, "Come, and let us cut them off from being a nation, That the name of Israel may be remembered no more." (Psalm 83:4)

My book, *Isralestine—the Ancient Blueprints of the Future Middle East*, has caused many eschatologists to rethink their end-time model. However, not all the experts agree with my end-time equation that Psalm 83 precedes Ezekiel 38-39. There are those who still sweep the prophecy into the catchall closet of the seven-year tribulation or simply deposit the event into the file thirteen trash bin of historical fulfillment.

Why Psalm 83 doesn't belong in the seven-year tribulation period is a subject for a future article; however, this piece is intended to pull the prophecy out of the annals of historical fulfillment and place it back into the pending event category. Furthermore, this article is not intended to serve as a substitute for reading *Isralestine* in its entirety, which covers all the above and volumes more.

## The 2 Chronicles 20 Argument:

Nathan Jones, the up-and-coming eschatologist extraordinaire and webmaster for Dr. David Reagan's *Lamb and Lion Ministries*, asked me to participate in an ongoing blog. The argument was raised by some gentleman identified as Don, that 2 Chronicles 20:1-37 likely describes the final fulfillment of the Psalm 83 prophecy. You can read my blog comments and review some of the other assorted blogs made by others at the following link: http://www.lamblion.us/2009/01/gaza-conflict.html.

## Here is my comment on the subject:

"Nathan and Don- 2 Chronicles is not likely the episode Asaph describes in Psalm 83. The 2 Chronicles account primarily describes only three, possibly four, of the ten-member populations enlisted in the prophecy of Psalm 83. These are the Psalm 83:6-8 confederates: The tents of Edom and the Ishmaelites; Moab and the Hagrites (Hagarenes); Gebal, Ammon, and Amalek; Philistia with the inhabitants of Tyre; Assyria also has joined with them; They have helped the children of Lot.

Now compare all of the above to 2 Chronicles 20:1-37 in your Bible.

> 2 Chronicles 20:1—It happened after this that the people of Moab with the people of Ammon, and others with them besides the Ammonites, came to battle against Jehoshaphat. (Following *Masoretic Text* and *Vulgate*; *Septuagint* reads Meunites see 2 Chronicle 26:7)

> 2 Chronicles 20:1; ASV—And it came to pass after this, that the children of Moab, and the children of Ammon, and with them some of the Ammonites, came against Jehoshaphat to battle. (Verse 1 enlists Moab and Ammon, and possibly the Meunites.)

The NKJV suggests that "others" were involved besides them, but that likely refers to the Meunites, a much smaller grouping than those of Psalm 83:6-8. The Meunites, if that is who verse 1 references, were an Arab tribe that dwelt about twelve miles southeast of Petra, which still puts them in modern-day southern Jordan. I cited the *American Standard Version* in addition to the *New King James Version* to illustrate that it only identifies Ammon, and Moab. Verse 2 references Syria, according to some *Masoretic Text*, *Septuagint*, and *Vulgate*; some Hebrew manuscripts and Old Latin read Edom.

Edom or Syria, or both—this still is only a portion of the ten populations of Psalm 83. Verses 10, and 22-23 of 2 Chronicles 20 lists Moab, Ammon, and Mt. Seir. Mt. Seir identifies primarily with the people of Edom. Thus, the populations referenced primarily would be modern-day Jordan, with a slight possibility of Syria having been involved. Moab is today central Jordan, Edom is southern Jordan, and Ammon is northern Jordan. Petra, Mt. Seir, and the Meunites, would also be clustered in and around southern Jordan today.

Due to the fact that less than half of the required ten Psalm 83 populations are referenced, it is not possible that 2 Chronicles 20 could be considered as the source of Psalm 83 fulfillment. In addition, several scholars like Dr. Arnold Fruchtenbaum, Chuck Missler, Hal Lindsey, Dr. David Reagan, Jacob Prasch, David Dolan and many others believe that Psalm 83 has yet to find its final fulfillment."

# The 1948 and 1967 Arab-Israeli War(s) Argument:

There are those who believe that the Six-Day war of 1967 occasioned the final fulfillment of the prophecy. I have this suggestion presented to me often, and below is a recent email I sent to a friend in response to his concern that this could be the case.

> I have recently been informed that you believe Psalm 83 may have found its fulfillment in the Six-Day war of 1967. Interestingly Dr. David Reagan and I discussed this possibility recently, while visiting together at a Calvary Chapel Chino Hills conference hosted by Pastor Jack Hibbs, in February 2009. We concurred that the better argument for fulfillment was the 1948 war commonly considered by the Israeli's as "The War of Independence;" however neither of these truly meets the description in our estimation. There are ten populations involved in Psalm 83:6-8 and not all of them were involved in 1967; and more than all of them, at least peripherally, were involved in 1948.
>
> Additionally it is important to note that the "tents of Edom" are the first population listed in the Psalm 83:6-8 grouping, and a careful study demonstrates that the Edomite descendants became tent-dwellers only in the aftermath of the 1948 Arab – Israeli War. This abrogates the possibility that Psalm 83 found fulfillment in the 1948 "War of Independence."

Biblically the "tents of" condition alludes to either refugees or military encampments. In the Edomite instance their refugee condition became a troubling reality in 1949, when the Palestinian refugee crisis commenced. Up until that time, they were known as the Arabs of Palestine; ever since they have been referred to as refugees.

*Isralestine* devotes an entire chapter to this topic called, "Whodomites"—Who are the Edomites Today. Inside the "Whodomite" chapter the Edomite – Palestinian refugee connection is clearly made. The chapter traces several historical waves of Edomite migration out from their original homeland into Israel. They generally settled in and around Hebron, which today exists in the modern-day West Bank. Ultimately they became known as the Idumeans, which is the Greek word for Edomites. The territory they developed inside of Israel assumed the name Idumea.

It appears that from 1949 to the present day the Palestinian refugees, the apparent antagonistic star of the Psalm 83 show, have a descendant Edomite contingency residing within their ranks.

However, the additional argument against either of these two Arab – Israeli wars being the fulfillment is the fact that Asaph is petitioning God to utterly destroy this confederacy as per Psalm 83:17, an event that has not yet occurred. He petitions God to fashion their demise in the similar format of the historic examples he lists in Psalm 83:9-11 and the allegorical illustrations of Psalm 83:13-16. The fact that these populations still exist, seek possession of the Promised land in Psalm 83:12, and continue to collectively possess the antagonistic attitude toward Israel of Psalm 83:4 conclusively evidences, in my estimation, that this prophecy has yet to find fulfillment."

For the brevity sake of this appendix, I'll let the reader do his or her own homework on the participants of the 1948 and 1967 wars.

# Conclusion:

The two arguments listed above are the primary ones forwarded by today's top scholars who believe that Psalm 83 has already found its fulfillment. Having previously deposited Psalm 83 into the historical fulfillment file thirteen, these advocates tend to then center their focus upon Ezekiel 38-39 as the next Mideast Bible prophecy set to find fulfillment. I disagree with this thinking and express my opinions further in the appendix called, *Psalm 83 or Ezekiel 38, Which is the Next Middle East News Headline?*

We must consider the fact those mere rumblings today between Russia and Iran in the epicenter of the Middle East, as Joel Rosenberg aptly refers to them, does not constitute, but rather simply suggests the nearby fulfillment of the Ezekiel 38-39 invasion. Oddly, many military experts are predicting just the opposite, that Israel may be forced to invade Iran in order to forestall their nuclear aspirations. This could temporarily sideline Iran and render them of little immediate utility to Russia, and may be one of the reasons ancient Persia is not listed among the Psalm 83 confederates.

Anyway you "prophe-size" it up, some big, world-changing Middle East event is certainly about to happen, just like the Bible predicted it would. The fact that the Psalm 83 confederates live on today and embrace the ancient hatred of Israel, signals the likelihood that Psalm 83 is the next Mideast prophecy to find fulfillment.

# Appendix 11
## Is Ezekiel 38 Imminent?

*(Appendix is based upon an article from the author written on 6/18/10. Linked at: http://prophecynewsstand.blogspot.com/2010/06/10-reasons-ezekiel-38-isnt-imminent.html)*

Current Middle East events are definitely stage-setting for the final fulfillment of the Israeli War prophecies of Psalm 83 and Ezekiel 38-39. Throughout much of 2010, Turkey distanced itself from Israel. This moved many of the "Ezekiel 38 Now"[20] advocates to the edge of their seats, because it meant that Turkey and Iran, both members of the Ezekiel 38 coalition, shared a common enmity toward Israel.

Certainly, there is just cause to consider the Ezekiel 38-39 prophecy in light of Turkish and Iranian anti-Israel sentiment; but, what about Hezbollah, Syria, Hamas, and the Palestinians? They also are at odds with Israel. Curiously, Ezekiel 38 describes nine distinct populations by their ancient names, including Russia, Iran, Turkey, and Libya, but omits the historic name equivalents of Hezbollah, Syria, Hamas, and the Palestinians

In light of the fact that these omitted populations are presently among Israel's most observable enemies, some "Ezekiel 38 Now" advocates have attempted to identify them in Ezekiel 38:6 among the *many peoples with thee* of the Ezekiel 38 Magog confederacy. However, there are three potential problems with this line of teaching.

- Hezbollah, Syria, Hamas and the Palestinians along with Egyptians, Saudis, and Jordanians are identified in a distinctly different Israeli War prophecy described in Psalm 83. The Psalm lists ten entirely separate members not included among the Ezekiel 38:1-6 invaders. Thus, it is probable they are not the *many peoples with thee* in Ezekiel 38:6, but are "many peoples distinct from thee" not listed in Ezekiel 38 among the invaders.

- The hordes of Ezekiel 38 invaders must cross over much of the land possessed by these Psalm 83 nations and territories presently occupied by the terrorist populations in order to invade the nation of Israel. This beckons the question: why aren't these nations, terrorists, or refugees specifically listed among the Ezekiel 38 invaders?

- Most importantly, Ezekiel 38 identifies nine specific invading populations, but oddly doesn't mention any of the Psalm 83 Arab confederates among them. This conspicuous omission makes no sense when you consider that Ezekiel references all of the Psalm 83 members numerous times elsewhere throughout his prophetic book.

Case in point: Ezekiel lists Tyre twelve times. Tyre is a member of Psalm 83 and likely represents the Hezbollah today. He alludes to Philistia or Philistines four times. They are probably the Hamas. Edom or the Edomites are referenced seven times. Asaph, the author of Psalm 83, calls them the tents of Edom and I interpret that as today's Palestinian refugees. The other Psalm 83 members like, Moab or Moabites, Ammon or Ammonites, Amalakites, Egyptians, Assyrians, Gebal (Lebanon), and the Saudis under the ancient banners of Dedan or the Ishmaelites, are also referenced elsewhere in the book of Ezekiel. In fact, all together the above Psalm 83 confederates are mentioned eighty-nine times by Ezekiel.

Not one of those eighty-nine "enlisted" references shows up in Ezekiel 38-39, with the exception of a potential Saudi contingent represented by Dedan, in Ezekiel 38:13. But in this instance, Dedan appears to abstain from enlisting with the Ezekiel invaders. This suggests they want no further part in an invasion of Israel. Ezekiel 25:13 declares many in Dedan will be killed in a war, which appears to be the result of the Psalm 83 war. If so, this could be the reason they apparently opt out of the Ezekiel invasion.

I believe the glaring omission of the Psalm 83 Arab confederates from the Ezekiel 38 list of invaders suggests they are not part of the Ezekiel 38-39 invasion. It is highly possible that they are defeated prior to the Ezekiel 38-39 Israeli War prophecy. Listed below are a few of the reason I believe Psalm 83 precedes Ezekiel 38.

Ezekiel 38:8-13 mandates that Israel must be dwelling securely, without walls, bars, or gates, and in the center of the land, probably alluding to the Genesis 15:18 landmass. Additionally, the Jewish state must be in receipt of great spoil. In my estimation, Israel today is not fulfilling these conditions.

Israel is unable to dwell securely as a result of their surrounding Psalm 83 hostile Arab neighbors. Walls, bars, and gates exist in Israel today in order to protect them from being terrorized by certain members of the Psalm 83 confederates, like Hamas, Hezbollah, and the Palestinians in general. Additionally, the goal of the Ezekiel 38 invaders is to destroy Israel and take plunder and great spoil. Israel doesn't presently appear to possess the great spoil that Russia and their coalition will someday covet.

However, in the aftermath of an Israeli conquest over the Psalm 83 confederates all of the above requirements could easily be met. A safe-dwelling Israel could temporarily emerge. Arab spoils of war could be had, additional territory annexed, and walls, bars, and gates could be swiftly brought down.

Another important distinction between the prophecies of Ezekiel 38 and Psalm 83 is found in their differing motives. Psalm 83:12 declares that the Arab confederates want to destroy Israel to take over the Promised Land. Ezekiel 38:12-13 states the Ezekiel invaders seek to destroy the Jewish state and confiscate plunder and great spoil.

Also an important difference between Psalm 83 and Ezekiel 38 may be understood by identifying the purpose of the *exceedingly great army* of Ezekiel 37:10. The Ezekiel invaders are destroyed divinely, but the Psalm 83 Arab confederates appear to be defeated by the Israel Defense Forces according, to Ezekiel 25:14, Obadiah v. 18, and elsewhere.

Interestingly, an exceedingly great army of Israel is mentioned in Ezekiel 37:10. This reference seemingly segues into the Ezekiel 38-39 prophecy. Logically, a reader might assume this army plays an instrumental role in the war of Ezekiel 38. However, Ezekiel 38:18- 39:6 teaches that this army plays little to no part in Ezekiel's invasion.

Upon closer investigation, this army appears to be the tool empowered by God to defeat the Psalm 83 Arab confederacy. If so, the fact that the army of Ezekiel 37:10 is referenced prior to the Ezekiel 38-39 war passages infers that chronologically Psalm 83 precedes Ezekiel 38. For more information about the exceedingly great army of Ezekiel 37:10 refer to the appendix called, *Is Ezekiel's Army About to Face Off with the Arabs?*

In conclusion, the fulfillment of a Bible prophecy mandates that the episode meets the prophetic description of the event entirely and exactly. There can be no overlooking even the slightest detail given. The growing tendency among eschatologists to recognize that current Mideast events are stage setting for the coming Psalm 83 and Ezekiel 38 wars is to be commended. However, newspaper exegesis can often cause us to overlook significant prophetic details, and should be avoided.

Perhaps Ezekiel 38 will come soon and precede Psalm 83, but from the numerous points made above it is doubtful. There are ten members listed in Psalm 83 that are not listed in Ezekiel 38. These ten represent Israel's most observable modern-day enemies, since becoming a nation in 1948.

For the reasons above and those included in the appendix called, *Psalm 83 or Ezekiel 38 Which is the Next Middle East News Headline*, in my estimation, Ezekiel 38 cannot be considered an imminent event until after Psalm 83 occurs.

# Appendix 12
## Israel Strikes it Rich Someday!

*(Appendix taken from the article of the same name written by the author on 6/18/2011. Link location: http://prophecynewsstand.blogspot.com/2011/06/israel-strikes-it-rich-someday.html)*

The Bible predicted the coming of a reestablished and extremely prosperous Israel. Ezekiel 36:24 and elsewhere foretold that the Jews would be re-gathered from the nations of the world into their own homeland. What had begun as a trickle around the turn of the century and then accelerated in the aftermath of WWII, the return of the Jews to the land as prophesied became official on May 14, 1948.

Ezekiel 36:8-12 informed that upon their return, the land of Israel would be tilled, sown, and become extremely fruitful. Ezekiel declares the historic ruins would be rebuilt and the ancient cities repopulated. In these passages, he predicts the Jews will be more prosperous than at any prior time in their history. This is a startling prediction considering the land of Israel lay mostly desolate between AD 70 and May, 1948, when Israel was restored as the Jewish state.

Equally as impressive is that Israel's abundance appears to proportionately exceed the national treasures King Solomon accumulated nearly 3,000 years ago. According to 1 Kings 10, King Solomon was the wealthiest king on Earth during his reign over Israel.

> So king Solomon exceeded all the kings of the earth in riches and in wisdom. (1 Kings 10:23; ASV)

1 Chronicles 22:14-16 informs that Solomon owned a seemingly limitless supply of gold, silver, bronze, and iron. The *International Standard Bible Encyclopedia* says Solomon possessed "A sum greater than the national debt of Great Britain." We are told in 2 Chronicles 9:13, that one year Solomon's estimated income was 666 talents, which is the approximate equivalent today of $708,400,000.[21] These earnings represented a monumental amount of annual wealth at that time. Presently, the cities are being rebuilt and repopulated and Israel is becoming very prosperous, but have they accumulated all the riches predicted?

In 2009 and 2010, Israel discovered large natural gas resources. Some eschatologists believe the Israelis will also someday discover crude oil underneath their fertile soil. Natural gas and crude oil could certainly become contributors toward Israel's foretold fortunes, but what does Scripture point to, possibly in addition to these resources?

Ezekiel 38:1-13 informs that a major alliance will form to invade Israel to confiscate Israel's riches. Ezekiel 38:13 specifically states this confederacy comes for Israel's great spoil. This prophecy, commonly referred to among scholars as the Gog of Magog invasion, remains unfulfilled. Should no unforeseen circumstances prohibit, this means Israel has more time to amass an even greater fortune beforehand.

The Hebrew words utilized for the Magog invaders goal to capture great spoil are *shalal gadol shalal*. According to the definitions given in the *New America Hebrew and Greek Dictionaries*, these words can be translated successively to read, "Plunder the great spoil of the despoilers." Despoil means to deprive someone of something valuable by force.[22] It suggests that the invaders are coming to plunder the spoils Israel previously captured from another. Widely respected eschatologist, Dr. Arnold Fruchtenbaum, teaches that the Magog invaders are coming to, "To take a spoil of a spoil."

In the prior verse, Ezekiel 38:12, the prophet says the Magog invaders are coming after acquired, or gotten, cattle and goods. The Hebrew word is *asah* and suggests that Israel has acquired livestock and commercial goods externally, perhaps more-so than developed them from their own natural resources and / or commercial endeavors.

If the enticing great spoil spoken of is acquired, rather than homegrown, then where does it originate? Zechariah 14:14 appears to hold an important clue in this regard. Apparently Israel acquires it from the Arab nations round about them.

> And Judah also shall fight at Jerusalem; *and the wealth of all the* (Arab) *nations round about shall be gathered together*, gold, and silver, and apparel, in great abundance. (Zechariah 14:14, ASV; emphasis added)

Zechariah declares that Israel gathers great abundance from the neighboring Arab nations "round about." Zechariah 14:14 appears to find connection with Zechariah 12:2, 6. To get a greater understanding of this connection, compare this appendix with the attached appendix called *Those Surrounding Israel to be Devoured!*

Zechariah chapters 12 and 14 find connection in that, portions of each chapter address the wars between Israel and its hostile Arab neighbors, and the subsequent conflict fought by Jesus Christ against the Antichrist and his armies during the campaign of Armageddon. These are two distinct wars, that are intricately interwoven between Zechariah's chapters 12 and 14. Zechariah 12:6 below, and 14:14 above, specifies that the IDF, represented as Judah, fights the Arab nations round about for possession of Jerusalem.

> In that day will I make the chieftains of Judah like a pan of fire among wood, and like a flaming torch among sheaves; and they shall devour all the peoples round about, on the right hand and on the left; and *they of* Jerusalem shall yet again dwell in their own place, even in Jerusalem. (Zechariah 12:6; ASV)

The IDF is instrumental in Israel's fight against the Arab confederacy of Psalm 83, but does not appear to get involved in the war waged between Christ and the armies of the Antichrist. Isaiah 63:1-6 informs us that the Messiah, as the one who is mighty to save, goes into battle alone. The absence of the IDF in the battle of Armageddon is reinforced by Zechariah 13:8, which points out that two-thirds of the Jewish population in the land of Israel will not survive. Zechariah's prophecy infers the IDF will flee from the armies of the Antichrist, rather than fight against them.

## Conclusion

According to Bible prophecy, Israel is on route to striking it rich someday. Their blossoming portfolio appears to include Arab spoils of war. Once obtained, the Ezekiel 38 Magog invaders are enticed to coalesce in an attempt to capture Israel's new national livelihood, which should by then include the acquired Arab resources, including oil and natural gas, plundered by Israel after their decisive victory over the Psalm 83 Arab nations round about.

Psalm 83 is a prophecy formatted into an imprecatory prayer. It foretells the coming of a climatic concluding conflict between the IDF and the Arab nations that share common borders with Israel. Presently those Arab nations are using the Palestinians as pawns in their ongoing war against Israel. This plight of the Palestinians also appears to have been predicted. Refer to the appendix called *Palestinians to be Forced to Israel's Borders*.

# Appendix 13
## Is the Church Identified in Psalm 83?

*(Appendix is based upon an article from the author written on 8/13/2010. Linked here—*
*http://prophecydepot.blogspot.com/2010/08/is-church-hiding-in-psalm-83.html)*

Recently I received an email asking a very interesting church-related question regarding the *hidden ones* of Psalm 83:3.

> They [Arab confederates] have taken crafty counsel against Your people [national Israel], And consulted together against Your sheltered [hidden] ones. (Psalm 83:3) Some translations use the word "hidden" instead of sheltered.

**Question:** I have a question concerning Psalm 83:3 and its link with Isaiah 26:20. The last section of the Psalm verse reads, "and consulted against thy hidden ones," and Isaiah explains who these are that are hiding. I understand these passages refer to the Saints/Church. That being the case would not the inference in the Psalm be that the Church has already been taken before the fulfillment of that prophecy? Kindest Regards– Garry M.

**Bill's Answer**: Brother Garry, I don't believe the church is identified anywhere in Psalm 83. Furthermore, since the rapture is an imminent event, Psalm 83 is about to occur, and the church is still present, it is very possible that Christians may witness the final fulfillment of Psalm 83.

In Psalm 83:3, the Hebrew word for "hidden" in "hidden ones" is *tsaphan*. This word does not appear in Isaiah 26:20 or anywhere else in the book of Isaiah. The first usage of *tsaphan* is in Exodus 2:2-3, alluding to the baby Moses being hidden by his mother from Pharaoh's edict of death in Egypt. At the time, all Hebrew males were being killed at birth in order to keep the Hebrew ethnicity weak and enslaved. However, a remnant led by Moses ultimately survived and departed for the Promised Land.

Typologically, from an end-time perspective, the mother of Moses likely represents national Israel, and Moses the faithful end-time remnant that eventually emerges from within it. Similarly, the next usage of *tsaphan* is found in Joshua 2:4, wherein Rahab was hiding the two spies. These two also typologically signify a select sub-group or remnant of Israel.

I believe that Psalm 83:3 alludes to both national Israel (Your people), which exists today in a condition of unbelief, and the faithful remnant (hidden ones) that comes out from national Israel in the end times in a condition of belief. Although the faithful remnant hasn't emerged yet from within Israel, one will in the tribulation period. Today, they are *tsaphan* within national Israel. Presently, they remain unidentified, but probably exist on the world scene somewhere unknowingly. However, omniscient God knows who and where they are.

Psalm 83 represents a genocidal attempt of the Jews and the final destruction of the Jewish state, that the name Israel be remembered no more (Psalm 83:4). Geo-politically, the Arab confederates want to destroy Israel and confiscate the Promised Land. We see this stage-setting in the Middle East today. Geo-prophetically, Satan wants to destroy all Jews worldwide, especially the infamous coming faithful remnant, to prove God is not a covenant-keeper. In Genesis 13:15, 22:17 and elsewhere, God unconditionally promised Abraham, Isaac, and Jacob, descendants forever. In Genesis 15:18 these patriarchs were promised land from the Nile River in Egypt to the Euphrates in Iraq and Syria. The Psalm 83 Arabs dwell upon a majority of this "Holy Land" today. They want to destroy the Jews and possess the land (Psalm 83:12).

Psalm 83 represents the first of three end-time genocidal attempts against the Jews. Ezekiel 38-39 appears to follow soon and sequentially on the heels of Psalm 83. In Ezekiel's prophecy, Russia, Iran, Turkey, and several other nations will confederate to kill the Jews and confiscate the plunder and booty that Israel will possess after they defeat the Psalm 83 confederacy.

Lastly, the Antichrist will muster up his Armageddon forces in the tribulation period in a final Jewish genocidal attempt. This is when the *tsaphan*, the faithful remnant, of Israel will emerge. They become the saved remnant of Romans 9:27 and 11:26. They are also the "sons of the living God" in Hosea 1:10 and Romans 9:26. I believe the Psalmist Asaph was informing us that Israel's Arab enemies will attempt to kill all Jews, even the hidden faithful, the end time's remnant, so that God's promises to Abraham, Isaac, and Jacob would be broken.

Although the church may be here to witness Psalm 83, it does not appear to be identified anywhere in the Psalm. Psalm 83 is Satan's attempt to inspire the Islamic Arabs that hate and surround Israel to destroy the Jews and the Jewish state in order to prove God is a promise-breaker. In fact, the church needs to come out of hiding regarding Psalm 83 and preach the possibility that it's about to find final fulfillment.

# Appendix 14
## The Treasured Ones of Psalm 83

*(Appendix is based upon an article from the author written on 2/9/2011. Linked here: http://prophecynewsstand.blogspot.com/2011/02/treasured-ones-of-psalm-83.html)*

**C**omment—Dear Mr. Salus—I regularly receive emails from Bible Prophecy and as a matter of fact, I pray Psalm 83 every night for the total defeat of Israel's satanic enemies. Regarding your article "Is the Church Identified in Psalm 83?" I would like to bring the following to your attention. In my Bible Ps.83.3 reads as follows: "They are making secret plans against your people; they are plotting against those you protect." I feel that this translation of vs. 3 is far more descriptive, especially in light of current events that are leading up to Psalm 83, which I believe will be the next "happening" in the prophetic Mideast calendar. It never ceases to amaze me how much different Bible translations differ. *Yours in Christ – J.M. - South Africa*

**Bill's Response** – Dear J.M., thanks for your comment. In 2010, Chuck Missler and I discussed this topic at a southern California prophecy conference we were speaking at. Chuck is studying the possibility that the "hidden" or "treasured" ones in Psalm 83:3 could represent true, born-again Christians. He presented a couple arguments in support of this view. However, for the reasons expressed in (refer to the appendix called, *Is the Church Identified in Psalm 83?*) and those listed below, I believe the "hidden ones" probably represent the faithful remnant inside national Israel.

- To make the "hidden ones" the church implies the confederacy of Psalm 83:6-8 wages a multi-front war against Israel and true Christian believers. It seems that geography alone would defeat this plan. The Psalm 83 confederacy is centered in the Mideast, but true believers are scattered throughout the world. The confederates surround Israel, making it an easy target. However targeting Christians would require a worldwide campaign headquartered in the Middle East, which is unlikely.

- The mandate of Psalm 83:4 is to destroy the Jewish state, "that the name Israel be remembered no more." This mission is very specific regarding Israel.

- The motive of Psalm 83:12 is the capture of the Promised Land of Israel. Thus, the mandate and motive of the Psalm 83 confederacy are entirely regarded with the Jewish people and the land of Israel.

- The Hebrew word for "hidden" is *tsaphan* and is first used in Exodus 2:2-3, identifying Moses being hidden in the basket from Pharaoh's persecution.

- The second usage is in Joshua 2:4 describing Rahab hiding the two spies.

In these initial usages the Hebrew word *tsaphan* best represents the faithful inside national Israel. Therefore, I suggest the "hidden ones" of Psalm 83:3 represent the faithful remnant that will surface out of today's national Israel and survive both Psalm 83 and ultimately the tribulation. The caveat is that if there is a significant generational gap between Psalm 83 and the tribulation, *which I doubt*, then the hidden ones in Psalm 83 probably represent the Messianic Jewish community dwelling inside Israel when Psalm 83 occurs.

# Appendix 15
## Is Egypt in Psalm 83?

*(Based on an article written by the author on 2/9/11. Linked at: http://prophecynewsstand. blogspot.com/2011/02/is-egypt-in-psalm-83.html)*

Most modern-day equivalents of the Psalm 83:6-8 participants are easily identifiable today. Clearly, the territories of Edom, Moab, and Ammon represent modern-day Jordan. Furthermore, Tyre still exists in Lebanon and the Gaza Strip is located in ancient Philistia. However, Egypt is more difficult to identify, causing some scholars to question its existence in the Psalm. Among them is the respected broadcast journalist David Dolan. He authored a book in 2001 entitled *Israel in Crisis, What Lies Ahead*. Dolan's book, along with Dr. Arnold Fruchtenbaum's *Footsteps of the Messiah*, were among the first books published that addressed Psalm 83 as a future war between Israel and its bordering Arab enemies. Dolan excluded, but Fruchtenbaum included, Egypt in the Psalm 83 confederacy.[23] Probably motivated by the February, 2011 crisis in Egypt, David Dolan wrote the following.

> Will Egypt eventually break its peace treaty with Israel? I suspect that in the end, the American-funded and trained army will not allow this to take place. I noted in my latest book, *Israel in Crisis*, that Egypt is not listed in Psalm 83 as being among a host of regional Arab powers that will attempt to destroy Israel in the prophesied end days, while Jordan, Lebanon and Syria are mentioned, along with the Palestinians. David Dolan 2/7/11

As much as I respect Dolan's work, I respectfully disagree with his assessment on Egypt's non-participation in Psalm 83. Here is what the Psalm says:

> O God, keep not thou silence: Hold not thy peace, and be not still, O God. For, lo, thine *enemies* make a tumult; And they that hate thee have lifted up the head. Thy take crafty counsel against thy people, And consult together against thy hidden ones. They have said, Come, and let us cut them off from being a nation; That the name of Israel may be no more in remembrance. For they have consulted together with one consent; Against thee do they make a covenant: The tents of Edom and the Ishmaelites; Moab, and the Hagarenes; *Gebal*,

and Ammon, and Amalek; *Philistia* with the inhabitants of *Tyre*: *Assyria* also is joined with them; They have helped the children of Lot. Selah! (Psalm 83:1-8, ASV; emphasis added)

(Refer to *The Psalm 83 Confederates* image (appendix 26) to discover who the author believes are the modern-day equivalents of the Psalm.)

## The Enemies vs. The Haters

Asaph seems to identify two distinct groups inside the ten-member confederacy. He says "thine *enemies* make a tumult; And they that hate thee have lifted up the head." *The New American Standard Version* translates; "Your *enemies* make an uproar, And those who hate You have exalted themselves."

Who are the *enemies* and *haters* of God listed inside the Psalm? I cover this extensively in my book, *Isralestine, The Ancient Blueprints of the Future Middle East* in the chapter called "Olam Ebah, The Ancient Arab Hatred of the Jews."

The Psalmist says the Lord has those who hate Him, but unlike the general carnal hatred characteristic of sinful humanity described in Romans 8:7, it is a deeply rooted hatred dating back almost 4,000 years. These haters listed by Asaph include the Egyptian matriarch Hagar, alongside the ancient patriarchs: Ishmael, Edom (Esau), Moab, Ammon, and Amalek. These all had familial relations with Abraham and histories of aggression against Abraham, Sarah, Isaac, Jacob, and their Hebrew descendants.

Hagar mothered Abraham's first son Ishmael. Esau was Abraham's grandson from Isaac. Moab and Ammon were the children of Abraham's nephew Lot. Lastly, Amalek was Abraham's great-great grandson through the line of Esau.[24] Esau fathered the Edomites according to Genesis 36:1.

These individuals coveted the rich contents of the Abrahamic Covenant and entered into family feuds with the true Hebrew recipients of the covenantal promises. These individuals, along with their Hebrew counterparts, were the Benjamin Netanyahus, King Abdullahs, and Hosni Mubaraks of their time; from their loins nations were formed.[25]

These jealous "haters" incubated an enmity against the Lord that manifested throughout the region against the Israeli descendants of Abraham, Isaac, and Jacob. The Bible calls it an "ancient hatred," also translated as a "perpetual enmity." Ezekiel 35:5 tells us it was spawned by Esau.

The two Hebrew words used by Ezekiel are *olam ebah*, which when used together can be translated as, "a condition stemming back long ago in ancient times, perpetuated throughout time, manifesting into hostility with no apparent end in sight." As time progressed, the Hebrews staked their covenantal claims throughout the Middle East. These claims included:

- Our God is the only God and you shall have no others before Him, (Exodus 20:3)

- We will be a "great nation" above all others, (Genesis 12:2)

- Arabs must bless Hebrews or be cursed, (Genesis 12:3)

- You Arabs are trespassing on our Hebrew lands. (Genesis 15:18)

Suffice it to say the other four members of Psalm 83, *Gebal, Philistia, Tyre*, and *Assyria*, found it favorable to their religious, real estate, and cultural needs to resist these Hebrew claims and embrace the ancient hatred, well established throughout the region. Thus, these four populations probably represent the *your enemies* group in Psalm 83. The family feuds that developed can be studied in the chapters depicted in the image. (Refer to the image called, *The Family Feuds, Appendix 26*).

Hagar's jealous behavior toward Sarah is one of the reasons we can include her among the Psalm 83 haters. Considering Hagar was an Egyptian, according to Genesis 16:1, and had her son Ishmael marry an Egyptian bride in Genesis 21:21, we can safely conclude the Hagarenes represent Egypt in Psalm 83, through her and Ishmael's family tree. However, it's not quite that simple. Some Bible translations list Hagarites or Hagrites, rather than Hagarenes. This has caused many to believe Psalm 83 is describing another ethnicity than Egyptians. This is because the Hagrites or Hagarites show up in 1 Chronicles 5:10,19-20 and elsewhere as a tribe dwelling approximately 300 miles northeast of Egypt, east of Gilead.

The Hebrew word used by the Psalmist to identify the Hagarenes was *Hagri*. Both the *Strong's Hebrew and Greek Dictionaries*, and the *New American Standard Hebrew and Greek Dictionaries* suggest *Hagri* has a possible matronymic relationship to "Hagar," the Egyptian matriarch.

Additionally, listed below are other reputable quotes supporting the Psalm 83 Hagar - Egyptian connection:

### Holman Bible Dictionary —
HAGARITE (Hag' ahr ite) Name of nomadic tribe whom the tribe of Reuben defeated east of the Jordan River (1 Chron 5:10, 19-20). Reuben won because they called on and trusted in God. The tribal name is apparently taken from Hagar, Sarah's maid and mother of Ishmael (Gen. 16).[26]

### International Standard Bible Encyclopedia—
Hagarenes / Hagarites / Hagrites

An Arab tribe, or confederation of tribes (1 Ch 5:10, 19, 20 the King James Version "Hagarites"; 1 Ch 27:31 the King James Version "Hagerite"; Ps 83:6 "Hagarenes"), against which the Reubenites fought in the days of Saul. In Gen. 25:12-18 are recorded the descendants, "generations," of Ishmael, "whom Hagar the Egyptian Sarah's handmaid, bare unto Abraham."[27]

### New Commentary on the Whole Bible: Old Testament—
Ps. 83:6-8 tabernacles—i.e., tents. Edom—Esau's descendants; they were located southeast of the Dead Sea and repeatedly attacked Israel (Psa. 137:7; Obadiah). Ishmaelites—descendants of Hagar and Abraham (Gen. 25:12ff.) as are the "Hagarenes."[28]

### Barnes, Notes on the Old Testament – Ps. 83:6-8 –

And the Hagarenes—The Hagarenes were properly Arabs, so called from Hagar, the handmaid of Abraham, the mother of Ishmael. Gen. 16:1; 25:12. As connected with the Ishmaelites they would naturally join in this alliance.[29]

Due to the confusion caused by the Hagarene verses Hagrite translation in Psalm 83, I emailed my friend Dr. Arnold Fruchtenbaum of Ariel Ministries in 2008. Dr. Fruchtenbaum, a graduate of Dallas Theological Seminary, ranks among today's most respected eschatologists. I asked him how certain he was that Psalm 83 identified Egypt through the Hagarenes. His email response to me confirmed that he felt comfortable that Egypt is identified through the Hagarenes in Psalm 83.

Lastly, those who omit Egypt from Psalm 83 need to explain Egypt's apparent future confrontation with Israel in Isaiah 19:16-18. Isaiah 19:16 declares Egypt will someday greatly fear Israel. From Isaiah's time until now, this fear has only been in place since Israel's defeat of Egypt in the wars of 1948, 1967, and 1973. It is this fear that drove former Egyptian President Anwar Sadat to make peace with Israel in 1979.

Isaiah 19:17 states this fear evolves into a terror of Israel that overtakes all of Egypt. Isaiah 19:18 predicts this terror results in Egypt allowing Hebrew to be spoken in five Egyptian cities. One of these cities will be renamed the "City of Destruction." These three passages encourage the possibility that Egypt's participation in Psalm 83 provokes the wrath of the Israel Defense Forces against at least five Egyptian cities. In the aftermath of an IDF victory over Egypt, five cities promote Hebrew as the spoken language. This suggests Jews migrate into these five cities taking their language, religion and culture with them.

Some suggest Isaiah 19 deals with the Antichrist's invasion of Egypt, specified in Daniel 11:42-43. Although portions of Isaiah 19 may find partial association with Daniel 11:42-43, it is doubtful that Isaiah 19:16-18 finds any association.

Why would the Antichrist take over five Egyptian cities and allow Hebrew to become the spoken language? It is commonly understood the Antichrist will be attempting Jewish genocide at the time. If this is the case, it would be contrary to his overall purposes to allow five cities in Egypt to promote the language of Hebrew.

For the above reasons I strongly believe that Egypt is identified in Psalm 83. Therefore, unlike David Dolan, I believe Egypt will someday break its peace treaty with Israel and join the Psalm 83 confederacy.

# Appendix 16
## Is the Arab Spring Setting Up for a Winter War?

*(Appendix drawn from an article written by author on 5/26/11. Linked at: http:// prophecynewsstand.blogspot.com/2011/05/is-arab-spring-headed-for-mideast.html)*

At the onset of 2011, many inside the liberal media applauded the widespread Arab protests. They hypothesized the protesters were merely the by-product of a regional youth bulge tired of tyrannical rule. They credited Internet social network sites like Facebook, YouTube, and Twitter for giving the activists a glimpse at freedom. Simply put, the demonstrators were desperately crying out for life, liberty, and the pursuit of happiness. The left-wingers anticipated that a wellspring of Muslim democracies would crop-up across the expansive North African and Middle East regions. However, by early spring actions taken by repressive regimes in Libya, Syria, Iran, Bahrain, Yemen, and Saudi Arabia quickly silenced these ideologues. These partisan pundits apparently forgot about the countless pages of bloodstained history demonstrating that the Arabs are accustomed to deadly power struggles.

Barely digesting the unsettling events of the Arab Spring, the media's attention has now been drawn back to the Arab-Israeli conflict and the genuine possibility of a Mideast Winter War. Presently, Israeli borders are fortified rather than redrawn, Arab arsenals are replenished rather than dismantled, and the prospect for the "Mother of all Mideast Wars" is extremely high. Mideast peace between the Jews and Palestinians has never been more elusive. Although politically brokered *land-swaps* for *peace-pacts* were intended to create unity between Israelis and Palestinians, they have had a reverse effect.

Instead of providing Israel greater security, these proposed land schemes have eventuated in the formation of a unity government between Hamas and Fatah. This is problematic, considering neither of these terror groups - turned Palestinian political parties recognizes Israel as the Jewish state. In fact, Hamas's charter calls for the destruction of Israel.

Interestingly, the evidence suggests that the majority of Middle East and North African countries plagued by the 2011 Muslim unrest are involved in end-time Israeli war prophecies.

Psalm 83 identifies an "*inner circle*" confederacy of Arab populations sharing common borders with Israel. Their mandate is to wipe Israel off the map, and their motive is the reclamation of "Palestine." They are listed in Psalm 83:1-8, and their mandate in verse 12. Conversely, Ezekiel 38-39 describes an "*outer ring*" confederacy destined to invade Israel in the last days. Ezekiel presents a separate set of invaders from those described in Psalm 83. Additionally, they are driven by a different motive, which is the promise of plunder and great spoil. (Ezekiel 38:1-13)

In May, 2011, in a seemingly desperate attempt to broker an Arab state of Palestine, President Barrack Obama suggested that Israel cede the territory it gained in the 1967 War. However, Israeli Prime Minister Benjamin Netanyahu quickly rebuffed this suggestion. On May 24, 2001, before the US Congress, Netanyahu declared that the land in question was not on the table for negotiation; specifically addressing the land acquired by Israel in the aftermath of their war victory in 1967. This land is often referred to as "disputed" territory by the US White House administration and much of the International community. However, Israel considers it their heritage, according to Genesis 15:18."

Summarily, Netanyahu addressed several additional key points relative to Israeli demands for peace:

- Jerusalem WILL be the undivided capital of the Jewish state,

- Millions of Palestinian Refugees WON'T be returning inside Israel,

- The Palestinians MUST recognize Israel's right to exist as the sovereign Jewish State,

- The Hamas – Fatah unity agreement MUST be abolished,

- Palestinian unilateral attempts at statehood through the United Nations MUST cease,

- Israel maintains the RIGHT to defensible borders,

- The Israeli demographic population changes since 1967 MUST be accepted,

- And, Israel WILL monitor Palestinian organizations and operations for national security purposes.

In essence, he put all of Israel's trump cards on the table and called the Palestinians' bluff. His laundry list above hits at the heart of the Palestinian wish-list. Every condition is a point of Palestinian contention. To the Palestinians, this was Netanyahu's declaration of war.

When we consider that Mideast diplomacy has failed, Arabs generally hate Jews, Arab governments have little to no democratic track record, and the Arab protests have primarily occurred in countries listed in end-time Bible prophecies, we can reasonably conclude that the Arab Spring could morph into a Mideast Winter War.

# Appendix 17
## Blockade the Waterways;
## Gog of Magog's "Evil Plan"

*(Appendix is revised from an author article posted on 5/8/10. Linked at: http://prophecydepot.blogspot.com/2010/05/trouble-on-seas-gogs-2-pronged-strategy.html)*

In the summer of 2009, Russia and Iran conducted joint naval maneuvers in the Caspian Sea for the first time.[30] In April 2010, Iran test-fired five new coast-to-sea and sea-to-sea missiles during their "Great Prophet Five" war game in the Persian Gulf. Shortly thereafter, during their "Judgment Day" war games in May, 2010, Iran demonstrated its fitness for sole responsibility over the security of the Persian Gulf, through which thirty-five to forty percent of the world's crude oil is channeled.[31] Since then, in August 2010 Iran opened up its nuclear facility at Bushehr and stocked it with Russian-made fuel rods. Additionally, in June 2011, the Iranian Revolutionary Guards conducted their "Great Prophet Six" war games. The Prophet Six exercises evidenced Iran could launch powerful missiles deep inside Israel.

Evolving military events like these involving Russia and Iran are among the reasons scholars are justifiably stirring over the possibility that the Ezekiel 38-39 Bible prophecy is about to find final fulfillment. The Hebrew prophet predicted approximately 2,600 years ago the coming of a Russian – Iranian led, nine member strong coalition seeking to destroy Israel and confiscate its great booty. (Ezekiel 38:13).

This appendix develops the possibility that the Russian – Iranian led coalition of Ezekiel invaders implements a two-prong "choke and capture" campaign. Step one involves a possible political boycott of Israel's booty, and step two matures into a military campaign to capture that booty.

International coalitions formed to level economic sanctions against a country have become politically expedient. Boycotting a country's imports and exports is a common first step to accomplish the will of a coalition. An excellent example was the Persian Gulf War of August 2, 1990 – February 28, 1991. Saddam Hussein had invaded Kuwait and in so doing brought down international economic sanctions upon the Iraqis. American

President George H. Bush skillfully assembled a sizable coalition that ultimately invaded Iraq, when the sanctions didn't work. The boycott matured into an invasion.

In the case of the Russian – Iranian coalition, this two-step process appears to occur. Identifying the modern-day equivalents of the Ezekiel 38:1-5 invaders, suggests this coalition is strategically assembled. There are geographic and religious commonalities to consider in their case. Apart from Russia, all of the other members hail from predominately Muslim countries. The religious overtones are noteworthy, and detailed in the commentary of chapter 13 called, "Gog Forms an Evil Plan to Invade Israel."

Additionally, locating the invaders geographically on a map, (see *Ezekiel 38 Invaders* image, Appendix 26), provides another interesting clue into the coalition's campaign. All of the Muslim members border the major bodies of water surrounding Israel. Is this coincidence or calculated on Russia's part? Israel will desperately need access through these waterways in order to export its plunder and great booty to global markets. We know with some certainty that Israel will be conducting international commerce because the theme of merchants is introduced in Ezekiel 38:13.

The *merchants of Tarshish* and all *their young lions* are listed, and they appear to be upset with Russia. A suitable modern-day translation of these merchants would be the "customers from Tarshish."[32] These international clients seem to abstain from joining the Russian consortia. Comments they make evidence concerns about Russian intentions to destroy Israel for its great booty. Their protests could be altruistic, but more likely show that they don't want their commercial interests invested in Israel disrupted.

The Mediterranean Sea, Red Sea, and Persian Gulf could easily be blockaded to Israel at Russia's command, once the coalition is set in place. Israel would be forced to truck its exports through the Arabian Peninsula, into the Arabian Sea, on into the Indian Ocean in order to distribute goods to market. All other transportation corridors would be choked off to Israel, since they connect through coalition territories. The image *Ezekiel 38 Invaders* evidences that Israel becomes completely boxed in by an outer ring of countries comprising this coalition.

Once Israel's economic knees buckle from disrupted commerce, the Ezekiel invaders could initiate the military portion of their campaign. Historical war campaigns have often been conducted in this fashion. First the enemy surrounds its target, prompting those under attack to circle the wagons in defense. Once surrounded, the enemy sits it out, forcing their foes to sustain themselves upon stored supplies. When fatigue sets in, the enemy attacks.

The other potential component of interest to add into the Ezekiel 38 equation is the untapped oil wealth landlocked in the Caspian Sea. Estimates suggest the world's largest lake hosts enormous amounts of untapped oil. Presently littoral rights are a major matter of tension between the nations of Russia, Iran, Kazakhstan, Azerbaijan, and Turkmenistan, which all surround the Caspian.

The Russian - Iranian joint naval exercises referenced earlier suggest they ultimately intend to share domination of this potential oil fortune. They will want to transport Caspian oil out into world markets and presently the main distribution is the BTC pipeline running through Baku, Azerbaijan; Tbilisi, Georgia; and Ceyhan, Turkey. Russia and Iran presently lack the necessary exclusive control of this critical pipeline. However, that could easily change, since Turkey ultimately enlists with the Ezekiel invaders.

Additionally, the border countries of Azerbaijan and Turkmenistan may join Russia's coalition, easing regional tension over the littoral rights to the Caspian Sea. This would give the Russian coalition the ready means and access to control the Caspian oil and its exportation. Only Georgia would possibly stand in the way and we know Russia can overpower Georgia; Russia temporarily shut this pipeline down during its invasion of Georgia in August of 2008.

Sovereignty over all major oil export pipelines and distribution waterways in tandem with control of robust Iranian and Caspian oil reserves will make Russia's coalition a commercial force to be reckoned with. Unfortunately, they will not be content with that, but will also seek Israel's plunder and great spoil. If Russia and Iran control all the Caspian and OPEC oil supplies in the future, they could possibly become unstoppable in their bid for collective world control. It is probably this goal that partially allures the other members to join in the Ezekiel coalition.

# Conclusion

It appears Russia will formulate a comprehensive "choke and capture" campaign, involving strategically located allies intent on invading Israel. This effort involves an outer ring of nations not presently sharing common borders with Israel. The inner circle of Arab states are likely not included in Russia's consortia, because they have probably been defeated previously in the Arab – Israeli war of Psalm 83:6-8.

In the war's aftermath, Israel seemingly annexes more territory and captures Arab spoils of war, making it potentially a very wealthy nation. Russia then forms its campaign and alliance to prevent Israel from burgeoning into a significant commercial goods and oil-exporting nation. Russia strategically assembles Muslim nations sharing a hatred of Israel. This coalition seems to be strategically selected in order to blockade Israel's exports first, and then destroy the Jewish State afterward. Perhaps the ominous phrase, "I will turn you around, put hooks into your jaws, and lead you out . . .," in Ezekiel 38:4 has something to do with a waterway related campaign against Israel. However, instead of catching fish on the seas, it may involve exporting oil through them.

# Appendix 18
## Iranistan, The Coming Shiite Crescent

*(Appendix drawn from an article written by author on 10/14/10. Linked at: http://www. prophecydepot.net/2010/iranistan-the-coming-shiite-crescent-2/)*

Israeli Prime Minister Benjamin Netanyahu's October 11, 2010, pre-condition for Mideast peace may be the shot in the arm Iran needed to accelerate its move to form a Shiite Crescent inside the Fertile Crescent.[33] Netanyahu proclaimed that in order to extend the moratorium settlement freeze on building in the West Bank, the Palestinians must recognize Israel as a Jewish state. Mideast peace talks subsequently and predictably dissolved shortly after this freeze expired on September 26, 2010. Additionally, Netanyahu's proclamation followed one day after the Israeli cabinet passed the controversial "loyalty oath."[34] If this bill passes into law it will require new Israeli citizens, Jew and non-Jew, to pledge allegiance to a "Jewish and democratic" state.

The call for recognition of a Jewish state and the oath of loyalty hit at the heart of the Palestinian predicament. The Palestinians are a displaced population of renegade refugees. Much like the Kurds scattered in adjacent parts of Iran, Iraq, Syria and Turkey, the Palestinians remain stateless and scattered in the Gaza, West Bank and border lying areas of Israel. The Palestinian refugee crisis resulted from the failure of the defeated Arab states surrounding Israel to resettle the Arabs of Palestine back into their ancestral Arab homelands after Israel won the War of Independence in 1948.

Rather than "Resettlement," "Right of Return" is the favored policy of the Arab supporters of the Palestinian refugees. The Arab states cringe at the hint of resettlement. Jeremiah 12:14-17 foretold they would be uprooted in order to be resettled; however, the Arab states vehemently oppose this. Seldom has the resettlement topic arisen in diplomatic peace talks. The talks always propose the right of the Palestinian refugees to return into Israel. If Israel becomes the *bona fide* Jewish state and all new citizens are forced to pledge allegiance to it, Palestinian refugees will be forced to resettle into the Arab states that generally reject them.

Presently, peace talks have hit a stalemate, opening a window of opportunity for Iran to make its move on the Middle East. It is commonly understood in the region that the present Iranian regime seeks the formation of a Shiite Crescent, starting with

Lebanon and Syria and subsequently moving deeper into the Sunni Arab states of Jordan and Saudi Arabia. Iran has been building inseparable relations with Hezbollah and Syria, and developing a nuclear program that should facilitate the Crescent's formation in the foreseeable future.

Iran's plans to subjugate Lebanon seem imminent at this point, and likely include a Hezbollah-backed revolution, if deemed necessary. Having seized power in Iran through revolution in 1979, the present Iranian regime is adept at accomplishing the same in Lebanon. However, instead of exercising proven revolutionary tactics in Lebanon, Iran could incite its proxy, Hezbollah, to instigate violence against Israel. By provoking Israel to attack Lebanon, seemingly as an aggressor, the Lebanese are expected to rally around Hezbollah for protection. Lebanon is a proven battleground, having been plagued with wars throughout modern history.

Making matters worse for Israel, Hezbollah has the backing of Iran, Syria and the Hamas, should another conflict occur. Iran has feverishly worked with Syria to arm Hezbollah with skillfully trained troops and 60,000 rockets over the past four years.[35] In the summer of 2006, Hezbollah lobbed 4,000 rockets into northern Israel, averaging 117 strikes per day. Presently, Hezbollah has fifteen times as many more advanced rockets, and arrogantly boasts it can hit any target inside of Israel, including Dimona, Israel's main nuclear site.

In its bid to revive the ancient Persian Empire, Iran could achieve the killing of three birds with one stone in a coming conflict: the destruction of Israel, the establishment of a Palestinian state in its place and the allegiance of Lebanon to Iran. Iran seeks a Palestinian state in their Shiite pocket. Iranian president Ahmadinejad's continued threats to wipe Israel off the map hint of a greater plan to control Jerusalem, Islam's third holiest city, by establishing a Palestinian proxy state to replace Israel. Here are some prior pertinent quotes from Hassan Nasrallah, Secretary General of Hezbollah: "We do not believe in multiple Islamic republics; we do believe, however, in a single Islamic world governed by a central government." "Jerusalem and Palestine will not be regained with political games, but with guns." "Hezbollah can destroy one-half of Israel's army."

Considering Palestinians comprise sixty-five percent of the Jordanian population, Jordan could easily become Iran's subsequent target, should Hezbollah be victorious over Israel.[36] At this point let me emphasize there is no biblical reason to believe, nor do I believe, that Hezbollah would win over Israel; however, the point being made is this is likely the logical thinking of the present Iranian regime.

Furthermore, Jordanian King Abdullah II has expressed his concern about this Shiite Crescent[37] possibility on numerous occasions. Lebanon, Syria, Palestine, Jordan and possibly Iraq, falling like dominoes into Iran's grand Shiite scheme, puts Saudi Arabia and the other smaller OPEC Arab nations of Kuwait, Qatar, and the United Arab Emirates in a precarious position. OPEC presently provides one-third of the world's oil supply, and Saudi Arabia is ranked number #1 within OPEC. This makes Saudi Arabia a prime down-the-road target on Iran's hit list. Saudi King Abdullah is extremely concerned about the prospects of Iran taking over the Middle East. In addition to its oil surplus Saudi Arabia also hosts Islam's two holiest cities, Mecca and Medina. If Iran first controls Jerusalem through a proxy Palestine and subsequently captures Mecca and Medina, it can possess the oil and tourism wealth of the Middle East and promote Shiite theology on a wider scale within Islam. Seemingly, for this reason Saudi Arabia has temporarily allowed Israel a strip of airspace to pre-empt a strategic strike against Iranian nuclear sites and contracted to purchase 60 billion dollars worth of advanced American aircraft.[38]

It appears as though Iran wants to turn Isralestine into Palestine and the greater Mideast into a region called Iranistan.[39] According to Bible prophecies contained in Psalm 83, Ezekiel 38-39, and Jeremiah 49:34-39 this doesn't find fulfillment; however, the breakdown of Mideast peace talks primes the pump for an Iranian attempt to revive the Persian Empire.

# Appendix 19
## The Fallible Assumption of Mary

Some believe she has redemptive power, others suspect she is the demonic impostor called "Mother of Harlots" in the biblical book of Revelation—the Catholic "Virgin Mary." Why has she become one of the most controversial religious figures of our time?

While Iranian president Mahmoud Ahmadinejad is praying for the return of the Shiite Islamic Messiah called the Twelfth Imam, also called the Mahdi, Catholics by the millions continue to pilgrimage annually to Marian apparition sites scattered throughout various parts of the world. Even more pray to her daily for guidance and spiritual intercession. Many Catholics believe the apparition is Mary, the mother of Jesus, in the Bible. Several of her supernatural sightings like, Our Lady of Guadeloupe (Mexico City) in 1531 and Our Lady of Fatima (Portugal) in 1917, are officially accredited by the Roman Catholic Church.[40]

## What is her extra-biblical story in a nutshell?

On November 1, 1950, Pope Pius XII, exercising papal infallibility, declared in "Munificentissimus Deus," (*most bountiful god*) that the Assumption of Mary is a dogma of the Catholic Church. He announced "That the Immaculate Mother of God, the ever Virgin Mary, having completed the course of her earthly life, was assumed body and soul into heavenly glory."[41]

As a dogma, the *Assumption* is a required belief of all Catholics; anyone who publicly dissents from the dogma, Pope Pius XII declared, "has fallen away completely from the divine and Catholic Faith." His statement accuses "anyone" who believes Mary died, rather than was assumed up into heaven while still living, is an apostate "fallen away completely" from the "divine" things pertaining to God.[42]

The Pope Pius XII declaration was made in direct correlation with the infallible statement issued ninety-six years earlier by Pope Pius IX in "Ineffabilis Deus" (*ineffable god*). His predecessor's statement pertained to the Immaculate Conception of the Virgin Mary.[43] This prior Pope's statement became the basis for Pope Pius XII Assumption of Mary dogma.

The Immaculate Heart of Mary, formerly called "The Sacred Heart of Mary," probably finds its early beginnings around the time of St. Augustine who stated: "Mary was not merely passive at the foot of the cross; she cooperated through charity in the work of our redemption."[44] Similarly, even though Saint Epiphanius of Salamis stated in AD 377 that no one knew whether Mary had died or not, apocryphal accounts of the Assumption of Mary have circulated since at least the fourth century.[45]

It is generally understood that Pope Pius XII exercised his papal authority in this matter to connect the Immaculate Heart of Mary with her bodily assumption into heaven. After years of controversy, he was left only two options. He could connect the two events officially through dogma or discredit all Catholic-accredited Mary apparitions.

The argument points surrounding the dilemma Catholicism faced were as follows:

- If Mary *died, she received* the wages of her sin. (Romans 6:23)

- If she died, she was simply *a sinner* in need of a Savior, which she admits in Luke 1:47.

- If she was *in need of a Savior*, then she *cannot be venerated* as having an *immaculate heart*. (Sin dictated the need for an "Immaculate Conception" in the first place, in order to override the powerful grip of death or in the case of our redemption, repay death its due wage.)

- As a sinner in need of a Savior she possessed *no redemptive power*.

- As a sinner who died, she *could not* subsequently *reappear randomly in apparitions*, making self-exalted redemptive claims.

These above points are crucial, considering several Catholic-accredited Mary visionaries report the apparition has made both self-exalting and co-redemptrix claims. Thus, the only possible way for Pope Pius XII specifically, and Roman Catholicism generally, to override the above sound Scriptural objections was to address them at their roots. Mary's death needed to be disproved and her assumption to heaven validated. If this could be done, then the immaculate nature of Mary's heart could be substantiated. Predictably, neither Pope Pius XII nor Pope Pius IX could provide such proof. However, Catholics are expected to accept papal infallibility in lieu of the need for proof in this matter. If the Vicar of Christ, the Pope in this case, exercises papal infallibility, his interpretations of the Scriptures are to be esteemed on even par with the Holy Scriptures themselves.

The inference to be understood by the Assumption of Mary dogma is that Mary was assumed directly into heaven, avoiding death's grip entirely, which she could only have done by having a sinless or immaculate heart. Thus, since she didn't die, but was assumed, she possesses an unrestricted right of random planetary return through apparitions, or whatever other means she chooses, throughout time.

As stated above, the Assumption of Mary dates back as far as the fourth century. Early references to the Assumption of Mary include Timothy of Jerusalem around 380 AD, who wrote: "Wherefore the Virgin is immortal up to now, because He who dwelt in her took her to the regions of the Ascension."[46] The uninterrupted tradition of the Catholic Church feast celebrating the Assumption of Mary dates back at least to 549

AD, as witnessed by Gregory of Tours and other Fathers of the Church.[47] Below is a quote that appropriately summarizes the connection between the Immaculate Heart of Mary and her assumption.

> On this special Feast, we are reminded of the flawless nature of Mary, the Mother of God. As the New Eve, Mary was created flawless, remained flawless throughout her life and was elevated to Heaven in her flawless state at the end of her earthly life. Consequently, the Holy Catholic Church proclaimed the dogmas of the Immaculate Conception and the Assumption of Mary in support of these truths.[48]

Some estimate that during the past forty years there may have been thousands of alleged apparitions every single year![49] This is an enormous number, rivaling even the number of reported UFO sightings, and complicates the controversy over the Catholic dogma of the Assumption of Mary and the Immaculate Heart of Mary.[50] The Bible predicts that there will be an increase in deception in the end times and many will be deceived by lying signs and wonders. It is not surprising to see an increase in the number of apparitions appearing in more and more places throughout the world. Ultimately, Satan will use these Marian impostors to unite the world in a global religion.[51]

> Then one of the seven angels who had the seven bowls came and talked with me, saying to me, "Come, I will show you the judgment of the great harlot who sits on *many waters*, with whom the kings of the earth committed fornication, and the inhabitants of the earth were made drunk with the wine of her fornication." ... (Regarding the waters verse 15 informs) Then he [the angel] said to me, "The waters which you saw, where the harlot sits, are peoples, multitudes, nations, and tongues. (Revelation 17:1-2, 15; emphasis added)

These Revelation passages inform that the great harlot will preside over many world leaders and inhabitants of the earth. At the apparent pinnacle of her prestige, the great harlot of Mystery Babylon will be destroyed by "Ten Kings." These kings surface in the end times according to Daniel 7:24, wherein he eludes to them as "Ten Horns." They come out of the kingdom Daniel 7:23 says will take over the whole earth. Many believe this kingdom represents a global government that emerges in the last days. The global government appears to at some point split into ten kingdoms, which gives rise to these ten kings.

> And the ten horns which you saw on the beast, these will hate the harlot, make her desolate and naked, eat her flesh and burn her with fire. For God has put it into their hearts to fulfill His purpose, to be of one mind, and to give their kingdom to the beast, [Antichrist] until the words of God are fulfilled. (Revelation 17:16-17)

Once the pagan religious system the harlot represents is devastated, *the beast* [Antichrist] will establish the final world religion, and along with a False Prophet force her forsaken followers to worship the beast.

It was granted to him [Antichrist] to make war with the saints and to overcome them. And authority was given him over every tribe, tongue, and nation. All who dwell on the earth will worship him, whose names have not been written in the Book of Life of the Lamb slain from the foundation of the world. (Revelation 13:7-8).

Whereas before, the great harlot sat over diverse tongues and nations, here we see that the Antichrist exerts his power over her former spiritual subscribers. The Antichrist will team up with a False Prophet and force people to worship their final world religious system.

He [False Prophet] causes all, both small and great, rich and poor, free and slave, to receive a mark on their right hand or on their foreheads, and that no one may buy or sell except one who has the mark or the name of the beast [Antichrist], or the number of his name. (Revelation 13:16-17).

# Conclusion

To discredit the Catholic Mary, her immaculate heart, assumption, and sightings, would destroy the centuries-old traditional teaching of the Catholic Church, discredit papal infallibility, and adversely affect Catholicism. Not only would the denial of Mary's Assumption cripple Catholicism, it would also detrimentally damage all groups still celebrating the assumption of Mary alongside Roman Catholic Church; such as, Eastern Catholic Churches, Eastern Orthodoxy, Oriental Orthodoxy, and parts of the Anglican Communion and Continuing Anglicanism.

Much like Shiite eschatology predicts the return of the Twelfth Imam (Mahdi) who died well over 1,000 years ago, Catholicism teaches Mary has returned to Earth on numerous occasions. To teach that either Mary or the Mahdi has conquered or escaped the power of death, and are able to return to Earth is heretical. Only Jesus Christ has authority over the power of death and the resurrection from death.

The veneration of this "Mary" impostor could be what the letter to the Church of Thyatira warns against.

Nevertheless I have a few things against you, because you allow that woman Jezebel, who calls herself a prophetess, to teach and seduce My servants to commit sexual immorality and eat things sacrificed to idols. And I gave her time to repent of her sexual immorality, and she did not repent. Indeed I will cast her into a sickbed, and those who commit adultery with her into great tribulation, unless they repent of their deeds. (Revelation 2:20-22).

As pointed out in the appendix called, *The Final Century—Christian Survival versus Pagan Revival,* the seven letters to the seven churches in Revelation have prophetic applications. The letter to Thyatira appears to address Catholicism within the church age. The passages above issue a stern warning about a seductive feminine figure that masquerades as a prophetess. If Catholicism is being addressed in the letter to Thyatira, then the worship of Mary may represent "that woman Jezebel" in the letter.

The allusions to her sexual immorality and adultery likely have idolatrous spiritual connotations.

This apostate Catholic component, seduced by this false prophetess, is severely punished. These misguided souls get cast into "great tribulation," which seemingly finds association with the last half of the tribulation period. Those individuals presently seeking to elevate this "Mary" impostor to the stature of a "mediatrix" or "co-redemptrix" on even par with Christ, need to be reminded that there is only one name through which mankind can be redeemed and it's not Mary. It's Jesus Christ!

> Nor is there salvation in any other, for there is no other name [than Jesus Christ] under heaven given among men by which we must be saved. (Acts 4:12).

Many of the apparitions appear to be genuine; however, unless hard proof can be provided that Mary didn't die, but was assumed up to heaven, the obvious conclusion to be made is that the apparitions are demonic in nature and intended to deceive humanity. This isn't about Mary, the mother of Jesus; it's about Satan's attempt to dupe mankind.

> And no marvel; for Satan himself is transformed into an angel of light. (2 Corinthians 11:14, KJV)

Some demonic being is masquerading as Mary in these last days, and the segment of the Catholic Church that is seduced by her enchantments is in danger of being cast into the "great tribulation" unless they repent of their deeds, according to Revelation 2:22.

# Appendix 20
## The Sinner's Salvation Prayer

"In an acceptable time I have heard you, And in the day of salvation I have helped you." Behold, now *is* the accepted time; behold, now *is* the day of salvation. (2 Corinthians 6:2).

The most important life decision one can make is to receive Christ as his personal Lord and Savior. It is the sinner's passport to a forgiven and changed life, so that they can enter paradise. However, sin is not allowed in heaven; therefore, Christ came to remedy the sin problem confronting mankind. He was sent because God so loved the world that He wished none would perish, but all would inhabit eternity.

For God so loved the world that He gave His only begotten Son, [Jesus Christ] that whoever believes in Him should not perish but have everlasting life. (John 3:16).

And this is eternal life, that they may know You, the only true God, and Jesus Christ [Begotten Son of God] whom You have sent. (John 17:1-3).

These passages point out that people are perishing, to the great displeasure of God, Who loves them immeasurably. He wishes that none would perish, but that everyone would inhabit eternity with Him and His only begotten Son, Jesus Christ. Of the utmost importance to eternal life is the knowledge of these two.

## Sin Separates Us from the Love of God

The apostle John reminds us in 1 John 4:8, 16 that God is love; but, man lives in a condition of sin, which separates him from God's love. Romans 8:5-8 explains how sin manifests into carnal behavior, that creates enmity between God and man. So then, those who are in the flesh cannot please God. (Romans 8:8).

The book of Romans also instructs us that sin entered into the world through Adam, and spread throughout all mankind, thereafter. Additionally, Romans informs us that sin is the root cause of all death, but through Jesus Christ eternal life can be obtained.

Therefore, just as through one man [Adam] sin entered the world, and death through sin, and thus death spread to all men, because all [men] sinned. (Romans 5:12).

All we like sheep have gone astray; We [mankind] have turned, every one, to his own way; And the LORD has laid on Him [Jesus Christ] the iniquity of us all. (Isaiah 53:6).

For the wages of sin *is* death, but the gift of God *is* eternal life in Christ Jesus our Lord. (Romans 6:23).

If this makes sense to you, and you:

- Will humble yourself and recognize you are a sinner, separated from your Creator and living under the curse of sin,
- Believe that Jesus Christ took your punishment for sin so that you could be pardoned, as the only way to be saved
- Want to repent and start letting God make changes in your life, to be in right relationship with Him,
- And, want to do it right now,

Then you have come to a right place spiritually. It is the place where millions before you, and many of your contemporaries alongside you, have arrived.

By the grace of God, you have only one final step to take to complete your eternal journey. This is because salvation is a gift of God. Christ paid the full price for all sin, past, present, and future, when He sacrificed His life in Jerusalem about 2,000 years ago. Your pardon for sin is available to you through faith in the finished work of Jesus Christ completed upon His bloodstained cross. His blood was shed for us. He paid sins wages of death on our account.

You must now take the final leap of faith to obtain your eternal salvation. It is your faith in Christ that is important to God.

But without faith *it is* impossible to please *Him,* [God] for he who comes to God must believe that He is, and *that* He is a rewarder of those who diligently seek Him. (Hebrews 11:6; emphasis added).

In this you [believer] greatly rejoice, though now for a little while, if need be, you have been grieved by various trials, that *the genuineness of your faith, being much more precious than gold that perishes*, though it is tested by fire, may be found to praise, honor, and glory at the revelation of Jesus Christ, whom having not seen you love. Though now you do not see *Him,* yet believing, you rejoice with joy inexpressible and full of glory, receiving the end of your faith—the salvation of *your* souls. (1 Peter 1:6-9; emphasis added).

Before the necessary step to salvation gets introduced, it is important to realize and appreciate that salvation is a gift provided to us through God's grace. We didn't earn it, but we must receive it. If you are one who has worked hard to earn everything you have achieved in life, then you are to be commended. However, there is nothing you as a sinner could have done to meet the righteous requirement to cohabit eternity with God. In the final analysis, when we see our heavenly Father in His full glory, we will all be overwhelmingly grateful that Christ's sacrificial death bridged the chasm between our unrighteousness, and God's uncompromising holiness.

> But God, who is rich in mercy, because of His great love with which He loved us, even when we were dead in trespasses, [sin] made us alive together with Christ (*by grace you have been saved*), and raised *us* up together, and made *us* sit together in the heavenly *places* in Christ Jesus, that in the ages to come He might show the exceeding riches of His grace in *His* kindness toward us in Christ Jesus. *For by grace you have been saved* through faith, and that not of yourselves; *it is the gift of God,* not of works, lest anyone should boast. (Ephesians 2:4-9; emphasis added).

# The Good News Gospel Truth

The term gospel is derived from the Old English "god-spell," which was understood to mean "good news" or "glad tidings." In a nutshell, the gospel is the good news message of Jesus Christ. Jesus came because God so loved the world that He sent His Son to pay the penalty for our sins. That's part of the good news, but equally important is the "Resurrection."

This is the entire good news gospel:

> For I delivered to you first of all that which I also received: that Christ died for our sins according to the Scriptures, and that He was buried, and that He rose again the third day according to the Scriptures (1 Corinthians 15:3-4).

Christ resurrected which means He's alive and able to perform all of His abundant promises to believers. The Bible tells us that He is presently in heaven, seated at the right hand side of God the Father, waiting until His enemies become His footstool.

> But this Man, [Jesus Christ became a Man, to die a Man's death] after He had offered one sacrifice for sins forever, sat down at the right hand of God, from that time waiting till His enemies are made His footstool. For by one offering He has perfected forever those who are being sanctified. (Hebrews 10:12-14).

The resurrection of Christ overwhelmingly serves as His certificate of authenticity to all His teachings. He traveled through the door of death, and resurrected to validate His promises and professions. This can't be said of the claims of Buddha (Buddhism), Mohammed (Islam), Krishna (Hinduism), or any of the other host of deceased, human, non-resurrected, false teachers. All the erroneous teachings they deposited on the living side of death's door were invalidated when they died and lacked the power to conquer death itself, as Jesus had done. One of Christ's most important claims is:

APPENDICES

Jesus said to him, "I am the way, the truth, and the life. No one comes to the [heavenly] Father except through Me." (John 14:6)

This is a critical claim, considering eternal life can only be obtained by knowing the heavenly Father, and Christ, whom He (the Father) sent, according to John 17, listed at the top of this appendix. Most importantly, the resurrection proves that death has an Achilles heel. It means that its grip can be loosed from us, but only by Christ who holds the power over death.

"O Death, where is your sting? O Hades, where is your victory?" The sting of death is sin, and the strength of sin is the law. But thanks be to God, who gives us the victory [over Death and Hades] through our Lord Jesus Christ. (1 Corinthian 15:55-57)

# How to be Saved —You Must Be Born Again

Jesus answered and said to him, [Nicodemus] "Most assuredly, I say to you, unless one is born again, he cannot see the kingdom of God." (John 3:3)

Jesus told Nicodemus, a religious leader of his day, that entrance into the kingdom of God required being born again. This is a physical impossibility, but a spiritual necessity, and why faith plays a critical role in your salvation. You can't physically witness your new birth; it is a spiritual accomplishment beyond your control, that happens upon receiving Christ as your Lord and Savior. God takes full responsibility for your metamorphosis into a new creation at that point.

Therefore, if anyone is in Christ, he is a new creation; old things have passed away; behold, all things have become new. (2 Corinthians 5:17)

You must trust God to perform on His promise to escort you through the doors of death into eternity, and to process you into the likeness of Christ meanwhile. This is the ultimate meaning of being born again; and alongside Christ, it is a responsibility undertaken by the third member of the Trinity, the Holy Spirit. Christ holds the power over Death and Hades, but the Holy Spirit is your "Helper" that participates in your spiritual processing.

I am He [Jesus Christ] who lives, and was dead, and behold, I am alive forevermore. [Resurrected] Amen. And I have the keys of Hades and of Death. (Revelation 1:18)

"If you love Me [Christ], keep My commandments. And I will pray the Father, and He will give you another Helper [Holy Spirit], that He may abide with you forever—the Spirit of truth, whom the world cannot receive, because it neither sees Him nor knows Him; but you know Him, for He dwells with you and will be in you. (John 14:15-17)

"These things I have spoken to you while being present with you. But the Helper, the Holy Spirit, whom the Father will send in My name, He will teach you all things, and bring to your remembrance all things that I said to you. (John 14:25-26)

In order for you to successfully cross over from death to eternal life, *at the appointed time*, God has to work His unique miracle. Christ's resurrection demonstrated He possesses the power to make your eternity happen. Death wasn't eliminated in the resurrection, it was conquered. Death still serves its purpose on Earth by providing the sinner his due wage. Death continues to serve its purpose even in the Messianic Kingdom, where Christ reigns over a restored Earth for 1,000 years.[52]

> "No more shall an infant from there *live but a few* days, Nor an old man who has not fulfilled his days; For the child shall *die* one hundred years old, But the sinner *being* one hundred years old shall be accursed. (Isaiah 65:20; emphasis added)

This is why the full gospel involves both God's love and power. His love for us would be of little benefit if it ended with our deaths. His love and power are equally important for our eternal assurance. Therefore, we see in Romans 10, the following:

> But what does it say? *"The word is near you, in your mouth and in your heart"* (that is, the word of faith which we preach): that if you confess with your mouth the Lord Jesus and believe in your heart that God has raised Him from the dead, you will be saved. For with the heart one believes unto righteousness, and with the mouth confession is made unto salvation. For the Scripture says, *"Whoever believes on Him will not be put to shame."* For there is no distinction between Jew and Greek, for the same Lord over all is rich to all who call upon Him. For *"whoever calls on the name of the Lord shall be saved."* (Romans 10:8-13)

These Romans verses sum it up for all who seek to be saved through Christ. We must confess that Jesus Christ is Lord, and believe in our hearts that God raised Him from the dead.

## The Sinner's Prayer for Salvation

Knowing that confession of Christ as Lord, coupled with a sincere faith that God raised Him from the dead, are salvation requirements, the next step is customarily to recite a sinner's prayer in order to officiate one's salvation.

## Definition of the Sinner's Prayer

A sinner's prayer is an evangelical term referring to any prayer of humble repentance spoken or read by individuals who feel convicted of the presence of sin in their life and desire to form or renew a personal relationship with God through His son Jesus Christ. It is not intended as liturgical like a creed or a confiteor. It is intended to be an act of initial conversion to Christianity, and also may be prayed as an act of recommitment for those who are already believers in the faith. The prayer can take on different forms. There is no formula of specific words considered essential, although it usually contains an admission of sin and a petition asking that the Divine (Jesus) enter into the person's life.[53]

## Example of the Sinner's Prayer

Below is a sample Sinner's Prayer taken from the Salvation Prayer website. If you are ready to repent from your sins, and to receive Jesus Christ as your personal Lord and Savior, read this prayer will all sincerity of heart to God.

> Dear God in heaven, I come to you in the name of Jesus. I acknowledge to You that I am a sinner, and I am sorry for my sins and the life that I have lived; I need your forgiveness.
>
> I believe that your only begotten Son Jesus Christ shed His precious blood on the cross at Calvary and died for my sins, and I am now willing to turn from my sin.
>
> You said in Your Holy Word, Romans 10:9 that if we confess the Lord as our God and believe in our hearts that God raised Jesus from the dead, we shall be saved.
>
> Right now I confess Jesus as the Lord of my soul. With my heart, I believe that God raised Jesus from the dead. This very moment I receive Jesus Christ as my own personal Savior and according to His Word, right now I am saved.
>
> Thank you Jesus, for your unlimited grace which has saved me from my sins. I thank you Jesus that your grace never leads to license for sin, but rather it always leads to repentance. Therefore Lord Jesus transform my life so that I may bring glory and honor to you alone and not to myself.
>
> Thank you Jesus, for dying for me and giving me eternal life.
>
> Amen.[54]

## Congratulations and welcome into the household of God!

Below are the congratulatory words and recommendations also taken from the Salvation Prayer website. If you just prayed the Sinner's Prayer please be sure to read this section for further guidance.

"If you just said this prayer and you meant it with all your heart, we believe that you just got saved and are born again. You may ask, "Now that I am saved, what's next?" First of all you need to get into a Bible-based church, and study God's Word. Once you have found a church home, you will want to become water-baptized. By accepting Christ you are baptized in the spirit, but it is through water-baptism that you show your obedience to the Lord. Water baptism is a symbol of your salvation from the dead. You were dead but now you live, for the Lord Jesus Christ has redeemed you for a price! The price was His death on the cross. May God Bless You!"[55]

Remember, being born again is a spiritual phenomenon. You may have felt an emotional response to your commitment to Christ, but don't be concerned if fireworks didn't spark, bands didn't march, sirens didn't sound, or trumpets didn't blast in the background at the time. There will be plenty of ticker-tape for us in heaven, which is where our rewards will be revealed. If you meant what you said, you can be assured God, Who sent His Son to be crucified on our behalf, overheard your every word. Even the angels in heaven are rejoicing.

> "Likewise, I say to you, there is joy in the presence of the angels of God over one sinner who repents." (Luke 15:10).

## *Welcome to the family...!*

# Appendix 21

## Old Testament Allusions to the Rapture—
## by Jim Tetlow

Several Old Testament allusions to the rapture exist and are helpful to argue for a pre-trib rapture timing. Many eschatologists have used Old Testament models like these below written by Christian author Jim Tetlow, to validate the rapture and its pre-Seventieth Week timing. Normally, I author all the appendices in my books, but in this unique instance I obtained permission from my good friend Jim Tetlow to use his excellent work previously performed on this subject. [56] —Bill Salus

Perhaps some of the strongest arguments in favor of a pre-tribulation, pre-Seventieth Week of Daniel rapture are found in the Old Testament. In the Old Testament we see "a shadow of the good things to come, and not the very image of the things" (Hebrews 10:1). The Holy Spirit explains that these Old Testament types are preserved for our learning:

> For whatever things were written before were written for our learning, that we through the patience and comfort of the Scriptures might have hope. (Romans 15:4)

> Now all these things happened to them (Old Testament characters) as examples, and they were written for our admonition, upon whom the ends of the ages have come. (1 Corinthians 10:11)

Bible students are well aware that there are numerous Old Testament types that foreshadow a New Testament fulfillment. A classic example is when Abraham took his son, his only son Isaac, whom he greatly loved, to the land of Moriah to offer him there as a sacrifice – concluding that God was able to raise him from the dead (Genesis 22; Hebrews 11:17-19). Abraham is a beautiful type of our heavenly Father, and Isaac, his beloved son, is a striking picture of Jesus, who willingly laid down His life on Mount Moriah 2,000 years later. Though the rapture was hidden in part from Old Testament believers, the types found throughout foreshadow a future rapture when God removes His people prior to pouring out His wrath on a Christ-rejecting world.

Let's now review some of these beautiful types that foreshadow the rapture:

- In Noah's day there were those who passed through the flood (Noah and his family in the ark); there were those who perished in the flood (the unbelieving world); and there was Enoch who was "translated" or "caught up" before the judgment of God was poured out. Enoch walked with God (Genesis 5:24) and pleased Him (Hebrews 11:5), just as Christians who abide in Christ please God (1 John 3:22). Interestingly, from the time God told Noah to enter the ark, until the time when the waters of the flood were on the earth, God granted seven more days for the world to repent (Genesis 7:1-10). Perhaps this is a foreshadow of the final seven-year period culminating in the final judgment (Revelation 19:11- 21).

- In Lot's day, Lot and his family were "removed" before God rained down His judgment on Sodom and Gomorrah (Genesis 19). God did not just "preserve" them through His wrath, He removed them prior to judgment. Jesus said that just before His return it would be like the days of Noah (Luke 17:26) and like the days of Lot (Luke 17:28). Judgment in Sodom *could not* occur until Lot was removed (Genesis 19:22)! Remarkably, "while [Lot] lingered, the [angels] took hold of his hand, his wife's hand, and the hands of his two daughters, the Lord being merciful to him, and they brought him out and set him outside the city...Hurry, escape there. For I cannot do anything until you arrive there (v. 16, 22). In other words, they were forcibly removed prior to judgment, and judgment could not commence until they safely arrived in the new city!

- Joseph (a type of Christ in many ways) takes a Gentile bride before the seven-year famine begins (Genesis 41:45). Notice in the account of Joseph, that after he received his Gentile bride, his brethren (the Israelites) and the entire world suffered a seven-year famine. (Genesis 41:54-57). During this time of famine many came to Joseph for food. Similarly, after Jesus receives His bride, His brethren the Jews (and many in the world), will turn to the Lord Jesus for relief (Revelation 7). How fitting that the great tribulation is called the "the time of Jacob's trouble, but he shall be saved out of it" (Jeremiah 30:7). It is also referred to as "the time of the Gentiles" (Ezekiel 30:3) and many Gentiles will also be saved out of it (Revelation 7). The famine is a type of the tribulation (Amos 8:11), and Egypt is a picture of the world. This account strongly suggests that Jesus will get His bride before the Seventieth Week of Daniel – before the famine that will come upon the entire world.

- In Joshua chapter 2, Rahab trusts the Lord and befriends the Jewish spies. By faith, Rahab puts a scarlet thread in her window (a symbol of Christ's blood), and she and her family are "brought out" of Jericho before the city is burned with fire (Joshua 6). Rahab is a prostitute (Hebrews 11:31) and a Gentile woman (Joshua 2), yet she is found in the Messianic line (Matthew 1:5). Rahab is therefore a beautiful picture of the church (the bride of Christ). Though formerly a prostitute, Rahab, by faith, was made clean and delivered from God's wrath. Amazingly, in this account, we again see seven days of warning preceding judgment (God's gracious delay to encourage repentance). The armies of God marched around the city six days, and on the seventh day they marched around the city seven times, and then the city was finally destroyed (Joshua 6).

- In 1 Samuel 25:39-42 Abigail is informed that King David (foreshadowing King Jesus) wants to take her as his bride. She immediately responds and "rose in haste" with five of her damsels to "depart" and go to David for the marriage. Compare this with Matthew 25:1-13, where five wise virgins who truly had, oil went forth to meet the Bridegroom (Jesus) away from their dwelling place (earth). Interestingly, the name Abigail means the Father's joy!

- The Song of Solomon is an amazing picture of Christ and His church (Ephesians 5:29- 32). In the Song of Solomon 2:8-13, the bride (the church) hears the voice of her beloved (Jesus) coming for her, then in verse 10 and 13, the Bridegroom speaks and calls His bride to "Rise up, my love, my fair one, and come away." This is a beautiful foreshadow of our marriage and honeymoon in heaven!

- Isaiah 26:20-21 also gives us a possible picture of the rapture preceding the tribulation: "Come, my people, enter your chambers, and shut your doors behind you; hide yourself, as it were, for a little moment, until the indignation is past. For behold, the LORD comes out of His place to punish the inhabitants of the earth for their iniquity; the earth will also disclose her blood, and will no more cover her slain." Apparently, believers are tucked away in heaven before the tribulation falls on the earth. This may also apply to the Jews who hide away in Petra during the tribulation.

- In Daniel chapter 3, King Nebuchadnezzar (a type of the Antichrist, cf. Revelation 13) demands that the entire population bow down to his image. Daniel's three friends (Jews) are preserved through the fiery tribulation, but Daniel is nowhere to be found. Daniel was "ruler over the whole province of Babylon, and chief administrator over all the wise men of Babylon" (Daniel 2:48), yet he is missing from the account. Why? Daniel was apparently away. Might he be a type of the church?!

- In Zephaniah 2:2-3 we read: "Before the decree bring forth, before the day pass as the chaff, before the fierce anger of the LORD come upon you, before the day of the LORD'S anger come upon you. Seek the LORD, all you meek of the earth, who have upheld His justice. Seek righteousness, seek humility. It may be that you will be hidden in the day of the LORD'S anger." Believers will be hidden in the day of the Lord's anger (cf. Isaiah 26:20-21). See also: Zephaniah 1:7.

- Malachi 3 deals with the day of the Lord. Interestingly, Malachi 3:18 implies two comings: "Then shall ye (believers) return, and discern between the righteous and the wicked, between him that serveth God and him that serveth him not." It becomes clear when we read the entire context of Malachi 3 that believers shall return to the earth. In order to return and discern, believers must have first been caught away to heaven. Isaac and Rebekah, as well as Ruth and Boaz, also provide beautiful pictures of Christ taking a Gentile bride—one who counts the cost and leaves their own family—but is not required to suffer through great tribulation or famine. Other examples could be expounded on, but these should be sufficient to show that Christians will be removed before God's wrath is poured out, and likely before the Seventieth Week of Daniel.

- An additional example of the rapture is pictured by Elijah, who was translated to heaven while being alive.

> Then it happened, as they continued on and talked, that suddenly a chariot of fire *appeared* with horses of fire, and separated the two of them; and Elijah went up by a whirlwind into heaven. (2 Kings 2:11)

# Appendix 22
## I Will Set Egyptians Against Egyptians

*(Appendix is based upon an article from the author written on 1/28/11. Linked at: http:// prophecynewsstand.blogspot.com/2011/01/i-will-set-egyptians-against-egyptians.html)*

These are the days when the Bible is its own best commentary. Imagine Isaiah the prophet standing on the streets of Cairo today, speaking in front of a mainstream news camera declaring:

> The burden against Egypt. Behold, the LORD rides on a swift cloud, And will come into Egypt; The idols of Egypt will totter at His presence, And the heart of Egypt will melt in its midst. "I will set Egyptians against Egyptians; Everyone will fight against his brother, And everyone against his neighbor, City against city, kingdom against kingdom. The spirit of Egypt will fail in its midst; I will destroy their counsel, And they will consult the idols and the charmers, The mediums and the sorcerers. And the Egyptians I will give Into the hand of a cruel master, And a fierce king will rule over them," Says the Lord, the LORD of hosts. (Isaiah 19:1-4)

Like a swift moving cloud, Isaiah predicts the rapid deterioration of events in Egypt. Civil unrest causes Egyptians to fight against each other. This fighting spreads from household to household and grows into a kingdom war. Probably quoting Isaiah 19:2, Christ warned that kingdoms would rise against each other in Matthew 24:7. Unlike nation coming against nation, which alludes to world wars, "kingdom against kingdom" refers to regional conflicts. Christ taught these prophecies would come upon the world like birth pains. Like a woman about to deliver her newborn, these events are foretold to come with increased frequency and intensity each building upon the other.

Rumors of regional kingdom wars presently abound in the Middle East. Egypt and Saudi Arabia reportedly conducted joint military exercises in 2010 preparing for a possible confrontation with Iran. Iran represents the Persian kingdom, and Egypt and Saudi Arabia the Arab kingdom. Additionally, the apocalyptically-minded president Ahmadinejad of Iran has threatened on several occasions to wipe Israel, representing the Jewish kingdom, off of the map. Psalm 83 predicts the Arab kingdom will someday rise against the Jewish kingdom to banish the name of Israel forever. Both Egypt and Saudi Arabia along with eight other Arab populations join the Arab kingdom in this pending prophetic war. (Also see the appendix called, "*Is Egypt in Psalm 83?*")

Isaiah's prognosis for Egypt worsens as you read the rest of his chapter 19. Isaiah 19:5-12 tells us unprecedented religious and economic strife plagues the nation, according to the purposes of the Lord. Apparently, this disastrous condition befalls Egypt because of its future involvement in Psalm 83, since we read in Isaiah 19:16-18 that Israel will take over five cities in Egypt and cause Hebrew to be the spoken language inside their city limits. One of these cities will be called "the City of Destruction," implying the IDF destroys this city.

> In that day Egypt will be like women, and will be afraid and fear because of the waving of the hand of the LORD of hosts, which He waves over it. And the land of Judah will be a terror to Egypt; everyone who makes mention of it will be afraid in himself, because of the counsel of the LORD of hosts which He has determined against it. In that day five cities in the land of Egypt will speak the language of Canaan and swear by the LORD of hosts; one will be called the City of Destruction. (Isaiah 19:16-18)

The Arab Spring of 2011 has potentially put Egypt in alignment with Isaiah's predictions. President Hosni Mubarak has been overthrown and a new government is forming. Anti-Semitic sentiments toward Israel are feared to surface, causing increased tension between Egypt and Israel. Some fear that the fragile peace treaty between the two countries will be broken.

Will the Muslim Brotherhood fill the vacuum left by Mubarak's departure, potentially fulfilling Isaiah 19:4? The Muslim Brotherhood, which was banned in Egypt during Mubarak's tenure, hates Israel and supports jihad against the Jewish state. Hamas, also participating against Israel in Psalm 83, is their political arm inside of the Gaza. Hamas, like the Muslim Brotherhood, calls for the destruction of Israel.

Will the social revolution inside Egypt metastasize into the fulfillment of Isaiah 19? If so will the coming cruel leader be the one who leads Egypt into the Psalm 83:6-8 confederacy? All of this is unknown, but entirely possible. One thing is for certain; the Middle East appears to be on the verge of going apocalyptic. January 2011 has seen the governments of Lebanon, Tunisia, and Egypt become severely challenged. The government of Jordan is expected to be next (also see appendix called, *Jordan to Soon Sever Ties to Israel*).

Lebanon, Egypt, and Jordan are involved in Psalm 83, and Tunisia appears to take part in the Ezekiel 38-39 prophecy. It appears to be high time for Christians to familiarize themselves with the prophecies of Isaiah 19, Isaiah 17, Jeremiah 49, Psalm 83, and Ezekiel 38-39. These are a few of the world changing prophecies stage setting on the prophetic horizon.

# Appendix 23
## Jordan to Soon Sever Ties to Israel

*(Appendix is based upon an article from the author written on 2/2/11. Linked at: http:// prophecynewsstand.blogspot.com/2011/02/jordan-to-break-ties-with-israel.html)*

The Arab Spring has pundits pondering the fate of Jordan. Will the Jordanian government collapse alongside Lebanon's, Tunisia's, and Egypt's? Interestingly, Jordan can be found in end time Bible prophecy. If the prophecies centered on Jordan are about to find fulfillment, then the best days of the Hashemite Kingdom are behind it.

Someday Jordan will break ties with Israel. It's simply a matter of time, according to Psalm 83:6-8. Making matters worse, Jordan will befriend Israel's worst enemies in the process. Rather than calling on America and the west at the time of dire need, Psalm 83 predicts they will call on Assyria, which incorporates modern-day Syria and Iraq. Syria is already a proxy of Iran's and Iraq has been inclined to become one ever since the summer 2010 US troop withdrawal. Thus, allegiance with Syria, Iraq, and by proxy, Iran, could wind up being Jordan's prophetic endgame.

Psalm 83:6-8 lists a group of ten Arab populations that will someday confederate in a final attempt to destroy the state of Israel. The goal of the confederacy is to wipe Israel off of the map and set up one last Arab state, called Palestine. Jordan is identified inside the list of nations as Edom, Moab, and Ammon. To Jordan's credit, it appears the Arab nation possibly gets drawn into the war with Israel reluctantly, rather than voluntarily. Psalm 83:8 tells us that Jordan is one of the weaker members of the confederacy.

> Assyria also has joined with them; They have helped the children of Lot. (Psalm 83:8)

Asaph, the Psalmist, informs us the children of Lot who were Moab, the eldest, and Ammon require assistance in the war effort. They need Assyrian military support. The Hebrew word used for "helped" is *zeroa* and means forces, power, might, strong arm or shoulder, or strength. Loosely translated, the verse reads Assyria has joined the Psalm 83:6-8 confederacy and become a strong shoulder of military support for Jordan. Note that Assyria's military support is only given to Jordan. This suggests the other Psalm 83 confederates are not lacking in strength at the time.

In 2010, King Abdullah II of Jordan warned on several occasions that the Middle East was on the verge of war. He told the *Chicago Tribune* in April, 2010,

> The chance of conflict is always very high. War would be disastrous for the Israelis, for the Arabs, for all of us. If we hit the summer and there's no active (peace) process, there's a very good chance for conflict.

When a summertime war was averted, he suggested in September 2010 that it could still occur by the end of 2010. The point he was making on both occasions is that a Middle East war could break out at any time. This imminent possibility exists presently, with even greater probability.

In December of 2010, King Abdullah II met with Iranian President Ahmadinejad in a rare meeting, to improve bilateral relations between the two nations. One month later, in January of 2011, he phoned Israeli Prime Minister Netanyahu to alert him of his concerns about Iran's clandestine goals for the Middle East. The Jordanian King warned Netanyahu that Iran aims to form a Shia Crescent inside the Fertile Crescent.

Then in February of 2011, due to protests inside of Jordan, King Abdullah sacked his government in order to avoid escalating protests inside his homeland. King Abdullah's recent pinball reactions remind us of "Humpty Dumpty's" sad tale: Humpty Dumpty had a great fall and all the king's horses and all the king's men couldn't put Humpty together again.

Jordan is the fish out of water in the Middle East. If Egypt falls, then Jordan will likely soon follow. Egypt's and Jordan's treaties with Israel are earning them billions of dollars of American aid. However, many Egyptians and Jordanians are ready to throw their peace treaties out with the baby's bath water. Even King Abdullah said in 2010 that his country's economy was better off before his father made peace with Israel, in 1994.

If Psalm 83 is racing full speed ahead upon humanity's horizon, then Mideast events are going to heat up, rather than cool down. Understanding the low ranking status and primary purposes of the Jordanian Armed Forces (JAF) sheds light on their need for military support in Psalm 83. On the Southern Front of Psalm 83 is the Egyptian army that is world ranked at number #17, with an active military personnel strength of 450,000 and active reserves of 254,000. This doesn't include Hamas units, with about 10,000 personnel, located out of Gaza and untold scores of Qassam and other assorted rockets, some of which Hamas boasted in 2010 could reach Tel Aviv. On the Northern Front of Psalm 83 there is Syria, Lebanon, and Hezbollah, inside of Lebanon. Syria's army is world ranked at #34 and has active military of personnel of 296,000 and active military reserve of 132,500. Additionally, many experts believe Saddam Hussein transported his weapons of mass destruction into Syria prior to America's invasion of Iraq in 2003. Lastly, Syria is thought to have the most advanced scud missiles in the world.

Lebanon's army is world ranked at #42. Their active military personnel number about 72,000 as of 2008. Hezbollah units in Lebanon have about 1,000 active personnel and reserves estimated at 6,000 to 10,000, and according to Netanyahu has 60,000 rockets. Additionally, in April of 2010 Syria reportedly supplied Hezbollah with scud missiles. The Eastern Front of Psalm 83 consists of Saudi Arabia, Iraq, and Jordan. The Saudi army is world ranked at #24 and consists of 124,000 active military personnel with an additional estimated 20,000 reservists. Additionally, the Saudis are attempting to procure $60 billion in arms from America and two nuclear weapons from Pakistan.

Information about Iraq's army and arsenal is difficult to access due to its burgeoning relationship with Iran. Much like Hezbollah, Syria, and Hamas, some military analysts suggest Iran is covertly arming the pro-Iranian factions inside Iraq with advanced weapons, as well. It appears Iraq is world ranked at #37. They have a relatively new US-trained army of about 100,000 soldiers with zero reserves, and a goal to reach a 200,000-man force. It remains an army under construction.

The Jordanian Armed Forces (JAF) has descended from the 1940s era British-led "Arab Legion." This force is purely defensive in nature and thus lacks any ranking among the world's armies. The JAF active military personnel number about 100,500 and reserves are estimated at 70,000. Their military mission objectives are to defend:

1.  The borders of the Hashemite Kingdom,

2.  The people within the Hashemite Kingdom,

3.  The reigning Monarch.

This means the JAF is a combat-ineffective force at best, because as a whole it is not designed for and does not train for offensive operations of the type that Psalm 83 has declared will occur. The Jordanian's receive US Army assistance of a technical and hardware nature, which is overwhelmingly orientated toward defensive command and control (C2).

Therefore, it is of little prophetic wonder that Israel will literally conquer most of Jordan as a result of the Psalm 83 war, as confirmed by the prophecy in Jeremiah 49:2. Even with the assistance of Syrian and Iraqi forces, the Jordanians will lose against Israel. Furthermore, America has taught the new Iraqi military a lot in counter insurgency (COIN) and defensive operations, rather than how to go on the offense against another nation state.

Lastly, we can't forget the Palestinian Authority, a/k/a "Palestine," is a lightly armed paramilitary police force known as the "Palestinian National Security Forces" organized into ten battalions and trained by the US in Jordan.

In contrast to their Psalm 83 enemies, the Israel Defense Forces are world ranked at #11 and their active and reserve forces in Israel number about 600,000, with another 2.8 million immediately available for military service. These additional reserves include those with prior service or some partial training. Suffice it to say, Israel is outnumbered, outmanned, outgunned, and needs divine empowerment when it comes time to face off with the Psalm 83 confederacy. In my book *Isralestine, The Ancient Blueprints of the Future Middle East*, I describe the prelude, event, and aftermath of this climatic concluding Arab-Israeli battle.

\*\*\* Military specifics above and JAF comments provided by Sean Osborne of the Northeast Intelligence Network. The Information was primarily collected from the U.S. Library of Congress; Central Intelligence Agency, GlobalSecurity.Org, and Wikipedia. Sean Osborne's web/blogsite is http://eschatologytoday.blogspot.com/

# Appendix 24
## The True Content of Antichrist's False Covenant

*(Appendix drawn from an article written by author on 11/17/10. Linked at: http://www.prophecydepot.net/2010/the-true-content-of-antichrists-false-covenant/)*

Covenants made between men are not a new phenomenon. War pacts, peace plans, and territorial treaties have been commonplace throughout human history. The Treaty of Versailles signed on June 28, 1919, ended World War I. United Nations Resolution 181 of November 29, 1947, i.e., the Partition Plan, reestablished the Jewish State of Israel. The December 13, 2007 Treaty of Lisbon, established the constitutional basis for the European Union. These are three, among thousands, crafted by mankind to mediate regional and world matters.

World wars, the reestablished State of Israel, and the revived Roman Empire are topics of prophetic importance. Thus, these three world impacting treaties ratified in modern history have biblical significance. Yet the Bible foretells of a coming covenant to be confirmed between the Antichrist and Israel that will undoubtedly make all prior peace pacts, partition plans and territorial treaties pale in comparison. According to Bible prophecy, this forthcoming covenant causes the world hourglass to make one final seven-year turn. Most scholars correlate these seven years with the tribulation period wherein the Lord enters into judgment with Christ rejecting sinful humanity. Therefore, something within the content of this covenant serves as the straw breaking the camel's back, provoking the Lord to dispense His wrath upon mankind. Thus, understanding the *true content* of the *false covenant* becomes an important undertaking.

This end time covenant is spoken of in Isaiah 28:15, 18 and Daniel 9:27. Daniel informs us it will span seven years. Additionally, he declares it will be confirmed by the Antichrist of Roman descent. Isaiah, speaking from the Lord's perspective, calls it a covenant with death, an agreement with Sheol. According to Isaiah, Israel ratifies this covenant believing that a period of peace will follow. By confirming this covenant, Israel believes it's protected from some *overflowing scourge* threatening the Jewish state at the time.

Additionally, the activation of this treaty creates a sense of worldwide security according to 1 Thessalonians 5:3. This suggests that the *overflowing scourge* may have a much broader reach than just the Middle East. It implies that the world is in a chaotic state of flux at the time, in dire need of stability. Therefore, understanding the nature of the *overflowing scourge* additionally helps to identify the content of this all-important covenant. However, that's a topic for book two of this series. This appendix intends to dispel six decades of seemingly erroneous teaching about the actual content of the false covenant.

The volatile Middle East is the focal point of many world leaders. The Arab Spring of 2011 has many pundits and politicians concerned that regional instability could lead to war between the Arabs and the Jews, if power shifts into the hands of Islamic extremists.  Since Israel became a nation in 1948, it has been at war with most of the Arab states and Arab terrorist populations surrounding it. This has caused many end-time experts to put the plight of the Palestinians and their Arab state sponsors somewhere upon the pages of the Antichrist's false covenant. However, this inclination seems primarily driven by geo-political events, rather than biblical discernment.

Arab fingerprints upon this covenant are nowhere to be found in Scripture. If anything, this treaty appears to be regarded with broader revived Roman Empire concerns, rather than Pan-Arab nationalistic needs.

# False Content of the False Covenant— Process of Elimination

By understanding the geo-political circumstances in the Middle East at the time the covenant is confirmed, we can determine what won't need to be addressed inside the document. In part, discovering what the true content of the false covenant is can be accomplished through this process of elimination.

Three powerful prophetic Mideast events will probably find final fulfillment prior to the issuance of the false covenant. These are Isaiah 17:1, Psalm 83, and Ezekiel 38-39. These Israeli war prophecies profoundly affect the geo-political landscape of the Fertile Crescent. Damascus will be destroyed, and the Palestinians along with their Arab state sponsors Syria, Lebanon, Saudi Arabia, Jordan, and Egypt will be defeated by the Israel Defense Forces in a massive war. Additionally, hordes of troops from Russia, Iran, Turkey, Libya, Ethiopia and several other of the Ezekiel 38:2-6 invaders will be divinely decimated by the God of the Jews, according to Ezekiel 38:18-39:6.

Should these events take place prior to the confirmation of the false covenant as Scripture suggests, then we can safely eliminate the following possible contents from the covenant:

- A Palestinian state with East Jerusalem as its capital.

- The "Right of Return" of Palestinian refugees into Israel.

- The receding of Israel to pre-1967 borders.

- The return of the Golan Heights to Syria.

- The Iranian nuclear threat in the Middle East.

- The consideration of Jerusalem as Islam's third holiest site.

- Lebanese littoral claims to all Israeli energy discoveries in the Mediterranean Sea.

These are just a few issues that will not likely appear on the pages of the false covenant of the Antichrist.

Therefore, if peace in the Middle East is achieved militarily through these prophesied wars rather than through politically brokered land for peace deals, then what will the *true content* of the *false covenant* contain?

# Appendix 25
## Egypt's Forty Years of Desolation

*(Based on an article written by the author on 3/1/11. Linked at: http://prophecynewsstand. blogspot.com/2011/03/end-times-egypt.html)*

This article was written in a question-and-answer format in response to an inquiry about Egypt's forty-year desolation period prophesied in Ezekiel 29:12. The pertinent Ezekiel verses are as follows;

> "I will make the land of Egypt desolate in the midst of the countries that are desolate; and among the cities that are laid waste, her cities shall be desolate *forty years*; and I will scatter the Egyptians among the nations and disperse them throughout the countries." 'Yet, thus says the Lord GOD: "At the end of *forty years* I will gather the Egyptians from the peoples among whom they were scattered. *I will bring back the captives of Egypt* and cause them to return to the land of Pathros, to the land of their origin, and there they shall be a lowly kingdom. It shall be the lowliest of kingdoms; it shall never again exalt itself above the nations, for I will diminish them so that they will not rule over the nations anymore. No longer shall it be the confidence of the house of Israel, but will remind them of their iniquity when they turned to follow them. Then they shall know that I am the Lord GOD."'" (Ezekiel 29:12-16; emphasis added).

**Comment to author:** Dear Mr. Salus, in reading some of your articles it is clear you believe Psalm 83 precedes Ezekiel 38. I'm puzzled about some prophecies regarding Egypt in the end times. Could you please answer the following questions?

**Question**—Ezekiel 29:12-13 says Egypt is made desolate for forty years, has this happened in history?

**Answer**—I believe Egypt's forty-year desolation period, which corresponds with the forty years of Egyptian deportation into world nations, remains an unfulfilled prophecy. However, some expositors believe this has already been fulfilled. To argue their point, they often refer to the writings of the Jewish historian Josephus in *Antiquities*, Book 10, Chapter 11, Section 1. Book 10 is titled, "From the Captivity of the Ten Tribes to the First of Cyrus" and Chapter 11 is titled, "Concerning Nebuchadnezzar and His Successors, and

How Their Government was Dissolved by the Persians; and What Things Befell Daniel in Media; and What Prophecies He Delivered There."

In this section Josephus appears to quote Berosus from "the third book of his Chaldaic History" that a young Nebuchadnezzar was sent by his father to conquer Egypt due to rebellion by the Egyptian governor, appointed by Nebuchadnezzar's father. Deportation is spoken of as follows, "the captive Jews, and Phoenicians, and Syrians, and those of the Egyptian nations, and having committed the conveyance of them to Babylon . . ."[57]

Adding support to the argument that Egypt's forty years of desolation found fulfillment during the Babylonian period are the prophecies in Ezekiel 30:20-26, which predict that the king of Babylon will conquer Pharaoh of Egypt resulting in the exodus of Egyptians into other nations.

> "Thus I will strengthen the arms of the king of Babylon, but the arms of Pharaoh shall fall down; they shall know that I *am* the LORD, when I put My sword into the hand of the king of Babylon and he stretches it out against the land of Egypt. *I will scatter the Egyptians among the nations and disperse them throughout the countries*. Then they shall know that I *am* the LORD.'" (Ezekiel 30:25-26; emphasis added).

The Egyptian forty-year captivity could have been fulfilled at this time; however it is hard to find historical or archaeological proof that this past deportation spanned forty years. Thus, Ezekiel 29:12-16 may still be pending prophetic events.

I recently emailed the following comments to a friend regarding the forty-year Egyptian deportation.

> There is the inference of Egyptian deportation by Josephus, but it seems to be for an unspecified time. Some estimated dates of importance in considering the length of the Egyptian deportation are: Nebuchadnezzar invaded Egypt in 568 BC and Cyrus of Persia, defeated Babylon in 539 BC. The time span between these two events is approximately twenty-nine years. From these dates, it is difficult to speculate how the 40 forty-year deportation could have occurred at that time. In order for the deportation to have been historically fulfilled then, it would require that the re-gathering of the Egyptians into their homeland specified in Ezekiel 29:13-14 commenced around 528 BC.

> Portions of Ezekiel 29-30 seem to find connections with Nebuchadnezzar's time; however, Ezekiel 30:3 alludes to the "day of the Lord," which is commonly associated with the tribulation period. Additionally, Ezekiel 30:5 speaks of more than Egypt being attacked. It alludes to Ethiopia, Libya, Lydia, and Chub. The expanse of Nebuchadnezzar's kingdom seems to not have included all these countries. Therefore, this part of Ezekiel's prophecy seems to connect better with Daniel 11:42-43, which is also often taught to be a tribulation event.

> Thus, we have to consider the possibility that Ezekiel 29-30 contains both near (fulfilled during prophets lifetime) and far (to be fulfilled after the prophets lifetime) prophecies. Some events Ezekiel describes clearly found fulfillment during Nebuchadnezzar's time (near), whereas others seem to be reserved for future fulfillment.

Isaiah 19:16-18 and Daniel 11:42-43 are far prophecies and could trigger the forty years of Egyptian deportation. If so, then forty years could commence after either Psalm 83 or Daniel 11:42-43. In either instance, the deportation could carry over somewhat into the Messianic kingdom.

It is hard to imagine how eighty-two million Egyptians today, minus those slain and those who remain in Egypt after both Psalm 83 and Daniel 11:42-43, could be deported in the future. But, that could be what Ezekiel 29:12 implies.

Additionally, the widely respected eschatologist, Dr. Arnold Fruchtenbaum, discusses these topics briefly in his book *Footsteps of the Messiah*. The pertinent pages to study, regarding Isaiah 19 and Ezekiel 29, are 497-509. In a nutshell, he states that because of Egypt's longstanding hatred of Israel . . . they will suffer desolation similar to that of Edom according to Joel 3:19. This desolation will lead to the forty years of Egyptian deportation. At the end of the deportation an Egyptian remnant will be re-gathered and Egypt restored. But, Egypt will be a lowly kingdom throughout the 1,000-year Messianic Kingdom. Dr. Fruchtenbaum believes the first forty years of the Messianic Kingdom could find the land of Egypt in a desolate condition and Egyptians dispersed throughout the world. Thus, he appears to believe the forty-year deportation is still a pending prophetic event and could overlap into the Messianic Kingdom.

I agree with Dr. Fruchtenbaum; the deportation could extend into the Messianic Kingdom, but if the deportation commences after Psalm 83, then I don't believe there will be a full forty-year overlap. If Israel's victory over Egypt in Psalm 83 begins the forty-year Egyptian deportation process, then I believe much of this forty-year period could elapse before the Messianic Kingdom even commences.

**Question**—Isaiah 19:23 says there will be a highway out of Egypt to Assyria and the Assyrian shall come into Egypt. When do you believe this finds fulfillment?

**Answer**—I believe this finds fulfillment during the 1,000-year Messianic Kingdom period.

**Question**—Isaiah 19:18 says five cities in Egypt will speak the language of Canaan. Has this happened in history?

**Answer**—The language of Canaan was Hebrew. I believe this remains an unfulfilled prophecy. Contextually, these five cities speak Hebrew after Egypt has a terrorizing encounter with Judah (Israel). I believe this encounter has to do with Egypt's participation in the climactic, concluding Arab - Israeli war described in Psalm 83. Egypt is identified in Psalm 83 under the banner of the "Hagarenes." Hagar was the Egyptian matriarch who mothered Ishmael to Abraham.

However, some teach this may have already found fulfillment. Here is what the *New Commentary on the Whole Bible; Old Testament* says—"By Jeremiah's day, 130 years later (Jer. 44:1), four places are addressed by the prophet as having Hebrew speakers: Migdol and Tahpanes, both in the northeastern delta; Noph (Memphis), located at the base of the delta; and Pathros, upper Egypt. Elephantine Island, at Egypt's southern border, was inhabited by Jews in the sixth century B.C."

For more information on this topic, listen to Bill Salus two-part radio show on the Internet at this link: *http://www.prophecydepot.net/2011/ezekiel-predicts-40-years-of-egyptian-deportation/* (posted on 2/25/11).

# Appendix 26
## Images

# Ezekiel 38 Invaders

**Russia &
So. Steppes**

**Turkey
Iran
Ethiopia
Sudan
Somalia
Libya**

**Algeria
Morocco
Tunisia**

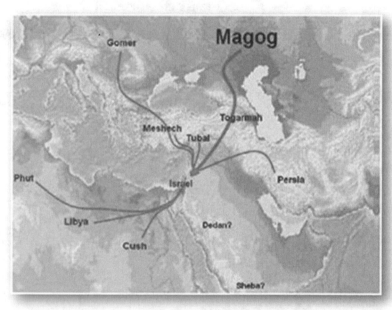

*Image #1 Map obtained from Chuck Missler's Koinonia House Ministries. Text imposed by the author. Some people believe Gomer represents Germany, but many others teach that Gomer settled in Asia Minor.*

## The Psalm 83 Confederates

| | |
|---|---|
| *Tents of* **Edom** | Palestinians & Southern Jordanians |
| **Ishmaelites** | Saudis (*Ishmael father of Arabs*) |
| **Moab** | Palestinians & Central Jordanians |
| **Hagarenes** | Egyptians – (*Hagar Egypt Matriarch*) |
| **Gebal** | Hezbollah & Northern Lebanese |
| **Ammon** | Palestinians & Northern Jordanians |
| **Amalek** | Arabs of the Sinai Area |
| **Philistia** | Hamas of the Gaza Strip |
| **Tyre** | Hezbollah & Southern Lebanese |
| **Assyria** | Syrians and Northern Iraqi's |

*Image #2 – Provided by the Prophecy Depot Ministries*

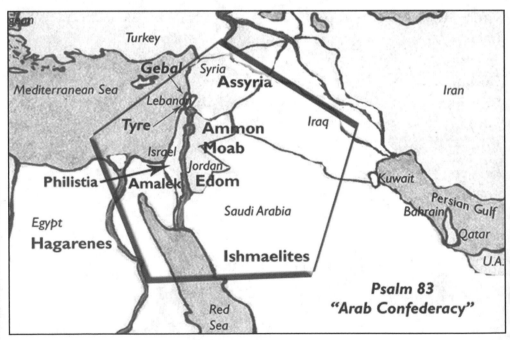

*Image #3 – Inner Circle of Psalm 83. The Psalm 83 Arab nations and/or terrorist populations are located inside the pentagon figure on the map. Map provided by Lani Harmony Salhus*

APPENDICES

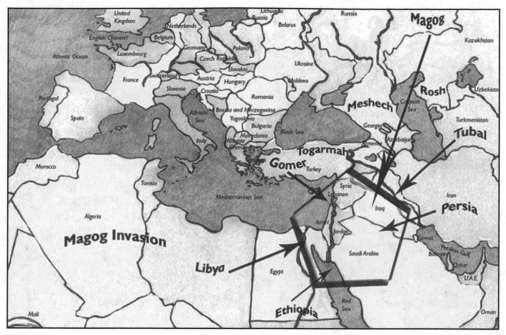

*Image #4 – Outer Ring of Ezekiel 38. The Psalm 83 Arab nations and/or terrorist populations are located inside the pentagon figure on the map and are part of the "inner circle." The arrows pointing toward the pentagon represent the Ezekiel 38:1-5 Gog of Magog invaders. Tubal most likely should be positioned between Togarmah and Gomer. Map provided by Lani Harmony Salhus*

# The Family Feuds

| The Mothers | Sarah vs. Hagar | HAGARENES | *Genesis 16 & 21* |
|---|---|---|---|
| The Sons | Isaac vs. Ishmael | ISHMAELITES | *Genesis 16, 17 & 21* |
| The Twin Brothers | Jacob vs. Esau | PALESTINIANS | *Genesis 25-28 & 32-33* |
| The Cousins | Israelites vs. Ammonites & Moabites | JORDANIANS | *Numbers 22- 25, Judges 3 & 10-11, 2 Kings 3, 2 Chron. 20* |
| The Great Grand Kids | Hebrews vs. Amalakites | AMALAKITES | *Numbers 14, Judges 3* |

*Image #5 The Family Feuds of the Patriarchs and Matriarchs. Created by Prophecy Depot Ministries.*

# End Notes — Appendices

1.  Revelation 3:14-22. Some commentators, as do I, teach that this seventh and last letter to the seven churches has multiple meanings. One of these meanings is a warning that the Christian church will fall apostate, "lukewarm" in its final stage of organizational development.

2.  *Isralestine* was released in 2008 by Highway, a division of Anomalos Publishing, and is available at the author's website http//:www.prophecydepot.com

3.  Iranian President Mahmoud Ahmadinejad declared on October 26, 2005, at the World Without Zionism conference that Israel must be "wiped off the map."

4.  *Epicenter* was published through Tyndale in 2006 and is available at http//:www.tyndale.com.

5.  Haiti earthquake casualty statistics gathered over the Internet on 8/14/11 at this link: http://en.wikipedia.org/wiki/2010_Haiti_earthquake.

6.  Death toll estimates from Japan's earthquake gathered over the Internet at this link: http://earthquake-report.com/2011/08/04/japan-tsunami-following-up-the-aftermath-part-16-june/.

7.  Cost estimate of Japan's 2011 earthquake were gathered on the Internet on 8/14/11 at this link: http://news.smh.com.au/breaking-news-world/japan-quake-damage-to-cost-up-to-309-bn-govt-20110323-1c6w4.html.

8.  The understanding of "kingdom against kingdom" as referring to regional conflicts rather than world wars is established in Isaiah 19:2 and elsewhere.

9.  Revelation 3:15-16 describes the church of Laodicea in a "lukewarm" condition.

10. Daniel 9:24-27 predicted a period of seventy "weeks of years," with the seventieth week being a time when Antichrist reigns. Other passages identify this as a period of tribulation—i.e., Matthew 24: 9, 15, 21 and Revelation 2:22, 7:14. Thus, many eschatologists call this the "tribulation period" and furthermore suggest that many of the judgments described in the book of Revelation occur in this final, seven-year period.

11. For further study into the prophetic interpretation of the seven letters to the seven churches of the book of Revelation, refer to the Revelation commentaries of Dr. Arnold Fruchtenbaum of Ariel Ministries at (http://www.ariel.org)or of Chuck Missler of Koinonia House Ministries at ( http//:www.khouse.org)

12. The date associations for the purposes of this appendix were quoted from http://www.midnightcry.net/PDF/Seven%20Letters%20to%20Seven%20Churches.pdf on 2/28/09.

13. These are not necessarily clichés of that period, but serve this author's purpose to convey his ideas and understanding of the Pergamos period.

14. 2 Thessalonians 2:8-13

15. http://www.blueletterbible.org/commentaries/comm_view.cfm?AuthorID=1&contentID=6877&commInfo=25&topic=Daniel (Internet accessed 12/16/2010). Chuck Smith's quotes are abbreviated and paraphrased by (parentheses).

16. The expression "in that day" is used in the Bible over fifty times to indicate the last days, the day of the Lord, and the time of judgment. Here are some examples: Isaiah 2:11, 17, 20; 4:1, 2; 10:20; 11:11; 12:1; 24:21; 25:9; 26:1; 27:1, 2, 12, 13; 28:5; 52:6; Jeremiah 30:8; Ezekiel 38:19; 39:11; Hosea 2:16, 18, 21; Joel 3:18; Amos 8:3, 9, 13; Obadiah v. 8; Micah 4:6; 5:10; 7:11, 12; Zephaniah 3:11, 16; Zechariah 2:11; 3:10; 9:16; 12:3, 4, 6, 8, 9, 11; 13:1, 2, 4; 14:4, 6, 8, 9, 13, 20, 21; Matthew 7:22; Luke 10:12; 17:31; 2 Thessalonians 1:10; etc.

17.  http://www.nydailynews.com/news/national/2007/09/19/2007-09-19_israel_to_syria_use_chem_
     weapons__well_w.html  accessed 2/15/2011

18.  It may refer to the nations in general and Damascus in particular. Read Isaiah chapter 17 for
     context.

19.  For a timeline of key last days events refer to: http://www.eternal-productions.org/PDFS/Time%20
     Line%20-%20Key%20events%20from%20Rapture%20to%20Second%20Coming.pdf

20.  Nickname given by the author to those who believe Ezekiel 38 is an imminent event.

21.  Internet accessed on 6/16/2010 at http://wiki.answers.com/Q/How_rich_was_Solomon—"In
     the Bible at 2 Chronicles 9:13 it says that Solomon had a basic yearly revenue of 666 Talents or
     22,000 kilograms of gold. A talent weighed between 20 and 40 KG, but the average estimated is
     33kg. The price today of one kilogram of gold is estimated at $32,200 so his yearly income was
     $708,400,000 a year. Seven-hundred eight million, four-hundred thousand dollars a year."

22.  Definition of despoil accessed on the internet at this link on 6162011http://www.thefreedictionary.
     com/despoil

23.  Fruchtenbaum, Arnold, *The Footsteps of the Messiah* (San Antonio, TX: Ariel Ministries, Revised
     Edition, 2003), p 498

24.  Esau grandfathered Amalek according to Genesis 36:12

25.  Nations promised to Abraham Genesis 12:2, to Ishmael Genesis 17:20, to Jacob and Esau Genesis
     25:23

26.  Parson's Technology Software, *Quickverse Version 6.0, Holman Bible Dictionary,* under "Hagarite,"
     (Austin, TX; n.d.)

27.  Parson's Technology Software, *Quickverse Version 6.0, International Standard Bible Encyclopedia*,
     under "Hagarenes/Hagarites/Hagrites," (Austin, TX; n.d.)

28.  Parson's Technology Software, *Quickverse Version 6.0, New Commentary on the Whole Bible, Old
     Testament,* under "Ps. 83:6-8 tabernacles," (Austin, TX; n.d.)

29.  Parson's Technology Software, *Quickverse Version 6.0, Barnes, Notes on the Old Testament,* under
     "And the Hagarenes," (Austin, TX; n.d.)

30.  Caspian Sea Naval exercises information accessed over the Internet on 8/5/11 at: http://www.
     israelnationalnews.com/News/News.aspx/132634

31.  Oil information about the Strait of Hormuz gathered over the Internet on 8/5/11 at: http://
     en.wikipedia.org/wiki/Strait_of_Hormuz.

32.  The Hebrew word for merchants is *sachar.* Ezekiel uses it in connection with Tarshish in Ezekiel
     27:12 also. *The New American Standard Exhaustive Concordance* translates the word in this
     instance as customers. Also refer to this concordance in Ezekiel 27:16,18,21 for other customer
     translations of the word.

33.  The Fertile Crescent is a geographical area of fertile land in the Middle East stretching in a broad
     semicircle from the Nile to the Tigris and Euphrates wordnetweb.princeton.edu/perl/webwn
     accessed 10/13/10

34.  Information about the passage of the loyalty oath was gathered over the internet as recently as
     7/18/11 at this link: http://www.msnbc.msn.com/id/39603969/ns/world_news-mideastern_africa/

35.  Missile quantity information was gathered over the internet as recently as 7/18/11 at this link:
     http://www.worldtribune.com/worldtribune/WTARC/2010/me_israel0448_05_24.asp

36.  Information about the Jordanian Palestinian population was gathered over the internet as recently
     as 7/18/11 at this link: http://www.cuttingedge.org/news/n2095.cfm

37. Information about Jordanian concerns with Iran's Mideast hegemonic goals was gathered over the internet as recently as 7/18/11 at this link: http://www.washingtonpost.com/wp-dyn/articles/A43980-2004Dec7.html

38. Information about Saudis opening airspace to Israel was gathered over the internet as recently as 7/18/11 at this link: http://www.upi.com/Top_News/World-News/2010/06/12/Report-Israel-can-cross-Saudi-air-space/UPI-78771276378954/

39. A neologism intended to describe a fictitious Iran controlling the greater Middle East. It is used only for the purposes of this appendix

40. Accredited Mary Apparitions can be seen at this Internet link as of 8/12/11 http://www.catholicdoors.com/isit/approved.htm

41. Quote accessed over the Internet on 8/12/11 at: http://en.wikipedia.org/wiki/Assumption_of_Mary

42. Quote accessed over the Internet on 8/12/11 at: http://www.vatican.va/holy_father/pius_xii/apost_constitutions/documents/hf_p-xii_apc_19501101_munificentissimus-deus_en.html

43. Information accessed over the Internet on 8/12/11 at: http://www.papalencyclicals.net/Pius09/p9ineff.htm, and http://en.wikipedia.org/wiki/Immaculate_Conception

44. St. Augustine quote accessed over the Internet on 8/12/11 at: http://en.wikipedia.org/wiki/Immaculate_Heart_of_Mary

45. Information about Saint Epiphanius of Salamis was accessed over the Internet on 8/12/11 at:

46. Quote from Timothy of Jerusalem gathered over the Internet on 8/12/11 at this link: http://www.ourladyweb.com/mary-defended.html

47. Information from Gregory of Tours was accessed over the Internet on 8/12/11 at: http://www.thesacredheart.com/feastmar.htm

48. Quote gathered over the Internet on 8/12/11 at: http://catholicdoors.com/homilies/2011/110702.htm

49. Michael H. Brown, *The Last Secret*, Ann Arbor, MI, Serva http://en.wikipedia.org/wiki/Assumption_of_Mary nt Publications, 1998, p. 281.

50. For a thorough examination of apparitions, refer to: Jim Tetlow, *Messages From Heaven*, Fairport, NY (book and DVD).

51. Comments contributed by Mike Gendron for the purposes of this Appendix. Mike's website is http://www.pro-gospel.org/.

52. The Messianic Kingdom was the high-point of Old Testament prophecy. Revelation 20:4 informs that is lasts for 1,000 years.

53. Sinner's Prayer quote taken from Wikipedia over the Internet on 8/13/11 at this link: http://en.wikipedia.org/wiki/Sinner's_prayer

54. Sinner's prayer example was copied from the Internet on 8/13/11 at this website link: http://www.salvationprayer.info/prayer.html (slight emphasis was added in this appendix)

55. Quote welcoming those who prayed the sinner's prayer into the family of God copied over the Internet on 8/13/11 at this link: http://www.salvationprayer.info/prayer.html

56. Jim Tetlow hosts the website located at http://www.eternal-productions.org/. Jim graciously permitted this part of his transcript located on the web at http://www.eternal-productions.org/PDFS/articles/Rapture.pdf, to be included in *Revelation Road*.

57. Research provided by Danny Isom of Moriel Ministries. Moriel Ministries website is: http://www.moriel.org/

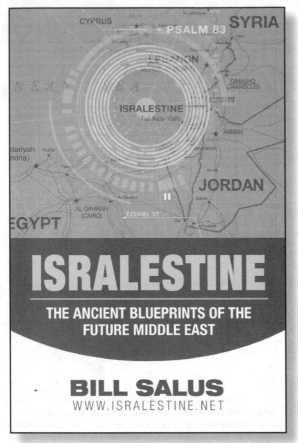